*Weak States
in a
World of Powers*

WEAK STATES
IN A
WORLD OF POWERS:

THE DYNAMICS OF INTERNATIONAL RELATIONSHIPS

Marshall R. Singer

THE FREE PRESS, NEW YORK
COLLIER-MACMILLAN LIMITED, LONDON

THIS BOOK IS DEDICATED TO STUDENTS EVERYWHERE,
WHO WILL INHERIT THE KIND OF WORLD WE LEAVE THEM.

IN PARTICULAR IT IS DEDICATED TO MY TWO FAVORITE
STUDENTS: MY SONS, SHEPHERD AND PAUL.

The Free Press
A Division of The Macmillan Company
866 Third Avenue, New York, New York 10022

Collier-Macmillan Canada Ltd., Toronto, Ontario

Library of Congress Catalog Card Number: 70–158070

printing number
1   2   3   4   5   6   7   8   9   10

Acknowledgments

How does one acknowledge the ideas that he has absorbed from other scholars over the years and that have come to permeate his thinking so completely it becomes impossible for him to discern which are theirs and which are his? Certainly in many ways this book is possible only because of the work of Harold Lasswell, Karl Deutsch, Erik Erikson, Heinz Eulau, and Robert McIver, to mention only a few of the authors who have had a profound effect on my thinking. Although this book will probably be viewed as an attack on Hans Morgenthau, it has been brewing in my mind since I read his *Politics Among Nations* for the first time, and that, I think, is one of the greatest compliments anyone can pay any man.

In the early stages of actually setting words to paper, my colleagues at the University of Pittsburgh and what is now Carnegie-Mellon University who formed a group called the "Tender Scholars" (which met monthly to nurture and cultivate those fragile, tender seedlings of ideas that had not yet been fully thought through) came to deserve many thanks for helping some of my tentative ideas to take root. Alex Weilenmann and Richard Cottam, joined later by Tom McCormack, Rolland Robertson, and Steven Schecter, met with me in a fortnightly Seminar on Weak and Powerful States (made possible by a grant from the Pittsburgh University Center for International Studies, under Carl Beck's direction), and read and reread the early drafts, offering some of the most constructive criticisms. The detailed comments of Joseph Coffey, Gaylord Obern, Warren Bennis, and Barton Sensenig on parts or all of the manuscript were also extremely useful. At every step of the way Alvin Roseman, Daniel Cheever, Hamlin Robinson, and Nick Caruso of the Graduate School for Public and International Affairs provided all of the logistical, financial, and library support any academician could hope for. James Rosenau, now at Ohio State University, provided positive feedback at a crucial stage of the work to give me the confidence to go on and complete the study. James Cron of The Free Press was most understanding and helpful in allowing me to surpass my deadline by more than a year and finish the book in

Malaysia. In addition, the Ford Foundation in Malaysia and Dean Yip Yat Hoong of the Faculty of Economics and Administration of the University of Malaya were extremely kind to allow me the time to finish this work while I was on a totally different assignment for them.

In the dedication, and throughout the book, I make reference to my students, who have taught me far more than I could ever have taught them. The reader will see the degree to which I have relied on their research in writing this book. What the reader cannot see is how much I have relied on their constructive criticisms, in class and out, to formulate, clarify, and rethink my sometimes outrageous ideas. In particular, I want to thank Daniel Rich, Steven Schecter, Mary Emeny, Paul London, Cecil Ee Kuang Yong, Martin Singer, Jeffrey Singer, and Bruce Pachter, who not only collected data, proof-read with me, and corrected some of my many mistakes, but who also had the insight and the guts to tell me when I was wrong, and who would not settle for anything less than what they felt was the best that I could do.

For all the help and encouragement I have received, I am extremely grateful. But none of the people or institutions mentioned here can bear any of the blame for errors of judgment, interpretation, or fact the book may contain. They tried their best to prevent those errors. It is I who must bear full responsibility.

One last word of acknowledgment must be made. It is hard on any family when the man withdraws to his study to write a book. It is not just that he devotes less time to them, but he also devotes considerably less psychic energy. The circumstances surrounding the writing of this book were particularly hard on my family. Not only did I "hole-up" for hours on end in Pittsburgh, but the burdens of preparing for the move to Malaysia, settling in when we got there, and preparing for the return to the States after eighteen months in Kuala Lumpur fell almost entirely on my wife Susan. At best she had to operate with only a part-time husband, and a part-time father for our boys. Not only did she survive, she prevailed. No man could ask for more.

Marshall R. Singer

Kuala Lumpur, Malaysia

Contents

List of Tables

List of Figures

SECTION I

Changing Relations Between States: Some Concepts

Introduction

The study of power is central to the study of human affairs. But power cannot be studied in a vacuum. It makes sense only when viewed as a process that operates in a relationship. The central focus of this work is the dynamics of changing relationships between weak and powerful states. In a very real sense, this means it is a study of changing power relationships. But the same power dynamic operates in all relationships, whether among individuals, groups, or states. What is more, the power relationship at each of these levels interacts and affects the other levels.

One cannot understand the relations among states without understanding the behavior of people. States are, after all, legal entities made up of people. The "affairs of state" are conducted by people. It is, of course, necessary to explore the decisions and actions of states as such. What a "state" does—or does not do—can often have an enormous impact on the lives of people in any number of other states. But many, many more international transactions occur on a nongovernmental level—among individuals, business corporations, and private organizations of all kinds—than occur on an official, state-to-state level, and these often overlooked transactions deserve at least as much attention as do "official" international relationships.

For example, American foreign aid rarely accounts for more than 3 to 4 percent of the Gross Domestic Product (G.D.P.) of any country, but private trade between corporations in the United States and corporations and/or individuals in other countries often accounts for between 10 and 20 percent of the weaker country's G.D.P., and in some cases has accounted for as much as 40 percent. A decision on the part of a private firm in the United States to invest $100,000,000 abroad is uncontestably one which will have major international ramifications. So will a decision on the part of that same firm *not* to invest abroad. For a deeper understanding of international affairs, it is important to know what factors influenced that decision.

There is little that occurs "domestically" in any country—but particularly in those countries that are major powers—that does not have simultaneous international implications. A seemingly private, domestic decision on the part of an American tire company to increase the synthetic content of its new line of tires could destroy much of the economy of Liberia, Malaysia, and several other rubber-exporting countries. A decision on the part of an American steelworkers' union to demand a $2.00-an-hour increase in wages—whether granted or denied—has enormous international ramifications, particularly to the major steel importing and exporting countries of the world. In a similar vein, as long as there are people in the world who think of other people living in another country as part of their particular group—as "one of us"— what happens to those people will inevitably become a concern in international affairs. It does not matter whether we are discussing the treatment of blacks in South Africa or South Chicago; the treatment of Chinese in Indonesia or the Philippines; the treatment of Catholics in South Vietnam; or the treatment of businessmen in Cuba: to the degree that they belong to a group with whom it is possible for people living in a variety of states to identify, their treatment will have international ramifications.

To deny the importance of these various factors merely because they make consideration of the problems in international relations more difficult, is equivalent to looking for the lost coin only under the streetlight—not because it was lost there, but because there is more light. To consider the behavior of states, without simultaneously considering the actions of people and groups, borders on the superficial, if not the sterile. To consider intergovernmental relations as the only legitimate concern in the study of international affairs is to consider only a small part of a much more rich and complex system of international interactions. A true understanding of the workings of the international political process requires that we first understand the individual and group decisions and actions that have repercussions beyond the boundaries of single states.

With these premises as my guide, I have approached this study with interdisciplinary tools, venturing to apply not only the perspectives of political science, but also my understanding of economics, communications theory, sociology, and psychology. My purpose is to try to illuminate the multiple dimensions of subjects that too often in the past have been treated as one-dimensional. Traditional discussions of power all but ignore interpersonal and intergroup relations. This study is an attempt to remedy that distortion. No student of domestic affairs would say that only the actions of the government were important to the political life of a country. Business, labor, mass media, political parties, the church, and the military, to mention only a few groups, are all recognized as important actors. Yet, when it comes to discussions of the international political process, these same groups are usually left out or underestimated.

Similarly, traditional discussions of power presume that its principal, most common, and most effective instrument—both domestically and internationally—is coercive force. In actual fact, that is not the case, save in very limited wartime situations. The inadequacies and counter-productive aspects of coercive instruments of power are usually ignored or underestimated, as are the strengths of the various "attractive" (noncoercive) means by which power is actually more frequently exercised. This study is an attempt to remedy that distortion, as well.

Generally, this study is concerned with the broad characteristics of power relationships and the ways in which the parties involved tend to behave. Specifically, it analyzes the nature of the ties that actually exist between weak and powerful states; the effects of these ties on the elites in the weaker countries; and the ways in which, and reasons why, ties between states tend to loosen or tighten.

The analysis focuses primarily on the relations since World War II between five major Powers—the United States, the Soviet Union, Japan, Great Britain, and France—and the weak states that are legally independent but are, in various ways, "associated" with them. While Britain and France today are not on a par with the other three, which are the world's most powerful nations now, they have been retained in the category of Powers in order to study what has happened to the relationships between them and their many former "dependencies" as their own power has declined. The functions once performed by Britain and France for the weaker states have increasingly been taken over by the United States, the Soviet Union, and Japan, and also by the European Economic Community (E.E.C.) Indeed, if the E.E.C. can achieve the kind of political integration it has achieved economically, it will itself be one of the world's major Powers. Therefore, wherever possible, data on the European Economic Community has also been included, as has data on China, another potential Power. When referring to a Power in relation to its associated states, I often call it a "Mentor" in order to signify its special role in the affairs of the weaker countries.

In determining which countries to include in the category of associated states—an extremely difficult matter at best, since there is no commonly held definition of what dependency or association means, and thus subjective criteria must be used—I have tried to avoid the extreme of considering nearly all states associated with all other states merely because perhaps one percent of their Gross Domestic Product is accounted for by trade with those other countries. On the other hand, I have also tried to avoid legalistic definitions that would place weaker countries in dependent relationships with only one Power even if they were actually associated in some ways with other Powers as well. There are innumerable variations in the relationships between weak and powerful states, and these relationships are constantly changing. Thus, my criteria for determining association have been the degree and kind of perceptual, communication, economic, military, and political ties that exist between states and elites of states. On the basis of these criteria, I have tried to include in this study those states that historically have been closely tied to the major Powers, and those states that are today closely tied.

Where possible, quantitative data are used. But because of the paucity of such data on many of the crucial variables in the relationships explored, and because of the crudeness of some of the measures that do exist, no highly sophisticated analysis has been attempted. Rather, the data are presented merely as indicators of gross trends and relationships. In some instances, I have used no data at all, but merely suggest relationships that I believe to exist. In trying to paint with a brush as broad as the one I have chosen, it is inevitable that detail—and sometimes significant detail—will be obscured. But, my object has been to discover the broad relationships, and how they *tend* to operate. Hopefully, other scholars will become interested in refining some of the very crude data I have been forced to use in lieu of none, and will test my premises and assumptions.

I realize that my use of materials from disciplines in which I am not a specialist, my reliance on limited data and subjective criteria, and my effort to draw from my study not only scholarly conclusions but specific recommendations for policy makers, invite accusations of unorthodoxy and presumptuousness. But the imperative need for a new approach to the relations between weak and powerful states has made me willing to accept this risk. Throughout the more than six years during which this study was in preparation, I witnessed the most powerful country in the world (the United States) tear both itself and one of the weakest countries in the world (Vietnam) to pieces—presumably to achieve a goal that was in the American "national interest." Throughout the entire period, I saw policy makers and a not insignificant number of otherwise brilliant scholars argue that since we are so powerful and Vietnam is so weak, all we need do is employ more of what is presumed to be the ultimate instrument of power—coercive force—and eventually our goal will be achieved. Yet, after all that time, all that force, somewhere in the order of $150 billion, over 50,000 American deaths, the death of possibly a million Vietnamese, and the damaged lives of countless others, we now appear no nearer that goal—whatever it is—than when we began. It seems clear to me that one of the main reasons for this failure is that many policy makers and many scholars have misunderstood the very nature of power and how it works. In the light of this, it seems necessary to offer my perspectives and recommendations, however unorthodox and presumptuous, in the belief that they are valid contributions toward correcting that tragic misunderstanding.

I hope that decision makers, as well as scholars, will be provoked to test some of my unorthodox policy recommendations. I am aware that the risk of the unorthodox for the policy maker is far greater than it is for the scholar. But building a world order in which the Powers recognize the long-term value to themselves of helping the currently dependent weaker countries to become stronger, more developed, and more interdependent seems worth the risk. Recognizing the utility and the effectiveness of the attractive instruments of power, and using them in place of the coercive instruments—even if it only helps avoid one more Vietnam, or Hungary, or Algeria, or Ireland, or Third Reich, or "Greater East Asian Co-prosperity Sphere"—seems like a very minor risk when placed next to the consequences of continuing the old approaches. If this work succeeds in inducing just one policy maker in just one powerful country—hopefully in the United States—to base his decisions on these new perspectives, it will have achieved its purpose.

Chapter 1

Perceptions and Communications

In his book, *The Behavioral Persuasion in Politics,* Heinz Eulau says, "A study of politics which leaves man out of its equation is a rather barren politics." In that same work Eulau goes on to say:

Small units like the individual or the small group, and large units like the organization of the nation-state, can be treated not as polar but as continuous variables . . . . all units small or large, should be subject to ordering on a single continuum. . . . from whatever point on the macro-micro continuum one proceeds, the task of research is to build, by patiently linking one unit with another, the total chain of interrelations that link individual to individual, individual to group, group to group, group to organization, organization to organization, and so on, until one gives the entire network continuous order.[1]

As an attempt to analyze the relations between states from just such a perspective, this study must begin by discussing the central concepts of individual and group behavior: perception, communication, and identity.

Perceptions

It may be said that man behaves as he does because of the ways in which he perceives the external world.[2] Perception is used here to mean the process by which an individual selects, evaluates, and organizes stimuli from the external environment.[3] While individuals

[1] Heinz Eulau, *The Behavioral Persuasion in Politics* (New York: Random House, 1963), pp. 3, 126.

[2] This perceptual model originally appeared in my article, "Group Perception and Social Change in Ceylon," *The International Journal of Comparative Sociology,* Vol. VII, No. 1–2 (Mar. 1966), pp. 209–226.

[3] Thus, my use of the term "perception" includes "memory" in the cybernetic sense and "cognition" in the interpretative sense.

and the groups they constitute can act or react only on the basis of their perceptions, the important point is that the same stimuli are often perceived differently by different individuals and groups. Whether or not an objective reality exists apart from man's perception of it need not concern us here. In terms of human behavior, only subjective reality exists—that is, the universe as individual men perceive it.

Man is inescapably a social animal. Particularly in the earliest years, but throughout life as well, he must exist in relationships with other human beings. Each human being brings to a relationship his own view of the universe. Essentially, his view is an individual compound of the perspectives of the groups in which he has been raised. What is more, each human being is raised in many different groups simultaneously, and each group will have conditioned him to view the world from its perspective. Will he regurgitate or salivate at the thought of eating the flesh of a cow or a kitten? It will depend upon how thoroughly he has internalized the attitudes and values he has been taught by his groups. Not only the language he speaks and the way in which he thinks, but even *what* he sees, hears, tastes, touches, and smells, are conditioned by the groups in which he has been raised. Benjamin Lee Whorf, the noted linguist, has written: "We are thus introduced to a new principle of relativity, which holds that all observers are not led by the same physical evidence to the same picture of the universe, unless their linguistic backgrounds are similar, or can in some way be calibrated." [4] I would go a step further and substitute the word "perceptual" for the word "linguistic." [5]

A Perceptual Model

The questions then are: How does man form his perceptions of the external world, and how do his perceptions affect his behavior? The model by which I try to answer these questions is based on

[4] Benjamin Lee Whorf, *Collected Papers on Metalinguistics,* quoted by Franklin Fearing, "An Examination of the Conceptions of Benjamin Whorf in the Light of Theories on Perception and Cognition," in *Language in Culture,* ed. Harry Hoijer (Chicago: University of Chicago Press, 1954), p. 46.
[5] I would argue that every group has its own language or "code," and that the language is a manifestation—verbal or nonverbal—of the perceptions the group holds. Language, once established, further constrains the individual to perceive in certain ways, but it is merely one of the ways in which groups maintain and reinforce similarity of perception. (I am using language in the broadest sense, to include, for example, the jargon or symbols used by social scientists or mathematicians to express the concepts peculiar to their groups.)

the following set of premises. Some of the premises are quite generally accepted; some are, at this stage, merely hypotheses; and some are definitional.[6]

1. Individual patterns of behavior are based on individual perceptions of the external world, which are largely learned.[7]

2. Because of biological and experiential differences, no two individuals can perceive the external world identically.

3. The greater the biological and experiential differences between individuals, the more disparate their perceptions are likely to be. Conversely, the more similar the biological and experiential background, the more similar their perceptions are likely to be.

4. A *perceptual group* may be defined as a number of individuals who perceive some aspect of the external world more or less similarly,[8] but who do not communicate this similarity of perception among themselves.[9]

5. A number of people who perceive some aspect of the external world more or less similarly, and recognize and *communicate* this similarity of perception, may be termed an *identity group*.

6. Other things being equal, the higher the degree of similarity of perception that exists among a number of individuals:
   a. the easier communication among them is likely to be;
   b. the more communication among them is likely to occur, and;
   c. the more likely it is that their similarity of perception will be recognized—that an identity group will form.

[6] These premises draw heavily on the work of cultural anthropologists, sociologists, psychologists, communications theorists, and linguists. In particular, the model is strongly influenced by the concept of "perceptual constancies." See F. F. Kilpatrick, ed., *Explorations in Transactional Psychology* (New York: New York University Press, 1961). As the model is refined and further developed, modifications will doubtless be made. While I believe that the approach is more important than the specific components, the premises are presented in order to make the model as explicit as possible.

[7] Perception includes the process by which attitudes and values are formed.

[8] The terms "more" and "less" are, of course, vague indicators of quantity. They are clearly inadequate for a precise science of social action. In much of the serious research being done by psychologists today, however, ways are being found to measure perception more precisely. For some suggestive approaches to this problem, see B. Berelson and G. A. Steiner, *Human Behavior: An Inventory of Scientific Findings* (New York: Harcourt, Brace and World, 1964).

[9] There are those social scientists who would argue that no collectivity of people who do not communicate can legitimately be called a group, and thus the term "perceptual group" is a misnomer. Strictly speaking that is true, and for the sake of precision those individuals who perceive some aspect of the external world more or less similarly, but who do not communicate that similarity of perception among themselves, should be called "perceptual potential group." This is one of those cases, however, where I prefer some imprecision in order to avoid cumbersome jargon.

7. Ease of communication allows for a constant increase in the degree of similarity of perception (through feedback mechanisms). This in turn allows for still further ease of communication. Thus, there tends to be a constant reinforcement of group identity. Conversely, where there is little or no communication among individuals there tends to be a *decrease* in similarity of perception, which in turn tends to make further communication more difficult.

8. The greater the number and intensity of perceptual groups individuals share—the more overlapping of important perceptual groups that exists among a number of individuals—the more likely they are to have a high degree of group identity.[10]

9. A pattern of perceptions and behavior that is accepted and expected by an identity group is called a culture. Since, by definition, each identity group has its own pattern of behavioral norms, and its own language or code (understood most clearly by members of that group) each group may be said to have its own culture.[11]

10. Since communication tends to be easiest among individuals who identify most closely with each other, and most difficult among individuals who perceive more or less dissimilarly, this tends to reinforce and exacerbate awareness of group differences. Any "we" (identity group) comes into much sharper focus when juxtaposed against any "they" (a different identity group).

11. To the degree that the people who inhabit a particular territory share some similarity of perceptions as subjects of that specific legal entity, they can be considered members of the perceptual group called the "state." [12]

---

[10] In most societies the family enjoys the highest degree of group identity. One reason is that the members of the family group are also concurrently members of so many other perceptual groups. Thus, with rare exceptions, all adult members of the family speak the same language, are from the same locality, are of the same religious persuasion, have approximately the same educational level, are of the same socio-economic class, are very likely to be employed in the same occupational grouping, and so on. Where the family members share fewer similarities of perception, as in the mobile societies of urban, industrial areas, family identity as the primary identification for the individual tends to break down.

[11] I have found that there is more analytical utility in considering each identity group as having its own culture, than in considering an entire society as having one culture and then having to account for deviations from that pattern in terms of subcultures. For a more complete discussion of this, see my "Culture: A Perceptual Approach," in *Vidya*, No. 3, Spring 1969, pp. 15–22.

[12] Not all inhabitants of a state necessarily become part of a statewide perceptual group. Indeed, it is possible that in many states the vast majority of the population may not share any similarity of perceptions as members of the statewide political units. In those cases they are one step further removed from becoming a nation. That is, the people in those states have first to develop some similarity of perception before they can become a statewide perceptual group and then a national identity group. See A. F. K. Organski, *The Stages of Political Development* (New York: Alfred A.

12. In those cases where there is a high degree of similarity of perception among the members of the state with regard to the existence and the symbols of the state, and that similarity of perception is communicated among themselves, the state (perceptual group) is also a "nation" (identity group).[13]

13. A nation may be defined as a number of people (usually large) who share and communicate a high degree of similarity of perceptions with regard to the symbols of either an existing state, or of a state they feel should exist.[14]

14. An individual must inevitably be a member of a myriad of different perceptual and identity groups simultaneously. However, he shares a higher degree of similarity of perception and a higher degree of group identity, with some than with others. Consciously or otherwise, he gives his various group identities a rank ordering. That ranking is what is commonly referred to as a "value system." Each individual's rank order is unique, and may vary, within narrow limits, from situation to situation.

15. Some identities are clearly more important to behavior than others. Because of this, it is useful to differentiate among primary, secondary, and tertiary identities. Although the ranking of these identities can and does change with time and circumstance, to understand individual behavior at any given moment, it is important to know which identities are primary and which are only secondary or tertiary.[15]

16. It often happens that individuals and groups have internalized elements of several different, even conflicting, value systems simultaneously. They are able to survive and function under this condition primarily because:

   a. they are able to identify in different degrees—and at different levels of consciousness—with each of the value systems, and

   b. most simultaneously held group identities only rarely come into direct *conscious* conflict.

17. When two equally valued identities do come into direct conflict, a high degree of anxiety (conscious or otherwise) may result.

18. In order to alleviate that anxiety, the individual or group often

---

Knopf, 1966). Although he does not use this term, he is referring to a similar phenomenon when he discusses the "Stage of Primitive Unification."

[13] For an interesting discussion of these relationships, see Karl Deutsch and William Foltz, eds., *Nation-Building* (New York: Atherton Press, 1963), particularly the article by Hermann Weilenmann, pp. 33–55.

[14] Thus nations such as Germany, Italy, or Israel can be said to have existed prior to the existence of the states by the same names.

[15] Thus, it becomes crucially important to the study of international affairs to know whether a decision maker in, say, the United Arab Republic, is acting on the basis of a primary identity as an Arab and only a secondary identity as an Egyptian, or vice-versa. What is more, it becomes crucially important that more study be devoted to how and why the salience of these identities can and does change. For this notion of differing level of salience I am indebted to Richard W. Cottam.

seeks some third identity which can accommodate, neutralize, rationalize, and/or synthesize these conflicting value systems.[16]

19. Because environmental and biological factors are ever changing, perceptions, attitudes, values, and identities are ever changing. Consequently, new perceptual and identity groups are constantly being formed and existing groups are constantly in a state of flux.

We know from the study of genetics that no two individuals are physiologically identical. Certainly, if the skin on the tips of the fingers is different for each individual, then each person's sense of touch must be presumed to be individual and unique. Even more important to the way men view the universe are the still unanswered questions of physical variations in other sensory receptors: the configuration of cones and rods in the retina of the eye, or taste buds on the tongue, or fibers in the ear. If no two individuals have identical receptors of stimuli, then it must follow, on the basis of physiological evidence alone, that no two individuals perceive the external world identically. Yet biological differences probably account for only the smallest fraction of the perceptual distinctions made by man.

Far more important in determining an individual's perceptions of the external world are the experiential factors involved in the reception, organization, and processing of sensory data. Genetically, we inherit from our parents those physical characteristics that distinguish us as their offspring. So, too, we inherit from our parents those environmental characteristics that distinguish us as their offspring. Admittedly, there is a good deal of individual variation, biologically and environmentally, but there is also a good deal of similarity. Given two white parents, the probability is that the offspring will be white. Given two English-speaking parents, the probability is that the offspring will speak English. The difference is that biological identity is, within a given range of probability, fixed, while environmental identity is not. The son of two white parents will always remain white no matter what happens to him after birth, but the son of two English-speaking parents may never speak English if from birth on he is raised by a totally non-English speaking group. Thus, while biologic inheritance cannot be changed, environmental inheritance is ever changing. But while there is, theoretically, an almost infinite number of possi-

[16] For some individuals and groups, the conflict could produce an inability to act. For still others, it might produce erratic behavior, with an alternative overstressing of one value system at the expense of another. All of these cases would probably be diagnosed as ambivalence. For a more detailed analysis of these situations see my article, "Group Perception and Social Change in Ceylon."

bilities for environmental conditioning the number of environmental factors to which most individuals are exposed is actually limited. Thus, for example, while there may be a whole world to explore, if not an entire universe, the vast majority of individuals who inhabit this planet never stray more than a few miles from their place of birth. Indeed, each of us is a member of a finite, and comparatively small, number of different identity groups.

If, for biologic and environmental reasons, it is not possible for any two individuals to perceive the universe in an identical manner, neither is it possible for them to have absolutely no similarities of perception. In a sense there is a continuum of similarity of perception among individuals. One extreme approaches—but never reaches—zero; the other approaches—but never reaches—100 percent. Actually, degree of similarity of perception can probably best be expressed not as a point on a continuum, but as a range of points. For example,[17] a Catholic from a wealthy third-generation Boston family and one from an illiterate and impoverished village in the Congo may share no more than perhaps a 10 to 15 percent similarity of perception as Catholics, but to this degree they are a part of the broad identity group called "Catholics." Teachers, considered as a broad group, may have a 20 to 25 percent similarity of perception. If we narrow the group to include only college teachers, the range of similarity of perception may increase to 40 to 50 percent. If we further specify that the group consists only of Irish-Catholic, American, middle class, urban, white, male, heterosexual college teachers of quantum physics, with Ph.D.'s from the Massachusetts Institute of Technology, between the ages of 35 and 40, the range of similarity of perception might well increase to 75 to 80 percent. Notice that while we have decreased the number of people who can be included in our group, we have increased the number of group identities the members share. By so doing, we have greatly increased the likelihood of easy communication among them and, thus, the likelihood of their sharing still greater similarities of perception in the future. It is no wonder that the smaller the group, the greater its cohesion is likely to be.

Communications

As the term "communication" is used here, it refers to the transmission from one individual to another of anything a human being is capable of sensing, thinking, or feeling. It follows from what was

---

[17] Any figures used in these examples are completely hypothetical, and are included merely to illustrate a concept. They are not based on any known research.

said above that since no two individuals can perceive the external world identically, no two individuals can communicate with 100 percent effectiveness. That is, it is simply not possible for one individual to transmit exactly to another an idea, a value, an emotion, a sensation that is to a greater or lesser degree outside the perceptual experience of the receiver. No amount of explanation, however good the communication effort, can convey the exact taste of pineapple juice, for example, if the receiver of the message has himself never tasted it. This is not to say, though, that he will realize he has not received the message exactly as the sender intended him to receive it. Since he has not, himself, had exacly the same perceptual experience, he has nothing with which to compare the explanation. Thus, he may receive a message very different from the one the sender intended, but, unaware that it is different, merely assumes that the message received is the same as the message sent. Unfortunately for the whole communication process, this is most often the case.

If the sender knows that what he is trying to convey is beyond the perceptual experience of the receiver, he might not bother to send the message at all, or he might attempt to convey it in terms (code) that approximate a perception which he knows the receiver has experienced. One of the major problems in communication, however, is that most of the time we have no exact knowledge of the perceptual experience of the intended receiver of our message. We have an unconscious tendency to assume, in most cases, that the other person's perceptions are more or less the same as ours. We must do this to function easily in everyday life. We assume a high degree of similarity of perceptions until proven otherwise. If someone asks us what we mean, or in some other verbal or non-verbal way indicates that he did not understand our message (in other words, provides feedback on the effects of the message), then we may consciously attempt to recode the message into terms we believe the receiver more likely to understand. But, since we can never know the exact contours of someone else's perceptual configuration, our new attempt is still only an approximation of similarities based on our own perceptual environment. This dependence on approximate similarities is equally true for the sender and the receiver. No amount of communication—regardless of the quality—can convey any perception *exactly,* since no receiver of the message is biologically or experientially exactly the same as any sender. Thus, no message is ever received exactly the way it was intended by the sender—which is another way of saying that there is inevitably going to be some distortion in every communication.

If a message is sent but not received at all, no communication has taken place. One may debate the philosophic question of whether a "sound" has been made when a tree falls in a forest in which there are no audio-receptors to "hear" it, but from the perspective of human behavior, a message that is sent but not received is simply not a communication. It does often happen, however, that messages are received that were not intentionally sent. That is, an individual (whether representing himself, his group, or his state) may say or do something that is meant to be received only by particular individuals and/or groups. Another individual, for whom the message was not intended, and who may not know the code in which the message was sent, may receive that message and may understand it in a totally different way from that intended by the sender. The receiver may then react on the basis of the meaning he has given to the message, rather than on the basis of the meaning intended by the sender.

A Model of the Communication Process

The concepts used in this discussion of communication require more systematic analysis. For that purpose a model of the communication process is presented here. My formulation borrows heavily from the work done by Claude Shannon,[18] Norbert Weiner,[19] Colin Cherry,[20] Karl Deutsch,[21] and David Berlo.[22] Although the model applies equally to communications between man and man, man and machine, and machine and machine, it is used here only to express the process of human communication. (See Figure 1.1 for a diagrammatic representation.)

The basic element in the process is man. He is, for every one of the twenty-four hours in a day, either a sender or receiver of messages. Although for most of those hours he is receiving ex-

[18] Claude Shannon and Warren Weaver, *The Mathematical Theory of Communications* (Urbana: University of Illinois Press, 1949).

[19] See particularly Norbert Weiner, *Cybernetics* (Cambridge: The Technology Press of the Massachusetts Institute of Technology, and New York: John Wiley & Sons, 1948); and his *Human Use of Human Beings* (New York: Houghton Mifflin, 1964).

[20] Colin Cherry, *On Human Communications: A Review, a Survey and a Criticism* (New York: Science Editions, 1961) published earlier (Cambridge: Massachusetts Institute of Technology Press, and New York: John Wiley & Sons, 1957).

[21] See particularly Karl Deutsch, *Nationalism and Social Communication* (Cambridge: The Technology Press of the Massachusetts Institute of Technology, and New York: John Wiley & Sons, 1953) and his *The Nerves of Government* (London: Free Press, 1963).

[22] David K. Berlo, *The Process of Communication: An Introduction to Theory and Practice* (New York: Holt, Rinehart and Winston, 1960). Berlo's summary of the writers in the field is most useful to the nonspecialist.

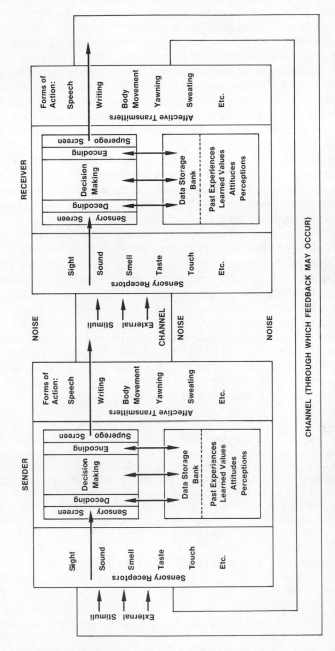

Figure 1.1 The Communication Process[a]

[a]Although taken primarily from the work of Claude Shannon and Karl Deutsch, this diagram is an adaptation of one done earlier for the author by Daniel Rich.

ternal stimuli from nonhuman sources, they are messages none-theless. The door closing in the next apartment, the wind blowing the trees, the light coming in the window—in short, anything that can be picked up by our sensory receptors—are messages when we receive them. Even when a man sleeps, he is receiving stimuli from the external environment and probably unconsciously re-cording them. If the room gets too cold or too warm, while re-maining asleep he adjusts the blankets accordingly. If a particu-lar topic is being discussed in the next room, the topic may find its way into his dreams. And if the message is loud enough (a car backfiring perhaps) or important enough (the baby crying) he might wake from his sleep to attend to the message. Indeed, in the course of every hour of every day from the moment of birth, man is bombarded with hundreds of thousands of discrete bits of information—stimuli of one sort or another that reach his sensory receptors from the world external to himself.

Obviously, man cannot attend equally to all stimuli to which he is exposed. For one thing, not all stimuli reach the sensory receptors at the same level of intensity. That is, some sounds are louder than others, some images are clearer than others. All things being equal, the louder sounds and the clearer images—the more intense stimuli—would probably be transmitted to the brain by the sensory receptors before the less intense stimuli. But all things are not always equal. Some stimuli are so important or so salient to us that, regardless of intensity, we are likely to pick them out first. Conversely, some stimuli are so repugnant to us or difficult for us to handle that, regardless of intensity, we are likely to pick them out last. As Berelson and Steiner explain:

Of all possible stimuli—i.e., all bits of energy capable of firing receptors at any given moment—only a small portion become part of actual experience; and that portion is not a random sample of what is objectively available . . . the observer, of course, plays an active part in determining what will be allowed to stimulate the re-ceptors at all: we look at some things, ignore others, and look *away* from still others ("selective exposure"). Beyond that, only a frac-tion of those stimuli that have gained effective entry to a receptor ever reach awareness ("selective awareness").[23]

The sensory screens through which stimuli picked up by our sensory receptors must pass, filter out all bits of data except those we are perceptually or emotionally prepared to receive. Thus, some stimuli will be received, but will be ignored because they dis-tract one's attention. When, for example, someone focuses his

[23] Berelson and Steiner, *Human Behavior,* p. 100.

attention on reading the words on a printed page, he has adjusted his screening devices to filter out of consciousness the multitude of other stimuli that are simultaneously coming to him and that would, if not filtered, impede the completion of his task. The stimuli are still there, but the reader's sensory screen prevents them from interfering with the primary task.

Some stimuli will be received, but will be essentially ignored because they contradict what the receiver wants, or expects, or is psychologically prepared for. Someone alone at home at night, having just finished reading or watching a murder mystery, is much more apt to be aware of every creak in every board and to be suspicious of strange noises outside than is someone who has been engrossed in a sex novel. More to the point of this work, much of what we know about the effect of stereotyping falls into this category. Twenty-five years ago G. W. Allport and L. Postman[24] conducted an experiment that graphically illustrated the effect of stereotyping on perceptions. The study consisted of showing a photograph of what appeared to be a subway car to a large number of Americans. In it, two men are standing, one black and well dressed and the other white and wearing working clothes. The white man in the picture is holding an open razor. The experiment consisted of showing the picture to a person and asking him to describe it to someone who could not himself see the picture. The second person would then describe to a third person what had been described to him. The third person, in turn, would describe it to a fourth, and so on through six or seven people. In over half the cases reported by Allport and Postman, the razor changed hands from the white to the black man, and the black man became the one who was poorly dressed. Indeed, in some cases the black man was reported to be "brandishing" it or "threatening" the white man with it. As Otto Klineberg points out, "This does not mean that half the subjects reacted in such a fashion, since one shift in a rumor chain might be reproduced by all who followed. It does mean that in 50% of the *groups* this phenomenon was observed."[25] In the study, the distortion was avoided in only two groups: among Negroes, for what were assumed to be obvious reasons, and among young children, who had not yet learned the stereotype. However, when this experiment was repeated approximately ten years ago at an all black high school in New York City, as much distortion occurred among the black students as was

---

[24] G. W. Allport and L. Postman, *The Psychology of Rumor* (New York: Holt, Rinehart and Winston, 1947), as reported in Otto Klineberg, *The Human Dimension in International Relations* (New York: Holt, Rinehart and Winston, 1964), p. 42.
[25] *Ibid.,* p. 42.

reported among whites in the original study.[26] One possible explanation may be that the black students participating in the experiment had subconsciously accepted the predominant white stereotype of the blacks.

These experiments illustrate two principles involved in any communication process. Most obviously, and most pertinently for any discussion of intergroup communication, they show the transmutation of sensory data to conform to expectation. But they also illustrate that in any process of communication, the more steps a message must go through from its original source to its intended recipient, the more distortion is likely to occur. Each person along the way will apply his own perceptual bias to the message as he receives it, and will pass it along not as it was sent to him, but as it was received by him.[27]

Joseph de Rivera says of the selection of stimuli in the process of communication:

Any stimulus is initially amorphous; it is not a psychological stimulus until the person attends to some aspect of it. In order to act, the observer selects an aspect of the stimulus which he can distinguish and thinks important. He determines the aspect of the stimulus to which he responds.

. . . both the perceptual and attentive processes are usually completely intertwined, so that both determine how a person constructs his world. A person cannot be said to attend to a stimulus unless he perceives it, and yet every perception involves a selective attention.[28]

Berelson and Steiner report that there are probably three major factors that determine which stimuli are selected, ignored, or missed:

The nature of the stimuli involved; previous experience or learning as it affects the observer's expectations (what he is prepared or "set" to see); and the motives at play at the time, by which we mean his needs, desires, wishes, interests, and so on—in short, what the observer wants or needs to see and not see. Each of these factors can act to heighten or to decrease the probability of perceiving, and each can act on both exposure and awareness.[29]

[26] This second experiment was reported to me in a personal communication.

[27] See Chapter 5 for a discussion of the effect of these communication principles on the way news of world events is received in the weaker countries.

[28] Joseph H. de Rivera, *The Psychological Dimension of Foreign Policy* (Columbus, Ohio: Charles E. Merrill, 1968), pp. 42–43.

[29] Berelson and Steiner, *Human Behavior,* p. 100.

It is the second of those three factors that is of primary concern in this study. As was noted earlier, learning occurs in the group into which one happens to be born or with which one happens to come into significant contact. Each group teaches somewhat different responses to the same stimuli. Learned responses are the perceptual culture of the group. Since each group teaches its own perceptual culture, two people from entirely different groups observing the same stimuli could respond so differently in some cases that one might wonder whether, in fact, it was the same stimuli to which they were responding.

I have been discussing the selection and perception involved in receiving messages, but it is also necessary to consider the factors that affect the sending of messages. Although the written word and the radio loudspeaker may be the most important forms messages can take in international affairs (largely because of distances involved), for group solidarity and influence on members, there is no more effective mode of communication than face-to-face contact. There are a number of reasons why this should be so, not the least of which is that when speaking to one person directly it is possible for the sender of the message to choose the code (perceptual language) he believes most likely to be understood by his hearer. Thus, if someone is trying to convince a dozen different people to take a particular action, he can present that particular message in twelve different ways—one to suit the perceptions of each of his hearers. What is more, using face-to-face conversation there can be instant feedback and thus he can refute or correct any distortions that may appear in his message. Also, he can convey the same message with his eyes, his body movements, his facial expressions, thus reinforcing the spoken message by using other transmitters simultaneously. Being able to bombard many of the receiver's sensory receptors with the same message, he is much more likely to get the message through, and to get it through at many levels of awareness.

One further point about the use of affective transmitters of messages: Not only must the individual select the message he intends to send from the experientially determined, culturally conditioned, finite number of possibilities available in his "data storage bank," but he must filter his initial internal reaction through a "superego screen" before expressing it as a verbal or nonverbal message. This screen sets the limits for the individual in terms of what is an acceptable reaction, given his personal interpretation of what the constraints of his environment (groups) are on his behavior. In essence, it sets the limits of his reaction to stimuli. While a detailed analysis of this aspect of the communication process is beyond the scope of this work, it is nonetheless important to note its existence. It has particular relevance to this work as a whole in this regard: the superego screen may regulate and set limits on responses of decision makers, official and nonofficial, of every country that is in some way dependent upon another and in which the dependence is both recognized and resented by the elite. Feelings of dependence often tempt one to react negatively and even violently, whether verbally or physically. Yet precisely because one recognizes his dependent position, he may not do so. What he judges he may and may not do is regulated by the superego filter. Without the existence of a superego filter, a member of a decision-making elite in a dependency might very well react to a derogatory slur from an officer of the powerful state with a fist to the jaw of the offender. With the superego monitoring behavior, that response may take no more violent a form than a curt departure from the scene—and, possibly, an internal resolve to work all the harder for independence.

Having discussed the two most important elements of the communications model—the sender and the receiver of messages—it is now necessary to consider the third element, the connecting channel. (See Figure 1.1, p. 17.) Every communication is sent via a channel. In the case of one individual talking to another, the channel is the air through which the sound travels. In the case of someone broadcasting, it is the airwaves and a radio tuned to the appropriate frequency. With a written communication the channel might be the postal system. If, in the first case, the sender whispers and the intended recipient is too far away to hear the message, no communication has occurred. If, in the second case, the intended recipient does not have a radio, or does not have it turned on or tuned in at the time of transmission, no communication has occurred. If, in the third case, the address is wrong and the letter never gets delivered, again no communication has occurred. But even if the channel between sender and recipient is adequate to the message and adequately utilized, there are still difficulties to overcome.

Every communication system operates in an environment full of what the communication specialist calls "noise." Noise is anything that interferes with the transmission of the message. It might be a car backfiring and drowning out the voice of the sender in a face to face conversation, or gum the speaker was chewing at the time he was talking, or the beautiful lady who caught the eye of the recipient and distracted his attention just at the moment the message was being sent. In the second example, the noise might be the electrical storm that interferes with the airwaves, or the jamming of certain frequencies that many governments practice, or the irritating accent of the speaker that causes the recipient to pay more attention to the speech than to the message.[30] In the third example, noise could be the poor handwriting that makes the message illegible, or the rain that smears the address and makes the letter undeliverable, or the psychological state of the recipient at the time he receives the letter that prompts him to throw it away unopened.

Fortunately, it is not imperative to the functioning of groups that communications be perceived with anything approaching 100 percent accuracy. Fortunately, too, there are corrective devices inherent in almost any communication system. One such device is redundancy. Most verbal languages are themselves more than one-half redundant. Note the last sentence with more than half the words left out: Most languages are redundant. Even if part of the message is lost, either due to differing perceptions on the part of sender and receiver, or to inadequacies or interference in the channel, enough of the message often gets through to convey the general meaning intended. But even if there is considerably more distortion of key words than presented above, the message is still likely to be received. Note the sentence: Mist languags ard redundent. Not only are more than 50 percent of the words used in the original message missing, each of the remaining words in the last sentence are themselves distorted. Still, it is possible to get the gist of the message. Because of the context of the other letters in the words, the other words in the sentence, and the other sentences in the paragraph, it is likely that most readers received the message despite the great distortion. There are only so many choices available in any language—cultural or verbal.

Now suppose the reader did not know the meaning of the word "redundant." Since that is a crucial word in the sentence, not knowing the code could prevent communication. However, since languages (and the authors who use them) tend to be redundant, merely having read the rest of the paragraph would probably have furnished the reader with some idea of the word's meaning.

Perhaps the most important device for overcoming the deficiencies of the communication process is "feedback"—the return to the sender of data about the results of his communication effort. This is built directly into some communication systems, particularly that of face-to-face communications. If the receiver of a message in a face-to-face communication does not understand

---

[30] It was reported to the author that at one time just after Radio Free Europe began operations, on a program beamed to the Ukraine and intended to stir the Ukrainians to revolt against the Russians, the announcer had such a heavy Russian accent that he outraged those potential revolutionaries who took the risks involved in listening to the station.

some portion of the message being sent, he can immediately convey that lack of understanding to the original sender, who can then attempt to correct the deficiency. This is precisely why face-to-face communication can be so effective.

Harold Levitt has devised an interesting and dramatic exercise to demonstrate the necessity for feedback in communications.[31] In that exercise, a volunteer is given a sheet of paper with five or six rectangles drawn on it. The drawing is the message, and the volunteer is asked to communicate that message to a group of people who will attempt to draw it from his instructions as precisely as possible. The exercise is done twice: once without any feedback and the second time with feedback. Invariably, without feedback no more than 20 percent of the people are able to approach correct representation in their drawing of the rectangles. With feedback—that is, with participants asking as many questions as they feel is necessary in order to draw it correctly—between 75 and 100 percent are able to draw a very close approximation of the rectangles. The exercise with feedback takes at least twice as long as the same exercise without it, but the results in terms of precision of communication are obviously worth the extra time.

What is most interesting about the experiment, however, is that when the sender estimates, immediately after he has attempted to communicate without feedback, how many in his audience got the message more or less accurately, he invariably overestimates the number whom he believes to have received his message; he thinks he has communicated quite well. Similarly, if the audience is asked, immediately after they have completed the exercise without feedback, how well they think they have drawn the rectangles, they too invariably overestimate; many more people think they have done the drawing accurately than actually have. Now, if no feedback were built into the system, both sender and receiver would believe they had communicated quite well, even though they had not. Only when the exercise is repeated, introducing feedback, do both sender and receiver begin to estimate realistically how well or poorly they are communicating. Unfortunately, there are many communication systems in the world—particularly mass media—into which it is impossible to introduce feedback.

I have outlined here a model of the communication process that is extremely bleak. Unfortunately, the actual communication process seems to approximate the model very closely. Indeed, the

[31] See Harold Levitt, *Managerial Psychology,* 2nd ed. (Chicago: University of Chicago Press, 1964), Chapter 9. I have used this exercise in a number of classes and training programs and have consistently received the same results.

failures of the communication process are one of the major reasons why, throughout recorded history, man has said he wanted peace and yet has found it impossible to attain. Perhaps if those who seek to minimize conflict—whether interpersonal, intergroup, or interstate—would pay more attention to improving communications than they have in the past, they could begin to attain their objectives.

Identity Groups: We vs. They

The most surprising thing about identity groups is that, aside from minor variations in style and values from place to place, they all exhibit similar characteristics. For example, regardless of the grounds upon which the common identity is based, once that identity is seen to exist, members of each group tend to make the same assumption that other members of their own group are good and members of other groups are suspect. "We" may recognize individual differences among ourselves and admit that not all of "us" are perfect, but by and large we consider ourselves intelligent, industrious, peaceful, kind, loyal, helpful, friendly, courteous, obedient, reverent, and clean. Regardless of what we may be engaged in at any particular moment in time, we genuinely believe ourselves to be acting from the best of motives. If we know nothing about two individuals save that one of them is a member of one of the groups with which we identify, and the other is not, we are likely to be trusting of the one who belongs to our group and suspicious of the other.

The operation of this phenomenon in domestic voting behavior has been amply demonstrated in studies of United States elections.[32] When the voter knows absolutely nothing about two candidates for the same office except their party affiliation (which is so often the case, particularly with respect to less important offices), the overwhelming likelihood is that he will vote for the candidate who belongs to the party to which he subscribes. In primary elections, when the contest is between two candidates of the same party, it is not an accident that ethnic candidates tend to carry ethnic districts.

It would appear to be one of the cardinal rules of group identity that "we" tend to recognize a common identity much more clearly when juxtaposed against a common "they." (See premise 10, p. 11.) Human beings may recognize and communicate some small

[32] See, for example, Bernard Berelson, Paul F. Lazarsfeld, and Hazel Gaudet, *The People's Choice* (New York: Columbia University Press, 1948).

degree of similarity of perceptions simply on the basis of their common humanity. But the focus tends to be on differences rather than on similarities. For most people, the list of "they" groups is probably longer than any list of "we" groups. Just as the Athenian word for non-Athenian—"barbarian"—conveyed a pejorative notion, so, too, does the very word "they." The degree of hostility expressed toward other groups increases as the group becomes more specific. Thus, while "they," "stranger," and "foreigner" have mildly pejorative connotations, words like *Spic, Mick, Honkie, Kike, Nigger, Wop,* or *Queer* are both specific and strongly hostile.

Otto Klineberg cites a study done in Princeton in 1933 by Daniel Katz and Kenneth Braly in which one hundred students were asked to select adjectives that they felt described different nationality groups. Among the adjectives chosen were the following:

. . . for the Germans, scientifically minded, industrious, passionate; the Negroes, superstitious, lazy, happy-go-lucky, ignorant; the Irish, pugnacious, quick-tempered, witty; the English, sportsmanlike, intelligent, conventional; the Jews, shrewd, mercenary, industrious; the Americans, industrious, intelligent, materialistic, ambitious; the Chinese, superstitious, sly, conservative; the Japanese, intelligent, industrious, progressive; the Turks, cruel, religious, treacherous.[33]

Note that this study was done many years ago, prior to Pearl Harbor. During and immediately after World War II, American attitudes toward the Germans and Japanese markedly changed. At that point in history, words like "treacherous," "cruel," "vicious," and "sly" were used much more frequently to describe Germans and particularly Japanese. On the other hand, the Chinese and Russians during those years were the ones viewed by Americans as "courageous," "brave," and "hard-working." But times and political alliances change, and so do our stereotypes. Still more recent studies show that Americans again picture the Germans and the Japanese as "intelligent" and "industrious," while the Russians and particularly the Chinese are again considered "treacherous," "sly," and "sneaky."

Studies of this sort have now been conducted in a great many countries of the world. Not surprisingly, each country has its pet "hate" groups. The Cambodians seem to mistrust the Vietnamese and the Thais more than any others, while the Nigerians mistrust the Ibos, the Sinhalese mistrust the Tamils, the Indians mistrust the Pakistanis, and the Chinese and the Nepalese mistrust the In-

[33] Otto Klineberg, *The Human Dimension in International Relations* (New York: Holt, Rinehart and Winston, 1964), p. 35.

dians.[34] While each country had a different enemy, they all agreed on one point: each one thought his own group was the most peace-loving of all! [35]

It should be noted, however, that it is not only important whether a specific group views itself as different; it is also important whether the society in which the group lives accepts its members as "one of us" or views them as alien. Thus, for example, while the Jew in Germany and the light-skinned Negro in America may have viewed themselves—or may have wanted to view themselves—primarily as Germans or Americans, their societies viewed them, at best, as particular kinds of Germans or Americans ("German-Jews" and "American-Negroes") and, at worst, as not German or American at all. Faced with that circumstance, regardless of personal preference most members of both groups had (or have) no choice but to see themselves as members of separate groups.

A great many identity groups cut across state and national boundaries. Sex, religion, occupation, race, class, language, ideology, age, education (to mention only a few of the identity groups that exist in the world), simply do not recognize international boundaries. Catholics, Jews, Muslims, Hindus, regardless of where they live, recognize and communicate a similarity of perception as Catholics, Jews, Muslims, or Hindus. Similarly, socialists, or anti-socialists, capitalists, or anticapitalists all over the world also recognize and communicate a high degree of similarity of perception. To be sure, national identity exists and in many cases is the identity to which an individual gives his primary allegiance. There have been times when religious, ideological, and even family identities have come into conflict with national identities, and the others frequently have had to give way. Modern history is filled with occasions when Christian has fought Christian, socialist has fought socialist, and even brother has fought brother, all in the name of a "higher" national identity. But the fact is that for much of the world, and particularly for most of the people in the weaker countries with which this work primarily deals, national identity may be far less developed than some group identities that cross state boundaries.

This cross lacing of group identities is represented diagrammatically in Figure 1.2. Of course, for the mass of the population of most countries the diagram does *not* apply. The world view of the village peasant rarely extends very far beyond the next village—

[34] The role that fear plays in the forming of such attitudes is discussed below in the section on "Misperceptions in Conflict Situations."

[35] W. Buchanan and H. Cantril, *How Nations See Each Other* (Urbana: University of Illinois Press, 1953), cited in Klineberg, *Human Dimension,* p. 36.

Figure 1.2   Multiple Group Identities: Relationships
             Between Individuals, Groups, and States[a]

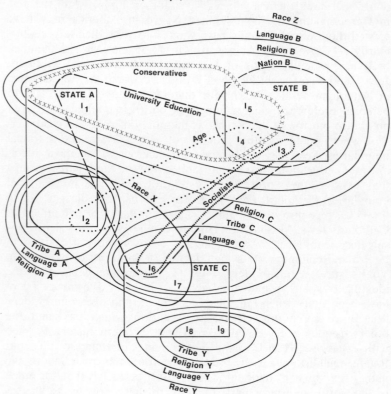

[a]*Although the diagram is the author's, the concepts underlying it are drawn heavily from Karl Deutsch. See particularly his* Nationalism and Social Communication: An Inquiry into the Foundations of Nationality, *2nd ed. (Cambridge: Massachusetts Institute of Technology Press, 1966).*

although this situation is changing with widespread use of the transistor radio. The family, the clan, the other villagers, perhaps co-religionists or the tribe or the caste, usually form the primary identity groups for the peasant, and these groups tend to be localized. That there may be other peasants, other co-religionists, other members of the same race with very similar perceptions of their own, tends to be simply beyond the reality world of most of these people. But this diagram probably represents the identity world of the literate, attentive portions of the populations quite accurately. Even if these latter people comprise only the smallest fraction of any given population, they tend to be the elite—the people who make the decisions—and thus, their group identities have a significance well beyond their numbers.

The diagram depicts nine individuals (I_1 I_2 . . . I_9) living in three states. The only state that is also a nation is B. While each of the individuals depicted would also be surrounded, in a more realistic representation, by a great many small circles representing local, peer, and familial group identities not shared by the other individuals, those more unique identities have been omitted here solely to avoid overcomplication of the diagram. What emerges is a picture of I_1 living physically in state A, but tied by a host of primary identities to state B. Indeed, in the diagram, I_1 is tied more closely (shares far more similarity of perception and identity) to the individuals in state B than he is to I_2 who also happens to be a resident of state A. I_3 and I_4, on the other hand, share as many group identities as do I_3 and I_1; but I_3 and I_4 share the important added identity of being members of the same nation. I_2 and I_6, while sharing some identity ties with individuals in other states, tend to share many more ties with individuals within their own states and, thus, are less likely to be drawn toward other countries. But since I_6 and I_8 share fewer identities than even I_6 and I_3, the likelihood is that I_6 will feel even less drawn toward I_8 than toward I_3.

With such relationships, it would be particularly easy for I_3 and I_4 to identify not only who "we" are but also to identify several possible "theys." "They" would probably be everyone outside of state B, with the possible exception of I_1. For I_7 and I_8, both the "we" and the "they" would also be fairly obvious. Indeed, if all other things are equal, the possibility that state C would become a nation seems quite remote. If, as simplified by the drawing, I_1 is a small minority in his country, in many ways his position in the country would be most ambiguous. Speaking the language of B, sharing the religious and racial perceptions of the majority of the population of B, the overwhelming probability is that he would be viewed by I_2 and others in state A as being more B than A, regardless of his own self-perception.

A person almost always belongs to at least one group of persons whose opinions he values. He cares what these particular persons think about him, and he tends to see things from their perspective. This perspective affects what is important to him and, therefore, what he attends to. Furthermore since changing his view of reality means losing emotional contact with the group, his beliefs are anchored in what the group perceives as real.[36]

Since men can act only on the basis of their perceptions, it follows that if they perceive their interests as more closely tied to some international identity than to a parochial national identity, when the two identities come into conflict the individuals or groups concerned might act in the perceived interests of the identity that crosses state boundaries. More likely, however—indeed much more commonly in such cases of conflicting identities—the indigenous elite will define national interest in terms compatible with their own international identity. Thus, to the Ceylonese tea-grower, it is in Ceylon's interest to maintain close ties with the West, which is, after all, the major market for Ceylon's tea. That it is also in his personal interest may not even enter his consciousness. Charles Wilson's axiom that what is good for General Motors is good for the United States is hardly unique. The point is that national interest is often defined by decision makers in terms of their own personal identity groups.

Misperceptions in Conflict Situations

That "we" are good and "they" are less than good in a great many situations is an attitude anyone studying intergroup or interstate relations must take into account. The student of intergroup or interstate conflict must also consider the likelihood that the more intense the conflict, the better *we* become and the worse *they* become. During times of relative calm it is fairly easy and often quite satisfying to consider ourselves objective enough to find fault with our own identity groups, and to find at least some merit in other groups. All that changes, however, when *we* perceive our group to be seriously threatened by the others.

In international affairs, particularly where national identity is strong, notice that *they* have "spies" while *we* have "intelligence men." Notice, too, that *we* have never declared an aggressive war; *they* fight aggressive wars while *we* fight wars of self-defense. It

[36] de Rivera, *Psychological Dimension,* p. 27.

was Britain and France, after all, who declared war on Germany in 1939, merely because *we* Germans went to the rescue of other Germans being massacred and mutilated by the Poles. What was Germany to do? *We* had to defend good Germans in the good German city of Danzig (at the time occupied by Polish troops) from destruction. And once the U.K. and France declared war, there simply was no choice for Germany but to defend itself.

The "Cuban Missile Crisis" of 1962 is another example. What was the United States to do? Was it to stand by and allow Castro to install "offensive" weapons just 90 miles from the Florida coast? Note the definition of "offensive weapons": the same weapons that we have pointed at them for protection become offensive weapons when *they* point them at *us*. Obviously, we had to insist that the Russians remove them merely in self-defense.

If such attitudes are the usual concomitant of strong national identity, how does one explain the widespread opposition to the Vietnam war on the part of many U.S. citizens who have a high degree of identification with the symbols and values of the American nation? The answer is not simply that those who oppose the war give a still higher ranking to their identity as pacifists or liberals or communists, although a few may do so. (Among those who identified themselves primarily as communists or fascists in the 1930's, some probably gave higher rankings to their ideological than their national identities.) But that is only a partial explanation. A less simplistic explanation would take into account the variety of responses that it is possible for the same symbol to elicit among different groups. Thus two highly nationalistic Americans who shared that group identity, but few others, might have very different images of what their country stood for. One might picture the America of the Bill of Rights, the Emancipation Proclamation, social welfare, and equal rights, an America that is liberal, humane, the friend of the downtrodden. The other might picture the America of the Mayflower, of the rugged God-fearing individuals who survived that first winter and went on to conquer a continent and create the wealthiest society the world has ever seen, an America that has always fought on the side of justice by manfully refusing to knuckle under to aggressive tyrants from George III down through Joseph Stalin. For the first, the American involvement in Vietnam is a shameful denial of everything that made us great in the past. For the second, America's refusal to do what is necessary to win is a shameful denial of everything that made us great in the past. Thus, two individuals, each with strong but different identities as Americans, could come to diametrically opposite views of what America should have been doing in Vietnam, and yet each would rightly think of himself as a "patriotic" American.

Ralph K. White, in a brilliant monograph entitled "Misperceptions and the Vietnam War," [37] has explored this subject in depth. In systematic fashion he has provided an analysis of six forms of misperception that commonly appear in intense conflict situations. While these forms of misperception are undoubtedly most intense during crisis periods, they probably exist to varying lesser degrees whenever any group perceives even minor threats to itself.

White's six forms of misperception are: (1) The Diabolical Enemy-Image; (2) The Virile Self-Image; (3) The Moral Self-Image; (4) Selective Inattention; (5) Absence of Empathy; and (6) Military Overconfidence. Numbers 1, 2, 3, and 6 are self-explanatory, and have been touched upon elsewhere in this chapter, although not necessarily under those names. Numbers 4 and 5, "Selective Inattention" and "Absence of Empathy," are not self-explanatory, and because of their importance to this study, deserve to be discussed in some detail.

The section on the communication process contained a discussion of selective attention. Selective inattention is, in a sense, the other side of that coin. Instead of analyzing which bits of data from the external world individuals with different perceptual sets choose to select and why, White asks which bits of data from the external world individuals with different perceptual sets choose to ignore, and why.

Call it resistance, repression, ignoring, forgetting, non-learning, inhibition of curiosity, evading, card-stacking, perceptual defense, blindspots, or just plain not paying attention. By whatever name, it is omnipresent. It has cropped up continually throughout this study. Absence of empathy—i.e., not paying enough attention to the thoughts of others is probably its most serious, most war-producing manifestation, but it has many others. Whatever is inconsistent with the black-and-white picture (that is, with the diabolical enemy-image and the moral self-image) and whatever is inconsistent with the virile self-image tends to drop out of consciousness. Space perspective, especially whatever has to do with distant onlookers (Western Europe, the USSR), tends to be restricted. Time perspective is restricted. Important distinctions (e.g., between different meanings of "aggression," between Munich and the present situation in Vietnam, between a holding operation and surrender) tend to be blurred or ignored. Individuals who raise issues that one does not want to think about are often not answered in terms of the issues; they are denounced as traitors, cowards or naive dupes of the diabolical enemy. Grounds for fear, including fear of atomic destruction, may be pushed out of the mind. . . . Elements of actual or potential strength in the ad-

[37] Ralph K. White, "Misperceptions and the Vietnam War," *The Journal of Social Issues,* Vol. XXII, No. 3 (July 1966), entire issue.

versary are often given less attention and less weight than they deserve. On each side of every acute conflict the tendency appears; we have seen it in the minds of the Austrians in 1914, in Hitler's mind in 1939, in the minds of Communists today, in the minds of non-militants in the United States, and in this chapter we have seen it, in many forms, in the minds of militants.[38]

Although, in the passage quoted above, White is referring to the misperceptions of American militants on the Vietnam issue, throughout his work he demonstrates the same process in operation, whether in reference to North Vietnamese misperceptions of the South or South Vietnamese misperceptions of the North, or Austrian misperceptions of Serbia. The fact is that, particularly in periods of intense conflict, but to some degree in all conflict situations, every group engages in this kind of distortion.

In discussing some of the incredible misperceptions that occurred among American decision makers during the Korean crisis, de Rivera says:

If there are differences in the perception of an event among persons similar enough to be high American officials, one can imagine how differently an event may appear to persons from different cultures. A person from a different culture lives in a different world of reality—so much so that a person who is thrust into a different culture actually experiences a kind of "culture shock" in which he is quite disoriented. This difference in worlds has two serious consequences for international relations. First, as Wedge has documented, a visitor to another country perceives events in a way that fits in with his own beliefs, and hence, often does not get a valid picture of that country. Second, in attempting to anticipate the reactions of other nations, officials often fail to view events from the other nations' perspective.[39]

It is precisely this inability to "view events from the other nations' perspective," that White refers to as absence of empathy.

To avoid misunderstanding it should perhaps be repeated that the word "empathy" as used here does not mean sympathy. It does not mean a sneaking sympathy for the Communist cause, but a tough-minded effort to understand the viewpoints of both enemies and onlookers as a basis for realism in coping with enemies (without war if possible) and achieving cooperation with onlookers. . . . One aspect, however, calls for further discussion: what Newcomb has called "autistic hostility"—the tendency to express hostility by cutting off communication (and with it, the possibility of achieving empathy), with the result that the hostility is perpetuated or even reinforced, and

[38] *Ibid.,* pp. 134–135.
[39] de Rivera, *Psychological Dimension,* pp. 31–32.

a vicious circle results. Autistic hostility is present to an extreme degree in the paranoid psychotic who believes himself persecuted and therefore cuts himself off from empathic communication with all or almost all of his fellow human beings. It can occur in any quarrel between individuals. It also tends to develop on both sides of any acute group conflict.[40]

Selective inattention and absence of empathy are just two of the more serious difficulties that occur when members of one group view members or actions of a different, hostile group. All the general problems of perception and communication inherent in any interpersonal, intergroup, or interstate relationship are invariably exacerbated in nearly direct proportion to the intensity of the threat perceived by the units in a conflict situation.

Because there is such a high degree of identity and great reinforcement of similarity of perception in some groups—particularly those that feel threatened—it is often extremely difficult to introduce change into those groups that might correct misperceptions or mitigate hostile attitudes. What is often overlooked in this generally unfavorable situation, however, is that group perceptions and identities are as a matter of course always changing, no matter how slightly. Because of changing factors in the environment, previously held identities fade while others are reinforced. What is more, new group identities are constantly forming. Each new exogenous stimulus that intrudes into an individual's awareness (conscious or otherwise) must be dealt with. If, for whatever reasons, a number of formerly unrelated individuals perceive this stimulus more or less similarly, a new perceptual group is formed. When an individual recognizes (again, consciously or otherwise) that another, or others, share the same perception and, either verbally or through some silent cue, communicates his shared perception, an identity group is formed. Whether the individual takes some action based on this perception of group identification largely depends on the ranking the identity acquires in his hierarchy of identities. But the point to be stressed is that the configuration of group identities and perceptions is ever-changing.

[40] White, "Misperceptions," pp. 132–133.

Chapter 2

Dependence and Independence: Two Views

A Political Continuum

What do the terms *dependence* and *independence* mean in international affairs? When does a state become "dependent" upon another state? When does it become "independent"? Hardly a year has gone by in the past two decades when one has not read of yet another state being granted, or seizing, formal independence. Hardly a book has been written about international relations in recent years without reference to the fact that since 1945, some seventy or so (depending on the method of counting) former "dependencies" have become "newly independent."

It has been fairly generally assumed that a country is either dependent or independent. The terms are treated by both scholars and practitioners as though they were dichotomous. If the country is independent, it is presumed to have the exclusive right to make decisions concerning its internal and external affairs, and, as a sign of this, to have diplomatic representation abroad and since 1956 to have a seat in the United Nations if it so chooses.[1] On the other hand, if it is not independent, it is considered to be dependent on some other country; that is, it is presumed to have no exclusive right to make decisions concerning its own internal and external affairs, and therefore to have no diplomatic representation abroad or in the United Nations. But is this really so?

India has been a member of the United Nations since 1945, although India and Pakistan did not formally receive independence until 1947. The Byelo-Russian and Ukrainian Soviet Socialist Republics have also been U.N. members since 1945 despite the fact that they are both also integral parts of the Soviet Union. As

[1] It has only been since 1956 that the Powers have generally agreed on the concept of universal membership in the U.N.

of this writing, the Peoples Republic of China has no diplomatic representation in many countries (including the United States) though it has been in existence since 1949 and controls the most populous country in the world.

Perhaps one should turn to international law for a definition of independence. J. L. Brierly, a leading expert in the international law of states, has said, "The proper usage of the term 'independence' is to denote the status of a state which controls its own external relations without dictation from other states . . . 'independence' does not mean freedom from law but merely *freedom from control by other states*." [2]

Since independence is defined there in terms of control, then presumably a state or an area that is in some degree controlled by another state might be said to be dependent upon the controlling state. What is more, the degree of that dependence should vary in direct proportion to the degree of control exercised by the other state. This was precisely the case during much of the colonial period. "Dependencies" had varying degrees of control over their own affairs and were treated accordingly. Some, like Algeria and the current "overseas provinces" of Portugal, were treated legally as integral parts of the metropole country.[3] Other areas were regarded by metropole Powers as colonies to be ruled by administrators sent out from the mother country and responsible only to the government of the metropole. Other areas were ruled more indirectly through indigenous governing authorities, who were still, however, ultimately responsible to the government of the metropole. "Leased areas," "colonial protectorates," and "trust territories" (called "mandates" prior to World War II) were presumably under less direct control. Still less dependent than a "colonial protectorate," but not yet considered independent were those places held under that form of dependence known as "suzerainty" or plain "protectorate." Finally, there were "spheres of influence." Nominally, these areas were independent, but the term meant that:

. . . a state, without establishing its jurisdiction . . . signifies that it regards certain territory as clearly closed to the ambitions of other powers. . . . The mere assertion of a sphere of influence gives the

[2] J. L. Brierly, *The Law of Nations*, 5th ed. (Oxford: Clarendon Press, 1955), pp. 121–122. (Emphasis added.)

[3] The term "metropole" is customarily used to describe the country that held legal control over another area. The control or influence some countries exerted (and still do) over others is not always legally recognized and thus the term metropole would be inappropriate. "Mentor" is a broader term of my own creation that will be used to denote those countries that have considerable influence over other countries regardless of the legal arrangements involved.

influencing state no right over the territory and is a political not a legal act; but in practice the claim is often protected by treaties with the states most likely to be affected. . . .[4]

In a *de jure* sense, territories were considered either dependent or independent—there was no middle position. In *de facto* terms, however, even international law recognized degrees of independence and dependence.

Brierly distinguishes between the legal limitations of an "independent" state's control over its own affairs when it is a sphere of influence or a protectorate, and the *de facto* control that some states exercise over others without benefit of this legal cover. He says:

> A relation of dependency sometimes exists between two states in fact, but for political reasons is not avowed either as a protectorate or a suzerainty. Thus, the United States at one time exercised far reaching control over some of the nominally independent states of Central America. . . . A similar *de facto* protectorate by Great Britain over Egypt also existed from 1882 until 1914, when a protectorate was openly declared.[5]

As in most international interactions, reality takes precedence over legality in the matter of dependence or independence. Therefore, I propose to view these apparent opposites not as dichotomous, but as points on a continuum. At one end of this conceptual continuum could be placed those states that are totally dependent on other states, while at the opposite extreme could be placed those that are totally independent. In between, a great variety of possible positions would exist. Indeed, one might rank order all of the geographical entities of the world along this *de facto* dependence-independence continuum.

In fact, of course, no state of the world falls at either extreme. No matter how dependent a colonial possession became, it was never completely subservient to the mentor Power. That is, decision making that affected the area was never *wholly* taken out of that area. To be sure, many major decisions were made in Paris, London, Madrid, Lisbon, or Washington, but many more decisions affecting the areas concerned were made locally—very often by local people.[6]

Similarly, it can be argued that no state was ever totally in-

[4] Brierly, *Law of Nations,* pp. 159–160.

[5] *Ibid.,* p. 126.

[6] Indeed, even New York City is not *totally* dependent on either Albany or Washington, and neither are Mississippi, Wales, Brittany or Uzbekistan dependent on their respective central governments.

dependent. That is, no state has ever had complete control over all the decisions that affect either its internal or external affairs. Some states may be politically independent, but at the same time be economically dependent on another state. Conversely, some states may be economically independent, but be militarily or politically dependent. Conceptually, of course, I am now implying a multi-dimensional continuum on which a country theoretically could rank low (or dependent) on one dimension and high (or independent) on another. Actually, however, the states of the world seem to function in another way. As will be shown subsequently, a country that ranks high on one dimension usually ranks high on all dimensions, while a country that ranks low on one dimension usually ranks low on all.

To be sure, there may be some countries so isolated and re-mote that most of the world is oblivious to their existence, and, therefore, they may be free to make all or almost all of their own decisions. But that is not a viable independence. If for some reason a major power should suddenly find it in its own interest to exercise influence in such a country, the likelihood is that it could do so rather easily. A country is independent, in terms of this study, only insofar as it has the power to enforce its freedom of decision making, regardless of which other countries want to influence it.

It is, however, a basic premise of this study that no country has total independence. Powerful countries often become mutually dependent (or interdependent), each needing something that the other has. The most powerful countries become involved in alliances and commitments far more than less powerful countries. The crucial difference lies of course in the ability of the most powerful countries to determine—*on the basis of their own perceived self-interest*—which commitments they will honor and which they will not. The less powerful countries of the world have far less choice in such matters. Thus, for each country, independence in international affairs—the ability of decision makers[7] in any country to make decisions affecting their own country without reference to the desires or wishes of decision makers in a foreign country—is a function of its power relationships with the other countries of the world.

In other words, independence—"sovereignty," as it is some-times called—is a relative concept. It implies the questions, "in-dependent of whom?" and "dependent upon whom?" Senegal, the Cameroons, Niger, and Chad (to mention only a few states), are all extremely dependent in various ways upon France despite their

---

[7] The term decision makers here is used in its broadest sense to include not only governmental elites, but also other individuals whose decisions affect broad segments of a country's population.

de jure independence. Costa Rica, the Philippines, Honduras, and South Vietnam are dependent upon the United States to a very considerable degree. Barbados, Jamaica, and Malta are dependent upon the United Kingdom, as are Bulgaria, Czechoslovakia, Poland, and East Germany upon the Soviet Union. On the other hand, Niger, the Philippines, Bulgaria, and Malta, for example, are almost totally independent of each other (indeed it is likely that 99 percent of the population of each has never even heard of the others); while in varying degrees France and the United Kingdom are themselves somewhat dependent upon the United States. Thus, while France and the United Kingdom are relatively independent via-à-vis the weaker countries mentioned, they are relatively dependent vis-à-vis the United States.

The realities of the international power situation are very difficult for many people to accept. Not only do they violate the egalitarian democratic notions so prevalent in the West but, more important perhaps, they violate the nationalist pride of the leaders and intellectuals of most of the countries of the world. At the time of the Suez crisis in 1956, Prime Minister Anthony Eden of Great Britain and Prime Minister Guy Mollet of France refused to see that reality and believed they could make policy for their countries independently of the wishes of the United States. Both men were wrong, and their error not only brought disaster to their policy, but ended the political careers of those gentlemen as well. Since 1956, at least, the United Kingdom seems to have come to terms with that reality, and now very carefully checks with the United States before embarking on any "independent" foreign policy objective. The U.K. can be as independent as the United States will allow it to be. The French, on the other hand, at least between 1958 and 1969, had greater difficulty in seeing the relative power relationship between themselves and the United States as immutable. President Charles de Gaulle embarked on a policy of strengthening his country specifically to make it more independent of the United States. France's *de facto,* though not *de jure,* withdrawal from NATO and its veto of Britain's entry into the Common Market (the former very much opposed by the United States, the latter very much favored) are evidence that de Gaulle's policy did have some success.[8] But France's manifest increase in strength

---

[8] The fact that Mississippi, Alabama, and other states in the southern part of the United States do not fully implement the federal government's orders on school integration does not mean that those states are "independent" of the U.S. It does mean that not every "dependent area"—whether a country, state, or city—does, or must do, everything that the more powerful unit wants it to do. Every dependent region has available some margin of independent action.

during the decade 1958–68 (due in no small measure to the spectacular progress of the European Economic Community) be-came a *relative increase in power* vis-à-vis the United States only because it coincided with something of a relative decline in Amer-ican power (due, in part at least, to the Vietnamese fiasco, and in part to the racial, political, and urban unrest at home). France is still far from totally independent. One need only read J. J. Ser-van-Schreiber's *The American Challenge,*[9] or review General de Gaulle's statements when the Soviet Bloc invaded Czechoslovakia in 1968, to realize that an economic, military, and political depend-ence on the United States continues.

To summarize the basic contentions: Independence (or, if one prefers to view the other end of the continuum—dependence) is both relative and contextual. To the degree that the power of a state increases, its relative independence vis-à-vis other states is also likely to increase. To the degree that the power of a state declines, its relative independence vis-à-vis other states is also likely to decline. To the degree that the power of some other state increases more rapidly than the power of one's own, that other state's independence—relative to one's own—is likely to increase as well. The *de facto* as well as *de jure* relationships of independ-ence and dependence among the states of the world are not im-mutable.

The Psychological Perspective

While there is some advantage in viewing the relationships among states in terms of a dependence/independence continuum, there is another approach that, on a different level of analysis, may better help explain the behavior of states and the people who run them. It is a basic premise of this book that any valid analysis of relations among states must take into account the psychological dimension. Therefore, in addition to viewing the question from a political perspective, it will be helpful to analyze it from the per-spective of individual human development and group relations. The insights of psychology—particularly those aspects that focus on individual identity—can be applied to the decision makers who define their states' national interests and determine their states' be-havior. The insights of social psychology—particularly those aspects that focus on group dynamics—can be applied to the in-ternational system, with each state considered as a member of the group.

[9] J. J. Servan-Schreiber, *The American Challenge,* trans. Ronald Steel (New York: Atheneum, 1968).

To speak of a state's behavior in terms of whether or not it ever successfully made the transition from the oral to the anal stage of development is obviously meaningless. But it is not meaningless to analyze in that way the behavior of people who make the crucial decisions affecting the state.[10] While this kind of analysis goes beyond what would be useful here, for the purpose of this work it does make sense to analyze the psychological nature of the relationships that the individual decision makers, sub-elites, and collective elite of a weaker state may have with a more powerful state or group of states. Such an analysis requires the set of terms, "dependence," "counter-dependence," "independence," and "interdependence."

A Set of Definitions

Dependence

Webster's defines dependence as: "(1) State of being influenced and determined by, or of being conditional upon something else. (2) State of depending, or being subject; esp. subjection to the direction or disposal of another. (3) Reliance; trust. (4) That on which one depends or relies." [11]

Essentially there are two kinds of dependence. One is the *objective dependence* inherent in so many life situations. Small children simply cannot do many things that adults can—including providing themselves with the food, clothing, shelter, and love necessary for their survival. Adults, too, are often objectively dependent. The worker may be dependent upon his boss for a job; the farmer may be dependent upon nature for a good crop; the citizen may be dependent upon the government for the maintenance of peace and order; and so on. Many of these are situations that people—individually or collectively—simply accept as in the "order of things." If a person accepts his situation on this basis, he is not likely to feel any resentment. Rather, he is likely to resign himself to that particular dependence and find or create other situations in which he is not dependent, thus providing psychological compensation and a feeling of inner worth. No man (or collective of men) is omnipotent, and most men do not expect to be so. Therefore, they feel no personal threat or lack of security in those objective situations in which they must be dependent.

[10] See, for example, Erik H. Erikson, *Young Man Luther* (New York: W. W. Norton, 1958), and *Gandhi's Truth* (New York: W. W. Norton, 1970); also A. L. George and J. L. George, *Woodrow Wilson and Colonel House* (Magnolia, Mass.: Peter Smith), 1956.
[11] *Webster's Seventh New Collegiate Dictionary*, S.V. "dependence."

On the other hand, while no man, group, or state is omnipotent, neither is any one totally impotent. Yet some individuals and groups feel that they are. For whatever psychological reasons, they do not possess adequate feelings of inner worth (are unable to find or create some situations in which they can be independent, or in which others can come to depend upon them) and find many (or most) situations of objective dependence demeaning. These people and groups can be said to be *subjectively dependent*. They resent their dependent relationships but feel incapable of doing anything to change them.

Certainly, some individuals and groups find themselves in positions of greater objective dependence than others, and simply do not accept this situation as unchangeable. Rather, they work to modify it. These individuals and groups are not likely to experience subjective dependence. There are many others, however, for whom the *feeling* of dependence becomes generalized and all-pervasive. For those individuals and groups there are two possible reactions. One is to develop feelings of inferiority, which stem from a recognition of the unequal power relationship—that is, the vulnerability to another's influence—and from his feeling that there is nothing he can do to change it. He may not accept the relationship as "preordained" and/or "just," and may wish to do something to alter it, but believing himself incapable of doing so, he resigns himself to the inevitability of the relationship and accepts it—but not without experiencing a sense of inferiority and/or impotence, whether he recognizes it as such or whether he rationalizes it, or in some other way disguises the feelings. The second possible reaction is to develop feelings of counterdependence. This can occur if the individual or group has, or can develop, enough ego strength (feeling of self-worth) to challenge the unequal relationship in an attempt to change it.

Counterdependence

As used here, counterdependence is the psychological state of individuals or groups in the process of altering a relationship from one in which they felt dependent and/or inferior, to one in which they feel equal. It is often an angry "lashing-out" to redefine an existing relationship. In psychological studies it is used synonymously with the word "rebellion."

Counterdependence is a very volatile state of mind precisely because it is usually a transitory stage. It is often a painful, violent, and confusing stage. Feelings of inferiority are often mixed with and mitigated by feelings of superiority, which themselves may be only half believed.

All change is painful, but when feelings of dependence become too painful to be endured and counterdependence occurs, it is often accompanied by resentment and anger directed at the individual or group upon whom one previously perceived himself to be dependent and who is viewed as the cause of the pain he experienced during dependence and is now experiencing during counterdependence. The individual or group one formerly felt dependent on often becomes the butt of intense hostility during counterdependence, which may have been building during the time that the person or group recognized the dependent nature of the previous relationship but felt incapable of changing it. Once counterdependence has occurred, no holds are barred. Indeed, it would appear that the more intense the feelings of dependence were (regardless of the objective situation) the more intense and violent the feelings of counterdependence are likely to be.

Once the dependence is no longer perceived to exist, there is no longer any need for counterdependence. But precisely because this is a phase in which relationships are in the process of change, it is sometimes difficult to determine exactly when the relationship actually has changed. Thus, counterdependent feelings sometimes continue considerably longer than needed. When the relationship has in fact changed and is perceived by *both* parties to have done so, then one of two possible relationships can follow: independence or interdependence.

Independence

In psychological terms, independence is a feeling of self-sufficiency. As with states, no individual is ever totally independent. Man simply cannot live in isolation from other individuals. He has, in greater or lesser degree, what Henry A. Murray has called "need affiliation": the need to associate with other individuals.[12] What is more, though no man was ever totally self-sufficient, modern man, living in societies of ever-increasing specialization, complexity, and technological innovation is even less so than his forefathers. Thus, man is led inevitably into recognizing the need for mutually dependent relationships merely in order to survive. However, there need not be a relationship with the individual or group upon which he formerly was dependent. Because of the availability of enormous numbers of alternative individuals, groups, and states in the world, and because of the residue of resentment that may be left from the counterdependent stage, the individual may choose to have no relationship whatever with the unit upon which

[12] Henry A. Murray, *Explorations in Personality* (New York: Oxford University Press, 1938).

he was formerly dependent and may thus become independent of it.

Interdependence

Interdependence is the psychological relationship between individuals, groups, or states that feel themselves autonomous, and more or less equal, but recognize the advantages of reciprocal dependence. Each unit in the relationship feels that it has something to contribute to the other, and that the other has something to contribute to it.[13] While each unit may feel that it could, if necessary, survive and perhaps prosper without the relationship, it believes it can prosper more in association with the other, and voluntarily enters into the relationship. Each unit perceives itself as in one way or another equal or nearly equal to the other, and treats the other as though it were in fact equal, whether it actually is or not. Thus, the actual power relationship that exists between the units may be less important than the *perceived* relationship of equality. In this circumstance, one unit is willing to become dependent upon some other unit for some things in the expectation that for different things, or at different times, the other will be dependent upon it. The perceived complementarity leads to the establishment of interdependence.

The Dynamics of Changing Relationships

The application of the psychological and sociological concepts of dependence, counterdependence, independence, and interdependence to an altogether different discipline, international relations, calls for strong reservations, of course. The units of analysis in the various disciplines are different (individual, group, and state, respectively). The concepts, even as used in their original disciplines, are only working formulations for investigating difficult questions, not precise and final answers. The basic analogy between an individual life and the life of a state cannot possibly be congruent in all its parts. Clearly, in using a psychological model to analyze international behavior, care must be taken to avoid oversimplification. Still, the growth and development of individuals and groups do parallel in some important ways the growth and development of weak states vis-à-vis powerful states.

[13] Note that interdependence is being used here in a somewhat different way than it has been used by Ernst B. Haas in his works on International Interdependence. See, for example, *The Web of Interdependence: The United States and International Organizations* (Englewood Cliffs, N.J.: Prentice-Hall, 1970).

No state in the world was ever as dependent upon another state as a child is upon its mother. Thus, the analogy is imperfect at the outset. In addition, there is a certain obnoxious quality of paternalism in comparing the dependency of former colonies with the child-parent relationship. Despite the odious nature of the comparison and the noncongruence of some of the parts of the analogy, I ask the reader to allow me to attempt to draw the parallel between the growth and development of individuals and groups, and, in some ways, the similar growth and development of weak states vis-à-vis powerful states. There is, after all, an element of changing power relationships in each circumstance, and that similarity alone may be worth investigating. In addition, it may be noted that it was the people who lived in the colonies who referred to the metropole as the "mother country"; who charged the administrators sent by the metropole with being "paternalistic" in their approach to the indigenous population; and who undertook in one degree of another some form of "rebellion" or counterdependent behavior against the metropole or mentor in order to change the nature of the relationship. Given even these superficial similarities, some comparison seems worthwhile.

Political concepts by themselves have failed to explain adequately the condition of *de jure* independence but *de facto* dependence of many states, the rebellious behavior of the elites of many weak states, and the mutual dependence exhibited by some states that are fairly equal in power. Despite these reservations it is nonetheless reasonable to hope that the concepts defined in this section can be utilized to gain new insight into the relationships between states.[14]

The Psychological Model

In terms of individual psychology, dependence has a very particular meaning. It implies a relationship in which one individual (A) relies upon another individual (B) for the fulfillment of his needs. It is a relative concept. In fulfilling the needs of A, B is assumed to be fulfilling other needs of his own. If B were not "getting something out of the relationship," he would presumably

[14] I should observe that I am not alone in this attempt. A number of relatively new books in the field of international affairs have attempted to apply the insights of other disciplines to the relations among states. See particularly Joseph H. de Rivera, *The Psychological Dimension of Foreign Policy* (Columbus, Ohio: Charles E. Merrill, 1968); David Singer, ed., *Human Behavior and International Politics* (Chicago: Rand McNally, 1965); Herbert C. Kelman, ed., *International Behavior: A Social Psychological Analysis*, Society for the Psychological Study of Social Issues (New York: Holt, Rinehart and Winston, 1965).

discontinue it. For example, while a parent may be satisfying the physical and emotional needs of a newborn baby, it is likely that the baby satisfies some needs of the parent, if only the need to be depended upon. Of course, it often happens that the parent did not want the baby at all and thus he derives little if any satisfaction of his own needs by satisfying the baby's needs. In extreme cases, the parent feels that he is getting so little from the relationship that the child is abandoned and the relationship is discontinued. But since the child cannot provide for its own needs, it must find a parent surrogate or die. Thus, the child is dependent upon the parent to a much greater degree than the parent is upon the child.

At birth all primates, particularly humans, are nearly totally dependent upon adult care. It is the parent, or parent surrogate who must supply all of the food, clothing, shelter, warmth, and protection a child needs. Psychologically, too, all of a child's needs must be met by the parent. Without love and affection, a child is almost as likely to die as he would without clothing or shelter. Indeed, in his earliest months a child is so dependent psychologically that he is incapable of distinguishing between himself and his parents. As the child grows, he begins to acquire both physical and psychological strength. By the end of the first year he can stand on his own two feet physiologically, but not psychologically. The process of establishing his own identity—his awareness of himself in relation to his parents, his siblings, his peer groups, his society—is long. Only through maturation does the child begin to delineate where his parents end and he begins. As growth progresses, the child continually tests his parents to determine the parameters of his autonomy. Although the lines drawn vary from culture to culture, each society sets limits to the child's autonomy. As the child becomes older—that is, stronger and, hence, more powerful—the area of freedom is usually expanded. As the child's ego develops, however, it becomes increasingly important for him to challenge parental authority, again so that he may learn the limits. Each society seems to prescribe just what forms of testing are permissible, but every society seems to countenance some form.[15]

Some societies avoid this later stage of testing precisely because they recognize that there comes a time (usually somewhere between the ages of twelve and sixteen) when the boy must become

---

[15] For a very comprehensive analysis of the psycho-social development of a child, see Erik H. Erikson, *Childhood and Society,* 2nd ed. (New York: W. W. Norton, 1963), particularly Chapter 7, "Eight Ages of Man," and part four, "Youth and the Evolution of Identity." It is to be hoped that some day Erikson or one of his students will attempt a more detailed analogy between the development of personal identity and national identity than it is possible to attempt here.

a man, with full rights, privileges, and duties. These societies normally celebrate the occasion with a "rite of passage" or an "initiation rite" that says to both the boy and the society: "Now you are a man; you will be expected to act accordingly." And he does, not because he is told to, but because he is now treated as a man by his family and his society. Father and son are now equals, and each accords the other the respect due his age, rank, and role. Each performs duties and receives rewards in a culturally prescribed fashion. Each assists the other while at the same time recognizing the other's areas of autonomy. The man and his father have become interdependent.

In American and Western European society, and perhaps in other societies, too, outright rebellion (counterdependence) during adolescence seems to be necessary, although the manifestations vary considerably. At this period in the individual's development, he is physically almost the equal of his parent but he is still learning how to become his parent's psychological equal. While his body is that of a man, his family and society seem unwilling to grant him equal status with adults. The changed physical power relationships are usually recognized but there is no formal recognition of a changed psychological relationship. In many Western homes it is just assumed that autonomy will eventually come—perhaps when the boy goes off to college, or goes into the army, or gets married—but nothing specific is done about it. It is at that stage, prior to the implicit acceptance into full and equal adult status, that counterdependence occurs. In lieu of a rite of passage, the boy (or girl) must rebel merely to determine how free he is.

Whatever else it may be psychologically, counterdependence is clearly in part a struggle for power, with the young adult demanding an area of autonomy and respect equal to that of the parent and trying to get it by testing the limits of his parents' authority. Once the young adult has achieved psychological autonomy, rebellion is no longer necessary. The outcome of the rebellion often depends on how radical or violent the transition stage has been. Parent and child may become completely independent, each—now totally self-sufficient—having little or nothing to do with the other. If the transition has been relatively smooth —that is, if the parent has encouraged, or at least not actively opposed the development of the child's autonomy—both parent and child may come to recognize a psychological as well as physical equality and establish a relationship of mutual assistance, respect, and affection. Each is independent in the sense that neither needs the other for survival, but each chooses to assist, love, and respect the other for mutual advantage. At that point, parent and child have become interdependent.

In human development, at the very period in life when the child is at the height of his physical and intellectual powers, and probably his earning power as well, his parents have already begun to decline. Eventually, if both live long enough, the parent may become as dependent upon the child as the child was once upon the parent. This is often a very difficult stage in the psychological relationship between parent and child. Western society has not really set up adequate cultural mechanisms to deal with this period. Often both sides are resentful of the role reversal, yet neither knows how to cope with that resentment. In traditional societies, age brings added respect and prestige; in a sense, the parent always has the power advantage. But in Western societies, old age is a liability.

The Political Application of the Psychological Model

In drawing analogies of the nature proposed here, it is tempting to be glib. One could say that while a country was a colony, it was dependent; that during its nationalist phase, it was counterdependent; and that having acquired its *de jure* independence, it became interdependent with its former metropole. But that kind of simplistic analogy would add no more to our understanding of the relations among states than the traditional legalistic argument discussed at the beginning of this chapter. If any new insights are to be acquired by utilizing this approach, the analysis will have to be specific.

As was noted earlier, it is possible for individuals, groups, and states to be simultaneously dependent in some respects, counterdependent in others, and interdependent in still others. Individuals, groups, and states all develop unevenly. For some, physical or economic growth may proceed more rapidly than perceptual or identity growth. For others, the reverse may be true. Americans are quite familiar with the phenomenon of the adolescent boy challenging his parents' authority while he willingly remains economically dependent. Similarly, Americans have become increasingly aware of counterdependent verbal attacks upon their country (or physical attacks upon its representatives), by countries, or groups within countries, that are highly dependent upon it economically. A weak country can be highly dependent upon a specific Power economically while simultaneously being quite counterdependent politically, or, conversely, two countries can be politically and perceptually interdependent, yet one may be economically dependent upon the other. There is ample statistical evidence, however, that with regard to the relations among states, dependence in one area tends to correlate highly with dependence in other areas, while counterdependence or interdependence in one area also tends to correlate with either counterdependence or interdependence in other areas. If a country is highly dependent economically upon another country, the likelihood is that it will also have a high perceptual, communications, military, and political dependence as well. Similarly, if the two countries are interdependent in one sphere, there will be a strong tendency for them to be interdependent in all other spheres.

Prior to the grant of *de jure* independence by the former metropoles, the elite groups in many of the former colonies seem to have gone through some stages of psychological development that resembles remarkably the stages of development one sees in both individuals and groups. Anyone familiar with the studies of leadership in colonial times (whether in the U.S. or in the newly independent countries) is aware of the repeated references to those indigenous individuals who, in their prenationalist stage, tried to identify themselves completely with the values, attitudes, and modes of behavior of the dominant country's elite group or culture. The example of the nineteen-year-old Gandhi in London in top hat, spats, striped trousers, a morning coat, a silver-mounted cane, silk shirt, and leather gloves, taking dancing lessons, is as painful and representative as any.[16] It is particularly in those cases where the psychological dependence was the greatest, that the counterdependence and rebellion seems to have been most extreme. It would appear that in both individual and group development, counterdependence varies in almost direct proportion to the degree of dependence experienced. Those individuals, groups, and states that experience the most extreme forms of psychological dependence seem also to experience the most extreme forms of counterdependence.

What is a nationalist movement, if it is not a challenge to the existing authority structure? Above all, it is a change in one's perception of oneself in relation to authority. Why and under what conditions those perceptions change need not concern us here. The catalysts for change are probably as varied as life's situations. The fact is that perceptions of self in relation to individuals, groups, and states upon whom there was some dependence constantly do change. And it is that change that moves people, groups, and states from dependence to counterdependence, from the prenationalist to the nationalist phases of development.

In the quotation below, W. G. Bennis and H. A. Shepard describe the dynamics of this changed relationship in a human development training group. The reader is encouraged to substitute the

[16] See Louis Fischer, *Gandhi: His Life and His Message for the World* (New York: New American Library, 1954), p. 14.

phrase "foreign power" wherever he sees the word "trainer." In so doing, he will have as good a description of indigenous attitudes toward the powerful state during the nationalist phase of a country's development as exists anywhere—despite the fact that the paragraph was written to describe counterdependence in a training group.

. . . power is much more overtly the concern of group members in this sub-phase. . . . Disenthrallment with the trainer proceeds rapidly. Group members see him as at best ineffectual, at worst damaging to group progress. [read: "national welfare"] He is ignored and bullied almost simultaneously. His interventions are perceived by the counter-dependents [read: "militants"] as an attempt to interrupt group progress; by the dependents, as weak and incorrect statements. His silences are regarded by the dependents as desertion; by the counterdependents as manipulation.[17]

In the Bennis and Shepard model, if and when the "rebellion" occurs, the trainer is either symbolically or actually thrown out of the group. However, in these training groups, as in the world at large, there is no inevitability about the counterdependence finally culminating either in rebellion or in the group's moving from one phase to another. Some groups never progress beyond the dependent stage; neither do some individuals or some states. Some individuals and states work out their counterdependent feelings easily and painlessly, as do some groups. Just as "the trainer's behavior is crucial in determining the group's ability to resolve the dependence issue," [18] so, too, the behavior of the foreign power is crucial in determining the weaker state's ability to resolve the dependence issue.

Many states in the world have experienced nationalist "counter-dependent" stages of development, but there was often no rebellion as such. In the vast majority of cases, the metropole Powers simply granted *de jure* independence without a fight on the part of the weaker states. Interestingly enough, however, this symbolic removal of foreign authority by a *de jure* transfer of political power —so analogous to the symbolic removal of the trainer in a human development training group—may in no meaningful sense move the metropole and the dependency any closer to interdependence. That stage comes only when both parties can perceive each other at least in some ways as equals. Legal niceties notwithstanding, interdependence in interpersonal, intergroup, and interstate rela-

[17] W. G. Bennis and H. A. Shepard, "A Theory of Group Development" *The Planning of Change,* eds. W. G. Bennis, K. Benne, and R. Chin (New York: Holt, Rinehart and Winston, 1966), p. 327.
[18] *Ibid.,* p. 337.

tions is a function of the perceived power relationships that exist between them. The symbolic grant of equal status may be a step in the direction of ultimate interdependence, but it is only a step.

Notice, however, that in almost all of those cases in which the British, French, and Americans agreed to nationalist demands for a symbolic "rite of passage" from *de jure* dependence to *de jure* independence—that is, from a *de jure* dominant/subordinate relationship to a *de jure* peer relationship—not only were the transitions nonviolent, but close relations between the former political mentor and the former dependency have been retained. Indeed, it would appear that dependence, consciously perpetuated, breeds counterdependence; while autonomy, consciously nurtured, breeds interdependence.

Changes in relations among units—whether individuals, groups, or states—are dependent upon both psychological and power factors. A change in the psychological relationship may produce a change in the power relationship. Similarly, a change in the power relationship may produce a change in the psychological relationship. Surely it is not mere coincidence that most of the former colonies of the European Powers entered their most intensely nationalistic (counterdependent) stage, and finally achieved at least *de jure* political independence, at the very moment in history when most of the European Powers themselves had just been beaten by an Asian Power and were weaker than at perhaps any other time in the previous two hundred years.

To repeat, it is a superficial analysis of the relations among states that ignores the psychological dimension of those relationships. It would, however, be equally as superficial to analyze the relations among states in purely psychological terms and to ignore the power dimension of those relations. The two are mutually reinforcing, and in some ways inseparable.

Chapter 3

On the Dynamics of Power

Definitions of Power

Webster's defines power as follows:

pow-er . . . 1 a: possession of control, authority, or influence over others b: one having such power; *specif:* a sovereign state . . . 2 a (1): ability to act or produce an effect (2): capacity for being acted upon or undergoing an effect b: legal or official authority, capacity, or right 3 a: physical might b: mental or moral efficacy c: political control or influence . . . syn POWER, FORCE, ENERGY, STRENGTH, MIGHT mean the ability to exert effort. POWER may imply latent or exerted, physical, mental or spiritual ability to act or to be acted upon; FORCE implies the actual and efficacious exercise of power; ENERGY applies to power expended or capable of being transformed into work; STRENGTH applies to the quality or property of a person or thing that enables him to exert force or withstand strain, pressure, or attack; MIGHT implies great or overwhelming power or strength.
    syn POWER, AUTHORITY, JURISDICTION, CONTROL, COMMAND, SWAY, DOMINION, mean the right to govern or rule or determine. POWER implies possession of ability to wield coercive force, permissive authority, or substantial influence; AUTHORITY implies the granting of power for a specific purpose within specified limits; JURISDICTION applies to official power exercised within prescribed limits; CONTROL stresses the power to direct and restrain; COMMAND implies the power to make arbitrary decisions and compel obedience; SWAY suggests the extent or scope of exercised power or influence; DOMINION stresses sovereign power or supreme authority.[1]

Clearly this is a definition supplied by lexicographers, not political scientists, and yet it has as much merit, covering as many meanings, as do those supplied by the scholars in the field.

[1] *Webster's Seventh New Collegiate Dictionary*, s.v. "power."

Power has been the subject of human study and the object of human striving from time immemorial. In the Western world, from Aristotle through Machiavelli, Hobbes, Rousseau, Montesquieu, and all the political writers of modern times, power and its control have been central themes of writings on the domestic political process.

Harold Lasswell, in *Power and Personality,* treated the relationship of the individual personality to the striving for power:

That men want power is a statement we can accept as true in every society where power exists; and this is not to say whether everybody wants it with the same intensity or whether the drive for power is innate or acquired. For the purpose of analyzing the social process, power is unmistakeably a value, in the sense that it is desired (or likely to be desired).[2]

In a later work, Lasswell and Abraham Kaplan made the point that "The concept of power is perhaps the most fundamental in the whole of political science: the political process is the shaping, distribution, and exercise of power (in a wider sense . . . of influence in general)."[3] What is more, Lasswell and Kaplan (in a sense setting the framework for my work) argued that power, like politics generally, is best understood as an interpersonal process. They quoted Tawney's definition, " 'Power may be defined as the capacity of an individual, or group of individuals, to modify the conduct of other individuals or groups in the manner which he desires.' " And they then said, "The making of decisions is an interpersonal process: the policies which other persons are to pursue are what is decided upon. Power as participation in the making of decisions is an interpersonal relation."[3a]

Notice, however, that neither Tawney nor Lasswell and Kaplan extend their analysis to include the influence of one state over another, although the latter do so implicitly when they define groups to include "territorial groups."[4] The role of power in the relations between states was made explicit by Hans Morgenthau (who, however, defines power differently from Lasswell and Kaplan, not viewing it as an interpersonal process). In 1948 Morgenthau published a book entitled *Politics Among Nations: The*

---

[2] Harold D. Lasswell, *Power and Personality* (New York: W. W. Norton, 1948, Viking Press Edition, 1962), p. 16.

[3] Harold D. Lasswell and Abraham Kaplan, *Power and Society: A Framework for Political Inquiry* (New Haven: Yale University Press, 1950), p. 75.

[3a] *Ibid.,* pp. 75–76.

[4] *Ibid.,* p. 35.

Struggle for Power and Peace.[5] The study of international affairs has not been the same since. If he did nothing else in that book, he established the crucial importance of power in considerations of international politics—a factor no international practitioner had ever dared forget, but one that many scholars of international affairs in modern times had ignored.

There simply can be no doubt that power exists as an operative factor at every level of interpersonal, intergroup, and interstate relations; that it has always existed and that it always will exist in these relationships. It is true that social scientists have been frustrated in their attempts to analyze power because it is so difficult to measure. Still, it must be analyzed and discussed and understood if man is ever to be in a position to cope realistically with the complexities of those relationships.

As used in this book, *power is a relative term.* In a positive sense, it is the ability to influence others to behave in a manner desired by the one wielding the power. In a negative sense, it is the ability to prevent others from exerting influence on one's own behavior. Is power, then, the same as influence? Not quite. Power is the *ability* to exercise influence and the *ability* to prevent influence from being exercised over oneself.

People, groups, and states tend to try to maximize their power in order to prevent others from being in a position to influence them, and because they want to be in a position to influence others when they perceive the need. Representatives of groups or states are chosen (by whatever process) to be leaders because the constituents believe that those individuals will protect and/or advance the interests of the group. If the leaders come to be seen by the people they are supposed to represent as not exercising maximum influence to obtain desired group goals, those leaders are very likely to be replaced by others considered more capable of doing the job. States seem to be the entities that make the broadest definition of what are "legitimate" ways to exercise influence. Every religion in the world and every state has some sort of "thou shalt not kill" proscription written into its basic law. An individual may not kill another individual from the same state, merely because he believes it is in his own interest to do so. But if he kills as an agent of the state to achieve what is believed to be in the state's interests, there is rarely any punishment. Under certain circumstances (such as in time of war) if one of "us" kills enough of "them," instead of being punished, he will be considered a hero, and may even get a medal. However, killing (coercion) is only one of the ways of

---

[5] Hans J. Morgenthau, *Politics Among Nations: The Struggle for Power and Peace* (New York: Alfred A. Knopf, 1948).

exercising influence—and in fact it is the way that is used least often. Every day of every year, every individual, group, and state exercises at least some influence over other individuals, groups, and states, and only rarely do they rely on coercion as the means of achieving their ends.

Because there are many different ways in which influence may be exerted, there are many different manifestations of power. One speaks of the power of the pen, or the power of the purse, or the power of an army. But *power is contextual*. That is, the pen, or the purse, or the army is powerful only if it is used in an appropriate context. A brilliant, logical discourse may influence the behavior of people who hear it in the quiet of a lecture hall, but it could not possibly have any impact on them if they were in the midst of a battlefield. Conversely, in a world where increasing attention is paid to the battle for the "minds of men," chemical mace, napalm, and nuclear weapons may be totally inappropriate as instruments of power in a great many contexts.

If power is relative and contextual, how then can one speak of "weak" and "powerful" states? One can do so in the same way one can speak of any relative term in an absolute sense. Relative to the universe of men, someone who is 7 feet tall is tall. This does not mean it is false to call someone who is 5 feet, 11 inches a tall man in comparison to someone 5 feet, 3 inches. It does mean, however, that when relative terms are used in an absolute way, they are inevitably somewhat imprecise. Thus, in a sense every reference in this work to a group or a state as weak or powerful is somewhat imprecise. But in this matter the concern is with orders of magnitude, and so it does not seem necessary to sacrifice readability to tedious qualifications.

In some contexts, A and B may both have power over C—the ability to make decisions that directly affect C or significant segments of C's population. But:

1. C may, in some contexts, have sufficient power to resist that influence;
2. C may, in some contexts, have some ability to influence A or B (or significant portions of their populations);[6]
3. A may, in some contexts, have the ability to influence B as well as C;
4. B may, in many contexts, have little ability to influence A.

[6] For an interesting treatment of the ability of weak countries to influence powers in some contexts, see Richard W. Cottam, *Competitive Interference and 20th Century Diplomacy* (Pittsburgh: University of Pittsburgh Press, 1967).

As long as A and B have considerably more power than C, both will be discussed here as Powers, relative to C, even though A has more power than B and even though the power of A and B, relative to C, is not total.

Johan Galtung has described the international system as analogous to a feudal system. At the top are a few powerful countries, which he calls, disarmingly, the "topdog nations." Ranked in order of descending power under each of them are different groups of countries he calls "underdog nations." By ranking each of these clusters of countries on a number of dimensions of power he has found that:

1. The *rankings* have a tendency to be *concordant* in the sense that a nation that ranks high on one dimension has a tendency also to rank high on other dimensions; and a nation that ranks low on one has a tendency to rank low on other dimensions as well. . . .

2. The *interaction* has a tendency to be *rank-dependent,* in the sense that there is much interaction between nations high in the ranking system, less between one nation that is high and another that is low, and much less between two nations, low in the system. . . .[7]

Essentially, he is postulating a number of nearly discreet subsystems within the large international system. At the top of each are some topdog states, which interact most among themselves, and more with the topdog states in other systems than with underdog states within their own systems. While there is relatively little interaction among underdog states within each system, there is, comparatively speaking, almost none between underdog states in different systems. This is really just another way of saying that a number of power blocs exist in the world, and that most international interaction occurs among the world's major Powers. Those who view the world as bipolar since 1945 are simply saying that there are only two major powers and all other states can be viewed as falling within one or the other of their systems.[8]

---

[7] Johan Galtung, "International Relations and International Conflicts: A Sociological Approach," International Sociological Association Plenary Session, September 4–11, 1966, cited in his "East-West Interaction Patterns," *Journal of Peace Research* (1966), p. 146.

[8] It is because these powerful countries are thought to interact most with each other and because they have the capacity to destroy much of the world, that most of the literature in international affairs tends to deal with relations between the Powers. When the so-called "newly independent states" are considered at all, they are not considered in terms of their individual situations, motivations, and behavior. They are sometimes treated as a segment of an international schema, as in the work of Galtung, J. David Singer, and others. Sometimes they are considered as a grouping with more or less unique attributes. See, for example, Peter Worsley, *The Third World* (Chicago:

While Galtung sees the power systems as essentially static—that is, he assumes implicitly that underdog states will remain weak, that topdog states will remain the most powerful, and that underdog states in a particular subsystem will remain in that subsystem —I see the relationships as constantly changing. It is true that most very weak states tend to remain weak, but historically it has not been true that very powerful states remain very powerful. In modern times Portugal, Spain, France, Britain, and the United States have all, in succession, experienced the zenith of power. But the power of each declined, either in absolute terms, or relative to the growth of new and stronger power centers.[9] And power, like a magnet, tends to attract. As the power of one state increases (relative to the power of other states) it tends to attract to itself those weaker states that were formerly "drawn" to other Powers. What is more, it is not necessarily true that weak states remain part of a particular power system even when the leading state in that system is at, or near, the height of its power. Cuba and Albania are only two extreme cases.

One further point on the nature of power should be made. It is often charged that power, or "power politics," is evil or immoral. Others sometimes argue that it is noble or virtuous. This simply is not a useful way of viewing the matter. Whether their ends are base or noble, there can be no doubt that men will use power to serve those ends. But power, as such, is neither good nor bad. Senator Fulbright is wrong when he argues:

University of Chicago Press, 1964); Irving Louis Horowitz, *Three Worlds of Development: The Theory and Practice of International Stratification* (New York: Oxford University Press, 1966); Lawrence Martin, ed., *Neutralism and Non-Alignment* (New York: Frederick A. Praeger, 1962). Sometimes they are treated as a set of regional entities. See, for example, Michael Brecher, *The New States of Asia* (London: Oxford University Press, 1963); Arnold Rivkin, *The African Presence in World Affairs* (Glencoe, Ill.: Free Press, 1963); Bruce M. Russett, *International Regions and the International System: A Study in Political Ecology* (Chicago: Rand McNally, 1967). And sometimes they are treated on a functional basis as the recipients of economic or military aid. See, for example, George Liska, *The New Statecraft: Foreign Aid in American Foreign Policy* (Chicago: University of Chicago Press, 1960); Asher Brynes, *We Give to Conquer* (New York: W. W. Norton, 1966); Joan M. Nelson, *Aid, Influence and Foreign Policy* (New York: Macmillan, 1968); Morris Janowitz, *The Military in the Political Development of New Nations: An Essay in Comparative Analysis* (Chicago: University of Chicago Press, 1964).

[9] This is not to say that there are now power centers in the world stronger than the United States. But American power—relative to other competing power centers—was at its apex in the years immediately following World War II when Britain, France, Russia, Germany, China, and Japan were all in nearly total collapse.

. . . power tends to confuse itself with virtue and a great nation is peculiarly susceptible to the idea that its power is a sign of God's favor, conferring upon it a special responsibility for other nations—to make them richer and happier and wiser, to remake them, that is, in its own shining image. Power confuses itself with virtue and tends also to take itself for omnipotence. Once imbued with the idea of a mission, a great nation easily assumes that it has the means as well as the duty to do God's work.[10]

Power does not "confuse itself" with anything. Men who have power may confuse themselves with Gods, but power itself is simply an existing capacity, to be reckoned with as a fact of life.

The Components of Power

A Critique of the Traditional Approach

It would appear that since 1948, at least, the traditional approach to the study of power in international affairs has been for most authors to attack the list of components of power that Hans Morgenthau presented in his *Politics Among Nations,* and then to proceed to construct another list, very similar in content to Morgenthau's.[11] In the process of their attack, many of the authors qualify, clarify, and/or refine Morgenthau's components, and adjust the importance attached to each. But these modifications notwithstanding, when they are finished it is clear that they have essentially accepted the basic premises of that original list.[12]

These premises ultimately lead to the conclusion—implied, but not stated by Morgenthau—that "Power, in the last analysis, must rest on the capacity of physical force." [13] Indeed, Inis Claude Jr., is even more specific. He says: "I use the term *power* to denote what is essentially military capability—the elements which contribute directly or indirectly to the capacity to coerce, kill and destroy." [14]

[10] J. William Fulbright, *The Arrogance of Power* (New York: Random House, Vintage Books, 1966), pp. 3–4.

[11] Since the first edition appeared, Morgenthau has made some major revisions of the work, but none of those revisions affect what is discussed here.

[12] See, for example, A. F. K. Organski, *World Politics* (New York: Alfred A. Knopf, 1958), chapters 6 and 7; and Inis L. Claude, Jr., *Swords Into Plowshares* (New York: Random House, 1959).

[13] John G. Stoessinger, *The Might of Nations: World Politics In Our Time* (New York: Random House, 1962), p. 28.

[14] Inis L. Claude, Jr., *Power and International Relations* (New York: Random House, 1962), p. 6.

It is this notion of power as relying ultimately on the ability to coerce that has been endemic to the traditional approach to the subject since 1948. This is a view I reject. If power is seen from this perspective alone, then of course those factors that enhance the coercive ability of a state will be seen as the components of power. A different view calls for a totally different list of components. The ability to coerce is one way to achieve influence, but power has many dimensions. Individuals, groups, and states have power in part and under some circumstances because of their ability to coerce, but in greater measure and in many more circumstances because other individuals, groups, and states want, both consciously and unconsciously, what those with power have. Thus, what the traditional approach fails to see is that *power rests as much, or more, on the ability to attract as it does on the ability to coerce.*

If the people of one country are hungry for food and another country produces far more than it can consume, leaders of the poorer country are likely to look to the more affluent to supply that food, at least in the short run. If people in a country are hungry for education and technological competence and another possesses advanced educational and technological competence, the leaders of the weaker country are likely to look to the more affluent to supply that education to their people. If the economy of a poor country is starved for raw material markets and for the finished goods it cannot produce itself, the economic leaders of the poorer are likely to look to the more affluent country to provide both the markets and the finished goods it needs. If the military of a poorer country is starved for the hardware and training the poor country itself cannot provide, the military leaders are likely to look to a country with advanced military hardware and technology to supply its needs. And while in the process of acquiring food, or education, or markets and finished goods, or military hardware and technology, the overwhelming likelihood is that the leaders of the poorer country will at the same time acquire an international political outlook that is not very different from the international political outlook of the people with whom they come in contact in the affluent country. In these dependent relationships, influence can be, and often is, exercised without the influenced persons even being aware that it is happening. Certainly the latter will also consciously do what the Power wants—within limits—in order to gain access to the things (material or nonmaterial) they desire. That is why, in relations between weak and powerful countries, coercion is for the most part not necessary to achieve the long-term policy goals of the mentor.

As early as 1934, Charles E. Merriam wrote:

Power is not strongest when it uses violence, but weakest. It is strongest when it employs the instruments of substitution and counter attraction, of allurement, of participation rather than of exclusion, of education rather than of annihilation. Rape is not an evidence of irresistible power in politics or in sex.[15]

What the Russians were not able to achieve by subversion in India, Afghanistan, Egypt, and a half dozen other countries during Stalin's day, Nikita Khrushchev and his successors have been able to achieve through the use of nonmilitary instruments of power. What the Japanese were not able to achieve militarily in South Asia in the 1940's they had achieved by the 1960's through the use of economic instruments of power. What de Gaulle was not able to achieve in Algeria militarily he was able to achieve in most of the rest of former French Africa through intelligent use of perceptual and economic instruments of power. Indeed, on the basis of the evidence that exists, the conscious use of these "attractive" instruments of power (for that is what these attributes of power become when used consciously to achieve policy goals) seems to be the most effective means available to the Powers. The fact is that the attractive attributes of strong countries in relation to the various, and varying, needs of the weak countries give the strong countries a great variety of instruments to tie the weaker countries to them.

An attractive instrument of power is anything (material or nonmaterial) possessed by one individual, group, or state that another desires, and seeks to obtain by doing what the possessor desires. Obviously, there are limits on what one will do in order to achieve certain goals, but those limits are relative and contextual. In order to achieve a higher education—if that is perceived by the individual as important and/or desirable—one may sacrifice a great deal (leisure, money, time), but rarely will one sacrifice his life. The hungrier an individual, group, or state is, the higher a "price" it will pay to get the needed food. A moderately hungry man is not likely to kill in order to obtain food, but a starving man is very likely to do so.

This is not to say that the coercive instrument never works. Obviously, it does—particularly in the short run. But it often creates counterdependence, which may be more damaging to the long-run interests of the Powers than the apparent short-term gain may have been worth. Hungary, Guatemala, and the Dominican Republic are often cited as successful instances of the use of coercive power. Perhaps they were, but it is also possible that insufficient time has elapsed to make a final judgment. Of course, the use of attractive

[15] Charles E. Merriam, *Political Power* (New York: Collier Book Edition, 1964), p. 179.

instruments of power to achieve goals that are perceived as damaging or demeaning to the interests of the weaker country can also produce counterdependence, but the use of the coercive instrument is much more likely to do so.[16]

A Suggested Different Approach

Looking at the subject of power from this perspective, one can argue that, either domestically or internationally, in terms of interpersonal, intergroup, or interstate relations, the three basic components of power are: wealth (either material or human), organization, and status. In presenting this analysis, the basic premise is that the exercise of power is a process. That is precisely what Lasswell and Kaplan discuss in their book. As a process, it should be possible to apply the model not only to interpersonal and intergroup relations, but to interstate relations as well. Thus, it is on all three levels that the components of power will be discussed.

Wealth: Material and Human

It is not coincidence that historically, the countries considered the most powerful were at the same time the most wealthy. Nor is it accidental that the individuals and groups possessing the most material wealth within their societies usually wield the most influence and are considered the most powerful.[17] Nor is it accidental that the poor or unskilled individual, the poor group, and the poor state normally wield the least influence in their respective spheres.

It is a basic fact of human existence that individuals, groups, and states having material wealth are usually in a position to influence others. The reason for this, of course, is that those who are

[16] If counterdependence is not produced among the ruling elites, then it may be among counterelites. Indeed one of the most effective ways to create or strengthen a counterelite in a weak country is for a powerful country to coercively intervene, with the consent of the ruling elite, in its internal or external affairs. (Recall the discussion of group identity above: the most effective way to create or solidify group identity is to juxtapose a threatening "them.") This is precisely what happened in Lebanon and South Vietnam after the American military stepped in; in Czechoslovakia after the Soviet intervention; and in every colony which France and Britain tried to maintain by force.

[17] To be sure, the heads of state in the United States, Japan, or the Soviet Union are not the wealthiest men in their countries, although they probably wield the most power. But this is the power of their office. When they leave that office, their power is gone. Interestingly enough, however, the village headman, the tribal chiefs, and, in recent times, the major contenders for the presidency of the United States have almost always been wealthy men—whether measured in terms of money or skill.

not wealthy usually want some of the things wealth can make possible. Thus, they will often do what the possessors of wealth want them to do, in order to have a share in that wealth. If the "have-nots" did not value the manifestations of wealth, there would be no chance for the "haves" to exert influence. In a sense, it is the "have-nots" who give the "haves" power by allowing themselves to be influenced.

There are, it is true, some individuals, groups, or states who make the conscious decision to rank something higher than material or human wealth. But these are minor exceptions. The sad truth for the idealist and the revolutionary is that almost always *both* the "haves" and the "have-nots" value wealth. In the light of that reality, it is clear that the "have-nots" often want change not for the sake of reorganizing the value structure of the society, but so that they can become the new "haves." How sad for the dreamer of the post World War I era to find that the "new socialist man" who was to emerge from the Russian October Revolution turned out to be indistinguishable from his American or European middle-class counterpart. How sad for the young idealist who went into union organizing in the United States in the 1930's to find in the 1970's that the very success of his efforts has given the now affluent white laborer the power to deny that affluence to black fellow laborers. The social realist is not sad, however, for he recognizes that in the political process, whether intergroup or international, he will have to take into account the realities of human nature. The social realist no more tries to change the laws of human nature than the aeronautical engineer tries to change the laws of gravity. The engineer very carefully studies the workings of gravity so that he can build a machine that will do what he wants it to do, not despite those laws, but because of them. In a like manner, if one wants to change societies or the international system itself, one can do so only by carefully studying the laws of human nature and learning to build a different system that works, not despite, but because of those laws. Reinhold Niebuhr once wrote:

The finest task of achieving justice will be done neither by the Utopians who dream dreams of perfect brotherhood nor yet by the cynics who believe that the self-interest of nations cannot be overcome. It must be done by the realists who understand that nations are selfish and will be so till the end of history, but that none of us, no matter how selfish we may be, can be only selfish.

The whole art of politics consists in directing rationally the irrationalities of men.[18]

[18] Quoted in *New York Times* (June 2, 1971), p. 45.

Overwhelmingly, individuals, groups, and states seek to maximize their wealth. And—though this may not be their conscious
goal—they are at the same time attempting to maximize their
power, since wealth is one of power's principal components.

Now, what is this wealth that is so universally sought? Wealth
in the broadest sense of the term is both material and human.
Material wealth includes mobilized natural resources, industrial
capacity, money, and all the manifestations that follow from the
possession of these things in abundance. Human wealth refers not
to the large size of a population, but rather to what other writers
have called the "quality of the population"; that is, it refers to a
population with a high percentage of skilled or trained people.

Like power, wealth is both relative and contextual. In an agricultural society it is land, in a nomadic society it may be horses, in
an industrialized society it may be factories, mines, and mills, and
in a technological society it may be technological skill. The skill
of a priest in moderating the forces of the unknown may be highly
valued by certain people, in certain societies, at certain times. At
those times, those priests could be said to possess wealth. At different times or in different societies, the same priest might be
considered to possess little or nothing of value. What one man,
group, or state values, another may despise. The explanations and
medications of the "witch doctor" may be highly valued by the
tribe taught to believe that he can cure, but may be scorned by
the Western urbanites, taught to value only the explanations and
medications practiced by the "medical doctor." Conversely, the
technological skill required to run enormous, complex industrial
organizations may be utterly scorned in a desert where survival is
dependent upon the ability to use a camel.

The individual, group, or state that controls whatever is both
scarce and sought after may be said to possess wealth. This is
simply a definition of wealth in terms of supply and demand, but
these are useful terms in which to consider it because they demonstrate the relative and contextual nature of wealth. If no one seeks
what you possess, you are not wealthy. Conversely, if there is a
great demand for what you possess, you are in a position to influence the behavior of the seeker. There may be a number of reasons
in any given situation why the possessor of wealth chooses not to
exercise his power, but so long as he possesses what others desire,
he is in a position to exercise his influence at any time.

Here a distinction must be made between "manifest wealth" and
"latent wealth." An individual, group, or country that possesses
vast resources of some sort but cannot use them is not wealthy.
When a way is found to utilize those resources the individual,
group, or state may indeed become quite "wealthy," but until

those latent material or human resources are mobilized (that is, made manifest) they cannot really be considered wealth. The former Belgian Congo and Indonesia are considered by geographers to contain probably the greatest concentrations of sought-after natural resources of any countries in the world, but that does not make these countries the wealthiest in the world. Let them convert that "latent" wealth into "manifest" wealth, however, and their position in a ranking of the world's wealthiest countries will change enormously. Notice that the economist defines a state's wealth as "total goods and services *produced* in the country." It is the act of converting latent resources into manifest goods and services that makes wealth in economic terms.

During the centuries when no one sought the "thick, black, liquid substance" that existed under much of the Arabian deserts, those lands were not considered wealthy. Only after that substance was found useful and oil was actually extracted from the ground, did those countries begin to become wealthy. But as more and more sources of energy become available, the bargaining position —relative wealth—of the possessors of that oil is lessened.

If manifest material wealth is one of the components of a state's power, it would be useful to know the relative division of the world's manifest material wealth. This is, of course, somewhat difficult to determine because of the relative and contextual considerations. When economists calculate the wealth of a country, they think principally, if not exclusively, in material terms. Thus, for example, while a country with a literate population is, in terms of manifest human resources, wealthier than one with a nonliterate population, that fact would show up only indirectly in an economist's estimate. Still, since only economists have thus far calculated the wealth of countries, we must rely on their estimates, however imperfect.

Table 3.1 is a rank ordering of the countries of the world according to their 1965 Gross Domestic Product (G.D.P.). It is meant simply as a crude index of their relative manifest wealth, not as a measure of their relative power.[19] It tells little about power relationships. Its purpose is to indicate how the estimated $2,050,827,-000,000 (read two trillion, fifty billion, eight hundred and twenty-seven million dollars) worth of manifest wealth produced in the world in 1965 was divided among 130 countries.

The division of these countries into four groupings is completely arbitrary. It was done to illustrate the enormous disparity among

[19] Like many others, in the past I have mistakenly equated the two. See Marshall R. Singer and Barton Sensenig, III, "Elections within the United Nations," *International Organization,* Vol. XVII, No. 4 (1963).

TABLE 3.1

Rank Order of 130 Countries by Estimates
of 1965 Gross Domestic Product[a]

Country	Estimated G.D.P. (in millions of dollars)	Per Capita G.D.P. (in dollars)
Group I[b,c]		
United States	$ 688,000	$3,536
U.S.S.R.	267,000	1,150
Germany (West)	116,713	1,977
United Kingdom	97,720	1,790
France	94,044	1,922
Japan	85,207	870
Subtotal for 6 countries: (66% of total world wealth)	$1,348,684	
Group II		
China (People's Republic of)	$ 58,046[d]	$ 84[d]
Italy	56,742	1,100
India	49,623	103
Canada	49,104	2,505
Poland	25,600	820
Australia	23,113	2,035
Brazil	22,173	273
Germany (East)	21,700	1,270
Spain	21,431	682
Mexico	19,705	482
Sweden	19,223	2,487
Netherlands	18,829	1,532
Czechoslovakia	18,400	1,300
Belgium	16,660	1,761
Philippines	15,209	156
Argentina	14,982	670
Switzerland	13,688	2,301
Rumania	11,800	620
South Africa	10,550	590
Denmark	10,040	2,109
Pakistan	10,028	97
Subtotal for 21 countries: (25% of total world wealth)	$ 506,649	
Group III		
Hungary	$ 9,500	$ 940
Austria	9,341	1,287
Turkey	8,745	279
Venezuela	8,466	971
Finland	8,054	1,747

TABLE 3.1 (Cont'd.)

Country	Estimated G.D.P. (in millions of dollars)	Per Capita G.D.P. (in dollars)
Group III (cont'd.)		
Indonesia	$ 7,371	$ 70
Yugoslavia	7,240	370
Norway	7,093	1,907
Iran	6,323	270
Greece	5,751	673
Colombia	5,427	305
New Zealand	5,345	2,025
Bulgaria	5,200	630
Chile	4,936	575
United Arab Republic	4,701	159
Peru	4,345	372
Cuba	4,055	530
Nigeria	4,040	92
Thailand	3,931	129
Portugal	3,689	400
Israel	3,602	1,407
Algeria	2,940	248
Malaysia	2,939	313
China (Taiwan)	2,835	228
Korea (South)	2,815	99
Ireland	2,719	951
Morocco	2,608	196
Iraq	2,268	275
Ghana	2,232	288
Kuwait	2,106	4,786
Saudi Arabia	2,025	298
Vietnam (South)	1,892	117
Burma	1,672	68
Uruguay	1,664	612
Ceylon	1,630	145
Guatemala	1,428	322
Sudan	1,393	103
Congo (Kinshasa)	1,334	85
Dominican Republic	1,220	337
Syria	1,210	228
Libya	1,142	705
Ecuador	1,134	223
Ethiopia	1,105	50
Ivory Coast	1,094	285
Rhodesia	1,064	250
Afghanistan	1,046	68
Subtotal for 46 countries: (8% of total world wealth)	$ 172,670	

TABLE 3.1 (Cont'd.)

Country	Estimated G.D.P. (in millions of dollars)	Per Capita G.D.P. (in dollars)
Group IV		
Tunisia	$ 960	$ 205
Jamaica	916	516
Singapore	915	489
Zambia	857	231
Kenya	806	86
El Salvador	800	273
Tanzania	798	76
Lebanon	775	323
Cambodia	760	124
Nepal	736	73
Uganda	697	92
Trinidad and Tobago	682	696
Senegal	676	194
Malagasy	674	105
Panama	646	517
Luxembourg	632	1,915
Bolivia	615	166
Cameroon	612	117
Costa Rica	602	421
Nicaragua	538	325
Honduras	514	225
Jordan	470	237
Paraguay	441	217
Iceland	403	2,121
Cyprus	398	676
Haiti	396	85
Sierra Leone	365	159
Albania	345	185
Niger	304	91
Liberia	300	280
Mali	298	65
Guinea	280	80
Yemen	255	50
Chad	243	72
Upper Volta	239	49
Guyana	210	323
Gabon	206	448
Mauritius	194	262
Central African Republic	184	136
Malawi	183	46
Dahomey	164	69
Burundi	161	50
Rwanda	156	50
Togo	156	95
Somalia	138	55

TABLE 3.1 (Cont'd.)

Country	Estimated G.D.P. (in millions of dollars)	Per Capita G.D.P. (in dollars)
Group IV (cont'd.)		
Mauritania	$ 126	$ 137
Laos	120	62
Malta	120	375
Congo (Brazzaville)	118	140
Barbados	103	412
Southern Yemen	80	70
Lesotho	61	73
Bahrain	51	268
Bhutan	39	50
Botswana	39	70
Gambia	31	94
Swaziland	27	70
Subtotal for 57 countries: (1% of total world wealth)	$ 22,824	
Total:	$2,050,827	

a These Gross Domestic Product estimates are figured in U.S. dollars in terms of the current market prices. The estimates are based on the work done by Mikoto Usui and E. E. Hagen, *World Income 1957*, Cambridge, Mass.: Center for International Studies, Massachusetts Institute of Technology, 1959. The 1965 figures presented here are an updated version of the same data, prepared by Prof. Hagen in 1967 for future publication. The unpublished mimeograph from which these figures were taken also included average annual growth rates of real G.D.P. for the 1955–60 and 1960–65 periods for selected countries. Later tables in this book that utilize G.D.P. figures are projections backward and forward made under my supervision by Michael Jewel. A word of caution: G.D.P. figures, particularly for the less developed countries, are often little more than "guestimates," and have value only in indicating orders of magnitude.

b The division of countries into groups is completely arbitrary and was done merely to facilitate comparisons. Some of the countries listed on this table were not independent in 1965 but had become so by 1970 and hence they were included here.

c Since 1965, the relative order of the top six states in Group I have changed significantly. By mid-1970 the United States and the U.S.S.R. were still in the first and second places respectively, but Japan had moved into the third place, ahead of West Germany, which was in the fourth place. France remained in the fifth place, while the United Kingdom had fallen to sixth place. See "Toward the Japanese Century," *Time*, Asia ed. (Mar. 2, 1970), pp. 22–40.

d Prof. Hagen's data did not include Mainland China. The figure given here is a projection for 1965 from the 1962 G.D.P. figure given in Karl W. Deutsch, *Nationalism and Social Communication: An Inquiry into the Foundations of Nationality*, 2nd ed. (Cambridge, Mass.: The M.I.T. Press, 1966), p. 252. For lack of more precise data we have arbitrarily assumed a 3% annual growth rate. An error of as much as 1% *in either direction*, would not markedly affect the magnitude of the 1965 figure given here.

the countries of the world in regard to manifest wealth. The United States, accounting for almost 34 percent, clearly should be in a category by itself. It produced more wealth than all 124 countries in Groups II, III, and IV combined! The material and technological wealth of the United States in the second half of the twentieth century is staggering to be sure. But so long as other sources of supply exist in the Soviet Union, Britain, France, Japan, and West Germany, the power that accrues from this wealth is not unlimited. Again reverting to economic terms, one could argue that the wealth of the world is not controlled in monopolistic fashion but, rather, in oligopolistic fashion.

Those who control huge stores of the world's capital-forming wealth have great advantages: the supply of this form of wealth tends to increase continually; worldwide demand seems always to run ahead of even rapidly increasing supply; it is convertible into a seemingly endless number of goods and services that are also highly valued around the world; and it makes possible the acquisition of technological skills, the form of human wealth that seems likely to be the most valuable for a long time to come. Those states with the largest stores of capital-forming wealth are able to produce more material wealth faster than the poor or underdeveloped countries can. In the twentieth century, the gap between the rich and the poor countries has been steadily increasing, at what appears to be an accelerating rate. What is more, as these countries' material wealth has increased, so has their human wealth. Larger numbers of their populations are receiving more training in technological skills. That there may come a time (after the bomb?) when knowing how to milk a cow or grow a turnip will be of more value than technological skill is little consolation at this moment in history. For as long as one can see into an uncertain future, the demand for technological skill will far outstrip the supply.

To repeat: Table 3.1 is *not* an index of power relationships. If it were, we would have to conclude that the United States is almost fifty times as powerful as Czechoslovakia, while the Soviet Union is only twelve or thirteen times as powerful, and that the U.S. should therefore have more influence over the government of Czechoslovakia than the Soviet Union does. We know empirically, however, that that is not true. And the reason it is not true is because this list indicates only relative mobilized wealth. It says nothing about which countries have "influence" with which other countries. In order to determine that, we would have to know the nature and degree of the perceptual, communication, economic, military, and political ties that exist among the various countries. Wealth is one principal source of power; but wealth and power are not simple equivalents.

Organization

That organization is a crucial component of power is not a new discovery. George Washington and Nikolai Lenin both knew that very well, as has every revolutionary before and since. Indeed, they are not alone in this understanding. Anyone who has ever done any political work, whether in a club or a fraternity, in city or country, has come to recognize the importance of organization to power. Writers in international affairs also have seen its value. The question is whether they have attributed to it the importance it deserves.

By organization, I do not necessarily mean formal structures with presidents, vice-presidents, committees, et cetera, although formal organizations of one sort or another (such as alliances in the international setting) certainly can be major factors of power. A group, to be organized, need not have a formal arrangement; sometimes informal organization can be equally effective. This is particularly true of small groups, the members of which can communicate with each other fairly rapidly, often on a face-to-face basis. They can thus easily calibrate their views on a particular problem and plan a common strategy. This is true, for example, of Latin American oligarchies, New York business groups, and hippy communities, where the members of each have a similarity of perception to begin with, and many opportunities for direct personal contact.

The basic role played by organization is in the mobilization of human and material resources for the achievement of particular goals. These goals may be clear and explicit, or poorly defined, or implicit. They may be understood differently by different segments of the group. But if most of the members can be mobilized for what each *believes* those goals to be, then the group can coordinate efforts in such a way as to maximize the influence it can have on its environment, national or international.

Just as with power itself, an organization's ability to exert influence is both relative and contextual. The European Economic Community wields considerable influence in European economic matters but is much less influential in political affairs. A political organization can exercise considerable influence getting someone elected to political office, but an organization of conservationists may be more influential in getting water pollution legislation passed. An organization of workers may exert some influence over its members' behavior as workers, but may exert little or no influence over their behavior as Catholics, or veterans, or sports fans or conservatives, or any of the perhaps dozens of other categories to which a worker might belong. Organizations compete with each other for the loyalty and attention of many of the same individuals. Before there can be *effective* organization a common identity must be established. That identity very often preceeds organization. The usual progression toward action in the political process is that a number of individuals perceive some aspect of the external world more or less similarly, communicate that similarity of perception among themselves, thus forming an identity group, and then organize for the accomplishment of certain goals thought to be important to the members. The crucial aspect of organization, from this perspective, is the establishment of channels of communication through which perceptions, values, goals, strategies, and so on, can be calibrated, synchronized, reinforced, and translated into concerted, directed action. In order for that to happen, however, the members of the group must understand the common language or "code." Words and symbols have to mean more or less the same things to the members of the group for effective communication to occur. That is why it is relatively easy for a number of people who already perceive some aspect of the external world similarly to coalesce into an identity group and ultimately to develop some form of organization that enables them to take part in the political process more effectively.

That is one of the basic differences between a nation and a state. Members of that entity called a nation recognize some common "codes" and symbols and are therefore—psychologically, at least —more easily organizable, than are members of a state who may share only very little similarity of perceptions and who, in fact, may be more hostile to other members of the same state than they are to members of some different state. Members of a nation acquiesce in and perhaps even actively support the decisions of their leaders precisely because the leaders are perceived as being *theirs*. Members of a state, on the other hand, may very well ask by what right the people attempting to make the state's decisions can claim to represent their interests. Indeed, they may not even know there are leaders beyond the village or tribe or clan level who claim to speak for them. Every study that has been done in the underdeveloped states has come to the same conclusion: large percentages of the populations are totally unaware of the existence of the state as such, and certainly share little similarity of perceptions with those who claim to speak for the state.

The "usual" progression in the political process was described above. Actually, that may have been somewhat inaccurate. Another pattern that occurs, possibly with equal frequency on the international level, is the imposition of an organization upon a disparate population, and the gradual development of some degree of similarity of perception among the members because of the encompassing organization. In this sense a state is a kind of organization. If the state—and most of the countries of the world are states, not nations—can be held together long enough, and if sufficient channels of communication can be developed within that organization, it is possible that a nation may emerge.[20]

The mere existence of a nation, however, does not ensure efficient organization of the inhabitants. Some would argue that China has been a nation for perhaps 4000 years, and that the Jewish nation, scattered throughout the world, has continued to exist for almost 5000 years. Even granting that these nations have existed for so long, one would be very hard pressed to demonstrate that their national identity made for effective mobilization of power. By itself, it did not. The Chinese nation and the Arab nation were strong when they had strong nation-wide organization which mobilized the human and material resources within their boundaries. The existence of a national identity may have made that mobilization easier, but no mobilization could or did take place without organization. China and Israel may have been nations, but they have had power only during periods when they were highly organized nation-states. The important consideration from the perspective of power is the ability to mobilize resources for the accomplishment of goals set by the leaders of the organization. To the degree that a national identity exists, that task may be made easier. But the crucial factor is degree of organization. China, despite its national identity, was a very weak country from the latter half of the nineteenth century until 1949. It was still a weak country in 1959, but by that time its Communist leadership had imposed upon the nation a tightly organized governing apparatus that attempted to mobilize every resource to maximize the power of the state. By 1969, experts were questioning the success of the Chinese Communists in their mobilization efforts since the Communist organization had broken down and various segments were mobilizing resources to fight other segments instead of directing all resources toward strengthening the state. If, and when, that internal struggle is fully resolved, however, China may be able to emerge as one of the most powerful countries in the world—perhaps the most powerful.

The question is why everyone agrees that an *organized* China could be the major power in the world. The answer is actually quite simple. Organization is a major component of power. The

---

[20] For an interesting discussion of how this process operated among the original American colonies, see Richard L. Merritt "Nation-Building in America: The Colonial Years," in Karl Deutsch and William Foltz, eds., *Nation Building* (New York: Atherton, 1963), pp. 56–72.

more effective the organization, the more resources are mobilized, and the more wealth is created. Wealth is a major component of power. One of the attributes of wealth is a highly mobilized, highly trained population. Should China be able to mobilize and train 700 million or 1 billion human beings, it would clearly be the major power in the world. The United Kingdom organized, mobilized, and trained a population of 20 to 30 million in the nineteenth century and was able to dominate much of the world because of it. The United States was able to organize, mobilize, and train between 150 and 200 million people and is able to dominate even more of the world in the twentieth century. If 200 million Americans can produce national wealth approaching $1 trillion, how much wealth might 1 billion equally trained Chinese produce? The experts are convinced that if those billion Chinese are ever organized, mobilized, and trained to the same degree as Americans, they will dominate an even greater portion of the world. This is not an attempt to raise the spectre of "Yellow Peril." The people who are most threatened by that image are the Americans who never realize how fearful the rest of the world is of the "Yankee Peril." It is merely a statement of fact about the relationships between wealth, organization, and power.

One thing is quite clear: Numbers alone are an insignificant factor in any power equation. Organized numbers, on the other hand, constitute a major component of power.

The effective coordination of the various segments of a society does not necessarily rest solely on the formal organizing efforts of the government or one particular group. The "interlocking directorate" of the industrial, military, academic, labor, church, and political sectors of American society has been criticized, but it is the similarity of perception and the ease of communication among those who exert substantial influence in each of these sectors that keeps the society producing at high efficiency. In the Soviet Union, the party hierarchy provides the similarity of perceptions and ease of communication among the major sectors of the society, thus serving the same organizing function. During a former era, Great Britain was similarly served by the "public school" ties of the British Establishment. However intangible these modes of coordination may be at times, they result in intragroup communication and a dovetailing of societal processes: organization in the broadest sense.

The need for organization to achieve power does not end at the national level. The vast majority of states with which this work deals are extremely weak, relative to the major powers of the world precisely because there are so many of the former and so few of the latter. Consider how different the world picture would be if, instead of bilateral relations between perhaps 125 separate units and the Powers, there were relations between the Powers and Latin America, Arabia, Black Africa, South Asia, or Southeast Asia? It is true that, at the moment, the manifest wealth of these units, if organized, would still be considerably less than the manifest wealth of the existing Powers. But this is one of those cases in which the whole, once organized, could be considerably greater than the sum of the unorganized parts. Indeed, there is every indication that if the individual weak states could effectively unite into larger units, these new entities would become major world Powers. Organization as a component of power should never be underestimated.

Status

There are some individuals or groups in every society who are able to influence the behavior of others because they have what is called prestige or status. In some societies, it is a caste or aristocracy that wields such influence. In others, it is certain families or individuals. Whether the prestige attaches to the person or to the office held by the person, in either case the person is able to influence behavior merely because of his high status. These people are said to have authority. Those with prestige have influence over others because both they themselves *and the people whom they influence* believe it is legitimate—that is, correct and proper—for those individuals to wield that power.

The most interesting aspect of status is that it depends as much on the beholder as the beheld. That is, an individual with a Ph.D. from Harvard may have a very considerable amount of status among college students, professors, and intellectuals generally, but almost none among, say, southern blue collar workers, to whom such a person is an "egghead," a pejorative term. Conversely, Mickey Mantle or Joe Namath may have high status among sports fans—and hence influence (fans *do* buy the cereals leading sports players tell them to buy on radio and TV commercials)—but presumably none among intellectuals, unless they happen also to be sports fans.

The sociologist, quite rightly, makes several distinctions among types of status. For example, he distinguishes between "ascribed" and "acquired" status. Ascribed status is that which accrues to an individual or group by birth. Someone born into an aristocracy in a particular society has high status merely by virtue of his birth and thereby is accorded the ability to exert influence in that society. Similarly someone born into a despised caste, class, or race has low status, and thereby no ability to influence others, merely by virtue of his birth. Acquired status is that which accompanies the attainment of some skill or position valued by a particular society (or segment of society). Someone who becomes a priest in a Catholic society acquires high status, and, thus, the ability to influence religious Catholics in that society. The Ph.D. holder and the athlete mentioned above have acquired high status, and the ability to exercise influence among their respective "constituents."

Another distinction the sociologist makes is between the status accruing to an office and that accruing to an individual. The office of President, King, or Pope carries with it high status and thus influence among particular populations, regardless of who the incumbent happens to be. Conversely, some individuals have high status—as did Ghandi, Robert Kennedy, and Martin Luther King —whether or not they hold a prestigious office. Of course, if the occupant of a high-status office happens also to be accorded high personal status by his group or state, he is in a much better position to exercise influence than if he brings to that office little personal status of his own.

Similarly, status perceptions exist among states. That is, people in all states view other states, and particular individuals and groups in them, as having varying degrees of status. In an interesting article on international status ordering, J. David Singer and Melvin Small say:

> In the international community, as in most others, status may take two closely related forms. First, there is that attributed to a given member by most of the community, or more likely, by those members whose own status is high enough to permit them to largely determine the status of others. Second, there is that attributed to a member by any other *single* member, and though this bilateral form may well depend largely upon the peculiarities of the attribu*ter* and its relationship to the attribu*tee*, it is also heavily influenced by the multilaterally assigned status. Be that as it may, the combined consequences of the bilateral and the collective evaluation processes will generally produce some sort of hierarchy or status ordering (not necessarily transitive) within the system, and that rank ordering will have important consequences for the nations themselves, as well as for the total system.[21]

Thus, to many people in the former British colonies, particularly in the so-called "Old Commonwealth," the country with highest status is clearly Britain. To many people in the former French colonies, the country with highest status is France. However, the newer elites in many of the newly independent countries now look to the Soviet Union or the United States or perhaps even to Egypt

---

[21] J. David Singer and Melvin Small, "The Composition and Status Ordering of the International System: 1815–1940," *World Politics*, Vol. XVIII, No. 2 (Jan. 1966), p. 238.

or India as the countries of highest status. Since there is considerably more agreement domestically than internationally on who has
legitimate authority to wield power, status as a component of
power is obviously more important domestically than it is internationally. Still, it is far from unimportant in the relations among
states. It is the high status of Britain in the eyes of some of the
leaders in some of the former colonies, as much as any other factor,
that keeps many countries in the Commonwealth. It is the prestige
of the United States in the eyes of many leaders in many parts of
the world that sparks much of the international political support
these leaders give to the U.S. For years Mr. Nehru of India played
the role of spokesman for many countries in Asia and Africa, not
just because India was the largest of those countries but also because of the high status accorded to India, and particularly to Mr.
Nehru himself, by the leaders of those countries.

Another point: Certain categories of individuals or groups—for
example, industrialists, military men of rank, and religious leaders
—seem to have high status and the ability to influence those who
recognize that status irrespective of national boundaries. Although
there is little empirical evidence to support this contention, it seems
to be an observable phenomenon on a subjective basis. Military
men tend to respect other military men with high military status,
regardless of the country in which they live; anticommunists tend
to respect others with high anticommunist status, no matter from
what country; and so on. This factor has been too long overlooked
in the study of international affairs.

Status and power are mutually reinforcing. That is, while it is
true that power accrues to those individuals and countries that
have high status in the eyes of some other individuals or countries,
it is also true that high status accrues over time to those individuals
and countries that have power. "Power seeks to project itself into
prestige, and prestige to transform itself back again into power." [22]
John D. Rockefeller and his robber baron counterparts in the U.S.
and elsewhere acquired great economic power in their own time,
but no one would have said that they had high status in the eyes of
their fellow citizens. As time passed, however, and hired public
relations experts did their jobs, the families gradually came to be
perceived as having high status.

Similarly, in international affairs, countries often acquire economic power before they acquire high status. Although the United
States may have had a preponderance of economic power prior to
World War I and certainly by World War II, it was not until after
1945 and probably not until after 1948, that leaders of noncom-

[22] Merriam, *Political Power*, p. 134.

munist countries consistently looked upon the U.S. as having the "right" and the "duty" to set policy vis-à-vis the communist world. Indeed, J. David Singer and Melvin Small observe the steady rise of the international status of the United States, which reached the number one rank briefly in 1914, and again in 1935 and 1940.[23] It is presumed that since 1945 the U.S. has maintained the number one position, despite what some have seen as setbacks caused by the invasion of the Dominican Republic and Cuba, the Vietnam war, the racial conflict at home, and the recent monetary crises.

The fear that the U.S. would lose its high status among its allies "if we abandon our South Vietnamese ally" may have had as great an effect upon decision makers in the Johnson administration as any other single influence. However, as leaders in other countries came to doubt the wisdom of the United States policy to fight a land war in Southeast Asia, and the American ability to cope with domestic problems, they began to question the "right" of the U.S. to set policies that they were expected to accept and follow. In a like vein, it was not just the power of the Soviet Union that—at least until 1956—induced Communist parties around the world to look to it for leadership. Those parties also perceived that the Soviet Union had the "right" to establish policy as the "motherland of communism." The invasion of Hungary in 1956 and of Czechoslovakia in 1968, while applauded in Moscow, East Berlin, and Sofia, seemed so irresponsible to leaders of other communist parties that the prerogative of the Soviet Union to set policy was severely damaged. While China today clearly does not have the economic power of the Soviet Union, a number of Communist parties—both in and out of office—look to it for leadership and not to the Soviet Union.

Clearly, status, like the other components of power, is relative and contextual. If Group A accords a person, group, or state high status, then that person, group, or state will be in a position to assert some influence, on some issues, among people in Group A. The degree of influence it can assert, however, varies in direct proportion to the degree of status it is accorded. Unless that same individual, group, or state is accorded similar status by Group B, however, it is not likely to have any influence among people in B.

The Effects of Perceptions

Power sometimes accrues to individuals, groups, and states from still another source, which, like status, depends not so much

---

[23] Singer and Small, *World Politics,* pp. 254–264.

on tangible attributes as on the viewpoint of others. In the chapter on perception above, it was argued that people can only behave on the basis of their perceptions of reality. It is possible that an objective, knowable reality does exist. But for determining the behavior of individuals and groups toward states, objective reality may be considerably less important than perceived reality. This is not to deny that the existence of the atom and hydrogen bombs in the stockpiles of states is an important aspect of their power. It is. However, various perceptions of those bombs may be as important as the bombs themselves. For example: The United States and the Soviet Union both have nuclear weapons. Each country assumes that its use of those weapons—whatever the circumstances—will probably trigger the use of them by the other. That perception may be sufficient to deter both of these powers from using nuclear weapons. What is more, each state perceives that there are limits to the actions it may take without provoking the other to use those weapons. Thus, the Soviet Union will not invade West Germany, not because it does not have the physical power to do so, but because it perceives that to do so would mean nuclear war (whether it actually does is relatively unimportant). It is the Soviet *perception* in this respect that prevents a Soviet invasion, just as it was American *perceptions* of likely Soviet retaliation that prevented an American attack upon China during the Korean conflict, or American intervention in Czechoslovakia in 1968.

Prior to the 1940's, the European powers were perceived in most of Asia and Africa to be nearly invincible. Thus, it was possible for less than 35,000 British bureaucrats and soldiers to rule a country of perhaps 500,000,000 Indians. To be certain, the British were masters at keeping their subjects divided—unorganized—and that was a major factor in their ability to control the subcontinent. But another major factor was simply that they were perceived to be unbeatable. The Indians did what the British wanted, not because the British actually had the power to force them to do so, but because the Indians perceived the British as having that power. They behaved toward the British *as though the British actually did have the power,* thus conferring that power upon them. The same was true of the Indonesians and the Dutch, the Vietnamese and the French, and the Filipinos and the Americans. When the Europeans actually collapsed at the hands of the Japanese in 1941 and 1942, the Asian perception of their former masters totally changed. At the war's end, nationalists in each of the Asian countries were ready to test the extent of European power. British subjects found their metropole unwilling to face a test of arms, and independence was immediately negotiated. The French and the Dutch, on the other hand, still maintained a prewar perception of their own power vis-à-vis "the natives" and fought to maintain political control over their colonies. It was only after the military defeat at Dien Bien Phu that the French revised their self-perception vis-à-vis the Vietnamese and sought a peace settlement. The Dutch never faced a similar military catastrophy, but due to American diplomatic intervention on the side of the Indonesians in 1949, they, too, came to perceive themselves as lacking the power to hold on to Indonesia.

The examples of how perceptions of power affect the behavior of men and states are endless. The point to be made here is that if one perceives another to have power, he will behave toward the other as though the other did in fact have power—regardless of whether objective reality fully supports his perception. Since power has been defined as the ability to influence behavior, the very perception of another as having power may thus be adding to that other's power.

The Notion of Balancing Power

There is a theory prevalent in the literature of both domestic and international political processes that "harmony" or "equilibrium" or "peace" can be achieved if only the power of A can be "balanced" or "countervailed" by the power of B, C, and D combined. In domestic politics one reads of "countervailing power" [24] or "checks and balances," while in international politics one constantly sees references to the "balance of power."

In the Constitution of the United States, the idea of dividing and balancing power was institutionalized and presumably made immutable. "All legislative powers herein granted shall be vested in a Congress of the United States." [25] "The Executive Power shall be vested in a President. . . ." [26] "The Judicial Power of the United States, shall be vested in one Supreme Court. . . ." [27] The power the founding fathers gave to the federal government was to be trifurcated to prevent any one branch from emerging "all powerful." In addition, the powers not delegated to the United States by the Constitution, nor prohibited by it to the states, were reserved to the states respectively, [28] thus assuring still another division of power, between the federal government on the one hand

---

[24] Galbraith's term for a notion that has been around at least since the middle of the 18th century. See John K. Galbraith, *American Capitalism, the Concept of Countervailing Power* (Boston: Houghton Mifflin, 1952).
[25] *Constitution of the United States,* Art. I, Sec. I.
[26] *Ibid.,* Art. II, Sec. I.
[27] *Ibid.,* Art. III, Sec. I.
[28] *Ibid.,* Tenth Amend.

and the states on the other. If that weren't enough to ensure tranquility, the *Federalist Papers* assured the population that their liberty would be guaranteed by the competition for power among the many groups existing in this vast country.[29]

In later years, it was argued that power in a democracy really was divided among interest groups. The notion of the plural society was brilliantly articulated by Harold Laski, who was followed by David Truman, V. O. Key, and David Easton, all arguing that each of the various groups that exist would organize to protect its own group interests. David Riesman took this argument to perhaps its logical conclusion: that decisions are not made by the United States government, but rather that they emerge out of the competition among contending "Veto Groups," each looking out for its own vested interests.[30]

Almost exactly the same argument is made on the international level by those who expound the theory of the balance of power.

The international balance of power is only a particular manifestation of a general social principle to which all societies composed of a number of autonomous units owe the autonomy of their component parts; that the balance of power and policies aimed at its preservation are not only inevitable but are an essential stabilizing factor in a society of sovereign nations; and that the instability of the international balance of power is due not to the faultiness of the principle but to the particular conditions under which the principle must operate in a society of sovereign nations.[31]

Whether it is a group of citizens banding together on the domestic level to defend its interests, or a group of states forming an alliance in the name of "collective security" to pursue its interests, several themes are constant:

1. Power is evil; absolute power is absolutely evil.

2. By keeping power divided, some good (whether peace or the collective well-being) will emerge.

3. The domestic or international system that is in equilibrium or balance is stable and peaceful.

4. All one need do in the face of existing power is organize those opposed to it and that original power will be balanced or countervailed.

[29] Madison, *Federalist Paper, No. 10, The Federalist: A Commentary on the Constitution of the United States,* Edward Mead Earle, ed. (New York: Random House, 1941), pp. 53–62.

[30] David Riesman, *The Lonely Crowd* (New Haven: Yale University Press, 1950).

[31] Morgenthau, *Politics Among Nations,* p. 167.

Early in this chapter the notion that power is evil was discussed
and it was argued that power itself is simply a neutral ability to
pursue goals, and that the goals bear the moral quality. The idea
that some "good" will emerge by keeping power divided is directly
related to this point. If power is evil, then obviously there is merit
in keeping evil divided. But if power is neutral then the argument,
as such, makes no sense. What does make sense, however, is the
idea of preventing "them"—whoever they happen to be—from
acquiring so much power that "they" can subject "us" to adverse
influence. People in the Western world have believed in both the
operation and the benefits of the balance of power in national and
international affairs for at least the last two centuries. There is
serious question, however, as to whether the facts have ever really
warranted this belief.

In a brilliant chapter in *World Politics,* A. F. K. Organski fairly
well destroys the entire theory that international peace depends
on a power balance by pointing out that peace does not exist when
units in the international system have approximately equal power,
but rather when one unit has a preponderance of power.[32] He
argues that conflict emerges at exactly the point when a competing
unit in the system believes itself to be approaching the power of
the first unit, and thus challenges the first. "A preponderance of
power on one side, on the other hand, increases the chances for
peace, for the greatly stronger side need not fight at all to get what
it wants, while the weaker side would be plainly foolish to attempt
to battle for what it wants." [33]

It is true that where the relative power of countries is more or
less equal, the attractive attributes of power exert a mutual pull.
That is, each country has some of what the other wants and thus a
situation of mutual dependence or interdependence can come into
being. But often governments, for what appears at the time to be
perfectly good political reasons, impose restrictions that prevent
the development of interdependence. The threatened tightening of
trade barriers during the economic recession in the U.S. in 1970
and 1971 is a good example of this. General de Gaulle attempted
to prevent interdependence in his actions regarding the entrance of
the United Kingdom into the Common Market. Stalin attempted
exactly the same thing in his insistence on Communist autarky,
and it wasn't until his death and the rise of the Soviet Union
to a position of relative power equal with Western Europe that
those artificially imposed restrictions began to break down and
Eastern and Western Europe began to recognize the mutual advantages of interdependence. Unfortunately, relatively equal power

[32] Organski, *World Politics,* pp. 299–338.
[33] *Ibid.,* p. 293.

and a degree of mutual dependence do not necessarily mean that the countries will "like" each other. Powers with relatively equal strength tend to be each other's major competitors, and this competition often becomes exacerbated into overt antagonism. Indeed, the history of world conflicts has shown that major wars are fought between Powers of relatively equal strength.

Organski's insight, which so completely destroys the notion that peace in the international system is maintained only when there is a balance of power, is equally applicable to domestic systems. Despite constitutional theory, one would be very hard put to demonstrate that there has been domestic "peace" in the United States when there has been a "balance of power" between states and federal government. Until the Civil War, power did overwhelmingly rest with the states, but the states were divided among themselves, thus giving to the federal government a preponderant influence. When the individual southern states organized (united) to achieve a "balance of power" with the Federal Government, war occurred. Perhaps since World War I, but certainly since World War II, the preponderance of government power in the U.S. has clearly lain with the executive branch of the federal government. There have been presidents who have chosen not to use this power, but that does not mean that the ability to exert influence was not within their grasp.

In terms of the nongovernmental groups that have had power in the United States, it is also clear that domestic tranquility has been greatest when some groups have had a preponderance of power, and that domestic turmoil has been greatest during those periods when other groups began organizing in order to increase their own power vis-à-vis the groups upon which they were formerly dependent. The history of the labor movement provides a paradigm. Prior to labor's organization, the preponderance of power was in the hands of the owners of industry, who were in a position to define the "national interest" as best served by high profits and low wages. Since they had overwhelming power, there was little labor could do. That period, prior to the organization of labor into trade unions, conforms closely to the psychological stage described in Chapter 2 as "dependence." The preponderance of wealth, organization, and status in the labor-management relationship was in the hands of management and, as a result, to a large extent, so too, were the instruments of government. There was "peace and tranquility," to be sure, but that was because of the nature of the power relationship that prevailed. Labor, or more correctly, individual labor leaders began to recognize that while one laborer in relation to management was impotent, all laborers organized to protect their perceived interests could negotiate from a position of some power. Labor began to change its self-image, and entered a period of counterdependence. The period of counterdependence was certainly not as tranquil as the period of dependence, but while management may have placed a higher value on maintenance of the status-quo and labor-management "peace," labor placed a higher value on sharing in the decision-making concerning its own interests. As labor began to organize, conflict and violence reached enormous proportions—largely because management (with the overt or covert assistance of local, state, and federal law enforcement agents) did everything possible to prevent labor from organizing. But labor had become, by that time, quite willing to sacrifice peace for a changed power relationship.

It was only after the relative collapse of business in the United States during the early 1930's and the ensuing change in the domestic political scene that labor was allowed, and even encouraged, to organize. Thus at the start of World War II, labor had organization, at least, with which to counter the power of industry. With the start of that war and the shortage of manpower that resulted, labor added the component of wealth to its power. That is, organized labor now controlled a scarce resource for which there was a very large demand; thus, in their relations with industry they now had two of the major components of power in wealth and organization. It is therefore not surprising to find the power relationship between labor and management totally changed by the 1950's. Relative peace was restored as each side began to recognize that areas of mutual dependence had developed from the changed relationship. Each side now recognizes its need for the other. Labor and management in the United States have become "interdependent." This is not to say that labor now has equal power with management in the making of decisions that affect both, or that there are and will be no points of conflict. But because of the changed power relationship between the two groups, mechanisms have now been institutionalized by which it is possible for the parties to reconcile their differences for mutual advantage. Such institutionalized mechanisms for the peaceful resolution of potential conflict situations tend not to be established until both competing units have substantial power and come to realize that neither can exert influence over the other unchallenged. That power relationship is not likely to be stable as long as one party is kept subordinate—and comes to recognize and resent that subordination.[34]

[34] The history of the black people's struggle for power in the United States is similar. As long as whites held an absolute preponderance of power in this country, the blacks were powerless, and for all practical purposes without rights. It was only after World War II and the beginning of black organization on a mass scale that the blacks began to be able to demand a

In international affairs, as in domestic affairs, there can be peace if unit A has an overwhelming preponderance of power relative to unit B, providing, of course, that B is willing to accept its position of dependence upon A. That is, if the people who govern B are willing to accept the fact that either the government of A, or powerful individuals and/or groups in A, can make decisions that vitally affect B or individuals and groups in B, and that there is little or nothing B can do to prevent A's influence, then there can be international peace. But if, for whatever reasons, the power relations between those units begins to change, or if the leadership in B consciously attempts to change that relationship (becomes counterdependent), then there may not be peace. Indeed, regardless of the wishes of A for peace and the maintenance of the *status quo,* as long as B values a change in the power relationship more than it values peace, there is not likely to be peace.[35] There could still be peace: First, if the power of A is such that it can put out of office B's counterdependent elites and replace them with other elites more willing to accept the *status quo* (as was done in the Dominican Republic, Guatemala, Iran, Hungary, and Czechoslovakia, to mention only the more obvious examples since 1945). Second, peace can be maintained if A utilized its power in such a way as to render the elite of B even more dependent than before (for example, by sending in large numbers of troops to "protect" B from its enemies or by offering huge amounts of much needed and wanted economic, technical, and/or military assistance, and forcing B to pay back the cost of that assistance at rather substantial rates of interest). The difficulty—and it is crucial—with both the first and second alternatives is that they tend to be short-run solutions and are *likely* to breed long-term discontent and counterdependence in the weaker unit. Third, there can be peace if A agrees to the change in the power relationships that the elites in B desire. For this to happen, the stronger has to be convinced that eventual interdependence with the other unit is more ad-

---

voice in decision making. The blacks had moved from a position of dependence to one of counterdependence. They have yet to see their movement reach the kind of fruition labor achieved, and it remains a moot question whether they will at all. Certainly the whites still have infinitely more power than the blacks. However, the reason there is a lack of tranquility in our urban areas is because the preponderance of white power is beginning to break down in the face of black organization.

[35] Just what form that breach of peace will take depends on the power ratio between the two units. It could be all-out war, as it often was in the 19th century and in World Wars I and II when the contending states (or coalitions of states) had nearly equal power; or it could be rebellion, or civil strife, or "insurgency," as it has been in much of this century when the battle has been between units of vastly unequal power.

vantageous in the long run than continued dependence. This does not imply that the two units in the relationship expect to have equal power and thus become interdependent. Rather, it means that the stronger acknowledges the desirability of changing the relationship. Perhaps the stronger also concludes that the cost of accepting the changed relationship is less than the cost of attempting to maintain the *status quo*. Whatever the motivations, the pattern for a peaceful change in relationship was actually followed by the United States vis-à-vis Mexico, after initial resistance; Britain vis-à-vis its former colonies, also after initial resistance; France vis-à-vis Guinea and its other less counterdependent former colonies in Africa, with the exception of Algeria; and the Soviet Union vis-à-vis Yugoslavia and now perhaps Romania.

In both domestic and international affairs, as long as one group or one state has the preponderance of power there may be peace, but it will be an imposed peace, with the terms defined by the holders of power. As other groups or states begin to acquire power —whether through organizing or other changes—conflict and, perhaps, violence are inevitable. What is overlooked in almost every equilibrium theory of power is that the normal state of affairs is *not* equilibrium, but change. Whether considering groups in the domestic system, or states in the international system, the one thing that appears absolutely constant is change in their relative power positions. Those with the most power invariably prefer to maintain the *status quo* as long as they are in a position to impose their will on others. But, just as invariably, the weaker groups or states are committed to changing the *status quo* to gain a greater voice in the decision-making that affects them. And since the perceptions of each group are bound not only to be different, but also to be in conflict, it is inevitable that conflict will emerge as soon as the challenging group or state feels itself strong enough to make that challenge.

Since it is inevitable that subordinate groups and states will eventually come to resent their subordination, they will ultimately challenge those exercising power over them. The best way to maintain peace, both domestically and internationally, is not by attempting to maintain the status quo—however attractive that may seem to those already powerful—but rather by finding some institutional mechanism whereby changes in the manifest power of groups and states can be reflected in their share of the decision-making that affects them. But power—the ability to exercise influence—is in fact, if not in rhetoric, often given a higher value than peace. Thus conflict is chosen over peaceful change, as the history of groups and states amply illustrates.

SECTION II

The Ties That Bind

Chapter 4

Perceptual / Identity Ties

While the focus in this and the ensuing chapters is on the ties—perceptual, communication, economic, military, and political—that bind individuals and groups across state boundaries, it should be remembered that the very ties binding individuals from one state to individuals and groups in another are often the barriers separating them from other states and from other individuals and groups within their own states. Central to this is the notion that men operate on the basis of their perceptions of the external world and that the individual is able to locate himself vis-à-vis that world on the basis of his personal and group identities.

Theoretically there are an infinite number of perceptual and identity groups to which men could belong, but in reality most men belong to surprisingly few, relative to the choices available. Membership in one group implies membership or nonmembership in certain others. To be a man proscribes a person's identity possibilities. It allows him to be a member of a host of perceptual and identity groups, and eliminates him from membership in a host of others. He cannot be a woman. He may perceive some aspects of the world like a woman, but that will not make him a member of the perceptual/identity group called "women." Rather it will make him a member of those perceptual and identity groups reserved for particular kinds of men who perceive some aspects of the world as do women. Similarly, to be Chinese implies membership in certain linguistic, racial, religious, and other identity groups but at the same time it proscribes membership in all those identity groups associated with being English. And while a Chinese individual can, during the course of his life, learn the English language, adopt the English religion (Anglicanism), and even go to live in England, he will never be an Englishman—with all the perceptions and identities that implies—but rather he will always be a member of those perceptual and identity groups reserved for particular kinds of Chinese who perceive some aspects of the world as do Englishmen.

So it is with many of the group perceptions and identities to be discussed in this section. Membership in one group often excludes the possibility of membership in others. This truism can be very useful to social science research for we can know a great deal about how people who belong to one or another identity group tend to behave. Once we know the most salient group identities of the world's elites, we are in a far better position to predict their behavior.

It can be argued that each chapter in this section is, in effect, an analysis of the ways in which various kinds of identity and perceptual ties are formed and reinforced. Certainly when we examine communication ties we are looking at the channels of communication that exist, or do not exist, and thereby enhance or restrict development and reinforcement of similarities of perceptions between individuals or groups in weak and powerful states. Certainly, too, in examining the economic ties of the elites of states, we are looking at the nature and extent of similarities of perception and identity concerning economic matters between economic elites in the weak states and their counterparts in the more powerful states. Why, then, a separate chapter devoted to perceptual and identity ties? The answer is that while communication, economic, military, and political ties can be seen as perceptual and identity ties, they are all functions of still more fundamental perceptual and identity ties. These are the historic, linguistic, religious, racial, class, ideological, and educational ties so basic to human behavior that they are simultaneously taken for granted and ignored. This chapter is devoted to these basic linkages. The effect of these identities in international affairs has been so little studied that this chapter can, at best, be a beginning.

Historic Ties

In a sense, all of the ties discussed in this chapter can be traced to the unique historical relationship that may have existed between a Power and an associated state. Shared historic memory, the legacy of this relationship, can link two countries long after other ties between them have been broken or eroded. The French were beaten by the British in North America in the late 1750's. Yet despite more than two hundred years of British hegemony in Canada, historic memories of France remain and influence both the domestic and international behavior of that state in discernible ways. Similarly, the country which is today called Cameroon is, in many respects, the result of the memory that the region was once ruled by the Germans, despite the fact that little of German influence remains, save the name.

While each historic relationship was unique, there are some historic factors that seem to be crucial in determining the strength or weakness of this tie for the various Powers and their associated states. One factor is the length of time the states were in contact. Others things being equal, the longer two states were in contact, the stronger the historic memory. It takes time to breed similarities of perception. Although this may appear so obvious as to require no statement, it is sometimes overlooked in assessing relationships.

The second factor is the degree of the mentor's involvement in the political affairs of its dependency. Certainly those areas that were ruled directly by mentors seem to have become much more intertwined with them than the areas ruled indirectly. In the former, the indigenous elite structure was often consciously replaced or recast to suit the needs of the mentor, and this often had profound effects both on the indigenous elite structure itself and on the relations between the mentor and the elite. In the latter cases the indigenous structures were sometimes almost totally untouched and in some places function today virtually the same way they functioned prior to the arrival of the mentor. In those cases, ties between indigenous and mentor elite are often minimal.

Also crucial to the strength of the historic tie was the degree of the mentor's involvement in the economic affairs of its dependency. Nothing seems to have disrupted the traditional social and political organization of a region more than massive economic involvement on the part of the mentor. Normally, of course, such an economic relationship was associated with direct political involvement and, in some cases, with fairly heavy migration from mentor to dependency. Nonetheless, no matter what political form the relationship took, or how long two areas were in contact, the greater the economic involvement, the more intense the historic ties seem to be.

The fourth factor was the degree and kind of mentor migration to the area. In some cases large numbers of families were transplanted into relatively underpopulated regions, creating colonies in the sense that bees and ants export portions of their own populations. In those cases, of course, the historical ties tend to be most intense, since the region is presumed to have had no history prior to the arrival of the settlers, and the history of the metropole becomes the prehistory of the colony. This appears to be true of the Russian colonization of Siberia, the French colonization of parts of North Africa, and the British colonization of North America, Australia, and New Zealand. The early Spanish and Portuguese migrations to Central and South America seem to have been somewhat different in that they originally sent out only men ("Conquistadores") who were supposed to conquer, convert, and plunder. Lacking women from home, however, they tended to marry and stay—or at least to populate. Thus the history of those areas became literally intermixed with the history of the mentor Power.

The final factor is the degree of violence associated with the relationship. Historic memories between states may create barriers as well as ties. It is the memory of Turkish rule that creates an almost insurmountable barrier between Turks and Greeks. The memory of five centuries of Franco-British hostility is probably as much a barrier to British entry into the common market as any other single factor. Conversely, the memory of nearly two centuries of Franco-American friendship was not easily erased by a decade of de Gaulle. What matters seems to be the way in which the past relationship is currently remembered by the population of a region.

The fact of a legal or quasi-legal relationship of subordination was itself crucially important in determining the degree of impact the Power had on the weaker area. Table 4.1 shows the types and duration of the subordination that existed between today's major Powers and the weaker states historically associated with them. The categories used are meant to be suggestive, not definitive. They describe the type of relationships that existed between the dominant Powers and the weaker states historically subordinated to them. Because of the difficulty in assessing precise dates and categories, and because different portions of the same country were often ruled differently, and the same country was sometimes ruled differently during different time periods, in many instances only approximate dates are noted, and only the range of categories in which a country may have belonged are indicated.

The relationship category "Direct-Formal" is applied to those countries under the direct, legally recognized political control of a Power.[1] Included are those areas ruled as an integral part of

---

[1] There are those, both in the weaker states and in the Powers, who would question the legality of all of those colonial relationships, but at the time, international law recognized and sanctioned them. Only with the spread of the democratic ideal in the 20th century has the legality of direct colonial rule come into question.

"Independent peoples have, of course, always been eager to preserve their independence; alien rule has always been resented, at least to begin with. Independence has been valued and alien rule resented by many more people than have aspired to democracy and individual freedom. But before these aspirations were common in the world, conquered peoples did not expect much sympathy in their predicament. The general rule was, in Asia and Africa as in Europe: Independence is for the strong, and those too weak to keep it must lose it. The weak were not condemned for fighting to prethe Power, as well as areas ruled as colonies. "Indirect-Formal" is used to denote legal protectorates or mandates. Since areas in this category usually had indigenous governments of their own, it was presumed that there was less direct interference by the Powers in the internal political process of the countries concerned than in the "Direct-Formal" areas, although in practice the differences were often more legal than real. "Direct-Non-Formal" accounts for those areas in which a Power directly intervened— usually but not always by direct military means—to establish the kind of government it wanted despite the absence of formal jurisdiction. "Indirect-Non-Formal" includes here only those countries for which some quasi-legal basis for the relationship could be found, such as the U.S. Monroe Doctrine, or the British-Russian agreement of 1907 concerning Afghanistan and Iran, both of which were announcements of the creation of spheres of influence. (Post World War II spheres have not been included because they will be considered separately in Chapter 8 on Political Ties, although they rightly belong in this category.) This type of political tie is the most difficult to identify since so many exist without sanction of international law, and the degree of political influence exercised by the Power varies so greatly from country to country and from period to period.[2]

The categories utilized in Table 4.1 were originally suggested by Richard Cottam in his analysis of various kinds of British colonial control in the Middle East.[3] Cottam's work deals only

---

serve their independence, nor the strong for depriving them of it. The conquered were thought unfortunate, and their conquerors fortunate. Not until democracy and individual freedom became common ideals was it thought wrong for the powerful nations to use their strength to force weaker nations into subjection."

John Plamenatz, *On Alien Rule and Self-Government* (London: Longmans, Green, 1960), p. 1. Note that the last remaining colonial empire on the 19th century pattern belongs to Portugal, perhaps the least "democratic" of all Western European countries.

[2] It is hoped that if other scholars see merit in this approach, those who know more about colonial history than I do will attempt to quantify much more precisely than has been possible here the kind and duration of relationships each of the Powers actually did have.

[3] Richard Cottam, "Colonialism and Middle Eastern Foreign Policy Perceptions," unpublished mimeo, Pittsburgh, 1967. Although in Table 4.1 most of the same categories as Cottam's have been used, the definition of the basis for which country belongs in which category is, of necessity, somewhat different for each. In addition, one of Cottam's categories ("infrequent, non-formal control") has been discarded, and another ("Direct-Non-Formal") has been added. For this modification I am indebted to Steven Schecter who compiled the first drafts on which Table 4.1 is based. See Steven Schecter, "Dominant-Subordinate Interstate Relations: A Case Study of 103 Countries," MPIA thesis, University of Pittsburgh, Pittsburgh, Pa., 1969.

TABLE 4.1

States Historically Associated with Major Powers[a]

Country[b]	Type of Relationship[c]				Year of Formal Indep.[d]	Predominant Population[e]
	Formal		Non-Formal			
	Direct	Indirect	Direct	Indirect		
States Historically Associated With Britain						
Afghanistan	(1780's–			1907–1919	Indep.	Indigenous
Australia	1627–1966		1931)[f]		1931	Settler
Barbados					1966	Slave
Botswana		1885–1966			1966	Indigenous
Burma	1826–1948				1948	Indigenous
Canada	(1620's–		1931)		1931	Settler
Ceylon	1802–1948		1796–1802		1948	Indigenous
China (Parts)		(1850's–		1941)	Indep.	Indigenous
Cyprus	1878–1961				1961	Indigenous
Gambia	(1750's–		1965)		1965	Indigenous
Ghana	(1750's–		1957)		1957	Indigenous
Guyana	1831–1966		1796–1831		1966	Slave/Immigrant
India	(1760's–			1947)	1947	Indigenous
Iran			(1907–1946)		Indep.	Indigenous
Iraq		(1917–1932)			1932	Indigenous
Ireland[g]	(1100's–		1921)		1921	Indigenous
Israel		(1918–1948)			1948	Immigrant
Jamaica	1655–1962				1962	Slave
Jordan		(1918–1946)			1946	Indigenous
Kenya	(1895–1963)				1963	Indigenous/(some settlers)

Country					Year	Identity
Kuwait	(1860's-	1914-1961		1899-1914	1961	Indigenous
Lesotho		(1870's-1964)	1966)		1966	Indigenous
Malawi					1964	Indigenous
Malaysia	(1796-	1887-1965		1957)	1957	Indigenous/Immigrant
Maldive Islands					1965	Indigenous
Malta	1814-1964		1802-1814		1964	Indigenous
Mauritius	1814-1968		1810-1814		1968	Immigrant
Nepal			1931)	1790's-1950	Indep.	Indigenous
New Zealand	(1840-		1931)		1931	Settler
Nigeria	(1860's-		1960)		1960	Indigenous
Pakistan	(1760's-			1947)	1947	Indigenous
Rhodesia	(1890's-		1965)		1965	Settler/Indigenous[h]
Saudi Arabia		(1915-		1927)	1902	Indigenous
Sierra Leone	(1780's-		1961)		1961	Resettler Slave/Indigenous
Singapore[i]	1819-1963				1965	Immigrant
South Africa	(1650's-		1931)		1931	Settler/Indigenous[h]
Southern Yemen	(1839-		1967)		1967	Indigenous
Sudan[j]		(1889-1956)			1956	Indigenous
Tanzania[k]		1919-1961			1961	Indigenous
Trinidad-Tobago	1802-1962		1798-1802		1962	Largely Slave
Uganda		1894-1962			1962	Indigenous
United Arab Rep.		(1882-		1936)	1922	Indigenous
U.S.A.	1620-1776				1776	Settler
Yemen		(1919-1934)			1934	Indigenous
Zambia		(1870's-1964)			1964	Indigenous

States Historically Associated With France

Country					Year	Identity
Algeria[g]	1831-1962				1962	Indigenous (some settlers)
Belgium[g]	1790-1815				1830	Indigenous

TABLE 4.1 (Cont'd.)

Country[b]	Type of Relationship[c] Formal Direct	Formal Indirect	Non-Formal Direct	Non-Formal Indirect	Year of Formal Indep.[d]	Predominant Population[e]
States Historically Associated With France (cont'd.)						
Cameroon[1]		1922–1960		1916–1922	1960	Indigenous
Cambodia		1863–1953			1953	Indigenous
Canada	(1534–		1763)		1931	Settler
Cent. African Rep.	1894–1960		1889–1894		1960	Indigenous
Chad	1910–1960		1891–1910		1960	Indigenous
Congo (Brazzaville)	1883–1960		1800's–1883		1960	Indigenous
Dahomey	1892–1960		1850's–1892		1960	Indigenous
Gabon	1888–1960		1830's–1888		1960	Indigenous
Guinea	1894–1958		1850's–1894		1958	Indigenous
Haiti	1677–1804				1804	Slave
Ivory Coast	1893–1960		1630's–1893		1960	Indigenous
Laos		1893–1954			1954	Indigenous
Lebanon		(1918–	1946)		1946	Indigenous
Malagasy Republic	(1700's–		(1960)		1960	Indigenous
Mali	1895–1960		1880's–1895		1960	Indigenous
Mauritania	(1903–1960)				1960	Indigenous
Mauritius	(1722–		1810–		1968	Immigrant/Mixed
Mexico			(1861–	1867)	1821	Mixed/Indigenous
Morocco		1912–1956			1956	Indigenous
Niger	1904–1960				1960	Indigenous
Senegal[g]	(1659–		1960)		1960	Indigenous

Country	Dates	Year	Identity
Syria	(1918–1946)	1946	Indigenous
Togo	1922–1960	1960	Indigenous
Tunisia	1881–1956	1956	Indigenous
United Arab Rep.	1904–1960; (1798–1870's)	1922	Indigenous
Upper Volta		1960	Indigenous
Vietnam (North)	(1883–1954)	1954	Indigenous
Vietnam (South)[m]	(1883–1954)	1954	Indigenous

States Historically Associated With the U.S.A.[n]

Country	Dates	Year	Identity
Argentina[o]	1824–1933	1816	Settler
Bolivia[o]	1824–1933	1825	Indigenous/Mixed
Brazil[p]	1824–1933	1822	Settler/Mixed
Canada[p]	Uncertain	1931	Settler
Chile[o]	1824–1933	1818	Settler/Indigenous
Colombia[o]	1824–1933	1819	Mixed/Settler
Costa Rica[o]	1824–1933	1839	Settler/Mixed
Cuba[o]	(1898–1934)	1902	Settler/Mixed
Dominican Rep.[o]	(1844–1960's)	1844	Mixed/Settler
Ecuador[o]	1824–1933	1822	Mixed/Indigenous
El Salvador[o]	1824–1933	1839	Mixed/Settler
Guatemala[o]	1824–1933	1839	Indigenous/Mixed
Haiti[o]	(1824–1934)	1804	Slave
Honduras[o]	(1824–1933)	1839	Mixed
Japan	1945–1952	Indep.	Indigenous
Korea (South)	(1945–Present)	1948	Indigenous
Liberia	1822–1847	1847	Resettled Slave/Indigenous
Mexico[o]	1916; 1824–1933	1821	Mixed/Indigenous
Nicaragua[o]	(1824–1933)	1839	Mixed/Settler
Panama[o]	(1903–1936)	1903	Mixed/Slave/Settler

TABLE 4.1 (Cont'd.)

Country[b]	Type of Relationship[c]				Year of Formal Indep.[d]	Predominant Population[e]
	Formal		Non-Formal			
	Direct	Indirect	Direct	Indirect		
States Historically Associated With the U.S.A.[n] (cont'd.)						
Paraguay[o]				1824–1933	1811	Mixed
Peru[o]				1824–1933	1821	Indigenous/Mixed
Philippines	1898–1946				1946	Indigenous
Uruguay[o]				1824–1933	1828	Settler
Venezuela[o]				1824–1933	1829	Mixed/Settler
Vietnam (South)			(1960's–Present)		1954	Indigenous
States Historically Associated With the U.S.S.R./Russia[q]						
Afghanistan				1907–1919	Indep.	Indigenous
Albania				1945–1962	1912	Indigenous
Bulgaria			(1944–Present)	1960's	1908	Indigenous
China[g] (parts)	(1850's–				Indep.	Indigenous
Czechoslovakia			(1944–Present)		1918	Indigenous
Finland[g]	1809–1919		1939–1941		1919	Indigenous
Germany (East)			(1945–Present)		1871	Indigenous
Hungary			(1944–Present)		1918	Indigenous
Iran			(1911–1947)		Indep.	Indigenous
Korea[r] (North)		1895–1898	(1945–Present)		1948	Indigenous
Mongolia		(1912–		Present)	1921	Indigenous
Poland[g]	1796–1919		(1939–Present)		1919	Indigenous
Rumania			(1944–Present)		1877	Indigenous
Yugoslavia				1944–1948	1918	Indigenous

States Historically Associated With Japan[a][b][c][d]

Country					
Burma		1941–1945		Indigenous	1948
Cambodia		1941–1945		Indigenous	1953
China (Mainland)		(1930's–1945)		Indigenous	Indep.
China (Taiwan)	1895–1945	1941–1945		Indigenous	1945
Indonesia		1941–1945		Indigenous	1945
Korea (North)	(1895–	1945)		Indigenous	1948
Korea (South)	(1895–	1945)		Indigenous	1948
Laos		1941–1945		Indigenous/Immigrant	1954
Malaysia		1942–1945		Indigenous	1957
Philippines		1942–1945		Indigenous	1946
Singapore		1942–1945		Immigrant	1965
Thailand			1941–1945	Indigenous	Indep.
Vietnam (North)		1941–1945		Indigenous	1954
Vietnam (South)		1941–1945		Indigenous	1954

a This table is based on an earlier draft compiled, under the author's direction, by Steven Schecter. (See his "Dominant-Subordinate Interstate Relations.") The placement of countries and the dates chosen here are mine, however, and I take sole responsibility for errors. Historians will undoubtedly take issue with many of the dates. Because of the complexities of European colonial history, and limited knowledge, we make no assertion of definitiveness. Rather, the dates should be viewed as approximations, subject to varying interpretations. The sources for this table, other than those used by Schecter, are: *Statesman's Year-Book 1968–69; Hammond's Historical Atlas, 1957;* Norris and Rose McWhirter, eds., *Dunlop Illustrated Encyclopaedia of Facts* (New York: Bantam Books, 1969); B. M. Russett, J. D. Singer, and M. Small, "National Political Units in the Twentieth Century: A Standardized List," *American Political Science Review,* Vol. LXII, No. 3 (Sept. 1968), pp. 932–951.

b Countries are listed according to their current names. A number of countries were arbitrarily omitted, such as Bhutan, Sikkim, Swaziland, and Western Samoa, because they were just too small or because there was insufficient data on them.

c See pp. 92–93 for definitions of categories. The categories of relations were suggested by Cottam, "Foreign Policy Perceptions," pp. 5–6, and modified by Schecter, "Dominant-Subordinate Interstate Relations." "Direct-Non-Formal" is a category that does not appear in Cottam's scheme, but was created by Schecter.

d For many countries the year of formal independence is disputed. Does one consider the date of U.S. independence to be

TABLE 4.1 (Cont'd.)

1776, when it was proclaimed, or 1788, when the British signed the document making it formal? When did the "Old Commonwealth" countries become independent? Was it 1911, 1931, or never? Countries like Afghanistan, China, Iran, and Nepal, on the other hand, never formally lost their independence, although the major Powers exercised what amounted to colonial control during the years listed. The attempt here has been to use the most commonly accepted dates.

e In order to distinguish various kinds of populations, several terms have been used. "Settler" refers to those people who came over *from the metropole country* (either exclusively or predominantly) and established the values, language, culture, and history of the metropole as the predominant ones in the country. Later, immigrants may have come from other countries, but they assimilated to the culture established by the original settlers. "Immigrant" refers to those peoples who came to an area *from a country other than the metropole* and who have not assimilated to the predominant metropole culture. The immigrants to some countries were originally brought over as indentured servants to work on large plantations (as in Guyana). "Slave" populations

are those descending from individuals involuntarily brought to a country (usually from Africa) by the earliest settlers. While there are some descendants of slaves in most of the countries of North and South America and the Caribbean, populations are listed as "slave" only where these descendants predominate. "Resettled slave/indigenous" refers to the populations of Sierra Leone and Liberia primarily, where Britain and the United States, respectively, resettled large numbers of freed slaves among the indigenous populations of those countries. "Mixed" populations refer to the offspring of indigenous and settler and/or settler and slave populations.

f Parentheses around dates spread across more than one column mean either that different portions of the country were controlled differently, or that the country as a whole has been subject to varying degrees of control. In many cases only a small portion of a country (often the coast) became associated with a Power at the date indicated, with the remainder subjugated years later.

g These countries, or portions of these countries, were incorporated as an integral part of the Power for at least some period during their history.

h The populations of Rhodesia and South Africa are overwhelmingly indigenous, but the governments are exclusively settler.

i Singapore was incorporated as part of Malaysia between 1963 and 1965.

j Sudan was ruled jointly with Egypt.

k Tanzania includes what were formerly Tanganyika and Zanzibar.

l Former British Trust Territory of Southern Cameroons (now Western Cameroon) voted to become a part of Cameroon in 1961.

m Cochin-China (the southern portion of present South Vietnam) was the only area in former French Indo-China ever governed directly as a colony.

n The states with which the U.S. has developed recent associations (i.e., treaties of protection, economic and military assistance, etc.) have been omitted here, but will be discussed under current political ties later. Countries (exclusive of those in Europe) in which U.S. troops have been active since 1945 are included under "Direct-Non-Formal." This does not include states in which the U.S. merely stations troops but rather includes only those countries in which the U.S. has been directly involved militarily. American involvement in Cambodia and Laos is too recent to have been included in our tables.

° Countries so designated are included in the "Non-Formal, Indirect" category of states associated with the U.S. by virtue of the Monroe Doctrine, which was issued in 1824 and repudiated by the U.S. in 1933.

[p] It is difficult to determine a precise date for the association of Canada with the United States because of the informality of the relationship, but there is no doubt that Canada should be included here.

[q] The Soviet Union's post World War II associations with Eastern Europe (including "Non-Formal, Indirect") are included in this table because of their importance to understanding current relations between the U.S.S.R. and other communist countries.

[r] Japan and Russia jointly occupied Korea from 1895 through 1898.

with the Middle East and his categorization is based on "the
perception of a substantial percentage of the politically aware of
a people that their governmental affairs are controlled by the
government of another people to such a degree as to constitute
a denial of independence." [4] For Cottam the major determining
factor as to the category in which a country should be placed is
the *perceptions* of politically aware people in each of the countries. Cottam illustrates this with the case of Iraq:

The British granted a great deal of freedom to the Iraqi government
under the mandate. After the mandate ended in 1932, the typical Iraqi
government differed little in composition and policy from its mandate
predecessors; the role of British advisers in government agencies altered very little; and the advice of the British ambassador was solicited
just as that of the high commissioner had been. After the 1958 coup
d'etat, however, the control the British could exercise in Iraqi affairs
was not sufficient to lead any substantial number of Iraqis to classify
the relationship as colonial. Were the formal definition of colonialism
to be used, the date of 1932 would mark the end of the colonial period
because British control was no longer exercised through institutions
overtly established for that purpose. However, the date that marked a
really substantial change in degree of control was 1958. Furthermore,
in the minds of not all but of a substantial percentage of politically
aware Iraqis, colonial control persisted until 1958. For a study of the
attitudinal impact of colonialism the date 1958 is clearly the critical
one.[5]

Cottam's analysis is in my view completely valid. Unfortunately,
however, until historians have done a great deal more research on
the perceptions of politically aware people in each of the weaker
countries of the world, historical analysis of this sort simply will
not be possible for most countries. Thus, while it would be highly
desirable to validate and refine the data on historical ties with
perceptual analyses like Cottam's, it is necessary to rely for the
time being on more formal records of relationships. Though only
tentative and rough, Table 4.1 can at least be viewed as a beginning toward providing the basis for a useful estimate of the degree
to which weaker states that are now legally independent were
and/or are historically tied to the Powers. From this, as well as
the data available about other perceptual/identity ties, it should
be possible to make some meaningful inferences about the historic perceptions of politically relevant sections of the populations
of these countries.

It becomes apparent with even a casual look at Table 4.1 that

[4] *Ibid.*, p. 4.
[5] *Ibid.*, pp. 3–4.

historically Britain and France have preferred the "Formal" mode of association (either "Direct" or "Indirect") with weaker states. That is, vast areas of the globe were ultimately made either colonies or protectorates of those two Powers. Except for Scotland, Wales, and the unsuccessful attempt in Ireland, Britain has never tried to incorporate these associated areas as an integral part of the country. Rather, most weaker areas were simply made legally subordinate to Britain. France followed much the same course, except that it attempted to assimilate Algeria and parts of Senegal after 1870 (that is, make them an integral part of France) and still rules Guadaloupe, Martinique, and several other small islands scattered around the world as integral parts of the Republic.

One major difference between British and French colonial history, of course, was the degree to which the former sent out settlers to populate relatively underpopulated regions of the world. Indeed, Alfred Milner and others have argued that as a result there never was one historic British Empire, but two. The Indian historian, S. R. Mehrotra, differentiates the two as follows:

[One was] white and self-governing, the other non-white and dependent. The former was "Greater Britain" an "expansion of England," "the sphere of settlement," "an empire of dwelling places," it was not really "empire" in the strict sense of the term but a "commonwealth." The latter belonged to "the sphere of rule," the English were in it but not of it; it was the true "empire" in the classic continental tradition.[6]

On the one hand, Englishmen went out to other areas of the world to live like Englishmen. Whether they went for religious freedom, economic opportunity, or sheer adventure, they took with them not only their families, but their language, religion, political traditions, and their memory of British history. They created little Englands wherever they went. By the time later immigrants and slaves arrived, these little Englands were so well established that the newcomers were forced to adopt as their own the language, life style, and the historic memories of the original British settlers.

The "other Empire" was not composed of Englishmen abroad, but rather of many different peoples controlled or influenced in greater or lesser degree by the British. John Plamenatz discusses European colonialism generally, but British relations with that other empire particularly when he says:

[6] S. R. Mehrotra, "Imperial Federation and India, 1868–1917," *Journal of Commonwealth Political Studies,* Vol. I (1961), quoted in K. E. Robinson, *The Dilemmas of Trusteeship: Aspects of British Colonial Policy Between the Wars* (London: Oxford University Press, 1965), p. 10.

. . . they went into thickly populated countries, often highly civilized and complicated in their social life; they went in small numbers, not to form new communities, but in search of trade and high and quick profits. Later, when to defend their profits they intervened in the native government, they went as tax-collectors, administrators, judges, and soldiers. They came from what were already strongly organized and powerful states. Militarily they were immensely stronger that the peoples they subjected; and they had evolved political methods enabling them to control vast populations and enormous territories more effectively, and often also more cheaply, than the native rulers could do.[7]

Within that empire over which Britain ruled, there were an incredible number of shadings or degrees of control, ranging from crown colonies ruled directly by a British governor appointed by the Crown and responsible directly and solely to the British government in London, to a *de facto* sphere of influence, as in Nepal or Tibet, where the indigenous government was kept intact and formally independent but where the British resident exerted influence of one kind or another (and with varying degrees of subtlety) in support of British interests.

It is because British and French colonial practice varied so greatly from time to time and from place to place that it is nearly impossible to determine in precisely what degree which countries, now formally independent, are or were in some way dependent upon these European Powers. How attached did a country have to be to be considered an associate or a dependency of another? To which Power, or Powers, were particular states actually most attached? For example, although Egypt was legally a part of the Ottoman Empire, there was no question in the mind of any scholar or policy maker—Egyptian or British—that for at least thirty years prior to the demise of the Ottoman Empire, Egypt was in fact a protectorate of the British Empire. Similarly, although Iran and Afghanistan never formally lost their independence, the Anglo-Russian agreement of 1907 effectively divided those states into British and Russian spheres of influence. The same could certainly be said of China prior to 1949, although in that case every one of the major Powers claimed its own sphere, while the United States demanded that the "door be kept open" to its penetration. Conversely, what about Scotland and Wales? Should they be excluded from a list of Britain's associated states merely because they have been incorporated into the United Kingdom? The same sort of questions can be asked of the United States and the Soviet Union, both of which incorporated vast portions of entire continents into their realms. Are those areas

[7] Plamenatz, *On Alien Rule*, p. 7.

to be excluded from the category of dependencies merely because they have become more effectively Americanized and Russianized than other associated states? The problem is further complicated by the time period in question. Certainly, the American colonies were as much a part of the British Empire as was any other colony. But does it make sense to include the United States in a list of states attached to Britain? Would not many argue that it makes more sense—particularly when one focuses on the Post World War II period—to include the United Kingdom in a list of states attached to the United States? Since this is a study of the relationships that exist between ostensibly independent weak states and the powerful states, I have excluded those areas that have been more or less effectively incorporated into the major states (such as Wales, Alsace-Lorraine, Hawaii and Estonia), and those areas that are still *de jure* dependencies (such as the Bahama Islands, Guadaloupe, and Micronesia).[8]

The myth that Britain or France—or any Power—ever ruled any dependency totally, has by this time certainly been destroyed. No governor governs without the acquiescence, cooperation, and even active support of at least some segments of the governed population. The ratio of European administrators, soldiers, and tax-collectors to the total population over which they were supposed to rule attests not only to the Europeans' governing skill (and perhaps of "playing off" rival factions) but also to the fact that they needed and received local assistance. What that ratio does not indicate is the number and significance of the decisions the British and French made relative to all of the major decisions concerning the governing of peoples made in the area during the period of European dominance. Nor does it indicate how many of the decisions made by the local people were made the way they were because the local people presumed either that the Europeans wanted those particular decisions, or that the Power would not tolerate different decisions and had the ability to reverse any it did not approve. Certainly, the promise of reward and the fear of coercion were a much more frequent mode of rule than direct control—regardless of the legal relationship of the area to the Power. What is more, it is extremely unlikely that European rule ever spread—even in those areas under the direct control of Britain and France—very far beyond the capital and major provincial cities. Almost always at the

---

[8] Note that it is even more difficult to determine objectively which areas are Soviet dependencies. This is because of the Soviet policy of either totally incorporating a region or allowing it to exercise at least nominal independence. There are, of course, very active Estonian, Latvian, and Lithuanian nationalist organizations that would argue that their countries fit precisely into the category of "dependency."

local level, and very often at the provincial level, as well, there was no awareness of foreign domination of any kind. Yet, the degree to which non-European peoples either were, or perceived themselves to be, politically dependent upon the European Powers seems to have been a crucial factor in determining their postcolonial relations with the Powers.

The United States and Russia, on the other hand, have for the most part avoided formal political control of the British and French variety. In the case of the U.S., through purchases and wars the original thirteen Atlantic states were able to expand physically to the shores of the Pacific Ocean and beyond to Hawaii and Alaska. Vast settler migrations and ever-increasing increments of real power over the past 150 years have insured actual, as well as political, assimilation of these areas. Indeed, only British power in the nineteenth century prevented the political absorption of Canada by the United States (which would have given the U.S. complete political control over all of North America) but it is only the *political* absorption of Canada that was prevented. Prior to 1945, the Philippines and perhaps Puerto Rico were ruled in the "Formal-Direct" mode, and since World War II, Micronesia has been ruled in the "Formal-Indirect" manner, but those are almost the only examples of American control in the British and French style.

For their part, the Russians seems to have had even fewer "Formal-Direct" colonial holdings than the Americans. Like the Americans, the Russians did not waste their efforts on colonial offices, but directly incorporated most of the areas over which they exercised political control. Some of the areas the Russians tried to integrate, however, were populated by groups with strong feelings of national identity. Thus the Russian Empire never succeeded in assimilating the Poles, the Finns, the Ukrainians, or the other "nationalities" within its borders. It would appear that the Communists have been more successful in their assimilation efforts than their Tzarist forebears, at least in the Ukraine, Byelo-Russia, Uzbekistan, and other constituent parts of what is now the Union of Soviet Socialist Republics, although by no means have they been totally successful.

To the degree that Russia and America did become involved in classical European-style colonial control, both countries seem to have done so most during the period from the late nineteenth century until World War I. But for the most part, both countries have seemed to prefer to exercise what has been defined here as "Non-Formal" political domination—either direct or indirect. "Non-Formal-Indirect" subordination to the Power is considerably more subtle than "Non-Formal-Direct," but the two are intimately related. These modes of domination, as practiced by the modern Super Powers, are closely analogous to what in a different era would have been called "spheres of influence."

The U.S. and the U.S.S.R. usually exercise their influence to maintain in office regimes favorable to their interests, and do not intervene *directly* in the internal affairs of the countries within their spheres unless there is a danger of the indigenous government doing something perceived by the Power as a serious threat to its interests. Then troops are normally sent in for a limited period to support a preferred regime, or to overthrow an uncooperative government, as in the Dominican Republic, Guatemala, Hungary, and Czechoslovakia in recent times—in which cases the non-formal control becomes direct. The point to be stressed is that the governments of the weaker countries associated with the Power are and have always been legally independent and indigenously ruled. But the elites who exercise the predominant decision-making authority within these countries are themselves inevitably tied, perceptually, economically, militarily, politically, and in matters of communication to the major Powers. What is more, the elites of these countries usually are aware of the threat of intervention should they antagonize the Power, and accordingly are likely to make the kinds of decisions they believe the Power wants them to make.

The "Monroe Doctrine" of the early 1800's warned European states that the U.S. would not tolerate their interference in hemispheric affairs. While the United States was not always strong enough to prevent such interference—particularly on the part of Britain—Latin America was viewed by both North Americans and Latin Americans as within the U.S. sphere of influence, and governments on both sides of the Rio Grande tended to act accordingly. Similarly, after World War II the United States did not attempt to impose any "Formal" subordinate relationships on the weaker states associated with it, but rather—particularly with the Truman Doctrine of the late 1940's and the broader "containment policy" of the 1950's—the U.S. announced to the world that certain parts of the globe were within its "defense perimeter" and that any encroachment by the Soviet Union or its allies would be viewed as a hostile act liable to produce nuclear war. The Soviet Union has done precisely the same thing. Eastern Europe, Mongolia, and (until the Sino-Soviet split) China, North Korea, and North Vietnam were declared Russian spheres of influence, into which no intrusion, by the U.S. and its allies, would be tolerated. Since 1948, both Super Powers have *tended* to respect the other's sphere. All of John Foster Dulles' verbiage about "freeing the captive nations of Eastern Europe" notwithstanding, the United States did nothing about the Russian invasion of Hungary in 1956 or Czechoslovakia in 1968. And for precisely the same reasons, Russia did nothing about the British-French-Israeli invasion of Egypt in 1956, and backed down in Cuba during the so-called "Missile Crisis" in 1962.

Thus for more than twenty years the world has been divided into two enormous "spheres" of "Non-Formal-Indirect" subordination to the two Super Powers. One has been called by its creator "the Free World," the other "the Socialist Camp." While most countries have been tied by treaty obligations of one sort or another to each of the Super Powers, some countries (which came to be known as the neutralist or nonaligned countries) have not been tied to either. But simply because a country has not been formally tied to either the Soviet Union or the United States does not mean that those Super Powers have not been able to exercise at least some degree of political influence over them.

Some of the more articulate counterdependent leaders of the weaker states have in recent years referred to this "Non-Formal-Indirect" mode of association between weak and powerful states as "neocolonialism." Admittedly, since World War II and the discrediting of formal political subordination that followed in its wake, Britain and France—to the degree that they have had the power to maintain any such relationships—have been forced to substitute the non-formal approach for the formal mode that historically has been their preference. But they had already practiced this mode of association in some parts of the world for more than two centuries. What those counterdependent leaders fail to see is that current forms of dependency and subordination are not new and—perhaps more important—that weak states have always been and presumably always will be in some ways dependent on, and subordinated to, powerful states. The mode of association, while important as an indicator of the nature of a relationship, is really a secondary matter. The primary questions are to what degree and to which Power has a state been subordinated? The answers to these questions provide the historic perspective from which to begin an analysis of current ties between a Power and its associated states.

Linguistic Ties

More blood has been spilled in the name of religious and linguistic identities than in the name of all other identities combined. Large numbers of people tend to focus their "we-they" differences in those terms. It is difficult to say why this is so with any certainty, but there may be a clue in the primacy with which these identities are held. In the next part of this chapter, religious similarities and differences will be considered. Here the purpose is to explore why linguistic identifications are often so central to men's behavior.

One explanation may lie in the fact that linguistic identity normally implies a cluster of identities. Certainly a common language implies a common culture, and often a common or at least intertwined history. It is also true that it is much easier to establish and reinforce similarities of perceptions and to communicate identities when people share a common language. It is not just a shared historical memory and a common culture that bind the Commonwealth and England, the Community and France, or Latin America and Spain.

Thanks to the educational work done by the British, French, and Spanish during their time as metropoles of more than three-quarters of the world, their's are still major languages in almost 100 of the world's countries. Indeed, of the perhaps 70 countries that have received *de jure* independence since 1945, English and French are spoken (to one degree or another) in at least 55. Though in many cases no more than .5 percent of the total population speaks one of those two "world languages," this .5 percent is almost invariably the elite. Since it is the elite that defines "national interest" and determines both domestic and international policy, it is the perceptions and identity of the elite that are crucial to the determination of policy.

Whether the mentor's language is the "first" or "second" language of those elites is central in determining the intensity of the linguistic identity. But the very fact that these languages are spoken, read, and/or understood to any degree tells us a great deal about the world view these elites are likely to have. While there is no inevitable linking of linguistic to other identities, there does tend to be a clustering of identity groupings, and language can be a major factor in determining which cluster is chosen.

How language leads to, and can reinforce the acceptance of other values, perceptions, and identities can perhaps best be shown by an example. If one wishes to study seriously some subject he believes to be of importance to his country, international affairs for example, one must choose from among relatively few languages in which to do so. Few, if any, texts in international affairs have been written in Sinhalese, Ashanti, Amharic, Hindi, Albanian, Laotian, or any of the perhaps thousands of languages that are spoken around the world, although many texts have been translated into these languages from the original English, French, Russian, German, Chinese, or Japanese in which they were written. These, however, are translations of foreign ideas, values, images, and perceptions. For extensive study, one must read the original languages in which most of the literature exists. Now, if one critically examines almost any book on international affairs, he will find that many or most of the basic premises of that book rest on value assumptions that are uniquely tied to the author's national identity. For a dramatic illustration of this phenomenon, the reader is encouraged to examine a British and a French scholarly text on the Napoleonic Wars. It is almost as though the scholars were writing on totally different subjects. The same is true of Soviet and American works on international developments since World War II, or some American and French scholarly texts on Vietnam. Scholars in different countries make completely different value assumptions upon which they then proceed to build their analysis.[9]

Thus, an individual who wants to study any subject seriously will be obliged to study that subject in the language in which the writings on it exist. While he is learning about his chosen subject, however, he will simultaneously be learning—largely unconsciously —other values, attitudes, and perceptions, which tend to be implicit in the work of each major linguistic group. He will learn about international affairs as interpreted by an American, an Englishman, Frenchman, Chinese or Russian. The "better" he learns his subject matter, the more likely he will be to have simultaneously imbibed the values, assumptions, and perceptions of the authors he has read. In short, for as long as scholarly work continues to emanate predominantly from the U.S., Britain, France, the U.S.S.R., Germany, China, and Japan (as it inevitably will for some years to come) elites in other countries of the world must learn one of the languages spoken in those countries.[10] In so doing they will be tying themselves linguistically to that country, and those linguistic ties will inevitably and concomitantly produce other ties as well.

General de Gaulle seemed to recognize this and to have made a concerted effort to expand the teaching of French throughout the world during his tenure as President of France. For their part, the Russians have made a concerted drive in selected countries of the

[9] It should be observed that this work is little different from most others in that respect. To the degree that there are differences, they rest with this author's conscious attempt to correct for value biases. But no one, including this author, can perceive "reality" differently from the ways in which he has learned to do so. There is no question that this work is being written in social science English, by an American social scientist, with all the perceptual biases that implies.

[10] While English-speaking members of an elite can read either British or American sources and are, thus, somewhat more fortunate in this respect than their French, Russian, Chinese, or Japanese-speaking counterparts, they are still essentially tied to one of those two Powers by the international language they happen to know. Similarly, if one knows French he will also be able to read some Belgian, Algerian, or Senegalese sources, but predominantly, he will be tied to sources from France.

underdeveloped world to bring students to the Soviet Union for higher education. Since the medium of instruction in Soviet universities is exclusively Russian, these students have first to spend a full year in the Soviet Union studying the Russian language. Thus the Russians are establishing, for the first time, linguistic ties with potential future elites of those countries. Similarly, it is not accidental that wherever American Peace Corps volunteers go, if their prime task is not the teaching of English (as it often is), it is very often their secondary job. This is not at all insidious, however. One of the basic facts of economic life throughout the world is that people who speak English tend to command better wages and more economic opportunity than people who do not. Thus Peace Corps volunteers often devote considerable time to teaching English to the people they work among not because they have been told to do so by the U.S. government, but because the people with whom the volunteers work ask to learn the language. (Here is one of those clear-cut cases of the attractive qualities of power.)

A common language among people in different countries tends to produce a number of side effects. One is that, other things such as distance, investment and market opportunity being equal (which, of course, they never are) businessmen are more likely to invest in a country where their language is spoken by at least some of the indigenous population. There are practical considerations for this, but there is also an unspoken feeling of trust—of "we-ness"—that linguistic similarities engender. Conversely, if all other things are not equal, and the economic opportunity is great enough to entice businessmen to cross the linguistic barrier, it very often happens that more and more indigenous individuals begin to learn the language of the investor. It also sometimes happens that the investor and the managers from the more powerful country learn the language of the country in which they are doing business and thus double linguistic ties may be created.[11]

Also, a country in which large numbers of people speak the language of the mentor tends to attract tourists and students from the mentor country. Although people are attracted by the exotic, they feel safe with the familiar, and tend to travel where their language will be understood. What is more, proportionally more individuals from the weaker countries who go abroad are likely to travel in the mentor country where they can understand and speak the language—thus further reinforcing similarities of perception. Of course, if the mentor happens to have a language little known to the elite of a weak associated state (as was the case for Cuba, for example, after it became associated with Russia, and for some of

[11] For a more complete discussion of the ties engendered by businessmen, see Chapter 6 on Economic Ties.

the Southeast Asian countries after World War II) the very act of travelling to the mentor country will not only create visual ties and impressions, but will also aid in the learning of the language.

While the next chapter is devoted to the communication ties that exist among countries, it is worth noting here that language is a crucial factor in determining the direction of communication ties. Individuals can listen to broadcasts from a state whose language they understand. They can subscribe to another country's periodicals and journals (either technical or popular) if they read the language. Since mentor countries tend to produce many more broadcasts and periodicals than do the weaker countries, the likelihood is that the weak countries will seek out some if they can understand them. Finally, and perhaps most important from the perspective of this study, countries tend to subscribe to the international news services of the foreign power whose language they know. If the elite or other segments of the population can understand the language spoken in the mentor country there is no need to have the "information" carried by those news services translated into the indigenous language. Thus the elite is likely to receive nearly the same interpretation of world news as the population of the mentor countries, thereby creating and reinforcing in the weak state a similarity of perception about world affairs.

Which weaker countries are linguistically tied to which major Powers? Table 4.2 is a listing of 131 countries and the principal languages spoken in each.

Note that while English is listed as the exclusive language in only five countries other than the United Kingdom and the United States (Australia, Barbados, Guyana, Jamaica, and New Zealand), it is at least one of the principal languages spoken in thirty other countries. All of those countries, with the exception of the Philippines, have at one time or another been British colonies. Obviously, the larger the number of British settlers (or British dominated slaves), the more widespread the use of English. In areas not predominantly settler or slave, the longer or more directly the colony was ruled by Britain, the higher the percentage of English-speaking population. This is not because the British pursued a conscious policy of assimilating subjected peoples. Quite the contrary. The British seem to have felt that no amount of English education could make someone not born in England an Englishman. (Hence the refusal to grant equal rights to the American colonists.) English was taught in the already populated colonies not from a desire to civilize the natives, but because it was cheaper to train natives for lower level military, government, and business positions than it was to import personnel from Britain. Indeed, it would appear that the

TABLE 4.2
Principal Languages Spoken in 131 Countries[a]

Country	Principal Languages
Afghanistan	Pushtu, Persian
Albania	Albanian
Algeria	French, Arabic
Argentina	Spanish
Australia	English
Austria	German
Barbados	English
Belgium	Flemish, French
Bolivia	Spanish, Aymara, Quechua
Botswana	English, African Languages
Brazil	Portuguese
Bulgaria	Bulgarian
Burma	Burmese, English
Burundi	Kirundi, French
Cambodia	Khmer, French
Cameroon	French, African Languages
Canada	English, French
Cent. African Republic	French, African Languages
Ceylon	Sinhalese, Tamil, English
Chad	French, Arabic, African Languages
Chile	Spanish
China (Peoples Rep. of)	Chinese
China (Taiwan)	Chinese
Colombia	Spanish
Congo (Brazzaville)	French, African Languages
Congo (Kinshasa)	French, Flemish, African Languages
Costa Rica	Spanish
Cuba	Spanish
Cyprus	Greek, Turkish, English
Czechoslovakia	Czech, Slovak
Dahomey	French, African Languages
Denmark	Danish
Dominican Republic	Spanish
Ecuador	Spanish, Quechua
El Salvador	Spanish
Ethiopia	Amharic, African Languages
Finland	Finnish, Swedish
France	French
Gabon	French, African Languages
Gambia	English, African Languages

TABLE 4.2 (Cont'd.)

Country	Principal Languages
Germany, East	German
Germany, West	German
Ghana	English, African Languages
Greece	Greek
Guatemala	Spanish, Indian Dialects
Guinea	French, African Languages
Guyana	English
Haiti	French, French Creole
Honduras	Spanish
Hungary	Hungarian
Iceland	Icelandic
India	Hindi, English, others
Indonesia	Bahasa Indonesia, others
Iran	Persian, Kurdish
Iraq	Arabic, Kurdish
Ireland	English, Gaelic
Israel	Hebrew
Italy	Italian
Ivory Coast	French, African Languages
Jamaica	English
Japan	Japanese
Jordan	Arabic
Kenya	Swahili, Kikuyu, English, others
Korea, North	Korean
Korea, South	Korean
Kuwait	Arabic
Laos	Laotian, French
Lebanon	Arabic, French
Lesotho	English, Sesotho
Liberia	English, African Languages
Libya	Arabic, Italian, English
Luxembourg	Letzeburgesch, French, German
Malagasy Republic	French, Malagasy
Malawi	English, African Languages
Malaysia	Malay, Chinese, Tamil, English
Maldive Islands	Maldivian
Mali	French, African Languages
Malta	Maltese, English, Italian
Mauritania	Arabic, French
Mauritius	Creole, French, English
Mexico	Spanish, Indian Languages
Mongolian Republic	Khalkha, Mongolian
Morocco	Arabic, French, Spanish
Nepal	Nepali, others
Netherlands	Dutch

TABLE 4.2 (Cont'd.)

Country	Principal Languages
New Zealand	English
Nicaragua	Spanish
Niger	French, African Languages
Nigeria	English, African Languages
Norway	Norwegian
Pakistan	Bengali, Urdu, English
Panama	Spanish
Paraguay	Spanish, Guarani
Peru	Spanish, Aymara, Quechua
Philippines	Tagalog, English, Spanish, others
Poland	Polish
Portugal	Portuguese
Rhodesia	English, African Languages
Rumania	Rumanian
Rwanda	Swahili, French
Saudi Arabia	Arabic
Senegal	French, African Languages
Sierra Leone	English, Creole, African Languages
Singapore	English, Chinese, Malay, Tamil
Somalia	Somali, others
South Africa	English, Afrikaans, African Languages
Southern Yemen	Arabic, English, African Languages
Spain	Spanish
Sudan	African Languages, Arabic, English
Sweden	Swedish
Switzerland	German, French, Italian
Syria	Arabic
Tanzania	English, African Languages
Thailand	Thai, Chinese
Togo	French, African Languages
Trinidad-Tobago	English, English Creole
Tunisia	Arabic, French
Turkey	Turkish
Uganda	English, African Languages
U.S.S.R.	Russian, Local Languages
United Arab Republic	Arabic
United Kingdom	English
United States	English
Upper Volta	French, African Languages
Uruguay	Spanish
Venezuela	Spanish
Vietnam, North	Annamese, Chinese, French
Vietnam, South	Annamese, French
Yemen	Arabic
Yugoslavia	Serbo-Croat, Slovene, Macedonian
Zambia	English, African Languages

[a] Taken from "Perspectives on U.S. Affairs," *Senior Scholastic* (Oct. 5, 1967), pp. 28–32.

greater the degree of British economic penetration, the more English-speaking natives were needed to service those enterprises. The exact percentage of the English-speaking population in each country is not known. It is known, however, that aside from the seven countries mentioned above, in which it was the only language spoken in 1967, English was the only official language spoken in eight countries,[12] and was one of the official languages in twelve other countries.[13] If it was British power that initiated the spread of the English language around the world in the sixteenth through nineteenth centuries, it is United States power that perpetuates and accelerates the use of the language in the twentieth century.

In almost all of the states historically associated with the United States and the Soviet Union languages other than English and Russian are the principal languages spoken. This is primarily due to the fact that the U.S. and Russia have historically tended to avoid the formal mode of political domination. Thus while they might intervene militarily, economically, and/or politically in the internal affairs of other states, they were rarely in a position (or rarely chose) to impose English or Russian as the language of instruction for the mass of the population. In those areas that were made integral parts of both countries, English and Russian have, of course, become ubiquitous. Hawaiian, Eskimo, and Sioux may still be spoken in some remote villages or reservations but, as the Puerto Ricans and earlier immigrant groups to the U.S. have learned, to "get ahead" one needs to assimilate into American culture, and the first step in the process of assimilation is learning English. In non-Russian parts of the Soviet Union, which were more populous than North America when they were integrated into the Russian Empire, so-called "national languages" continue to survive. Ukrainian, Uzbek and Lithuanian (to mention only three) are still spoken by large numbers of people in those "Republics." But how many of the children in those republics do not also speak Russian? In Russia, as in America, one must assimilate to get ahead.

As American and Russian power has increased throughout the world, so has the use of the English and Russian languages. While there are no precise figures available on languages spoken by elites in continental Europe, Latin America, and the Middle East, there is no doubt that prior to World War II French and German were the preferred second languages in those areas. (Indeed, the same was true for elites within the United States and the Soviet Union.)

---

[12] Botswana, Malawi, Nigeria, Rhodesia, Sierra Leone, Trinidad and Tobago, Uganda, and Gambia.
[13] Canada, Ghana, India, Ireland, Kenya, Lesotho, Malta, Pakistan, Singapore, South Africa, Tanzania, and Zambia.

Since that time, however, English has overwhelmingly become the preferred second language almost everywhere except in Eastern Europe, where ambitious people study Russian.

When French power in Europe was at its height the French language was not only the international language of diplomacy, but was also the mark of an educated man. With the decline of French power, the use of the French language has also declined. But for the French, at least, the ability to speak flawless Parisian French has remained a prerequisite for being considered civilized. This has been, and remains, particularly true of the French attitude toward the people who inhabited the lands France dominated politically. Only those natives who were civilized were treated as equals by the French, and the test—emotionally, if not officially— has been the ability of the natives to speak flawless French. This attitude was perhaps nowhere more succinctly expressed than by the famous seventeenth century French colonial governor of Canada, Louis de Buade de Frontenac, when in his dispute with the Jesuit missionaries he

. . . expressed to the Jesuits my great surprise at the fact that, out of all the Indians under their care at Notre-Dame de Foye, not one of them could speak French. I have told them that in their missions they should endeavour, whilst making Indians sons of Christ, to transform them also into subjects of the king. To reach this end, and give them sedentary habits, and induce them to abandon a life so opposed to the spirit of Christianity, since the best means to make Christians out of these poor creatures should be to persuade them to be men.[14]

More recently Georges Pompidou, while he was Prime Minister under de Gaulle, said:

Of all countries, France is the country which cares most about exporting its language and culture. This characteristic is genuinely specific to us. When a Frenchman travelling abroad meets someone who speaks French, who has read French authors, he feels as if he has found a brother. This is a need of our thought, perhaps of our genius. Our cooperation is undeniably oriented and ought fundamentally to be so, towards this expansion of our language and our culture.[15]

As a result of French and Belgian colonialism, French is today one of the principal languages in thirty-one countries outside of

---

[14] Quoted in Herbert I. Priestley, *France Overseas Through the Old Regime: A Study of European Expansion* (New York: Appleton-Century, 1939), p. 150.
[15] Quoted in Teresa Hayter, *French Aid* (London: Overseas Development Institute, 1966), pp. 9–10.

France. But the French never thought that entire populations could, or should, be taught the language. Rather, for the French, "assimilation" meant teaching French language and culture to a thin layer of the top elite in each of the areas they controlled. Regardless of numbers actually taught, however, French is a principal language in all twenty-three of the states to have achieved independence from France since 1945, and is the only official language in fourteen countries other than France itself.[16]

Even though relatively small percentages of the total population speak English or French in most of the newly independent countries, these are the official languages in many for two reasons. English or French is the language spoken by the elite of the country (and, indeed, often the first language of the elite). Often, English or French is the only medium in which the various segments of a multilingual population can communicate. This is particularly true for those states (often artificially created by Britain and France) in sub-Sahara Africa, where as many as one hundred different African languages and dialects are spoken by as few as five million people.

Interestingly enough, although there was often open hostility to the use of English and French as the official language in pre-independence days, particularly on the part of the more counterdependent nationalist elites, after independence many of these same leaders (like Nehru of India) fought to retain its use, recognizing it as a unifying factor in their struggle to build a nation out of disparate language groups. In a number of countries in which English or French is no longer one of the official languages—such as Malaysia, Ceylon, Sudan, and Lebanon—it is still used extensively to communicate across linguistic divisions in the country. In some of these former dependencies, dropping English or French as the official language may be the sign of the emergence of a less westernized elite into positions of power (as in the case of Ceylon). Or it may be a symbolic gesture of independence to placate nationalist sentiment among significant sectors of the population, who viewed the official use of these European languages as a sign of subservience or as a bar to their own possible mobility within the governing structure.

There is some evidence to indicate that despite the need for a

[16] I know of no comparative data on the percent of colonial populations taught English and French in their respective areas, but official French policies of assimilation notwithstanding, impressionistic evidence seems to indicate that at least as high and probably a higher percentage of the population in British-controlled areas learned English than did the equivalent populations in French-controlled areas. This, of course excludes the predominantly settler countries like Canada and Australia, and the predominantly slave countries like Jamaica and Haiti.

knowledge of a world language, for domestic political reasons English and French will cease to be the official language in an increasing number of weaker countries. As that happens, proportionately fewer people in those countries will speak English and French (and those who do, may speak them less well), and thus the linguistic ties with the U.K., the U.S., and France will be weakened. But this may be only a short-run phenomena. As the various national languages become entrenched as the only official languages of these countries, there is very strong likelihood that the domestic political pressure will switch from adoption of the national language to support for increased teaching of an international language so that the mass of the population may be brought into the mainstream of modern technological and economic advancement. Indeed, as will be shown in the section on "Educational Ties" below, the demand for, and the increase in, mass education in English or French as a second language has already begun in many countries. The preferred international language chosen by the mass of the population is almost always the language of the former metropole (particularly in states formerly associated with Britain and France). The reasons for this are clear: the elites already speak those languages, and it is in their interest to see to it that the language they already know remains the principal international language in their countries; learning the language spoken by the elite is often a prerequisite for entrance into economic and political decision-making positions controlled by the elite; the international language spoken by the elite because it is the elite language, is almost always the language given highest status by the mass of the population.

Thus, while short-term domestic political pressures seem to be causing a weakening of the linguistic ties between the mentor Powers and their associated states in some parts of the world, long-term trends seem to indicate a strengthening of the linguistic ties between the Powers and the associated states beyond that which existed prior to the grant of political independence.

Religious Ties

In past centuries in Europe, religious identification was the one over which men seemed most willing to draw swords. Today too, where religion is central to a society, religious identity assumes the position of the most highly valued of all identities. Nations such as Germany, Ireland, Bengal, and the Punjab have been ripped apart because religious identities took precedence over linguistic or national identities.

In the Middle Ages, despite the differences among them, it was possible to unite all of Christendom to oppose the Islamic "they" who were perceived as the major threat. Several hundred years later the more menacing threat became the Protestant or the Catholic, depending on one's own religious identity. Still later, as national identities came to have precedence over religious identities, members not only of the same religion but even of the same sect were perfectly willing to kill each other in the World Wars for the sake of their "higher" identity as nationals of this country or that.

It would appear that in Europe (with the exception of Ireland) religion no longer enjoys the prime identity ranking it once held. Despite the decline in rank, however, there is some evidence that it has not totally disappeared as a significant identity. Is it merely coincidence that the European Economic Community is composed of six predominantly Catholic countries? The Treaty of Rome creating the community was signed by leaders of six Christian Democratic (Catholic) parties, which all happened to be in office at the time, with the blessing and encouragement of the Pope.[17]

Islam is certainly one of the major factors uniting the people of North Africa and the Middle East. Indeed, recent research indicates that many Arabs are unable to distinguish between the words "Arab" and "Islam."[18] One may explain the feeling of unity among the Arab peoples on grounds other than religion, but certainly the Indian, Indonesian, Malaysian, Iranian, and Pakistani attitudes toward Israel must, at least in part, be explained by their religious identity. Note the Muslim—not Arab—summit conference that was called in late 1969 to consider action to be taken as a consequence of the fire at El Aqsa Mosque in Jerusalem.

Similarly, Jews the world over—whether Zionists or not—responded, largely on the basis of their religious identity, both to the Nazi threat in the 1940's and the perceived Arab threat to Israel in the 1950's and 1960's. There is, in fact, some evidence to suggest that the more deeply religious the non-Israeli Jew, the more intense his support of Israel is likely to be.[19]

More important than an analysis of the religious identity of the mass of the population in each country, however, is an analysis of the religious identity of members of the elite. In Latin America the elites are all Catholics of some sort, so it is difficult to assess attitudes based on religious identity. But what about Asia and Africa?

---

[17] Frans Van Wynsberghe, "The Vatican and the Idea of a United Europe," MPIA thesis, University of Pittsburgh, Pittsburgh, Pa., 1969.

[18] Personal communication to me from Richard Cottam.

[19] This is not meant to imply that some Jewish atheists are not Zionists. Some of them are among the most militantly Zionist. But as a general tendency, the proposition seems to hold true.

Except in the Arab countries where Christian missionary work was either prohibited or relatively ineffectual, a considerable proportion of the elite became Christian under various European colonial rulers. Almost invariably, the proportion of Christians among the elite was higher than the proportion in the whole population. This is no great surprise; often, conversion to Christianity was a requirement for acquisition of elite status. Some of the formerly Christian elites reverted to the religion of their precolonial forefathers when the metropoles relinquished domestic political power, but even today there is a higher percentage of Christians among the elites of many of the former dependencies than in the population at large.

Does this Christian identity tie those leaders to the power centers of modern-day Christendom (which, for purposes of this study, are Britain, France and the U.S.)? [20] It seems to, particularly in those cases where religious identity is important to those leaders. It is difficult to assess exactly how important the religious linkage is in specific cases. In some cases, it is yet another of those mutually reinforcing ties that bind elites in the weaker countries to individuals and groups in the more powerful countries. But it may be presumed to be particularly important where the elite is Christian and the majority of the indigenous population is not. Anything short of a detailed profile of the elite, however, preferably supported by attitudinal and perceptual questioning of individuals, is not likely to produce significant statistical evidence either to support or refute these contentions.

The elite studies that do exist, though not always exactly compatible, do suggest that religious identities may play a considerable role in tying the elites of the weaker states to the stronger (particularly in places like South Vietnam—where the accusation has been made that Diem and those around him sought and received the initial support they did because of strong Catholic ties). But much more research is necessary.

Religious ties between the Christian Powers and the states associated with them—and particularly the elites of these states— is an area very much in need of study. The Church of England is the official church of the United Kingdom, and many of the inhabitants of the associated states did either convert to Anglicanism or brought it with them when they came from England. Similarly, the U.S. is a predominantly Protestant (though not Anglican) country, while France is predominantly Catholic. But comparable, systematic data on the various types of Christians in the popula-

---

[20] Since no other country of the world professes the Russian Orthodox religion, and since the Communists tend to deny or negate religious identity, the Soviet Union will be excluded from this discussion.

tions of the weaker states (and in the decision-making elites in those countries) are, to this author's knowledge, nonexistent. Even more relevant, but equally nonexistent, is precise information about the saliency of religion to those people who profess to be Christians.

Religious animosity between Protestant and Catholic, and among Protestant sects, has been a major barrier among Europeans for centuries. Differences among Protestant sects was a direct factor in the migration of Quakers, Puritans, and others to the New World in the 1600's, while awareness of differences between Anglicans and Catholics was probably the major factor inhibiting the integration of Ireland into the United Kingdom, and remains even today the chief identity barrier to harmony in North Ireland. While it is possible to give numerous examples of differences in religious identities that have kept peoples apart, it is difficult to find examples of similarities in religious identities that have bound peoples together. Yet such ties must certainly exist. The questions are in which cases and in what degree?

Holding all other variables constant, it would seem that the greater the percentage and saliency of Christianity among the elite of a country, the stronger would be the religious identity between that elite and the U.S., U.K., and France. But until much more systematic and extensive research on this question is undertaken than has been possible here, information to support this hypothesis will not be available. Information is available, however (although it is extremely crude and imprecise), on the percentage of Christians in a total population, and while that information is not nearly as relevant as information about elites, still there may be some merit in examining it for possible hints about religious identification.[21] Some refinement of the data does already exist. For example, it is possible to determine, in most cases, what percentage of the Christian population is Protestant and what percentage is Roman Catholic. But, under what circumstances is being Christian more important an identity than being a specific kind of Christian? Is there more similarity of religious identity among Anglicans and other Protestants than among Anglicans and Catholics? If so, to what degree and under what circumstances? Unfortunately, there are no answers to these questions yet. But there are some hypotheses that may be worth further exploration. For example, I

---

[21] One of the major and most valid criticisms of social science research is that social scientists do not measure what is relevant, but rather take available measures and try to find relevance in them. This is an example of exactly that type of analysis. The only defense is the admittedly dubious argument that some indication of possible relationships is better than none. I therefore caution the reader to avoid attributing too much significance to the data.

would argue that in a country in which all Christians are a minority, the likelihood is that religious identities among them would be more significant than would be the differences. In fact, I hypothesize that the smaller the percentage of Christians in a country, the greater their identity as Christians is likely to be, regardless of sect. Conversely, the greater the percentage of Christians in the population, the greater the identity differences among the sects.

Table 4.3 lists estimated percentages of Christians in the populations of countries historically associated with the United Kingdom and France.[22] Note that in only twelve of the thirty-six countries associated with Britain, and in only three of the twenty-seven countries associated with France, do Christians of all varieties comprise more than 50 percent of the total population. In the remaining twenty-four British associated countries, and in the remaining twenty-four French associated countries, Christians constitute a minority. If the hypothesis is correct, differences among the latter would tend to be less significant than among Christians who constitute more than 50 percent of their population.

On the basis of very impressionistic evidence I estimate that in at least thirty-two countries on the list (those with an asterisk before the country name) Christians tend to constitute a significantly higher percentage of the decision-making elite, broadly defined, than they do of the total population. Indeed, studies indicate quite conclusively that when the British and French transferred political power in the former colonies, almost invariably the indigenous groups to whom they handed the reins of government contained a much higher percentage of Christians than did the population at large. In most of the former British and French colonies, the educated, rich, urban dwellers who were most favored by the colonial masters tended to be much more Christian than did their less educated, poorer, rural, fellow countrymen.

Where these countries have striven to assert their own identity since the grant of formal independence, indigenous religious identity has been a major factor. There are more Muslims in positions of political, military, and/or economic power today in Egypt, Pakistan, Malaysia, Cameroon, and Togo than there were at the time formal independence was first granted. This is true of Hindus in India today and of Buddhists in Burma, Ceylon, Laos, and Cambodia. There can be no question that this has meant a lessening of religious ties between the U.K. and France and their former dependencies. But at the same time it has meant an increase in the

[22] The United States has been left out of this table because none of the Christians in the populations of its associated states—save perhaps Protestants in the Philippines—can be directly attributed to the historic association between those countries and the U.S.

TABLE 4.3

Estimates of Percent of Christians in the Populations of States Associated with the United Kingdom and France[a] (Grouped by Historical Association[b] and Ranked by Percent of all Christians in the Population)

Country	All Christians as Percent of Total Population[e]	Roman Catholics as Percent of Total Population[d]	Muslims as Percent of Total Population[e]
United Kingdom and Associated States			
Ireland	100	94	0
United Kingdom[f]	97	8	N.D.
Malta	97+	97	N.D.
Barbados	95	20	0
Cyprus	82	1	18
Canada	81	44	0
New Zealand	80	12	0
*South Africa[g]	76	5	N.D.
Australia	75	19	0
*Lesotho[h]	70	40	N.D.
*Trinidad & Tobago	68	N.D.	6
*Guyana	59	14	8
*Malawi[h]	55	20	N.D.
*Mauritius[h]	47	35	N.D.
*Rhodesia[i]	35	13	N.D.
*Kenya	33	9	4
*Uganda	29+	29	N.D.
*Ghana	20	10	14
*Tanzania[j]	20	13	20
*Sierra Leone	16[k]	1	N.D.
*Nigeria	12	4	33
*Ceylon	9	8	7
United Arab Republic	7	1	92
*Burma	5	1	4
Jordan[l]	5	2	95
Pakistan	5	0+	86
Iraq	4[m]	4	96
*Malaysia[h]	3	1	51
Sudan	3	2	80
India	2	1	10
Israel[l]	2	2	9
Kuwait	1+	1	95[k]
Iran	1	0+	98
Southern Yemen	1	N.D.	98
Afghanistan	0	0	99

TABLE 4.3 (Cont'd.)

Country	All Christians as Percent of Total Population[e]	Roman Catholics as Percent of Total Population[d]	Muslims as Percent of Total Population[e]
United Kingdom and Associated States (cont'd.)			
Saudi Arabia	0	0	99
Maldive Islands[h]	0	0	99
France and Associated States			
France[f]	98	83	1
Canada	81	44	0
*Haiti	70+	70	N.D.
*Gabon	57	N.D.	1
*Congo (Brazzaville)	48	N.D.	1
*Mauritius[h]	47	35	N.D.
*Lebanon	44	39	42
*Malagasy	36	19	9
*Cameroon	27	N.D.	18
*Central African Republic	25	N.D.	4
*Togo	17	16	3
Syria	13	5	87
*Ivory Coast	11	N.D.	22
Algeria	10+[m]	10	90
*South Vietnam	8+	8	N.D.
*Dahomey	8	N.D.	12
*Chad	5	N.D.	52
Morocco	5+[m]	5	92
Tunisia	5+[m]	5	95
North Vietnam	4+	4	N.D.
*Mali	4	N.D.	75
*Senegal	3	N.D.	75
*Upper Volta	3	N.D.	15
*Guinea	1	N.D.	70
Cambodia	1+[m]	1	2
Laos	1+[m]	1	0
Niger	0	0	80
Mauritania	0	0	99

[a] Unless otherwise indicated, data are from Bruce M. Russett, et al., *World Handbook of Political and Social Indicators* (New Haven: Yale University Press, 1964), pp. 249–257. All percentages have been rounded to nearest whole number.

[b] See Table 4.1 above for complete listing of historically associated states.

[e] "All Christians" data, unless otherwise stated, are circa 1960–1963.

[d] "Roman Catholic" data, unless otherwise stated, are circa 1958.

[e] "Muslim" data, unless otherwise stated, are circa 1960–1963.

[f] The United Kingdom and France have been included for comparative purposes.

NOTES TO TABLE 4.3 (Cont'd.)

g Data from *United Nations Demographic Yearbook, 1956.* Figures are for total population.
h Data from *The Statesman's Year-Book, 1968–69.*
i Data from *United Nations Demographic Yearbook, 1964.*
j Data refers to Tanganyika only.
k Estimates are even more crude than the data in Russett.
l Data for Jordan and Israel were calculated prior to the 1967 war and do not reflect changes in boundaries and populations after that war.
m Some of Russett's figures were not consistent (i.e., he indicated a smaller percent for "All Christians" than for Catholics alone). These have been adjusted upward here.
N.D. = No Data.
+ in "All Christians" column indicates that there are at least that many Christians of all denominations because that figure is the percent of Catholics listed in the next column. 0+ means less than .5% of the population.
* indicates a subjective estimate that there is a higher percent of Christians in the decision-making elite—broadly defined—than there is in the total population.

religious ties among the weaker states that share the same religious identity. Buddhist governments in predominantly Buddhist countries throughout South and Southeast Asia have repeatedly protested the way in which predominantly Christian governments in South Vietnam have treated the Buddhist majority in that country, while Muslim leaders of predominantly Muslim countries have tended to side with Pakistan in its dispute with India.

Religious ties seem to correlate with the same factors as do linguistic ties. A higher percentage of Christians tend to be found in populations that were originally predominantly settler or slave. Excluding Ireland, Malta, and Cyprus, of the eleven remaining countries with more than 50 percent Christians in the population, four were predominantly or largely settler and four were predominantly slave countries.

Also there tends to be a close correlation between the directness of political control and the percent of Christians in the population. As Table 4.1 showed, of the ten countries with the highest percentage of Christians in the population, every one was for a major period of its history in a "Formal-Direct" political relationship with Britain or France, while of the ten countries with the lowest percentage of Christians in the population only India and Guinea ever had "Formal-Direct" rule, and even then this was not so for all of India.

Finally, there tends to be a high correlation between the length of political association and the percent of Christians in the population. With the exception of Cyprus, nine of the ten countries at the top of Table 4.3 have been associated with Britain or France for a minimum of about one hundred and fifty years. Ireland has been associated with England for almost four hundred years.[23]

Note that eight of the dozen states at the bottom of Table 4.3 are predominantly Muslim. Whether degree of political control or resistance of Islam to conversion is the crucial determining factor must await further research.

Racial Ties

As with religion, it is difficult to determine how important race is in the multitude of identities men hold. Indeed, it is even difficult to define race. A scientific definition of race is less important here, however, than the various perceptual definitions different peoples hold at different times. Amorphous as the concept may be, there is a real threat of misunderstanding if racial identities are not considered among those that tie states together, or keep them divided. People the world over seem to be aware of what they consider to be racial identities, and hence, this variable must be discussed as one of those that either unite or divide peoples.

Both blacks and whites in the United States accept skin color as the mark of racial differentiation. The Germans in the 1930's and 40's used the term to refer to what Americans would call ethnic or historic groups. In Ceylon, Tamils and Sinhalese (two groups Americans would also describe as ethnic groups) are both referred to as "races." The Chinese divide themselves into four races, based not at all on color, but on place of origin (and to some degree on language). In India, Dravidians and Aryans are differentiated less by color than by place of origin and culture, while color differences are often expressed in terms of caste (the Portuguese word for color), despite the fact that castes have traditionally been considered "occupational" groups.

One indication of just how limiting the American definition of race is, can be found in the data used by Rudolph Rummell for his study, "Dimensions of Conflict Behavior within and between Nations." In that study only three races were considered: "Caucasian, Negroid and Mongoloid." Because he used that breakdown, Rummell was simply unable to decide where to place all of the Arab countries, as well as India, Pakistan, and Iran, and thus figures for those countries were left blank. On the other hand, for some inexplicable reason he decided that the populations of

---

[23] Length of association in no way seems to have affected the number of Protestants in Ireland, although it must be remembered that England did not become Protestant until the reign of Henry VIII.

Ceylon, Burma, and Nepal can be considered "Mongoloid." [24] The difficulty Rummell had underlines a basic fact of life on the subject: when dealing with the universe of peoples who inhabit this globe, American notions of race are simply inadequate as a categorization scheme. Each definition of race is valid for the people who use it and is important in determining their attitudes and behavior regarding "we" and "they." Therefore, in order to accommodate divergent definitions, I would argue that racial identities are those immutable similarities or differences that people perceive themselves and others to possess and that are commonly associated with physical characteristics. Skin color, nose shape, height, hair texture, and eye shape have all, at one time or another, been used to differentiate people, and "race" is often the term given to this distinction. Cultural, religious, linguistic, class, and many other identities into which people divide themselves are subject to change and hence do not qualify under this definition. The distinction between racial, ethnic, and tribal identities—in behavioral terms, although not necessarily in biologic or anthropologic terms—is difficult to make. It is my feeling that these distinctions are more often semantic than real. The fear and hostility toward "them" in cases of extreme conflict seems to be equally great regardless of which differentiating term is used. What is more, many distinctions Americans would term "ethnic" are perceived by both groups in conflict as being racial, and they act on the basis of that perception.

Racial identity operates in the same manner as any other identity grouping. If one has some characteristic by which we can identify him as being "one of us" we are much more likely to trust him, to feel some degree of rapport, and to attribute credibility to what he says. If he is perceived as being "one of them" we are less likely to trust him and much more likely to have at least some doubts as to his credibility. Antagonism over perceived racial differences can become so extreme that one race is denied equal standing as humans—that is, one antagonist decides that the other is a subhuman species and therefore not entitled to the same treatment as groups that are considered human; or one antagonist decides that the other is a race so "bad" that mankind as a whole would be better off without it—and thus, for "humanitarian" reasons, decides to exterminate all of "them" from the face of the earth.

A whole range of less extreme racial attitudes tend to flourish

[24] Rudolph Rummell, "Dimensions of Conflict Behavior within and between Nations," *General Systems: Yearbook of the Society for General Systems Research*, No. 8 (1963), pp. 1–50. Those data were made available to me in part by the Inter-University Consortium for Political Research. Neither Rummell nor the consortium bear any responsibility for the analysis or the interpretations presented here.

around the world. We may grant a particular people equal status as humans, but may simply prefer not to live or work near them (as do the Australians and many West Coast Americans in relation to Asians). Or we may grant them equal status as humans, but decide to enslave them for a profit, as earlier European whites did with African blacks.[25]

Since racial identity is usually determined on the basis of what people decide are the important distinctions to be made, and since the colonial Powers, and especially the British, were for all practical purposes perceived as having divided the world into essentially two "racial" groupings—Europeans and non-Europeans—it is that differentiation we shall consider here. "European" really means "Western European ancestry" since Americans, Canadians, Australians, and New Zealanders would all be considered Europeans racially by the British and French and also the non-European peoples they dominated. "Non-European" is a much more heterogeneous identity, which at various times and under various conditions has included the essentially Caucasian, but Semitic, Arab peoples; the Aryan branch of Caucasians, who mainly inhabit the Indian subcontinent and its environs (and who range in skin color from white to dark brown); the Negroid peoples whose ancestors originated in sub-Sahara Africa; the Mongoloid peoples of Far Eastern Asia; and the Malay and Polynesian peoples of Southeast Asia and Oceania. Despite the enormous racial differences that actually do exist among the peoples included in this category, because they were all treated as equally unequal by the Europeans, particularly by the British, it is this broad racial division that has the most saliency for this study.

These racial divisions express the distinction between the two British Empires discussed under "Historic Ties" above. Australia, Canada, and New Zealand (and of course the United States) are the former British dependencies that most fit the description, in racial terms, of the countries that became "Greater Britain." South Africa and Rhodesia are two countries with heavy settler populations that subjugated the more numerous indigenous peoples, although increasingly South Africa has come under Afrikaaner rather than British settler influence. Still, in the eyes of the subjugated non-Europeans, the country is ruled by a racially homogeneous European settler population. Kenya, too, had a relatively large European settler population and it was the difficulty in working out racial harmony between European and non-European groups that delayed Kenya's independence by a few years. This

---

[25] It was only later, when the need arose to justify the existence of slavery, that American (and some European) whites evolved a notion of black inferiority.

same circumstance produced almost six years of bloody warfare in Algeria.

But not all of the British "other Empire" was non-European. Certainly Ireland, Malta, Cyprus, and now Israel are peopled predominantly by individuals who either are, or consider themselves, or are considered by others to be, Europeans. Thus among former colonies, the British dependencies at least can be divided into the two racial groupings of European and non-European. Within the former would be included at least the decision-making elites, if not the total populations, of the following states: the United States, New Zealand, Australia, Canada, Rhodesia, South Africa, Ireland, Malta, Cyprus, and Israel. There can be little doubt that British unwillingness to take military sanctions against secessionist Rhodesia stemmed in some (probably significant) measure from the similarity of racial identity on the part of politically potent segments of the British masses, and the ruling groups in Salisbury.

Within the non-European grouping, racial identity depends largely upon who the threatening "they" happen to be. Do lighter-skinned Indians and Semites view themselves racially as closer to the light-skinned European or to darker-skinned compatriots in other countries? I would submit that precisely because the British recognized no distinction based on lightness of skin and treated all non-Europeans as nonwhites, there is significantly greater similarity of racial identity among the leaders of the non-European peoples—regardless of skin color—than there is between them and the British. This tie has undoubtedly been strengthened by British nonwhite exclusion practices in the past few years.

In fairness to the British, it should be noted that their exclusivity is not based totally on skin color. Recall that it was because the British refused to grant equality of status to Englishmen born in the American colonies that the American Revolution was fought. To the English, anyone not actually born and bred in England simply cannot be English—that is, is somehow inferior.[26] The spectre of racial superiority was never raised in the case of the settler colonies and Britain, because both the English and the settlers perceived themselves as being of the same race. But when the British brought those same attitudes to heavily populated non-European lands, British attitudes of superiority were inevitably interpreted as attitudes of racial superiority.

The early settlers who immigrated to the United States and established the cultural norms to which all later settlers were assimi-

---

[26] This is a gross generalization, to be sure, which certainly does not apply to all Englishmen, but unfortunately it seems to apply to enough of them to make such a generalization not totally irresponsible.

lated brought with them not only the English language and religion but also the English attitude toward race. This was undoubtedly heightened by the American experience with black slavery and its aftermath. Whatever the causes, it cannot be denied that white Americans generally tend to have deep feelings of racial superiority, particularly toward black fellow Americans.[27] It should be noted, however, that Americans tend to be considerably less racist overseas than they are at home, and that the prime target of their superiority feelings are nonwhite Americans. While they are certainly less racist toward non-Europeans abroad then are the British, still some racism has been expressed. In places like Korea and Vietnam, American troops have referred to both enemy and ally alike with such pejoratives as "gooks" or "dinks," thus reinforcing the prevalent image abroad of the American as a racist. Many Americans, of course, do not like that image, but for purposes of this study, how Americans perceive themselves is much less important than the way in which they are perceived by people living in weaker states. Despite the lack of statistical data on the subject, there is no doubt that in areas where the people consider themselves non-European, the United States is considered to be anti-non-European. This can be inferred, for example, from how racial incidents in the U.S. are reported internationally. The murder of a white person by another white person gets little or no space (unless, of course, one of the parties is internationally known, like the Kennedy brothers or Sharon Tate), but the murder of a Negro by a white person, particularly if he is murdered for obviously racial reasons (if the Negro was a Civil Rights worker, or if the murderer was a member of the Ku Klux Klan), makes headlines throughout the world. Also, in speaking with Asian intellectuals one repeatedly hears it said that the United States would not have used the atomic bomb against the Germans, even if it had been ready for use several years earlier than it was (although, for a time, some Asians came to think the U.S. and the U.S.S.R. might actually use the bomb on each other). This belief that racial attitudes figured in the U.S. use of the bomb seems to have become less prevalent since the U.S. stopped testing its nuclear devices in the Pacific. Since the development of the Sino-Soviet split, the Chinese seem to be convinced—and many other Asians share the view—that racial identities are playing and will continue to play a significant role in cementing a Russo-American détente that is essentially anti-Chinese.

The effect of this perceived American racism on United States relations with weaker non-European countries is devastating to

[27] See *Report of the National Advisory Commission on Civil Disorders* (New York: E. P. Dutton, 1968).

U.S. relations with those countries. Although there are many ties
growing at ever accelerating rates between these countries and
the U.S., the perceived racism of the U.S. is perhaps the major
impediment to the possibility of building relationships of interdependence. Racism is America's Achilles' heel. Racial identities the
world over are so strong, and sensitivities to racial affronts, real or
imagined, are so high—particularly in the non-European world—
that the benefits to the U.S. of the numerous other ties are often
negated by this one barrier.

The Russians, for their part, have tried—and with some success,
at least until the split with China—to create the opposite perception of themselves. They have lost no opportunity to remind as
many people as they can reach that the greater portion of their
land mass is in Asia, and that significant portions of their population have non-European ancestry. Precisely how successful this
effort has been is, of course, impossible to assess. The fact that the
Russians tested their atomic devices on their own soil may have
been something of an assist to that image, but at least some people
noted that the tests were held in the Asian part of its territory, and
took offense. The allegations by some African students in Moscow
in the late 1960's that they were being discriminated against on
racial grounds received rather widespread news coverage, particularly in the "non-European" world, and probably further tarnished
the image the Russians tried to create as a non-European Power.
Even before the split with China the Soviet Union was excluded
from the Bandung Conference (and China was invited). As the
rift between China and the Soviet Union has widened, and actual
clashes have occurred, and talk of possible nuclear war between
the two communist giants has increased, it is this writer's impression that Russia is increasingly being perceived as a European
Power by both non-European and European countries alike. This
may aid Russia in its search for a détente with Western Europe,
but it certainly weakens the racial ties it has tried to nurture with
the non-European world.

Of all the European Powers that have exerted influence over
non-European peoples in the past two centuries, the French are
probably perceived as the least racist.[28] That Frenchmen—particularly intellectuals and elites—have a strong sense of cultural su-

[28] The Spanish and the Portuguese in an earlier period, with their conscious policy of assimilation and intermarriage, may actually have been
less racist than the French. But so many non-Europeans were killed by them
in their proselytizing zeal when colonialism first started, and the Portuguese
have been so tenacious in their holding of non-European colonies since
World War II, that considerable doubts seem to have been raised in the
minds of non-European peoples concerning Spanish and Portuguese racial
attitudes.

periority over all other cultures in the world, there can be no doubt. But one need not be Christian and white to be French: one need only have French culture. Anyone can become French—and therefore superior—simply by totally assimilating the French language and culture. This stood France in very good stead with the elites of its associated states. There was little of the racial resentment in the French colonies that one found in British colonies. Once the elites of the colonies mastered French culture they were treated as equals—or nearly equals. They were allowed (at least in the twentieth century) to vote in French elections, to serve in high-ranking military, business, and government posts, and even to serve in the French National Assembly. Indeed, the Vice President of the Fifth Republic during de Gaulle's first term of office was Gaston Monneville, a West Indian by birth, but a Frenchman by choice.

It would, of course, be an exaggeration to say that there was no racial discrimination on the part of the French, or that the natives perceived no racial barriers. Certainly the French displayed some feelings of racial superiority, particularly in the days of the slave trade. After all, the slaves the French bought and sold were all black. In Haiti prior to the Black Revolution racial awareness and animosity were intense and were the cause of the numerous uprisings led by free blacks or mulattoes that finally led to the creation of the first all-black state in the New World.[29] But aside from the examples of racial animosity in the slave economies, there is actually very little concrete evidence of French racism. Still there is equally little doubt that the Arabs of North Africa, the blacks of mid-Africa, and the Asians of Indo-China all perceived the French attitude of superiority as at least partly an attitude of racial superiority. There are innumerable hints of this in the speeches and writings of many of the leaders of these countries. Just how intense, and how realistic, those perceptions may have been is, of course, difficult to determine.

Like the broad racial identities of European and non-European, the more narrowly defined racial identities that the various non-European peoples perceive themselves to have play a major divisive role. One can cite the Arab/black conflict in the Sudan, the Sinhalese/Tamil conflict in Ceylon, or the Malay/Chinese conflict in Malaysia—all of which are considered *by the people involved* to be essentially racial in character.[30] In past centuries most of East and Southeast Asia came under one form or another of Chi-

[29] See Priestly, *France Overseas,* particularly pp. 273–275.
[30] Note that the Ibo/Hausa conflict in Nigeria was considered "tribal" and was apparently not perceived by those involved as "racial," although both groups acted in a manner indistinguishable from that seen in racial conflicts.

nese dominance, and in the 1930's and 40's most of the same area came under direct Japanese domination. Again, this is a topic on which no hard empirical evidence currently exists, but there are strong subjective indicators that both China and Japan are perceived by themselves and by their weaker neighbors as racially distinct. They seem to consider themselves racially superior and the people they have dominated believe them to hold this racist attitude. There is certainly no doubt that the Chinese have a deep sense of cultural superiority to most people, being proud of a civilization that has continued for approximately 4,000 years. Certainly, too, there is a deep sense of identity among Chinese as Chinese, whether they live in China itself or elsewhere. Even ideological differences tend to give way before this identity. Both the Communists on the mainland and the Nationalists on Taiwan are agreed that the two cannot be separated because they are both Chinese.

But to what degree is this Chinese identity racial? When the Chinese compare themselves to other Chinese, they may think of themselves as composed of four different races. But when they compare themselves to non-Chinese, there is little doubt that they perceive themselves as a racial unit. Regardless of religion, country of residence, language, or political ideology, a Chinese views himself—and, just as important, is viewed by others—as Chinese. Since that distinction is immutable, by definition the basic identity is a racial one.

In Southeast Asia, the racial differentiation between Chinese and non-Chinese appears to be equally as strong as the differentiation between European and non-European. Contrary to popular American usage, which lumps all Mongoloids together, the Chinese and Japanese see themselves as being of different races. The question for the future is how long that perception of distinction can be maintained in the face of the Western perception of similarity? Historically, China and Japan have been enemies. But if the Sino-Soviet conflict should continue to worsen, and if Sino-American antagonisms should intensify, and if U.S.-Soviet relations should improve—all of which could well happen, although there is nothing inevitable about such developments—what role will racial identities play in Japanese decisions about which side to join? The Japanese probably were sincere in their World War II call for an "Asia for the Asiatics." Was that an expression of geographic or racial identity? I would argue that it was an expression of the non-European racial identity. Couldn't that sense of identity be revived again if sometime in the future China is perceived to be the target of essentially racial hostility on the part of Russia and the United States? If American policies toward Japan were to alienate the

Japanese *politically,* there might be a "natural" tendency for two countries that are perceived by the "European" enemy as racially the same, to join in a common "non-European" cause.[31]

Class Ties

Marxist scholars have written at great length about the importance of class identities to "bourgeois" national and international behavior and argue, with considerable rigidity, that class interests *alone* account for most behavior in the capitalist international system. The non-Marxist scholar, on the other hand, rigidly refuses even to acknowledge the possibility that class identities exist as a factor in international affairs. Both extremes seem to me equally wrong and yet it is astonishing to find how uniformly "scholars" conform to party lines on both sides of the ideological curtain. To assert that perceived economic self-interest is the only factor important to international behavior is patently simplistic, but it is equally simplistic to argue that class identities play no role whatever.

What is "class identity"? There is no more commonly accepted definition of class than there is of race. Ralf Dahrendorf in his provocative work, *Class and Class Conflict in Industrial Society,* quotes a number of sociological definitions of class, all of which, he claims, are inaccurate:

Class "is a force that unites into groups people who differ from one another, by overriding the differences between them." [T. H. Marshall, *Citizenship And Social Class* (Cambridge: 1950), p. 114.]

"Class, as distinguished from stratum, can well be regarded as a psychological phenomenon in the fullest sense of the term. That is, a man's class is a part of his ego, a feeling on his part of belongingness to something; an identification with something larger than himself." [Richard Centers, *The Psychology of Social Classes* (Princeton: 1949), p. 27.]

"We shall then mean by a social class any portion of a community which is marked off from the rest, not by limitations arising out of language, locality, function, or specialization, but primarily by social status." [R. M. MacIver, *Society* (New York: 1937), p. 167.]

"According to the point of view here advanced social classes . . . are social groups determined by three factors, namely, (1) similar

[31] The major difficulty in prediction is the lack of information about the relative ranking of ideological and nationalist identities, and the lack of information about the relative saliency of racial identities among the parties concerned.

social conditions, (2) similar social status, (3) similar social values."
[Fritz Croner, *Die Angestellten In Der Modernen Gesellschaft* (Frank-
furt a.M. and Vienna: 1954), p. 185.]

"By class is meant two or more orders of people who are believed to
be, and are accordingly ranked by the members of the community, in
socially superior and inferior positions." [W. L. Warner and P. S. Lunt,
The Social Life in a Modern Community (New Haven: 1941), p. 82.] [32]

Dahrendorf argues that all of these are really definitions of
stratum, and not of class. " 'Stratum' " he says, ."is a descriptive
category. By contrast, the concept of class is an analytical category
which has meaning only in the context of a theory of class.
'Classes' are interest groupings emerging from certain structural
conditions which operate as such and effect structure changes."
Going back to Karl Marx for his own definition of class, he
argues that "classes are political forces based on the relations
of property and power." Further, he quotes Marx's notion that
" 'The struggle between two classes is a political struggle.' " For
Dahrendorf, as for Marx, "the formation of classes always means
the organization of common interests in the sphere of politics."
Thus, "classes are political groups united by a common interest."

Status, ranking by others, self-ranking, style of life, similar economic
conditions, and income level are all factors which define social strata
but not social classes. . . . *Class* is always a category for purposes of
the analysis of the dynamics of social conflict and its structural roots,
and as such it has to be separated strictly from *stratum* as a category
for purposes of describing hierarchical systems at a given point of
time.[33]

Observe that all of the definitions discarded by Dahrendorf,
as well as the one he puts forward in its place, define class in
terms of identity groups. For Marx, the crucial distinction was only
whether these economic identity groups were organized for political action to change the relative power positions of the competing
groups. The fact is, however, that merely by being aware of their
identity, as a group, they cannot but have a political effect, both
on their own societies, and across state boundaries. What that
effect will be in any specific instance would, of course, depend on
many other factors that'need not concern us for the moment. The
point is that once a group becomes conscious of its class identity,
the tendency will be for it to seek to defend and/or improve its
own perceived interests vis-à-vis other class groupings, both do-

[32] Ralf Dahrendorf, *Class and Class Conflict in Indusirial Society* (Stanford, Calif.: Stanford University Press, 1959), pp. 74–75.
[33] *Ibid.*, pp. ix, 16, 17, 76.

mestically and internationally, and for other class groupings to seek to defend and/or improve their own perceived interests vis-à-vis it.

Pitifully little comparative, empirical research on the class identities of elites has been done to date, particularly in the West, where class identities are all too often ignored. We do know, however, that governmental as well as nongovernmental elites of all countries—regardless of the political system—tend to be composed primarily of the "haves." Immediately after a major social revolution, to be sure, the elites that have just come to power often (but by no means, always) perceive themselves, and are sometimes perceived by their own populations, as "have-nots." It appears to take little more than a decade or two, however, before the governors begin to view themselves as the new "haves," and are so perceived by the governed.[34]

Since the term "haves" is relative—that is, its meaning varies according to the society in which it is being considered—it is impossible to provide an absolute definition of what constitutes a "have" class. But it is enough to say that so long as any group in any country perceives itself, and is perceived by others, to occupy the top economic stratum of that society, it can be considered the "have" group of that society. Those who occupy the top rungs of the economic ladder in any country are the "haves" of that society. This is so regardless of how high or low in absolute terms the top stratum may be. In a society like the United States, with an annual per capita income approaching $4,000, the wealthiest .5 percent of the society may have a minimum annual income of $100,000.[35] In a society like Ceylon, where the annual per capita income may be approaching only $150, the wealthiest .5 percent of the society perhaps has a minimum annual income of $800.[36] While there is certainly an enormous disparity between

[34] There is considerable speculation that Mao Tse-tung initiated the so-called "cultural revolution" in the late 1960's (using "have-not" Red Guards), precisely because he wanted to oust party bureaucrats who had begun to think of themselves (and who had come to be viewed by others) as "haves"; and to perpetuate the "have-not" identity of the elites. How often China can survive these periodic revolutions remains to be seen, but there is little doubt that eventually some Chinese governing elites are going to decide that political stability and sustained economic growth are more important for the welfare of the country than the "have-not" class identity of the governing elite.

[35] U.S. Bureau of the Census, *Statistical Abstracts of the U.S. 1969,* 90th ed. (Washington, D.C.: 1969), p. 333. Annual income is not the sole criteria of class, but in order to simplify the discussion, annual income figures are used for illustrative purposes.

[36] This figure represents an educated guess for 1970, based on my previous work with 1954 data.

the two groups in absolute terms, in relative terms both are the economic "haves" of their societies; both recognize their own positions; both are recognized by others as the "haves" of their respective societies; and hence both must be treated as such in this discussion.

There is a law of physical behavior which says that a body remains stationary or in uniform motion unless it is made to change that state by external forces. Similarly, a law of political behavior could be formulated saying that a group at the top of an economic structure in a society will tend to remain at the top unless it is made to change that state by external forces. There are two principal reasons why this is so. The first is the very characteristic of wealth itself, that it tends to generate increased wealth. ("It takes money to make money," says the proverb.) The second reason is the conscious effort on the part of the top economic strata in each of the world's countries to maintain their positions. It is precisely because of this that Dahrendorf's distinction between class and stratum is fictitious. In order for the upper economic stratum of any society to perpetuate its position, this group must become involved—directly or indirectly—in the political process to defend the economic status quo.[37] What is more, in almost every country of the world, again regardless of political system, top government decision makers tend to be drawn, if not from the few wealthiest families in the country, certainly from the wealthiest 1 or 2 percent of the population. Actually, there is very convincing evidence to indicate that the more underdeveloped a society, the greater the likelihood that the overwhelming preponderance of its political elite will be drawn from among its wealthiest citizens.[38] This, perhaps, helps to explain why, despite a great deal of talk in the underdeveloped countries about rapid economic development and the need for creating peaceful social revolutions, so little is actually done.

Since most of the weaker states considered in this work are

[37] The fact that certain individuals from this class may work to change the relative positions of the classes in no way diminishes the accuracy of this observation. Marx has said it is "quite possible that a man's actions will not always be determined by the class to which he belongs [I would say that it is quite possible for a man to rank other identities above his class identity]; but these individual cases are as irrelevant to the class struggle as the defection of some noblemen to the Third Estate was to the French revolution." Quoted in Dahrendorf, *Class and Class Conflict*, p. 17.

[38] For example, Ceylon, with a per capita annual income of approximately $136 in the early 1960's, recruited 93% of its political elite (defined as all members of parliament) in 1960 from less than .6% of its wealthiest citizens. See my *The Emerging Elite: A Study of Political Leadership in Ceylon* (Cambridge: Massachusetts Institute of Technology Press, 1964), pp. 95 and 176.

quite underdeveloped, it seems a fairly safe assumption, despite the absence of hard empirical data, that the governments of the great majority of these states are run by the tiniest fraction of the wealthiest people. It would not be totally unjustified to assume that these political elites share some similarity of perception as "haves" with the governing elites in the other underdeveloped countries, and also with the "haves" in the mentor countries. What may be even more important, the "haves" in the mentor countries (who, after all, have a considerable say in decision making in their own countries) probably have at least some sense of common identity with the "haves" in the associated states. Granted these assumptions, it is not difficult to see why an attack on the "haves" of any country by the "have-nots" of that society is likely to be perceived by all "haves" as a threat, in precisely the same way that members of any racial identity group tend to perceive an attack by a different race on any member of their group, anywhere in the world, as a threat to themselves. Further, there is a tendency for these "have" groups to take action, on the basis of that common identity, to assist other "have" groups that are perceived to be in danger.

As will be shown in the next chapter on Economic Ties, very often "haves" in the associated states derive significant portions of their personal income from economic activities either directly or indirectly connected with the economic activities of "haves" in the mentor countries. That is, the upper classes in Asia, Africa, and Latin America and, to a somewhat lesser extent, the upper classes in Eastern Europe, often hold the dominating heights on the economic ladder of their societies because of occupations or activities that exist to service the economic needs of "haves" in the mentor country.[39] The indigenous owners and managers of rubber estates and agency houses in Asia; of mines in Africa; of coffee, sugar, and banana plantations in Latin America; as well as the managers of the large state-owned enterprises in Eastern Europe (although perhaps to a lesser extent), derive their personal wealth and position in their societies in no small measure from the markets and other economic opportunities provided by the "haves" in the mentor Powers. Because of the common economic gain to be derived from working together and because of their common class identity, it frequently happens that the "have" classes in both weak and powerful states exercise whatever political influ-

[39] Djilas was absolutely correct in calling the new bureaucratic leaders of industry in Communist countries a "new class." They qualify under all of the definitions offered at the start of this section. See Milovan Djilas, *The New Class: An Analysis of the Communist System* (New York: Frederick A. Praeger, 1957).

140 THE TIES THAT BIND

ence they can—and it is often extensive—to protect the interests of the foreign "haves" within their own countries.

What about the class identity of the "have-nots"? As could be expected, the "have-nots" in a society center their identity as a class on a perspective of comparison with the "haves." Social scientists have given a great deal of attention to the "international demonstration effect" in increasing the expectations and aspirations of "have-not" people around the world.[40] To overlook that factor in both domestic and international affairs—particularly when there is a transistor radio in practically every village, and television sets in many—is to overlook a major catalyst for political change. An even more potent catalyst for change, however, may be the "domestic demonstration effect," in which a "have-not" group recognizes its identity as such relative to the domestic "haves" within its own society. This group does not normally perceive itself to be in competition for what it views to be limited resources with "have" groups outside the boundaries of its country, but rather seeks to improve its economic position vis-à-vis other groups within the same society.

To be certain, the "have-nots" may also come to believe that foreign "haves" operating within their country have an excessive share in the economic domination of their society, and may therefore call for the nationalization or expropriation of all foreign holdings in the country. While in some cases the "have-nots" are not aware of how great the foreign domination of their country's economy actually is, in many other cases the "have-nots" are led to believe that this economic domination by outsiders ("them") is considerably more extensive than it actually is. Often this is done by the domestic "haves" (usually, but not exclusively, prior to political independence) to distract public attention from the degree to which they themselves actually control the economy, and to gain the opportunity to acquire the foreign holdings in their country at less than what would otherwise be market price. In still other cases, of course, domestic "haves" who share a high degree of identity with the foreign "haves" staunchly oppose expropriation of any private property. They fear that if the property of foreign "haves" is nationalized, it may be only a short time before the "have-nots" will be demanding the expropriation of their property. Or their own personal wealth may depend on interests in the foreign country, and they fear that nationalization of foreign wealth might bring retaliation that would adversely affect their own. All

[40] See for example Daniel Lerner, *The Passing of Traditional Society: Modernizing the Middle East* (New York: Free Press, 1958), and Lucian Pye, ed., *Communications and Political Development* (Princeton, N.J.: Princeton University Press, 1963).

this having been said, the fact remains that in most cases it is the domestic "haves" who are most visible to the domestic "have-nots," and it is they who most often become the target of "have-not" discontent.[41]

"Have-nots" in any given country may recognize a marginal commonality of interest with "have-not" groups in other countries, and they may even, in some few cases, work with those other groups to obtain some limited common ends, but empirical evidence seems to indicate that Marx was quite wrong in his expectation that proletarians (industrial "have-nots") the world over would recognize their common interest and unite on the basis of that identity to overthrow the "bourgeois" states that everywhere kept them in bondage. "Have-nots" the world over may share a high degree of similarity of perception, but because they are usually incapable of communicating that similarity of perception across national boundaries, they rarely become an identity group (or, in Marx's terms, a class) internationally. To the degree that they are able to recognize or communicate any similarity of perception across state boundaries, it is usually a linguistic, religious, racial, or nationalist identity that they perceive first.

This is not to say that "have-not" class identities are never communicated internationally. Certainly the proliferation since World War II of "National Liberation Fronts" and similar organizations in underdeveloped countries in Asia, Africa, and Latin America attests to the growing awareness of common problems among "have-not" groups in many countries. But these groups are almost invariably nationalist in scope and sentiment. The groups may work together in some areas to achieve common aims, as in Laos and Vietnam (both North and South), but this is usually a matter of cooperation among separate national "have-not" groups, rather than integration of the groups into a single international unit. Similarly, individuals and groups from countries in which the "have-nots" have been successful (as in Cuba) will often go to other countries to help organize the "have-nots" there, but again this is a matter of cooperation rather than integration.

It is wrong, and dangerous in the extreme, to assume as many governments do that these *class* identity groupings are nothing more than internationally inspired and/or controlled *ideological* groups (usually labelled "communist" by anticommunist governments, and "imperialist" by communist and socialist govern-

---

[41] Note that when Prime Minister Indira Gandhi expropriated the banks in India in 1969 and 1970, it was only the domestic banks she wanted to nationalize. This was, of course, in no small measure because the domestic "haves" in India were thought to be substantially financing her opponents within the Congress Party.

ments). Even though communist ideology explicitly seeks to unite and lead "have-not" identity groups in their struggle to become "haves," scholarly research has clearly established that the identity of most of the individuals actively involved in such struggles is primarily a class identity, and only secondarily—if at all—an ideological identity. Most of the "communists" in Malaya in the late 1940's and early 1950's were recruited from among individuals with a strong sense of "have-not" class identity. Only later did some accept communist ideology, and most of the individuals involved never did accept any ideology. That was why it was ultimately possible to get them to put down their arms in return for land, jobs, and/or money.[42] Similarly, in Vietnam the Viet Cong (and their predecessors, the Viet Minh) eventually had among their ranks a significant percentage of ideological Communists, but most of the peasants who worked for and supported them did so not because of any ideological commitment but because of their awareness of their "have-not" position in Vietnamese society relative to the Vietnamese "haves" and their French and American supporters.[43]

In Cuba, the majority of the people who supported Castro (particularly in the early days of the revolution) did so because of their identity as "have-nots" in a society where only a small percentage of Cuban and American "haves" controlled most of the wealth of the society. (In the Cuban case particularly, but in many others as well, the "have-nots" were supported and indeed often led by "middle-class" intellectuals who supported the legitimacy of the "have-not" claims.) The Communists at first even refused to work with Castro because of his lack of ideological identification, and only later joined him, when the revolution had proved a success, and the Americans had proved incapable of recognizing and cooperating with a true "class" revolution.[44] What is more, a strong case could be made that the East German, Polish, and Hungarian uprisings in the mid-1950's were all manifestations of "have-not" discontent[45] and were only marginally, if at all, ideological (in this case "anticommunist").

There is very strong evidence to indicate that many govern-

[42] See Lucian Pye, *Guerrilla Communism in Malaya: Its Social and Political Meaning* (Princeton, N.J.: Princeton University Press, 1956).

[43] See Bernard B. Fall, *The Two Viet-Nams: A Political and Military History,* 5th ed. rev. (New York: Frederick A. Praeger, 1965); and Ralph K. White, "Misperceptions and the Vietnam War," *The Journal of Social Issues,* Vol. xxii, No. 3 (July 1966).

[44] For an insightful analysis, see C. Wright Mills, *Listen Yankee* (New York: McGraw-Hill, 1960).

[45] Mixed with fairly large doses of nationalism, to be sure, as were all the other examples cited here with the exception of the Malaysian case.

ments have difficulty in dealing with opposition groups precisely because they view them as "communists" or "imperialists" instead of recognizing the reality of the class identity interests of these groups. Usually these people really are economic "have-nots," and it is not at all surprising that they should want a greater share in their country's "economic pie." If the elites who control many of the underdeveloped countries of the world could recognize that many of the people opposing them within their own countries do so on the basis of an identity as "have-nots," it is possible that they could dissipate that opposition by directing their actions toward changing the identities of those people from "have-nots" into "haves." Unfortunately, because the interests of the "have-nots" often are perceived to be a direct threat to the interests of the decision makers, it is usually easier for the elites to see "international communism," "neocolonialism," or "international capitalism" instead of legitimate class interests. And because they see ideological rather than class identity as the cause of their problems, they tend to react by using the wrong instruments of power. That is, they tend to use coercive instruments of power, rather than persuasive instruments: they attempt to repress the opposition rather than attract it with economic rewards. Thus they reinforce the perceptions of the "have-nots" that the only way to become "haves" is to overthrow the existing elite, and that the only way to do this is to use violence. A spiral of violence and counterviolence, reinforcing preexisting images of the "hostile other," is set in motion, which all too often results either in a near police state if the elite is "successful," or in the violent overthrow of the regime, as in France in 1789, in Russia in 1917, and in China, Cuba, and Vietnam since World War II (to mention only a few instances).

What is most ironic in this whole situation is that the "have" elite very seldom is successful in the long term by using repression exclusively. In the first place, the cost of repressing widespread "have-not" discontent is often far in excess of the costs that would be involved in providing "have-not" peasants with land of their own or "have-not" workers with remunerative jobs, thus converting them into relatively contented "haves" likely to support the regime responsible for their improved position. Second, in the very process of strengthening the coercive arms of the government (the military, police, and "special forces") to repress opposition, the elite is increasing the ability, and thus the likelihood, that these agencies themselves will achieve what the "have-nots" could not achieve—the violent overthrow of the government.

Governments in underdeveloped countries—and in developed countries as well—often fail to recognize the significance of class

identity in another potentially destructive situation that commonly
confronts them. Very often the opposition "have-not" groups are
of a race distinct from the "haves." To the degree that a government recognizes the essential class character of the discontent
shown by these groups and attempts to deal with it from that
perspective (that is, attempts to convert "have-nots," regardless
of race, into "haves") the problem is probably amenable to
eventual solution. It is, after all, far easier to change the class
identity of a person than it is to change his racial identity. Unfortunately, however, many governments fail to recognize what
are, after all, the legitimate demands of these "have-not" racial
groups to achieve economic parity with other groups in the country, and tend to treat their discontent primarily as a racial problem. Because governments often fail to respond rapidly enough
to what begin as essentially economic demands, these groups come
to perceive the cause of their economic disadvantage in primarily
racial terms. Of course, racial identities often precede "have-not"
identities, but if "have" elites were able to recognize the class
aspirations of these groups, and were able to act vigorously enough
to satisfy those aspirations, race conflict as such could probably
be avoided or at least mitigated.

All of this is not to imply that a "classless" society in Marxian
terms is achievable. It is not, as the experiences of all of the communist governments have demonstrated. It is possible, however—
particularly in the more developed countries of the world—to
achieve a degree of egalitarian distribution of wealth in which the
disparity between the "haves" and the "have-nots" is dramatically
reduced.[46] Precisely how such an achievement would affect international relations is impossible to tell at this point since there is
so little comparative data on the class identities of both elites and
nonelites in all the world's countries. There is little empirical evidence on which to base analyses of the role of class identity in
international affairs. Certainly class identity is not, as the Marxists
claim, the major, if not the only, identity that motivates elites.
Just as certainly, however, it is considerably more important than
most American scholars of international affairs have been willing
to admit.

Ideological Ties

The definition of ideology that is relevant here can be taken directly from Webster:

[46] See Joseph A. Schumpeter, *Capitalism, Socialism, and Democracy*, 3rd
ed. (New York: Harper & Bros., 1950).

. . . (3) Manner or content of thinking characteristic of an individual or class; or bourgeois *ideology*. (4) The intellectual pattern of any widespread culture or movement; as exposure to Anglo-Saxon *ideology;* specif., the integrated assertions, theories, and aims constituting a politico-social program, often with an implication of factitious propagandizing; as Fascism was altered in Germany to fit the Nazi *ideology*. . . .[47]

There are those who have argued that in the twentieth century ideology has replaced religion as a major force in both uniting and dividing men, and a superficial analysis would tend to reinforce that view; no one could seriously contend that the major wars of this century were religious in origin,[48] while a strong case could be made that they were largely ideological. While any such monocausal explanation for a phenomenon as complex as a major war is bound to be insufficient, the fact does remain that twentieth century wars have been justified in ideological rather than religious terms. Thus, we have had wars to "make the world safe for democracy"; to oppose fascism, communism, socialism, capitalism, or imperialism. Indeed, some would go so far as to say that ideology has become the religion of the twentieth century. Certainly many ideological beliefs are held with a zeal equal to that with which religious beliefs were held in former times, but if ideologies may be considered as religions, may not religions be viewed as ideologies of a particular nature?

It can undoubtedly be argued that nationalism has replaced religion as the great ideological force of the twentieth century. Although nationalism tends to be confined within the boundaries of a state, it is the only "ism" that is.[49] Most of the other major ideological constructs that capture the imagination of men do so irrespective of country of residence. Although there may be a wide diversity of dogma from country to country, the more formally structured ideologies like capitalism, socialism, communism, or democracy (and even the more loosely structured conservatism, liberalism, anticommunism, anticapitalism, militarism, pacifism, and anti-Semitism) are recognized as such regardless of local modification.

[47] *Webster's Seventh New Collegiate Dictionary,* s.v. "Ideology."
[48] Except, perhaps, the Indian/Pakistan and Arab/Israel battles, but these could hardly be called major wars of the 20th century.
[49] Even nationalism crosses state boundaries in some cases, however. Notice that both Zionism and Arab nationalism have adherents in dozens of states and that one of the reasons given to justify Hitler's expansion into Poland, Czechoslovakia, the Sudetenland and elsewhere was the nationalistic goal of uniting the German people. Further, in many parts of Africa and Asia, people who identify themselves as members of a nation live in a number of states.

Clearly, ideologies are one of the bases for identity groupings. What is ideology if not a shared similarity of perception among people regarding certain ideas, particularly political ideas. And man, with his penchant for plural identities, is just as likely to identify with a number of ideological groups simultaneously as he is to identify with other kinds of groups. It is not uncommon for men to hold two or more conflicting, or potentially conflicting, ideological identities simultaneously. Indeed, it is not even uncommon (in practice, though not in theory) to find devoutly religious, communist, nationalists. One need think only of the Catholic French Communist who would have his child baptised in the morning, would attend a communist union meeting in the afternoon, and would cheer Gaullist nationalism in the evening. As long as a person's various identities do not come into direct and specific conflict, or as long as he has them clearly rank-ordered in his own mind, he can hold contradictory ones simultaneously without discomfort.

It would seem more accurate, then, to argue not that ideology has replaced religion, but that twentieth century man has tended to rank some political identities higher than religious identities; he still, however, holds both. Further, there is evidence that in most cases where a political ideology comes into conflict with a nationalist ideology, the nationalist ideology tends to be ranked more highly. Note, for example, the ringing phrases in which the delegates to the 1912 Second International Socialist Convention in Basel condemned the approaching capitalist war and pledged to unite all workers in opposition to it. When the war came, however, many of these same socialists, now back in the legislatures of their own countries, voted to approve the budgets that made the war possible. As Lane Lancaster, in his *Masters of Political Thought,* pointed out: "No matter how bitterly Lenin might denounce the German socialists for voting the war credits in 1914, their doing so showed beyond all doubt that patriotism is a primary force not to be exorcised by any assertion that 'working men have no country.' " [50] Indeed, of all groups, "working men"— particularly "blue collar" working men—in current day America, Western Europe, and elsewhere, appear to be among the most ardent supporters of nationalistic ideology. Also note that, just as Christianity in Europe did not prevent nationalist wars between Christian states, it appears entirely possible, as of this writing, that the two communist giants, Russia and China, may some day go to war over clearly conflicting nationalist interests.

Nonetheless, the power of transnational political ideologies must

[50] Lane W. Lancaster, *Masters of Political Thought,* Vol. 3: Hegel to Dewey (London: George G. Harrap, 1959), p. 171.

not be underestimated. Prior to June 1941, Communists around the world condemned the European war as a manifestation of capitalism in its last death throes. But once Russia was attacked, Moscow did not have to order Communists elsewhere to do an about face. Precisely because Communists in 1941 did share such a high degree of similarity of perception—whether Russian, French, Indian, or Liberian—they viewed the attack on Russia as an attack on communism generally, which had to be fought at all cost. Similarly, no word had to go forth to the Zionists of the world to support Israel in 1956 and 1967. To the Zionist, whether in the United States, Argentina, or the Soviet Union, it was the Arabs who attacked Israel and, therefore, Israel had no choice but to defend itself. '

Thus, while many or most of the elites of every country have a high nationalist identity, they may simultaneously hold a number of transnational identities. In particular, those elites who have studied or lived in a mentor country for any length of time may hold an ideological identity with that country side-by-side with a nationalist identity. So long as the two are not perceived by the individual as being in direct conflict (and it is, after all, often in the individual's interest not to perceive them as conflicting), holding the two simultaneously would present little difficulty. To use a crude example, a member of the commercial elite in one of the weak countries probably shares an ideological identity as a "capitalist" with other capitalists abroad. He may also have an identity as a nationalist. Therefore he would probably seek to find definitions of the national interest that combine his own capitalist and nationalist identities. The more intensely he identifies with the capitalist identity group, the more likely he is to define his country's interests in its terms, while the more intensely he identifies with the nationalist ideological group, the more likely he is to see a more nationalistic definition.

Conversely, but similarly, a communist member of the elite in almost any of the countries with which we are dealing probably shares an ideological identity as a Communist with other Communists, both in his own country and abroad. Even though he may also have an identity as a nationalist, he will probably seek to find a definition of the national interest that will combine his own communist and nationalist identities. Also, the more he identifies with the communist identity group, the more likely he is to see a more communistic definition of national interest, while the more intensely he identifies with the nationalist ideological group, the more likely he is to see a more nationalistic definition of national interest.

It is the ideologies of the more powerful nations that are usually held in the weaker states, and not the other way around. In the chapter on political ties we shall see more specifically how most of the weaker states tend to follow the ideological lead of their mentors. There are a few notable exceptions among the more counterdependent leaders of the weaker states, to be sure, but overwhelmingly the majority of the leaders of the weaker states tend to identify with the ideology of the mentor. In some measure, of course, this is because the major Powers use their influence to see to it that the people who control decision making in the weaker states are ideologically "pure." Or, if they do not demand 100 percent ideological purity, they certainly eliminate what they perceive to be cases of gross ideological impurity. Thus Juan Bosch and his followers in the Dominican Republic, and for a time Cheddi Jagan and his followers in Guyana, were prevented from coming to power because the U.S. perceived that they were being used by the communists, while Alexander Dubcek and his followers in Czechoslovakia and Nagy and his followers in Hungary were removed from power because the U.S.S.R. perceived that these officials were being used by the anticommunists.

Prior to World War II, the major ideological groupings that crossed national boundaries were fascism (in its various forms) and antifascism; communism and anticommunism. The German attack on Russia allied the communist and antifascist forces on one side and the fascist and anticommunist forces on the other. But that grouping of states on the basis of ideological identities did not survive more than three years after the end of World War II.[51] From the ashes of that war emerged the conflict between the communist and anticommunist (or "Free World") countries. Russia was acknowledged as the leader of the Communist ideological grouping while the United States became the leader of the "Free World." Note that it is the ideology of the most powerful states that became the foci of these ideological groupings.

Not all of the states of the world identified with either of these ideological groupings, however. Along with the emergence of the newly independent states there developed an ideology of neutralism and/or nonalignment with which a number of the leaders of these states identified. As could be expected, the perceived leader and major articulator of this ideology was the most powerful of the neutral states, India.

This more or less tripartite ideological division of the world held until the 1960's, when the Sino-Soviet dispute split the

---

[51] Horowitz argues that the anti-fascist coalition began to fall apart within a few months of Franklin Roosevelt's death. See David Horowitz, *The Free World Colossus: A Critique of American Foreign Policy in the Cold War* (New York: Hill and Wang, 1971).

communist ideological grouping into two camps that might, for convenience, be called the radical communist and the moderate communist groups. The major ideological questions for the 1970's seem to be whether the moderate communists are going to feel more threatened by the anticommunists or by the radical communists; whether the anticommunists will feel sufficiently threatened by the radical communists to make "peace" with the moderate communists; and whether the previously neutral states are going to remain nonaligned or whether they will feel sufficiently threatened and/or atracted by one or the other camp to abandon neutralism and take sides ideologically.

Educational Ties: Value Systems

A number of writers have noted that one of the most crucial determinants of a person's identity and self-image is the amount and type of education he has received.[52] C. P. Snow, among others, has written at length about what might be called the perceptual gap that separates those educated in the humanities and those educated in science. If one chooses a humanities education—from whatever motivation—he will learn the names and teachings of the gods and demigods in that area. The simple words "the Prince of Elsinore" convey a host of meanings, almost all implicit, to someone who has pondered the life of Shakespeare's great character. If the reader of that phrase has not read and studied *Hamlet,* it would require a full chapter to convey the implications of those four words, and even then only a start would be made toward comprehension. Similarly,

$$E = \frac{(2\pi)^2}{\lambda} \frac{A}{r} \sin\ \theta\ \frac{\cos\ 2\pi}{\lambda} (ct\text{-}r)$$

has a coded meaning that can be fully understood by physicists, whether in London or Lagos, but would require elaborate explanation to be even partially understood by someone without a scientific education, even if he should happen to be the brother of a physicist. There is not only a specific set of meanings that go along with each of these culturally coded messages, there is an entire value system—a way of approaching the universe. At school, one learns to order the world in a certain manner in the very process of learning the code language of a particular area

[52] In my earlier study, *The Emerging Elite,* on the Ceylonese political elite, these criteria, along with language spoken and mode of dress, were the most important indices in determining a person's value orientation and mode of behavior.

of human endeavor. Once learned, this value system is not easily unlearned. Indeed, it tends not to be unlearned precisely because, in order to communicate, the individual is forced to find other individuals who speak the same cultural language. These individuals, in their work and personal lives, tend to form an identity group that constantly reinforces their own values, attitudes, identities, and perceptions. The gulf between people with different educations thus tends to widen after they leave school and enter their chosen careers.

Education tends to weaken even ties to the family. If all of the adult members of the family are equally and/or similarly educated, this may not be a problem. But we are all familiar with the phenomenon of the boy going off to college and then returning only to discover that communication with his immediate family has become considerably more difficult than it was before he left. After he has inquired about Aunt Harriet's health and the health of her immediate relatives or friends, what can he say to her? Regardless of the closeness of family relationships, the likelihood is that for a discussion of the topics that interest him most he will seek out friends or associates—perhaps from very different family, religious, tribal, or ethnic group backgrounds than he— who have been similarly educated, and with whom he can therefore communicate.

Education Abroad

A person learns more than merely "science" or "humanities" when he goes off to study; he learns a way of life as well. At Oxford and Cambridge, above all else, one learns the definition of being an educated gentleman. At the Sorbonne, he learns the glory of a French education. At Harvard or Yale he learns more than mathematics or poetry. He learns, subtly and rather effectively, an upper class, egalitarian way of life. At Moscow, he learns not only the accomplishments of Russian space science, but a view of the way the "good life" is to be ordered. To be sure, there are individual exceptions in each case, but by and large, at each school in every country, one learns a preferred value system, world view and way of life. That aspect of one's education is as important, if not more important, than the facts or ideas he learns in class.

Thus, what is implicitly and explicitly taught at the schools attended by various segments of a country's elite becomes crucially important in understanding the perceptions, values, attitudes, and modes of behavior of these elites. To the degree that they hold values and perceptions espoused at the schools of a country other than their own, they are perceptually tied to that country. To the degree that they feel they must look to developments and innovations taking place primarily in the country in which they have studied in order to remain in the forefront of their field, they are tied perceptually to that country.

This is not to deny, that each person studying abroad brings with him totally different values, attitudes, and perceptions; and that, because of this, and because each student's experience abroad is different, each student will react to a foreign education somewhat differently. There are students who come away from a country more negative toward it than they were before arrival. But on the basis of the relatively little empirical evidence that exists, it seems quite clear that the vast majority of students who study abroad come away more positively inclined toward the country than they were before they went.[53] They may still criticize the country, but their criticism is more specific and focused once they know more about the country. They appear more able to separate their specific complaints from an over-all disposition toward the country.

It is sometimes argued that foreign students learn anti-capitalism in the U.S.A., Britain, or France, and anticommunism when in the U.S.S.R. To be certain, some may have learned their communism at the London School of Economics or the Sorbonne, but if they have, they often go home with perceptions strikingly similar to British or French Communists. That is, they are not anti-British or anti-French, but anti-British capitalism or anti-French capitalism. Given the opportunity, they would convert their societies into replicas of Britain and France—not as these countries are, but as they and the British or French communists would like to see them become.[54]

Nationalism seems to be a concept the leaders of the various nationalist movements learned while studying abroad. While nationalist ideas may have been appealing intellectually, there is strong evidence to suggest that these ideas gained the greatest acceptance among those individuals who were emotionally most

[53] Bryant Wedge, *Visitors to the United States and How They See Us* (Princeton, N.J.: D. Van Nostrand, 1965).

[54] A remark attributed to the president of Cameroon epitomizes the notion: "If I wanted my students to come back communists I would send them to study in Paris. If I wanted them to come back devoted to the free enterprise system I send them to Moscow." In reality, this notion does not stand up under investigation. To be certain, some students may become hostile to the dominant political values of the country in which they received their education, but the vast majority of students internalize the political values and perceptions of the country in which they have studied. Indeed, it has been reported (but not confirmed) that those Cameroonian students who did go to the Soviet Union to study were put into jail shortly after they returned home.

prepared to accept them. That emotional predisposition seems to have been a function of the degree to which these men aspired to be accepted as equals by the people of high status in the countries in which they studied. That is, had these Philippine, Indian, or Algerian sons of the elite in their own countries been accepted by the Americans, English, and French as Americans, Englishmen, or Frenchmen who happened to have been born in the colonies, there would probably have been little emotional predisposition to entertain nationalist ideas. But it was precisely because they were viewed as "the natives"—no matter how hard they tried to acquire the accoutrements of Westerners—that the future leaders felt a psychological need for a rationale for their difference.[55]

Once national independence has been achieved, and the notion of "different but equal" has been institutionalized by the creation of separate, "equally sovereign states," the leaders who brought about the creation of those states seem to strive very hard to transform their societies into at least partial replicas of the countries from which they just acquired independence. To be certain, they may have no interest in bringing about the social revolution that would be necessary to actually transform their societies. Indeed, the social revolutionaries seem to be recruited largely from those segments of the society that have not been as exposed to the mentor as were the nationalist leaders themselves. But that is precisely the point. These nationalist leaders do not tend to see themselves as social revolutionaries, but as gentlemen who will show their former political and social "superiors" that they can in fact be equals—if not as Englishmen or Frenchmen or Americans, then as prestigious leaders of "equally independent" states.

Not only the African and British leftists, but the scientist from London and the scientist from Lagos (if he is from a sufficiently wealthy family) probably went to the same schools in London. After all, how many really fine scientific schools exist in the world? Certainly, as of this writing, there is none in Lagos. And while there are excellent scientific schools in France, Russia, and the United States, the one to which the student from Lagos would most logically go would be in London. He would have to make a major effort to learn a new language in order to go to school in France or the Soviet Union. To go to school in the United States he would either have to win a scholarship or come from a very wealthy family with connections in exchange control, which would

[55] E. E. Hagen's work *On the Theory of Social Change: How Economic Growth Begins* (Homewood, Ill.: Dorsey Press, 1962) contains an interesting exploration of a parallel circumstance in which motivation for changed status comes from a denial of the status to which individuals feel they are entitled.

allow him to convert the local currency into dollars instead of the more easily available pounds sterling. Moreover, to the degree that an English education is perceived in his own country as a prestige education, the likelihood is that he will go to the United Kingdom. Only if the United States or the Soviet Union has projected an image of surpassing Britain in the field of science (as in recent years they have) will his family consider sending him to one of those countries.

Indeed, one of the more interesting questions to consider is how an education in certain countries is perceived by the population (particularly the elite population) of other countries. For example, when and why did Americans, who could afford to send their children anywhere (and who, in the 18th and 19th centuries, sent their children abroad to study), decide that they would get the "best" education in the United States and should go abroad only in their junior year or after school was completed? When did English families decide that American education had surpassed British education and begin to send their sons to the United States? Though large numbers of the British establishment still insist that their children be "educated" at Oxford or Cambridge on the undergraduate level they agree, perhaps reluctantly, to have them "trained" on the graduate level in the United States. Relatively more British students *do* come to the U.S. to study than American students go to Britain nowadays. There is no precise date for the turning point because data are incomplete, but probably it was after World War II, when the U.S. was perceived—even by Englishmen—as the most powerful country in the world, and therefore the one with the best educational institutions. Similarly, when did Latin American elite families perceive a North American education to be more prestigious or beneficial than a Spanish education? What are the implications of this in terms of one country's perceptions of another?

It has not been possible to acquire precise data over long time periods on the number or percentage of students from the weaker countries who have studied in the more powerful ones. The pre-World War II data that do exist suggest that although a larger number of students from more developed associated states studied abroad than did students from more underdeveloped states, a higher percentage of those who did go abroad for study from the underdeveloped countries went to mentor countries, than did students from the more developed countries. That is, the more economically developed the country, the greater the proportion of its students who tended to study abroad, but also the more diverse the countries in which they studied. There seems little doubt, however, that the United Kingdom and France were always the major recipients of foreign students from their respective associated states. In the late nineteenth and early twentieth centuries both the U.K. and France seem to have received upwards of 90 percent of the students from the more underdeveloped of their associated states who studied abroad. (Of course, it should be remembered that the absolute numbers involved were extremely small.)

The United States does not appear to have been a major recipient of foreign students prior to World War II, even from its own associated states. Canadians and English-speaking West Indians may have come to the U.S. in greater numbers than they went to Britain, but there is no hard evidence on which to base that assumption. Latin American elites seem to have sent their children in much greater numbers to European universities, particularly to Spain, France, and Germany, than to universities in the States. Indeed most people—including North Americans—seem to have looked to Western Europe as the repository of the collective wisdom of Occidental civilization and it was to universities there that students went to imbibe.

It seems equally clear that through the nineteenth and the first half of the twentieth centuries Russia, Japan, and China exported many more students to Europe, and even the United States, than they imported. After 1905 Japan undoubtedly began to receive a considerable number of Asian students, probably reaching a peak in the early 1940's, but at the same time Japan was exporting large numbers of its own students to Western Europe and the U.S. Of all the major Powers, Russia probably exported the most and imported the fewest students. France, on the other hand, appears to have been one of the major recipients of foreign students, not only from its associated states but from other states as well—both powerful and weak.

Since World War II, and the relative decline of British and French power, there has been a decline in the percentage of students from weaker associated states studying in the United Kingdom and France. (The decline in the percent going to England, particularly, has been startling.)[56] In part, of course, this is because

---

[56] The decline in percentage of students from French associated states has been appreciably more modest (see Table 4.4). This is largely because of the language ties to France; the recentness of formal independence (most achieved independence less than three years before the date the figures for the table were compiled); the success of France in inculcating the notion in its associated states that it was the center of the civilized world and therefore the "only" place to study; and the conscious effort on the part of the French government in the early 1960's to bring large numbers of students to France and thus to strengthen the ties among what were formerly colonies and are now the French Community.

the removal or decrease of British and French political, economic, and military presence has lessened the compulsion in terms of career advancement to study in those countries. Much more important in explaining the relative decline in percentage, however, is the great increase since World War II in the numbers of students from weak states who study abroad. Prior to World War II only a tiny fraction of a percent of the wealthiest portion of the populations could afford to send their children to study abroad, and almost inevitably they sent them to British and French universities. Some data for this period on students from Britain's associated states studying in the U.K. do exist. For example, around 1930 there was a total of 1,846 students from India (including what is now Pakistan), Ceylon, and Burma studying in universities in the United Kingdom.[57] In contrast there were 195 Indians (including Pakistanis), 1 Ceylonese, and 2 Burmese studying in the United States,[58] while perhaps a similar number were studying in all of Western Europe combined. In addition, perhaps a dozen students from those countries studied in Eastern Europe and Japan. By 1963, although the number of students from those four countries studying in the United Kingdom had risen to 2,545 (an increase of almost 38 percent over the number studying there in 1930), the number in the United States alone had risen to 7,631, while an additional 1,391 were studying in France and West Germany, another 245 were studying in Soviet Bloc countries, and 70 were studying in Japan.[59]

Table 4.4 shows for each country's university students studying abroad in 1963 the percentage studying in each of the major power centers. Because comparative data over longer periods of time are lacking, this table is somewhat misleading. For example, while it is true that 17 of the 21 countries listed as associated states of the United States sent the greatest bulk of their university students studying overseas to the United States, the 1963 figures, while representing a sharp increase over pre-World War II figures actually represent a sharp decline from comparable figures for 1958.[60] In 1958 Argentina sent 59 percent of its overseas uni-

[57] Paul London, "Ties Among Nations: A Case Study of Britain and Her Ex-Dependencies," MPIA thesis, University of Pittsburgh, Pittsburgh, Pa., 1968, p. 121.
[58] Institute of International Education, *Handbook on International Studies for Foreign Nationals* (New York, 1961), pp. 232–235.
[59] Figures are from those collected by Steven Schecter from the same sources cited in note [a] to Table 4.4.
[60] The figures for 1958 were collected by Steven Schecter from the same sources cited in note [a] to Table 4.4.

TABLE 4.4

University Students Studying in Major Power Centers as Percent of Each Country's Total Students Studying Abroad in 1963[a]
(Grouped by Historical Association[b] and Ranked Within Group)

Students from (Country)	United States	United Kingdom	France	E.E.C.[d]	Soviet Bloc[e]	Inter-Regional[f]
			Percent Sent to:[c]			
U.S.A. and Associated States						
United States	—	13.1	16.7	**32.3**	N.D.	27.2
Philippines	**89.2**	1.6	0.2	1.4	0.0	1.9
Liberia	**83.6**	1.2	N.D.	N.D.	1.5	N.D.
Mexico	**72.7**	0.7	4.4	8.2	2.5	1.4
Guatemala	**67.0**	0.3	N.D.	N.D.	3.3	12.1
Brazil	**56.7**	2.4	8.8	19.8	6.7	3.4
Venezuela	**55.9**	1.5	3.7	6.7	2.2	9.8
Panama	**55.1**	0.3	N.D.	N.D.	1.3	15.7
Colombia	**50.3**	0.8	3.0	7.2	1.5	10.7
Argentina	**49.6**	4.5	8.1	16.9	1.9	8.6
Chile	**49.4**	2.2	6.4	16.9	4.4	11.3
Costa Rica	**48.5**	0.0	0.7	4.3	4.7	19.9
Ecuador	**44.9**	1.0	2.2	7.1	5.1	23.6
Cuba	**44.0**[g]	0.0	0.5	0.8	**43.7**	1.2
El Salvador	**43.2**	0.2	0.2	4.7	3.2	33.1
Uruguay	**41.1**	3.3	7.9	12.6	7.0	19.2
Honduras	**41.0**	0.0	N.D.	N.D.	4.7	31.6
Dominican Republic	**40.1**	0.2	N.D.	N.D.	0.0	28.6
Nicaragua	**39.7**	0.2	2.5	4.8	0.9	25.9
Paraguay	32.2	0.5	2.0	7.9	5.0	**47.5**

Peru	27.2	0.4	1.8	5.6	1.6	**34.2**
Bolivia	19.5	0.7	0.8	7.7	7.5	**49.0**
U.K. and Associated States						
United Kingdom	**32.4**	—	15.8	22.3	N.D.	28.2
Malta	0.0	**85.2**	N.D.	N.D.	N.D.	5.6
Ceylon	22.5	**45.3**	0.7	2.1	10.0	6.0
Uganda	29.2	**40.6**	N.D.	N.D.	14.7	N.D.
South Africa	29.8	**36.7**	1.8	9.9	0.0	N.D.
Australia	**51.1**	35.6	2.4	4.9	N.D.	N.D.
Nigeria	**36.8**	33.0	N.D.	N.D.	12.3	N.D.
Cyprus	32.4	**32.9**	N.D.	N.D.	8.5	N.D.
Pakistan	**43.1**	32.8	1.5	7.4	0.0	3.5
Tanzania	**40.6**	29.8	N.D.	N.D.	13.0	N.D.
Sierra Leone	**35.6**	27.4	N.D.	N.D.	19.4	N.D.
New Zealand	27.5	25.3	2.2	3.6	N.D.	**37.6**[h]
Kenya	**46.7**	23.7	N.D.	N.D.	18.7	N.D.
Ireland	**41.8**	23.6	9.7	14.1	N.D.	6.9
Ghana	19.8	21.4	0.7	17.9	**29.5**	N.D.
Sudan	12.3	17.3	0.0	7.2	15.5	**46.5**[i]
India	**63.2**	15.3	1.0	11.9	1.3	1.1
Trinidad and Tobago	31.6	14.9	N.D.	N.D.	0.0	**46.6**
Burma	**44.9**	14.2	0.6	2.6	19.9	8.0
United Arab Republic	**30.7**	11.4	7.2	29.9	6.2	2.6
Malaysia[j]	8.7	10.6	N.D.	N.D.	0.0	**70.7**
Jamaica	**67.9**	10.1	N.D.	N.D.	0.0	20.7
Iraq	16.6	9.8	1.4	11.1	**41.1**	17.6
Nepal	27.7	7.6	N.D.	1.2	**44.2**[k]	4.0
Canada	**87.6**	6.8	2.9	3.8	N.D.	N.D.

TABLE 4.4 (Cont'd.)

Students from (Country)	United States	United Kingdom	France	E.E.C.[d]	Soviet Bloc[e]	Inter-Regional[t]
U.K. and Associated States (cont'd.)						
Israel	**61.1**	4.9	8.9	17.1	0.0	N.D.
Kuwait	35.1	4.0	N.D.	N.D.	0.0	**59.0**
Iran	36.9	3.4	9.1	**41.8**	0.0	2.2
Saudi Arabia	35.0	2.3	0.6	10.3	0.5	**48.7**
Jordan	13.0	1.1	0.0	10.2	0.0	**67.0**
Yemen	2.6	0.0	N.D.	0.7	**69.3**[l]	27.2
France and Associated States						
France	24.7	1.8	—	N.D.	N.D.	33.0
Malagasy	2.4	0.0	**94.9**	95.6	1.6	N.D.
Ivory Coast	2.1	0.0	**94.2**	94.5	0.0	N.D.
Upper Volta	3.7	0.0	**94.1**	N.D.	0.0	N.D.
Central African Republic	0.0	0.0	**92.9**	93.9	5.1	N.D.
Senegal	0.0	0.0	**90.1**	90.4	6.7	N.D.
Dahomey	4.5	0.0	**89.8**	90.4	0.0	N.D.
Congo (Brazzaville)	8.0	0.0	**88.2**	89.5	N.D.	N.D.
Gabon	0.7	0.0	**84.2**	84.9	0.0	N.D.
Tunisia	1.8	0.0	**82.5**	85.0	1.4	3.1
Morocco	3.0	0.0	**78.6**	N.D.	5.6	1.7
Vietnam (South)	16.3	0.0	70.7	72.1	N.D.	3.0
Algeria	3.4	0.0	69.5	70.9	19.1	2.6
Cameroon	6.7	1.0	66.5	69.1	18.1	N.D.
Mauritania	4.8	0.0	**54.8**	N.D.	28.9	1.9

Percent Sent to:[c]

Chad	1.1	0.0	53.3	N.D.	11.1	N.D.
Togo	7.0	0.0	46.3	50.9	40.2	N.D.
Mali	4.1	0.0	44.9	45.1	49.3	N.D.
Laos	5.1	0.0	41.9	N.D.	47.0	0.0
Belgium	22.5	2.6	34.3	45.4	N.D.	N.D.
Cambodia	42.2	0.0	31.7	32.1	13.5	1.3
Lebanon	26.8	1.8	30.5	40.5	0.0	17.2
Haiti	23.5	0.0	27.5	35.1	3.0	8.8
Guinea	10.8	0.0	22.2	23.6	63.0	N.D.
Niger	0.0	0.0	19.8	N.D.	63.7[1]	N.D.
Syria	9.3	1.4	7.6	30.9	6.5	42.6
Soviet Union and Associated States[1]						
U.S.S.R.	26.2	8.4	19.9	21.0	N.D.	N.D.
Finland	25.6	3.1	3.1	36.1	N.D.	N.D.
Yugoslavia	24.4	6.4	22.8	49.5	N.D.	N.D.
Afghanistan	41.1	1.7	7.2	23.3	14.9	0.0
Japan and Associated States						
Japan	86.2	1.8	2.9	7.9	N.D.	0.5
Korea (South)	41.6	0.5	N.D.	3.0	0.0	50.1m
China (Taiwan)	69.1	0.0	N.D.	2.4	0.0	20.3m
Indonesia	25.1	1.0	0.6	17.2	22.5	11.9m
Thailand	64.4	6.9	3.4	9.9	0.0	8.0m
Other European Countries (not ranked)						
Austria	12.6	1.0	6.9	72.2	N.D.	10.2
Denmark	43.3	4.6	23.7	37.8	N.D.	9.8
Germany (West)	14.3	2.7	16.1	N.D.	N.D.	19.2

TABLE 4.4 (Cont'd.)

Students from (Country)	United States	United Kingdom	France	E.E.C.[d]	Soviet Bloc[e]	Inter-Regional[f]
			Percent Sent to:[c]			
Other European Countries (not ranked) (cont'd.)						
Greece	19.3	2.7	7.8	**46.4**	N.D.	27.3
Iceland	22.7	19.2	N.D.	**51.5**	N.D.	3.5
Italy	21.2	2.7	19.0	**32.0**	N.D.	42.3
Luxembourg	0.8	0.0	**30.9**	58.6	N.D.	N.D.
Netherlands	23.2	3.3	13.1	**36.0**	N.D.	N.D.
Norway	16.3	7.4	5.8	**52.6**	N.D.	19.1
Portugal	20.2	8.6	**27.0**	39.9	N.D.	15.9
Spain	23.8	3.6	**31.4**	48.8	N.D.	12.2
Sweden	29.1	2.1	14.2	**45.7**	N.D.	20.8
Switzerland	20.9	4.5	22.8	**56.4**	N.D.	10.2
Turkey	30.9	5.2	7.7	**49.1**	N.D.	11.6
Other Non-European Countries (not ranked)						
Congo (Kinshasa)	8.1	0.0	**21.2**	21.9	N.D.	N.D.
Ethiopia	**45.8**	2.3	14.6	19.6	12.5	N.D.
Libya	16.3	11.2	4.2	16.0	1.4	**45.7**
Somali Republic	12.1	2.6	N.D.	1.3	**71.9**[l]	N.D.

Boldface figure indicates country or region receiving the highest percentage of students from the particular sending country. Regional totals that include a major Power (as does the E.E.C.) usually will be higher than the percentage for the Power itself, but if it is clear that the majority of students actually study in the Power within that group, the percentage for the Power has been set in boldface rather than the higher percentage for the group.

ᵃ Data compiled by Steven Schecter from: UNESCO, *Statistical Yearbook, 1964 and 1965*, Paris, 1966; U.S., Department of State, *The Education of Students from Developing Countries in the Soviet Bloc*, Washington, D.C., 1964; Pan American Union, *Annual Survey of the Interchange of Persons 1963-64*, Washington, D.C., 1965.

ᵇ Each country is listed in this table only once and hence for those countries historically associated with more than one Power, arbitrary decisions had to be made as to which Power they should be listed with.

ᶜ The category "Other" has been omitted. Therefore each line of percentages may total less than 100%.

ᵈ Figures for the European Economic Community (E.E.C.) represent only the combined totals of students studying in France and West Germany. Where no data were available for students studying in France, the figures in this column represent only students studying in West Germany.

ᵉ No data were available on students studying in the Soviet Union alone, but data were available for students from developing countries studying in the Soviet Bloc, which includes the Soviet Union, but excludes China and Cuba.

ᶠ Inter-Regional means selected countries in the same geographic region as the listed country, excluding the region's major Power. Thus for Western Hemisphere region this means Latin America and Canada only; for Europe it means the combined total for Belgium, Netherlands, Austria, Ireland, Spain, and Switzerland only; for the Middle East it means only the U.A.R. and Lebanon; for Asia it means Singapore, Hong Kong, and Taiwan.

ᵍ The percent listed in this column is misleading since most, if not all of the Cubans studying in the United States in 1963, were refugees and could not or would not return to Cuba in the foreseeable future. Normally "foreign student" means one who intends to return to his country of origin.

ʰ Studying in Australia exclusively.

ⁱ Sudan was considered here as a Middle Eastern country.

ʲ Figures do *not* include Singapore as part of Malaysia—hence the high percentage in the "Inter-Regional" column.

ᵏ There is reason to believe that these figures may be excessively high and may represent an error in computation.

ˡ While there are data available for students from Soviet Bloc countries studying in non-Soviet Bloc countries, there were no data available for this time period on how many students from Soviet Bloc countries were studying within the Bloc. This data would be necessary for determining percentages since the great majority of students from within the Bloc who go to universities in countries other than their own, study in either the Soviet Union or other Bloc countries. Thus Soviet Bloc countries have been omitted from this table.

ᵐ Studying in Japan exclusively.
0.0% = Less than 0.4%. All figures have been rounded off.
N.D. = No data available.

versity students to the United States and that was the lowest percentage sent by any of the U.S. associated states. At that time every one of the other associated states sent at least 75 percent of their overseas students to the United States, while 8 of the countries sent at least 90 percent. Similarly for the United Kingdom associated states, of the 23 countries on which there is comparative data for 1958, 15 were sending a smaller percentage of their overseas university students to the U.K. for study in 1963 than in 1958. But the implications of those figures for the two powers are quite different. In the British case the 1963 figures represent the continuation of a long-term trend reflecting the long-term decline of British power, relative to the other major power centers in the world. In the American case the figures represent something else entirely. For more than a decade after World War II the U.S. was almost the only major Power with the facilities to accept large numbers of foreign students. Thus in 1958 the U.S. received the greatest percentage of foreign university students sent abroad for study from 47 (55 percent) of the 85 countries independent at the time. By 1963 more countries had become independent; the European Economic Community (with assistance from the U.S.) was thriving; regional institutions of higher learning (supported and nurtured in large measure by the U.S.) were flourishing; the Soviet Union had begun to recognize the advantages of educational ties with the underdeveloped world; and hence the U.S. received the highest percentage of foreign students from only 39 of the 105 countries then independent on which comparative data exist. But this does not mean that there has been a decline in the number of students from weaker countries studying in the United States; quite the reverse. The underdeveloped countries have been sending students to study overseas at an ever-increasing rate, and the U.S. has been receiving more and more of them. Rather it indicates only that the U.S. was not receiving as great a percentage of all students sent abroad for study in 1963 as it was in the immediate post World War II period.

This comparative data should not obscure the major implication of Table 4.4, which is that in 1963 the United States was the country to which almost 40 percent of the independent countries of the world sent most of their overseas students for study. Even that figure under-represents the true picture of how dominant the United States has become as the educational center of the world. As best as can be determined, in 1963 there were somewhat over 174,000 students (other than Americans) studying in countries other than their own. The major receivers of students were, of course, the major Powers:

69,786 were studying in the United States;[61]
30,232 were studying inter-regionally;
23,605 were studying in France;
21,948 were studying in West Germany;
11,629 were studying in the United Kingdom;
11,485 were studying in Soviet Bloc countries; and
5,505 were studying in Japan.

Thus, almost three times as many foreign students were studying in the U.S. in 1963 as were studying in any other *single country* of the world.

Collectively the U.S., the U.K., West Germany, France, the Soviet Bloc, and Japan—the six major power centers of the world —in 1963 educated 82.6 percent of all the world's foreign university students. This figure gives only some indication of the degree to which the weaker countries are dependent for higher education upon the major Powers. For while the developed countries tend to send greater numbers of students abroad than do poor countries, these students from powerful countries form only a very tiny percentage of their countries' total university population. Most of the weaker countries, on the other hand, educate many more of their university students abroad than they do at home. In fact, as of this writing, many of the poorest countries do not have any universities of their own and must educate *all* of their university students abroad. And while many of the newly independent countries have started universities of their own since independence, because they do not have highly trained indigenous staffs they must rely on the powerful countries to supply the professors, the reading lists and books, the equipment, and the syllabi (as well as the basic unarticulated value systems all of this implies). What is more, until these newly independent countries become much more developed than they are at present, most technological and educational advances are likely to continue to come from the universities in powerful countries, and thus for the foreseeable future these weak indigenous institutions will have to rely on stronger institutions in one or another of the powerful countries merely to keep abreast in the field of higher education.

With the emergence of the United States as the dominant Power after 1945, its emergence as the principal educator of future elites of the world is no surprise. But the implications of that finding

---

[61] By 1965–66 the figure for foreign students studying in the United States had risen to 82,709. To this must be added an additional 11,000 students who had changed their visas so that they could remain permanently in the States. Institute of International Education, *Open Doors 1966: Report on International Exchange* (New York: I.I.E., Sept. 1966), p. 4.

deserve far more attention by students and practitioners of international politics than they have received to date. The implications of international educational ties, both as an indicator of the "attractive" qualities of power, and as an instrument of big Power foreign policy have been largely overlooked. As an indicator of power one need only consider which powerful countries are attracting what percentage of university students from which weaker countries. As an instrument of big Power foreign policy it is a means of establishing closer perceptual ties between the Power and the potential elites of the weaker countries of the world.

To be certain, the Powers have not been adverse to educating students from weaker countries, but relatively few have given this instrument of power the attention it deserves. The Soviet Union has always recognized the advantages of educating the elites of communist countries and has apparently educated the great majority of all post World War II university students from communist countries who have studied abroad. Since the death of Stalin it has also recognized the advantages to be gained by educating the potential elites of weaker noncommunist countries, and has embarked on a major campaign to educate the youth of the developing world. Although the major effort has been in a few selected countries in Africa and Asia (see Table 4.4) it has made impressive inroads in several dozen countries that formerly never sent any students whatever to the Soviet Union for higher education. The Patrice Lumumba Friendship University in Moscow, established specifically for the purpose of attracting students from the underdeveloped countries, has still further increased their headway in establishing educational ties with the newly independent countries.

As noted earlier, General de Gaulle, of all the recent leaders of the powerful countries, seemed to recognize most the utility of strengthening linguistic and educational ties with associated states. While there are no hard data available to demonstrate the magnitude of France's effort toward this end, indications are that large numbers of government fellowships and other types of assistance have been offered to students, particularly those from so-called "francophone Africa," for study in France.

The United States government seems to have done proportionately less than the governments of France and the Soviet Union to attract foreign students to America, and certainly much less than it could do. The U.S. government fully sponsored (that is, paid for) only 6.4 percent of all the foreign university students studying in the United States in 1965–66, and contributed partial sponsorship only to an additional 2.4 percent.[62] In contrast, more

[62] *Open Door 1966*, p. 10.

than one-third (37 percent) of all the foreign students in the
United States in 1965–66 paid their own way entirely. They came
to the United States to study not because the U.S. government
induced them to do so, but because that is where they believed
they could receive the best education.

For 20.9 percent of the foreign students, study in the U.S. was
made possible wholly or in part by the institutions of higher learning at which the students were studying. These institutions do not
bring foreign students to the U.S. for any reasons of international
politics, but because having foreign students on their campuses
gives them prestige. It lets them claim an international reputation
and a "cosmopolitan" atmosphere for their own students. In short,
these universities feel that foreign students help make them more
interesting places, and hence more likely to attract the better U.S.
students, and they are thus willing to divert a substantial proportion of their scholarship and fellowship funds—particularly on the
graduate level—to get those students. That they are at the same
time greatly increasing the perceptual ties between the U.S. and
the future decision makers of the weaker countries never even
enters the minds of the actual admissions committees making the
decisions to bring these students to the U.S. for study. Yet that
is precisely what they achieve, and in so doing they are inad-
vertently assisting the American government in its international
diplomacy. If these (mostly) private universities realized how
much they were aiding U.S. international interests, they would
surely insist that the government pay a larger portion of the bill
than it currently does.[63]

Private U.S. foundations, such as Ford, Rockefeller, Carnegie,
Mellon, Heinz, and hundreds of smaller organizations also contribute substantial amounts to the support of foreign students in
the U.S., again not consciously to assist the government in
strengthening ties with the weaker states, but primarily for reasons
of their own prestige. This desire for an international reputation
motivates the private foundations to support, either wholly or in
part, 11.8 percent of all the foreign students in the U.S. To the
degree that financial support is required by foreign students in
order to study in the U.S., it is overwhelmingly private universities
and foundations—not the government—that provide the support.
However, in comparing this situation to what happens in Britain,
France, Germany, and the Soviet Union, it must be remembered
that universities in those countries are almost completely govern-

---

[63] A distinction must be made here between the involvement of U.S. universities in government-sponsored projects overeas, and the rationale used
by the admissions committees of these same universities in attempting to
attract foreign students.

ment-financed. And while Britain, France, and the other E.E.C. countries all have private foundations that make grants to foreign students, those foundations are for the most part insignificant compared to their American counterparts. Thus, those governments must contribute the lion's share of the cost of bringing to their countries foreign students who could not otherwise afford to come.

The figures discussed so far represent only those individuals who go abroad for university and graduate study. They do not include the perhaps even more significant number brought to each of the Powers each year for short-term "training programs." Some of those programs may last only a week or two, while others may go on for as long as six to nine months. All of the major Powers have training programs of this sort. Unfortunately, no data are available on the scope or content of those programs except for the United States. While the U.S. program may be somewhat more extensive than those of other countries (although there is some evidence to indicate that the Soviet Union may put considerable emphasis on programs of this sort) the U.S. data are instructive nonetheless.

Excluding those in the military training program (which will be discussed in Chapter 7 on Military Ties) there are approximately 10,000 students from more than 70 underdeveloped countries training in the U.S. at any given time.[64] They are sponsored by the Agency for International Development (A.I.D.), which runs the so-called "Participant Training Program." The fields in which these participants are trained range from agriculture, through industry, transport, public safety, and public administration, to atomic energy. While the length of training is relatively short, it is usually intense: 6 to 10 hours a day, 5 or 6 days a week. The university students who go abroad to study are the next generation's primary, secondary, and tertiary elite; the participants in the A.I.D. program are most often this generation's elites. Harley O. Preston, in writing his semi-official report about the "Participant Training Program," says:

. . . the Agency for International Development contributes to their [the countries at "earlier stages of economic development"] growth in technical skills and human resources through the training of some of their citizens in technical, professional, and managerial skills and *in the attitudes and values that are believed to be essential* to social and economic development.[65]

[64] U.S. Department of State, Office of International Training, *Facts About the A.I.D. Participant Training Program* (Washington, D.C., 1967), p. 3.

[65] Harley O. Preston, *Operations of the Participant Training Program of the Agency for International Development*, U.S. Department of State, Agency for International Development (Washington, D.C.: Nov. 1966), p. 4. (Emphasis added.)

There is no study comparing the impact of training programs and university education as methods of establishing perceptual ties, but university education is probably more effective. As a university student the foreigner is exposed to the country for a longer period, at an earlier age. In this situation perceptual ties are established subtly—often very much below the level of consciousness—whereas the short, professionally oriented, intense participant training is so obviously designed to get the participant to think the way the host country wants him to think, that it is easier for the participant to resist the effort. On the other hand, because participant training is geared directly to the professional interests of the participants and supplies them with the information and concepts of most relevance to their own work in their home country, there can be no doubt that it has considerable effect, both in establishing the notion that the powerful country is the place where most knowledge exists on the professional matters of concern to them, and in establishing the impression that the Power is friendly and anxious to help the participants and their countries to do the jobs they want to do.

The weak countries must have education and training in order not to remain perpetually weak. The realities of power being what they are, the only place they can get expert knowledge is in the powerful countries. As long as all or most of the Powers offer educational opportunities, people in the weaker countries have some options as to which one they will become tied to educationally. Here is one of the many examples of mutual interest between weak and powerful states. It is in the interest of the Power to educate and train as many individuals from the weaker countries as possible, thus creating and/or reinforcing perceptual ties between thmselves and the elites and potential elites in the weaker countries. It is in the interest of the weaker countries to have as many of their nationals educated and trained as quickly as possible. But, while it is clearly in the interest of the Power to achieve as much of a monopoly as possible over the education of the weak countries' elites, it is in the interest of the weak countries to diversify their sources of education and training as much as possible to avoid becoming (or remaining) too dependent educationally on any one of the Powers.

Indigenous Education

There is little doubt that the perceptions, attitudes, values, and modes of behavior of a major Power will be more thoroughly inculcated in an individual from a weak state if he goes to the Power for study. In relative terms, however, few individuals have been able to go abroad for study. Therefore, the British, French, American, and Soviet educators have had to carry the value systems of their countries to the weaker states. Any educational system introduced by a Power into a dependent area was invariably patterned on the system "back home." More important, perhaps, the history, language, attitudes, and values of the mentor country were taught. Thus, the value and educational systems of each of the mentor Powers have become the models in each of their dependent states.

In order to get a true measure of the extent of the educational ties between the associated states and the European Powers, it would be necessary to know the percentage of the population educated in European-type schools in each country, the number of European teachers in the country relative to the total number of teachers, and the number of European-trained native teachers relative to the total number of teachers. Unfortunately, we do not have that information. We do know, however, that particularly in the countries the British and French controlled directly they did introduce European-type schools and did train significant numbers of the people in the English or French language, customs, manners, values, and attitudes. Often European church groups rather than the colonial governments founded and ran the schools, but the schools did exist and the natives were educated in a European-dominated system. And while they may not have educated as many natives as some of the modernizing local leaders wanted (and often educated more than the traditional local leaders wanted) the fact is that the Europeans trained a significant percent of the elites of the countries they controlled.

Although there are no data available on the degree to which British education has declined in the associated states since the grant of formal independence, there is no doubt that the decline has been rapid and drastic in many of them. One of the reasons for this, of course, is the emphasis many of the newly independent countries have placed on mass education. Since most of the masses do not speak English, teaching in English has increasingly been relegated to, at best, a secondary position. As the language of instruction has changed, so has the value content of the subjects taught. For one thing, it is no longer necessary for the school teachers to become thoroughly Anglicized before they can teach. Indigenous youngsters now become teachers in these associated states without having been exposed to teachers who are as Anglicized as were the teachers of their fathers. Even when students in these countries are exposed to foreign-trained teachers, there is much less likelihood now than in former times that the foreign training their teachers received was British training. As indicated above, as increasing percentages of those who study abroad train in countries other than Britain, they inevitably bring back with them attitudes, perceptions, values, and identities other than British. Consciously or subconsciously those non-British values—whatever they are— are being transmitted to the students they teach.

Of course, the British created an educational structure in many of their former colonies that will not easily be changed merely because the individuals who operate the structure are not as thoroughly British-trained as were their forerunners. Institutional and educational norms tend to persist long after the people who established them have passed from the scene. What is more, the British have in recent years made a concerted effort to increase the educational ties of weaker Commonwealth members to the U.K. The Commonwealth Education Conference of 1959 in Oxford and of 1962 in New Delhi established funds for scholarships for study in all Commonwealth countries, but more than one-half were for study in Britain. In addition,

. . . large numbers of teachers from Britain are recruited for service in schools, teacher-training colleges, technical colleges and universities overseas through various official and voluntary bodies in Britain. It is estimated that upwards of 2,500 a year have been taking up service, either permanently or on short-term contracts, in other Commonwealth countries including the dependencies. Since the Oxford Conference further steps have been taken. In 1959 Britain announced a scheme which, when in full operation after 1963, will provide some 400 additional teachers in Commonwealth countries. In 1962 an inter-denominational committee representing the churches in Britain launched a campaign to recruit 1,000 teachers a year for the next five years for service in Africa.[66]

Despite this belated British effort, however, and institutional proclivities toward self-perpetuation, the proportionately increasing non-British influence on the educational systems in the associated states will make a continued decline of British influence inevitable.

There is strong evidence that French education in its associated states has increased, not declined, since these states became independent. Since 1960, when they granted independence to fourteen African states, the French have made a strong effort to perpetuate and extend the educational links between these associated states and France. More teachers have been sent from France and more money has been spent on education in Africa since independence than before. Teresa Hayter, in her exhaus-

---

[66] Central Office of Information, *Consultation and Co-Operation in the Commonwealth,* Ref. Pamphlet 25 (London: H. M. Stationery Office, 1963), pp. 41–42.

tive study, *French Aid,* shows how closely the educational systems of those countries have been geared to the one in France:

. . . the educational system [in francophone Africa] has so far deviated only in minor respects from that of France. In higher education the syllabuses at the African universities are decided by their (French) directors, and ("rarely") by the French Ministry of National Education. . . . Decisions on the content of courses are also taken locally, and changes have been made. But, *ultimately, decisions are in the hands of the French Ministry of National Education;* the States could not take unilateral decisions without running the unacceptable risk of losing French recognition of the value of diplomas issued by the universities. This recognition has been granted in stages, as new universities and new faculties establish themselves, sometimes only for the first year or two in certain subjects, after which the studies can be continued without a break in France. When recognition has been granted by the Ministry of National Education the diplomas issued by the African universities are equally valid in Africa and in France, and give access to the same professions and institutions as diplomas issued in France. The structures of the universities are identical to those of French universities. *Their teaching staff is appointed and can be dismissed by the French Ministry of National Education. So far, between 1 and 2% of them are Africans.*[67]

When the French Ministry of National Education has the final say in the appointment and dismissal of teachers in these countries, and when only 1 or 2 percent of the teachers are Africans, it is clear how very dependent these countries are, educationally, upon France—despite the formal grant of political independence.

Since neither the United States nor the Soviet Union were major colonial powers in the traditional sense, their educational and value systems were spread in the traditional colonial manner only in limited areas of the world. In those areas that have been their political dependencies,[68] however, the impact of the American and Soviet educational and value systems seems to have been considerably more far-reaching than that of the British and the French in their dependencies. With the exception of the Philippines and possibly Puerto Rico for the U.S., most of the indigenous people

[67] Teresa Hayter, *French Aid* (London: Overseas Development Institute, 1966), p. 193. (Emphasis added.) Miss Hayter notes that "The adaptation [of the French system to Africa] that has occurred since 1961–2 has consisted mainly in painting faces in text-books black, changing oak trees into palm trees, and belatedly, suppressing such obviously unsuitable phrases as 'our ancestors the Gauls.' "
[68] The Philippines, Virgin Islands, Puerto Rico, and perhaps Alaska and Hawaii for the United States; Estonia, Latvia, Lithuania, and perhaps the Ukraine and several other Soviet Socialists Republics for the Russians.

in the other dependencies speak either English or Russian and value what is generally valued in the U.S. or the U.S.S.R. respectively.

American and Soviet educational influence around the world has increased enormously since World War II. While the United States and the U.S.S.R. emerged from that war as the two major Powers in the world (with the U.S. far in the lead), Britain and France emerged exhausted. Thus, while a newly independent country—or any underdeveloped country, for that matter—might have wanted help in building its educational system from its former colonial master, the likelihood was that the former Power was just too poor to be of much assistance. The United States, on the other hand, was not poor. In the years since the end of World War II, hundreds of millions of dollars in economic aid (both public and private) have been poured into the educational systems of the weaker countries. Economic aid has been accompanied by technical advisers trained in the American value and educational system. Of course, American educators believe that the American educational system is superior to any other (if they did not believe this, they would work to change the American system) and on this basis they are helping to remould the educational systems of perhaps seventy-five countries in the American pattern. And while they may not be free to institute carbon copies of their own system in their own language, as the British were able to do in the nineteenth and early twentieth centuries, and as the French seem to be doing since 1960, they are in a position to profoundly influence the educational systems in the underdeveloped countries by infusing them with American values, attitudes, perceptions, and modes of behavior.

No formal measures of American influence on education in the weaker states of the world exist, but some idea of magnitude can be obtained when it is realized that in addition to the hundreds of millions of dollars in aid to education spent abroad since 1945, and the thousands of advisers accompanying these funds, hundreds of thousands of students from the weak countries have studied in the United States and returned home as teachers and informal carriers of the American educational tradition. In addition, every major university in the United States is tied to at least one or two universities in weaker countries, helping them "improve" the quality of education in their universities. The quotation marks around the word "improve" are not meant to imply that they will not really do so. On the contrary, I am certain they will. But while they are in the process they will also, consciously or unconsciously, seek to change the methods and values of education in those universities to conform more closely to the American model.

One further source of American educational influence should be noted as well. Each year the Peace Corps sends out approximately 10,000 young Americans to live and work in the underdeveloped countries of the world. No country or village is too remote or too primitive to receive Peace Corps help. While teaching is not the primary job of every volunteer, it usually becomes one of his secondary tasks, simply because people have a vast appetite to learn and because teaching is necessary to the transmission of skills. But whatever his formal tasks, the volunteer himself (as a product of the American educational system) will be conveying American values, attitudes, perceptions, and modes of behavior, and will have a profound educational effect on his host community.

Soviet poverty and Stalinist ideology after World War II prevented the spread of Soviet educational values and methods beyond the limits of Eastern Europe and Outer Mongolia. In their educational aid to noncommunist countries since the death of Stalin, they have had much the same objectives as American educators. However, except in Eastern Europe and in Cuba since the 1960's, their poverty (compared to the U.S.) has continued to limit the depth of their involvement and, hence, their impact. Though Soviet educators are in a number of Asian and African countries (and are just as certainly convinced as the Americans of the merits and superiority of their educational system), there are probably too few of them at the present time to produce the kind of results Americans have achieved. As the Soviet Union grows richer, however, and extends more aid to more countries, it will surely effect substantial changes in those educational systems on the pattern of the Soviet model, and will succeed in inculcating Soviet values, attitudes, perceptions, and modes of behavior.

Changing Perceptual/Identity Relationships

Perceptual and identity relationships never are, and never can be static. They are constantly changing precisely because the perceptions and identities of every individual, group, and state are constantly changing. The degree to which a relationship affects the perceptions and identities of an individual, group, or states varies according to how significant or marginal the relationship is for the units involved. The nature of perceptual and identity relationships also depends on the nature of the power relationship between the units. If one is subordinate and the other dominant, it will produce a totally different perceptual/identity relationship than if both are of equal power.

In terms of the actual experience of states, prior to the colonial period the weaker states and Powers had no significant relationship whatever. They had little or no contact with each other and knew little of each other's existence. After the initial contacts between the Powers and the more settled regions of Asia and Africa, and the initial immigrations to the relatively underpopulated new worlds of the Western Hemisphere, Australia and New Zealand, relationships of dependence of the weaker upon the stronger came into existence. What form each perceptual/identity dependence took varied from country to country. Just as the history of no two individuals is identical, so, too, the history of no two countries is identical. Still, broad patterns can be discerned.

In the so-called settler areas the history, language, religion, race, class structure, ideology, and value system of their former homes came with the settlers along with the other provisions and supplies they brought from their former homes. Indeed, though these were lighter than other provisions, and took up less space (only a tiny corner of the brain), they were considered by many of the settlers to be the most valuable possessions they had, and were often the most important imports into the new lands. Since the indigenous peoples were totally overwhelmed or eliminated by the new arrivals, the regions were perceived by the settlers as having had no history prior to their arrival; the history of the mother country remained the salient history to them. Since the settlers knew no language other than the one they spoke, the language of the mother country became the linguistic identity of the new country, which all later settlers were expected to adopt. Since this was an objective dependence on the language of the metropole—and was not perceived by the settlers to be dependence at all—no linguistic counterdependence developed. For many of the settlers in the Spanish, Portuguese, and French colonies, the same was true of their religious identity. They knew no other religious identity and therefore did not perceive themselves to be religiously dependent on the more powerful country; thus no religious counterdependence could develop. The settlers in the British colonies were not likely to have feelings of religious dependence or counterdependence either, but for different reasons. Many of them perceived themselves to be of a different religion than their countrymen back home, even though all were Christians. The very act of migrating to a new land in order to practice their own creed had been an act of religious independence. Indeed, to the degree that there were any feelings of religious counterdependence among the nonconformist groups while still in England, those feelings were probably dissipated by the symbolic as well as the physical "rite of passage" to the new world.

European racial identity was undoubtedly highest among those settlers who met the most hostility and resistance from the non-

European inhabitants whom they were displacing. Indeed, particularly where the "savages" fought back, the Europeans clung tenaciously to their feelings of racial superiority.

Economic class identities no doubt also existed among the early settlers who populated the new lands, but they were not the same class identities the immigrants held prior to leaving Europe. Very few of the highest classes felt the necessity or the desire to leave the comforts and prestige they experienced in their homelands. Consequently, those who did leave Europe permanently were overwhelmingly from the middle or lower classes, but because there were no already established upper classes in the new worlds in which they settled, many were quickly able to acquire that identity there.

The prevalent political ideologies seem to have undergone some transformations in the voyages across the seas. Officially, all of the earliest immigrant colonization was conducted by the liege of one European monarch or another, and thus nearly all of the settlers were more or less dependent upon the favor of those monarchs. Monarchy and its related feudal structures may have been vaguely accepted by the earliest settlers. But the fact that the late eighteenth century and early nineteenth century revolutionary movements, which toppled only the French throne in Europe, led to the elimination of monarchy for every country in the Western Hemisphere, seems to attest to the existence of a high degree of counterdependence toward the *ideology* of monarchy, as such, among the later colonists of both North and South America. None of the newly independent countries of the New World chose to adopt a monarchical form of government after independence—though they certainly could have and still remained independent. That there had developed a high degree of counterdependence toward the *political domination* that the metropoles attempted to perpetuate goes without saying. Since all of the metropoles of the time were ruled by monarchs, it is reasonable to hypothesize that as resentment and counterdependence toward their political domination grew, those feelings were also directed at the type of political institution the metropoles represented.

Related to this ideological and political counterdependence is the change that occurred in the general value systems of the newly independent settler countries. During and after the revolutions everything (or nearly everything) European came to be considered "bad." All of the reverence for the old and the tried—the value system of prerevolutionary Europe—was now despised in the former colonies, and in its place there emerged a reverence for the new and the different. This is, of course, not really surprising since people who would emigrate in the first place must have had a value system that was not hostile to the new and different. Indeed, the likelihood is that those who held most tenaciously to the old value system—regardless of class or religion—probably stayed in Europe, while those who held the "new" value system were predominantly the ones who became settlers.

After the counterdependence of the revolutionary period subsided, and as the power of the former colonies increased relative to the power of the former metropoles—and given all of the similarities of perceptions and identities that had existed between the settlers and those who remained in the "mother country"—it is not at all surprising that a high degree of interdependence eventually developed between former metropole and former colony. Indeed, the similarities of identity and perception made this the "natural" development. In many cases, the act of successfully defying the metropole's authority was sufficient to defuse the counterdependence and to convert the relationship into one of interdependence. The metropole's rule had not been so universally perceived as unmitigated dominance and exploitation as to evoke total or even deep-seated counterdependence, and thus the transformation of the relationship into perceptual interdependence—rather than perceptual independence—was both politically and psychologically feasible.

In those areas that were heavily populated prior to the European contact, the situation was completely different. There the existing populations did recall a long and often a very proud history totally separate from the history of the Power that came to dominate them. Prior to the colonial contact, they spoke totally different languages, had totally different religious systems, and often very different class and prestige systems. All perceived themselves (and were perceived by their conquerors) to be racially different. In these areas the indigenous populations saw their own languages, cultures, and religions increasingly subordinated to the language, culture, and religion of the colonial Power, yet felt helpless to prevent this from happening. No matter how high the indigenous upper classes were in their own systems, they were almost always made to feel subordinate to the predominantly middle class Europeans who were sent out to rule them. And while the indigenous people prized their own ideological and value systems, which were so completely different from the Europeans', they were forced into the humiliating position that their ideologies and values must somehow be inferior to those of the colonial Power: how else could one explain the position of subordination in which they found themselves? In short, by every criterion that mattered, the indigenous person was made to feel humiliated, impotent, and frustrated by the overwhelming power of the metropole. No wonder he suffered feelings of subjective dependence and, finally, enormous counter-dependence.

In those areas in which the colonial Power had direct control for a long period of time, the feelings of counterdependence were in turn often frustrated and the indigenous person had no psychological option but to try to accept as his own the history, language, religion, ideology, and, where possible, race and class values of his dominator. Some became so perceptually dependent, and identified so completely with the colonial Power, that they were unable to differentiate themselves from the colonists. Admittedly, it was only a tiny segment of the top elite who were able to assimilate so completely, but those who could often did so gladly. The problem was—especially in the British-controlled areas—that try as they might to become British, to the British they were always "WOGs" (Western Oriented Gentlemen). As already noted, this attitude was not so marked in the areas the Spaniards, Portuguese, and French controlled. For example, Guadaloupins so completely subordinated their own indigenous culture (much of it African in origin) that they have not experienced—or at least, have not expressed—identity counterdependence. Instead, many have completely assimilated and now identity themselves, and are identified by others, as French. But in those areas of the world where the local people made the effort to assimilate and were rejected by the colonial Power, frustration, rage, and intensified counterdependence seem to have been the inevitable outcome.

The intensity of perceptual and identity counterdependence varies enormously from state to state, and from time to time in the same state. It always includes some rejection of the language, religion, ideology, and value system of the former dominator, but the degree of rejection also varies. Curiously enough, perceptual counterdependence seems to occur in its most intense forms in countries that were under an informal rule. Thus, for example, Iraq, Cuba, North Vietnam, and Albania—none of which was ever ruled in the "Formal-Direct" mode—are all exceedingly counterdependent toward their former mentors. One could argue that the relationship of these countries with their former mentors has moved from dependence, through counterdependence, to perceptual independence. But because these are all relatively weak countries, it is not possible for them to be completely independent of any Power—even perceptually—and so they increasingly identify themselves with different Powers.

What this means in concrete terms can be shown in the case of Iraq, for example. In rejecting a dependence on Britain and associating instead with the Soviet Union, the Iraqis are not likely to begin converting to Russian Orthodoxy. Rather, the implications are:

1. that for the first time the history of Iraq has become positively intertwined with the Soviet Union;
2. that more and more Iraqi elites are studying the Russian language;
3. that the class structure in Iraq is beginning to resemble more closely the Soviet model than the British model on which it was formerly patterned;
4. that communist ideology is widely accepted, at least in modified form, among the elite; and
5. that, as increasing numbers of Iraqis go for study in the Soviet Union (see Table 4.4), and increasing numbers of Soviet instructors teach in Iraq, Soviet values will more and more replace those of Britain for the elites.

The same could be said for Cuba's and North Vietnam's new relationships with the Soviet Union and for Albania's relationship with China. Though the manifestations may be less extreme, much the same could be said of a great many other countries that have experienced perceptual counterdependence. Most of those countries are simply no longer as perceptually dependent upon their former mentors as they were previously. But, to repeat, that does not mean that they have achieved absolute perceptual independence (no country—or individual—no matter how powerful could do that in today's world). Rather it does mean that they have achieved relative perceptual independence from their former mentors, but in the process have become increasingly linked perceptually to new mentors.

Chapter 5

Communication Ties

In order to act, man must have information about the external world. The information to which he is likely to attend largely depends on his perceptual conditioning and on the totality of information available to him. In an interesting article on the elements that comprise the decision maker's definition of an international situation, Dean G. Pruitt says,

. . . the decisions made by a policy-maker or the proposals, goals, and limits communicated to him by another citizen may be derived from a *definition of the international situation.* By this is meant a set of images possessed by an individual, representing his views of what other nations are like, what relevance they have to the goals of his own nation, and what behavior toward them would be appropriate for his own nation. Taking this approach it is possible to distinguish three broad classes of images that influence action toward another nation:

1. *Predictions about the future behavior of the other nation.* . . .
2. *Perceptions of the basic characteristics of the other nation.* . . .
3. *Conceptions of appropriate ways for dealing with the other nation.* . . .[1]

In discussing "selective inattention" in Chapter I, it was observed that the individual will choose from the vast amount of information available to him those bits he is perceptually disposed to accept, and will reject all others. The three factors mentioned by Pruitt are central in determining which messages will be received and which will be ignored. But the decision maker can only "selectively attend" to messages from among the universe of information to

[1] Dean G. Pruitt, "Definition of the Situation as a Determinant of International Action," in Herbert C. Kelman, ed., *International Behavior: A Social Psychological Analysis* (New York: Holt, Rinehart and Winston, 1965), p. 394.

which he is exposed. Suppose the decision maker in one country is exposed to a substantially restricted universe of information? What does that do to his decision-making capabilities?

One basic law of effective decision making is to acquire and evaluate all of the information that it is possible to obtain on a given subject. Presumably, the more information at the disposal of a decision maker, the more effective his decisions are likely to be. The less information, the more questions will exist about the wisdom (however defined) of his decision. Powerful countries are wealthy enough to be able to gather extensive information in order to make their decisions. Almost the exact opposite is true for the weak countries. The decision maker in the powerful country must guard against a communications "overload" whereby he has so much information at his disposal—much of it contradictory—that it is difficult for him to process intelligently what he has. The decision maker in the weak country, in contrast, must often make decisions of utmost importance to the well-being of his country on the basis of, at best, scanty information.

Further, if decision makers in two countries are exposed to very different universes of information, then, regardless of similarities or differences in their perceptual histories, they can only react to the information to which they are exposed. And the basic reality of international communication is that decision makers—particularly in the weaker countries—live in almost totally isolated "communication worlds," different from each others' and from those of decision makers in the powerful countries.

The decision maker in the weaker state lacks the *quantity* of information available to the decision maker in the more powerful state; he lacks the *diversity* of information available to his counterpart in the more affluent country; and he lacks the ability to acquire the *feedback* available to his counterpart in the powerful country. Given these limitations, decision makers in weak countries must rely for the most part on information supplied by or filtered through mentor countries. The international communication system thus determines the universe of information from which the decision maker in the weak state can select, and vastly restricts the possibilities of action open to him.

Channels of Communication

In simplified form, any communication media system can be described as having three basic steps: information is gathered, processed, and disseminated. Taking the last step first, how much information gets disseminated where?

Although in this work the concern is primarily with the information available to the decision-making elites of the countries involved and not to the total populations, the two are not unrelated. To the degree that a country has a literate population, there is likely to be a greater demand for written information. Laws of supply and demand being what they are, the greater the demand for written information (the higher the literacy rate), the greater the amount of written information likely to be attracted to that country. The countries of Western Europe, North America, and Japan have the highest literacy rates in the world, in many cases reaching 98.5 percent of their populations, while the weaker countries of Asia, Africa, and Latin America have the lowest literacy rates, ranging from 77 percent in a country like South Korea to only 1 percent in Mozambique.[2] But it is not illiteracy alone that prevents information from being disseminated in the weaker countries. Poverty seems to be one of the major factors. W. Phillips Davison notes that:

Poverty often makes it impossible for the press to reach even those who are literate. India's dailies, with a combined circulation of about 5 million, are not read by more than a fraction of the approximately 100 million literate people in the country. In the Philippines, where literacy is about 70% the total circulation of the daily press is only about 350,000 in a population of more than 27 million. In some countries of Africa, a subscription to a daily paper would require about 20 per cent of the average family's annual income.[3]

It is not only the written word that fails to come to the poorer countries because of lack of demand. The spoken word also tends not to reach those countries in anything approaching the quantity attracted to the powerful countries. In part, of course, this may be attributed to the multiplicity of languages spoken in many of the weaker countries. In still larger part, however, it must again be attributed to poverty.

None of the emerging nations comes up to the "minimum" standards for communication media suggested by UNESCO: namely, for each 100 inhabitants at least 10 copies of daily newspapers, 5 radio receivers, 2 movie seats, and 2 television receivers. As of 1961, as many as 100 states and dependencies in Africa, Asia and Latin America fell below in 3 categories. *Thus a large proportion of the world's inhabit-*

   [2] See Bruce M. Russett et al., *World Handbook of Political and Social Indicators* (New Haven, Conn.: Yale University Press, 1964), pp. 222–224.
   [3] W. Phillips Davison, *International Political Communication.* Published for the Council on Foreign Relations (New York: Frederick A. Praeger, 1965), p. 131.

ants lack adequate means of being informed about their own lands, let alone others.[4]

Not only are the number of people who have access to information about the external world much more limited in the weaker countries, but even those who do receive information, receive much less information than do their counterparts in the powerful countries. This is true whether one considers the amount of information delivered by international news media, number of books and periodicals available in the country, number of films available, number of telephone, telegraph, or Telex messages received, the amount of foreign mail received, the number of foreign diplomats sent or received, or the number of nongovernmental visitors sent abroad or received (including those who travel for study, business, or pleasure—all of whom are carriers, or potential carriers, of messages).[5] In short, no matter which channel of communication one chooses to examine, the findings are the same: weaker states have fewer channels of international communication available to them, and receive fewer messages over the channels that do exist, than do more powerful countries. In this chapter only a few of the governmental and nongovernmental channels of international communication will be examined, to see both the degree of disparity that exists and the degree to which weaker states are either dependent on or interdependent with more powerful states for international information.

International News Media

It was estimated by the International Press Institute in 1953 that the international news services alone then brought some 80,000 words of foreign news into the United States every day; that Western Europe received 135,000 words of "foreign" news a day; that India received 32,000 words per day, and that some of the smaller countries received amounts counted only in the hundreds of words per day, if they received any at all.[6] Thus, in terms of quantity of information disseminated by the international news media alone,

---

[4] *Ibid.*, p. 130. (Emphasis added.)

[5] Karl Deutsch, Bruce Russett, and others have done so much theoretical and empirical work on this subject that the point need not be elaborated here. For an interesting case study that demonstrates the effect of this situation on the making of foreign policy in a weak country, see Cecil Ee Kuang Yong, "Communications and Malaysia's Foreign Policy," Graduation Exercise, University of Malaya, 1970.

[6] *The Flow of News* (Zurich: International Press Institute, 1953), cited in Davison, *International Political Communication*, p. 328.

decision makers in the weaker countries are at a major disadvantage compared to their counterparts in the more powerful countries.

Even more limiting of the information available to decision makers in the weak countries are the international news gathering and processing mechanisms available to them. Most of the weaker countries consider themselves technologically rather advanced if they possess the facilities to effectively gather and process their own domestic news, let alone news of events that occur in other countries. Davison says of the facilities in these countries:

Telecommunication facilities are usually antiquated, where they exist at all. A recent survey found that Central American telecommunications were at a stage characteristic of industrialized countries 100 years ago. Facilities in Africa and some countries of South Asia and the Far East are still more rudimentary. A great many of the emerging countries have not yet developed national news agencies, and are dependent on international services for both domestic and world news.[7]

In contrast to this, every major Power has the headquarters for an international news gathering agency. The United States has not just one, but two such agencies. Those wire services have reporters in nearly every major city of the world, gathering information and sending it back to headquarters for processing and distribution to subscribers wherever they happen to be. The foreign subscribers may be national news agencies (where they exist), government information services, or the press. Since the press in many countries is officially or semi-officially controlled, its subscription can become a major source of governmental information as well. As of 1962, United Press International (UPI) delivered news to 111 countries; Associated Press (AP), the other American international news agency, sold news to subscribers in 80 countries; Reuters, the British news agency, serviced 110 countries, while Agence France-Presse (AFP) sold international news to subscribers in 104 countries. Tass, the fifth major international news service, sold news to subscribers in 65 countries.[8]

Now these figures may be misleading. At first glance it would appear that there is a totally interrelated system in which most of the world's countries subscribe to all of the major wire services, but that is not the case. Because of the poor market for international news in many countries, and because of the cost involved in these subscriptions, most of the weaker countries subscribe to only one or at most two of these services. Those that can afford

[7] Davison, *International Political Communication*, pp. 133–134.
[8] Figures cited are from UNESCO, *World Communication* (New York: UNESCO, 1962).

to subscribe to more than one service tend to be those big consumers of news in Europe, North America, Latin America, and Japan with very high literacy rates, and they subscribe to all, or nearly all, of the major wire services. Thus, thirty to forty of the countries listed as subscribers to each wire service are the same countries buying news from all the major suppliers. The other subscribers are not at all random, but follow clear-cut historical and/or political patterns.

Table 5.1 presents an index of the communications ties between the Powers and their associated states in 1960–62 with regard to international news agencies.[9] The table does not give anything approaching a complete picture of communications ties because to do so would require much more comprehensive data than were available for this study. But because the wire services are one of the most important single sources of international news, the percentages in Table 5.1 can be considered a rough indication of the degree of communications ties between weaker states and each major Power. The index takes into account the exchange of foreign correspondents, the existence of news service bureaus, subscriptions to the services, and exchange agreements. Thus a listing of 100 percent for a U.K. associated state does *not* mean that all the international news coming into the country is from Reuters. Rather, it means that insofar as there were any foreign correspondents in that country in 1960–62, they were exclusively from Reuters; if any correspondents were sent abroad from that country, they went exclusively to Britain; if there were any international news agency bureaus in that country, they were Reuters bureaus; if any local agency had a foreign bureau, it was in London; if there were any subscriptions or exchange agreements with an international news agency, they were exclusively with Reuters.

The countries that rely most heavily on Reuters seem to be former colonies and the more highly developed states that are large consumers of all wire services. The services of Agence France-Presse too are sought primarily in France's former colonies and in the big consumer countries, but many of the weaker countries not formally associated with France subscribe as well. Undoubtedly, one of the reasons is that the French Government makes their services available at only nominal cost. The services of Tass are bought by the big consumers, the communist governments, and those underdeveloped, noncommunist countries with which the Soviet Union has established special ties since 1952—

---

[9] This table is based on a weighted index constructed by Steven Schecter. See his "Dominant-Subordinate Interstate Relations: A Case Study of 103 Countries," MPIA thesis, University of Pittsburgh, Pittsburgh, Pa., 1969, pp. 100–103.

TABLE 5.1
Crude Index of International News Service Ties between Weak and Powerful Countries[a]
(Circa 1960–1962)
(Grouped by Historical Association and Ranked Within Each Group)[b]

Country	U.K.	U.S.	France	E.E.C.[c]	Soviet Bloc[d]	Inter-Regional[e]	Other[f]
United Kingdom and Associated States							
United Kingdom	—	7	6	27	15	44	7
Trinidad and Tobago	100[g]	0	0	0	0	0	0
Uganda	100	0	0	0	0	0	0
Malta	100	0	0	0	0	0	0
Sierra Leone	83	0	17	17	0	0	0
Cyprus	70	0	10	10	10	10	0
Sudan	69	0	0	0	8	23	0
Kenya	69	25	6	6	0	0	0
New Zealand	64	0	0	0	0	0	36
Barbados	50	50	0	0	0	0	0
Nigeria	47	47	7	7	0	0	0
South Africa	41	48	10	10	0	0	0
Ceylon	41	22	4	4	4	26	4
Jamaica	37	42	0	0	0	21	0
Ireland	36	29	7	36	0	0	0
Gambia	33	33	0	0	0	33	0
Iran	29	38	4	4	29	0	0
Canada	29	51	6	6	6	8	0
Australia	27	49	6	6	2	16	0
Malaysia	27	54	19	19	0	0	0

% Index of International News Services Exchanged With:

Burma	26	37	26	26	11	0	0
Ghana	26	5	14	14	42	14	0
Israel	23	23	21	37	17	0	0
Singapore	21	18	9	9	0	44	9
India	19	16	12	12	13	40	0
Pakistan	18	21	4	16	1	28	16
Iraq	13	26	0	0	61	0	0
United Arab Republic	3	6	0	19	46	18	8
Tanzania	0	0	20	20	80	0	0
Kuwait	0	0	0	0	0	100	0
Saudi Arabia	0	0	0	0	0	100	0
Nepal	0	0	42	42	0	58	0
United States and Associated States							
United States	9	—	9	41	19	19	13
Dominican Republic	0	100	0	0	0	0	0
El Salvador	0	100	0	0	0	0	0
Guatemala	0	100	0	0	0	0	0
Panama	0	100	0	0	0	0	0
Bolivia	0	93	7	7	0	0	0
Venezuela	0	93	0	0	7	0	0
Costa Rica	0	89	0	0	11	0	0
Honduras	0	89	11	11	0	0	0
Nicaragua	0	89	11	11	0	0	0
Ecuador	0	73	20	20	7	0	0
Paraguay	0	61	39	39	0	0	0
Peru	16	56	28	28	0	0	0
Philippines	35	48	13	13	0	0	4
Colombia	0	45	21	21	3	27	0

TABLE 5.1 (Cont'd.)

% Index of International News Services Exchanged With:

Country	U.K.	U.S.	France	E.E.C.c	Soviet Blocd	Inter-Regionale	Otherf
United States and Associated States (cont'd.)							
Mexico	0	**45**	21	45	0	9	0
Liberia	35	**40**	20	20	5	0	0
Argentina	18	**35**	18	18	30	0	0
Uruguay	16	**33**	16	26	7	19	0
Chile	10	31	10	10	3	**55**	0
Korea (South)	9	**25**	13	22	0	22	22
Brazil	7	22	7	24	13	**35**	0
Japan	8	14	8	N.D.	26	**41**	2
Cuba	6	11	6	6	**78**	0	0
France and Associated States							
France	8	10	—	**32**	21	32	15
Cameroon	0	0	**100**	100	0	0	0
Central African Republic	0	0	**100**	100	0	0	0
Chad	0	0	**100**	100	0	0	0
Haiti	0	0	**100**	100	0	0	0
Malagasy	0	0	**100**	100	0	0	0
Mauritania	0	0	**100**	100	0	0	0
Niger	0	0	**100**	100	0	0	0
Upper Volta	0	0	**100**	100	0	0	0
Laosg	6	44	**69**	69	0	0	0
Gabon	36	0	**64**	64	0	0	0
Congo (Brazzaville)	0	0	**61**	100	0	0	0

Dahomey	0	0	**58**	100	0	0	0
Syria	31	0	**54**	62	8	0	0
Senegal	38	14	38	**48**	0	0	0
Ivory Coast	17	30	**35**	52	0	0	0
Togo	33	0	33	67	0	0	0
Cambodia	28	6	28	28	28	6	3
Lebanon	16	**45**	23	26	13	0	0
Guinea	9	9	20	20	**63**	0	0
Tunisia	17	17	17	**30**	17	19	0
Vietnam (South)	5	14	17	26	0	**34**	0
Morocco	4	14	16	**36**	35	11	0
Algeria	16	16	16	16	2	**50**	0
Mali	8	14	14	14	**56**	0	**8**
Vietnam (North)[b]	11	0	11	11	**79**	11	0

Soviet Union and Associated States

U.S.S.R.	14	18	14	N.D.	**42**	42	12
Mongolia	0	0	0	0	**97**	0	3
Albania	0	0	0	0	**89**	89	11
Korea (North)	0	0	0	0	**73**	73	27
Rumania	7	14	8	N.D.	**63**	63	8
Hungary	7	6	7	20	**59**	59	7
Bulgaria	6	7	7	15	**58**	58	13
Germany (East)	9	12	6	12	**54**	54	12
Czechoslovakia	6	6	7	24	**49**	49	14
Finland	8	12	8	28	23	**34**	0
Afghanistan	0	20	20	20	**22**	20	20

TABLE 5.1 (Cont'd.)

Boldface figures indicate country or region exchanging the highest percentage of international wire services (as measured by Schecter's weighted index).

[a] Table 5.1 was constructed using the weighted index devised by Schecter, "Dominant-Subordinate Interstate Relations," Appendix III. Data for his index were drawn exclusively from UNESCO, *World Communications*, and refer to the 1960–1962 period only. As the title of the table indicates, the index is extremely crude. In some cases, the numbers upon which the percentages are based are very small. Therefore, *all figures should be treated with extreme caution*. The index is presented here because it is more sophisticated than many seen by this author, and because it does give some indication of relative orders of magnitude.

Percentage figures may total more than 100% either because of "rounding," or because of double counting (as in the case of France and the E.E.C.).

[b] Each country is listed only once in this table and hence for those countries historically associated with more than one Power, arbitrary decisions had to be made with regard to which Power they should be listed with. Not all countries are listed. Some were omitted for lack of data. Most European states have been omitted.

[c] European Economic Community (E.E.C.) figures include the wire services of all six members, including France.

[d] Soviet Bloc includes wire services of all East European Peoples Republics except Yugoslavia, and excludes China and Cuba.

[e] Interregional figures normally exclude the major Power in the region. Thus, the Western Hemisphere excludes the U.S.A.; Japan and China are excluded from Asia; Australia and New Zealand are considered a region themselves; the Middle East and Africa south of the Sahara are both considered separate regions. Western Europe excludes the U.K., and is synonymous with the E.E.C. The Soviet Bloc is synonymous with the Eastern European region.

[f] "Other" in this case includes only Mainland China and Japan.

[g] There is obviously a computational error in the figures, which it was not possible to correct. The figures are presented here nonetheless because the primary concern here is with orders of magnitude, and they are unaffected by the error.

such as the United Arab Republic, Iraq, Cuba, and Afghanistan. (It would appear that Tass, too, makes its services available at only a nominal charge.) The U.S. news agencies sell their services internationally not only to the big consumers and to Latin America, but also to the myriad of countries in which the U.S. has become increasingly involved since 1945.

Many of the countries included on Table 5.1 were either not yet independent, or had just recently achieved independence at the time the data on which the table is based were collected, and that surely explains some of the inordinately high percentages listed for some of the British and French associated states. But note that many of America's weaker associated states, which never were formal colonies of the United States, were just as dependent upon U.S. international news agencies. Twelve countries in the early 1960's had an index of 40 percent or above with the United Kingdom, and every one of them was a British associated state. Similarly, the fourteen weaker countries of francophone Africa (which had just received independence) were at least that tied to Alliance France-Presse. While no states had as high a percentage for Tass alone, nineteen countries were tied at least 40 percent to wire services in all Soviet Bloc countries combined.[10] On the other hand, twenty-six weaker countries were at least that tied to wire services in the United States.

Thus, not only is there a deficiency in the quantity of information received in most of the weaker countries, but, due to their lack of adequate information gathering services and the resultant reliance upon specific mentor Powers for information gathering, there tends also be different information disseminated in different countries. For example, the information available from the wire services to decision makers in Uganda, Kenya, Sierra Leone, Malta, and New Zealand overwhelmingly, if not exclusively, emanated from London in the early 1960's. On the other hand, the information available in Cameroon, Niger, Dahomey, Malagasy, and the Central African Republic overwhelmingly, if not exclusively, emanated from Paris. In short, many of the weaker states in the world are faced with a lack of access to information about events in the world except from the communication capitals of the powerful countries on which they are, in large measure, still highly dependent. The effect is to create four nearly closed communication systems, as shown in Figure 5.1.

The general pattern outlined above has been changing somewhat in recent years, of course. The major shift since pre-World War II days has been the stationing of AP and UPI correspondents

[10] Exclusive of Mainland Chinese wire services.

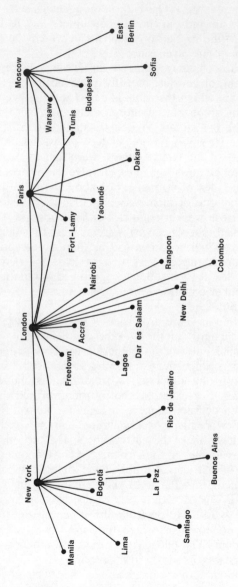

Figure 5.1 International Communication Systems

in the capitals of almost every country of the world, regardless of how remote from New York. In addition, a large number of newly independent countries now subscribe to AP and UPI wire services, as well as to Reuters or AFP. What is more, there is hardly a country in East, Southeast, or South Asia that does not today also subscribe to the Japanese wire services. Similarly, the number of countries subscribing to Tass or the Chinese news service has increased as well, but not nearly at the rate countries have subscribed to American or even Japanese wire services.

Another factor that has tended to modify the pattern somewhat is the development of regional news agencies which, although limited in scope, sometimes have an enormous impact on the areas they cover. Middle East News (MEN), the Egyptian news service, is subscribed to by only eleven countries, but in those countries its impact is presumed to be significant. Press Trust of India (PTI), the Indian news agency, is subscribed to in fifteen countries, while Informex, its Mexican equivalent, serves eight.[11]

Still another factor that has helped to modify this pattern since World War II has been the development of several fairly powerful regional radio stations, which are normally, but not always, associated with the regional news agencies. Radio Cairo, Havana, and Radio Colombo, for example, all can be received over many hundreds of miles, and have had a major communication impact not only on their own countries, but also on neighboring countries. While rudimentary compared to the international giants, these regional information services are still a step toward lessening the weak countries' reliance on the mentor Powers for world news.

Despite these developments the communication system in the world is in large measure still such that for news of an event occurring in, say, Accra to be reported in Lagos, less than 400 miles away, the information must travel almost 4,000 miles from Accra to London, and then back to Lagos. More important than the mileage covered, of course, is the perceptual screening through which this information must pass before it is made available to the decision makers and the news-conscious parts of the population.

Now it is precisely here that the question of selection and processing becomes so crucially important. As was noted earlier, each person selects from the vast amount of information available only those specific bits *he* perceives to be important. What gets reported to the wire service home office, therefore, are not "the facts" but rather the facts as selected and interpreted by the reporter in the field. Those selected bits of information are received in the home

[11] Figures from UNESCO, *World Communication*.

office where they are further screened by a staff editor, who selects from the relatively large amount of information that has been received from the field only those items *he* considers newsworthy; he then presents this limited material to the world, in the form *he* considers appropriate, as "the facts." Thus, what finally goes out over the wire services has been so highly screened and slanted by the conscious and unconscious perceptual biases of those who have handled it, that it may bear little resemblance to the "same" event reported on the wire services of another country.

The overthrow of President Kwame Nkrumah of Ghana for example, was reported from Accra in English by British reporters —with their British values, attitudes, and perceptions—back to London for screening and processing by the home staff of Reuters —with their British values, attitudes and perceptions. The story they sent out was picked up in Lagos by either British reporters working on Nigerian newspapers, or by Nigerians who probably studied journalism in London. It was again screened for what these local newspaper people interpreted to be the most salient points, and only then published. Hence, for the overwhelming majority of Nigerians, the only available information on which to base a reaction to Nkrumah's overthrow was a highly anglicized version of the event. Even if they refused to believe the anglicized version, where could they get a different one? To be sure, they may have gotten a slightly different version from the American wire services, but how different, in this case, were the perceptions of the American reporters from their British counterparts? Couple with this the fact that the majority of the Nigerian elite either studied abroad at American or British universities or at home under British or American teachers or teachers trained in the United Kingdom or the United States, and it is not difficult to understand that the information they received concerning the overthrow of Nkrumah would reinforce their previously acquired perceptions.

Compare this with the news of the overthrow of Nkrumah as reported in Warsaw. All of the same perceptual screenings that operated in the communication process from Accra via London to Lagos were present in the Accra via Moscow to Warsaw process, but the actors along each line chose to report different bits of information and, thus, two entirely different messages emerged. In the first instance, a cruel dictator was overthrown by a patriotic army to the cheers of the mass of the population. In the second, a popular leader was deposed by an American and British supported military junta to the dismay of the population. Which is reality?

Of course, for both the decision makers and the mass of the population in each of the countries, reality is not even in question.

Previously acquired perceptions have conditioned each to believe the reality that was reported to them. Even if they heard the other version, the likelihood is that they would screen it out as "enemy" propaganda.

The reporting of the negotiations to establish the South East Asia Treaty Organization in the 1950's is another case on point.[12] All, or almost all, of the reporting in the United States stressed that the arrangement was intended to resist the threat of communist invasion in Southeast Asia. It was reported that way because that is how most of the American reporters perceived it. One might question whether this was actually their view, or whether they were pushed by the government into reporting it that way, but that introduces an unnecessary element of suspicion. In this instance there was probably no need for the government to exert any influence. At the time there was clearly a high degree of similarity of perception among the major American news service reporters and America's foreign policy makers as to who were the "villains" in international affairs. For the *Time, Life,* AP, UPI, ABC, CBS, and NBC reporters, there can be little doubt that the Communists were not to be trusted and were out to damage the interest of the United States; anything done to counter that menace was probably more or less "a good thing." This is an oversimplification, of course, but one did not get to be a *Time, Life,* AP, or UPI reporter if he did not have essentially those perceptions. As a result, Americans —and others exposed to American wire services and mass media— were bombarded with information about how SEATO would avert and/or prevent aggression on the part of the Communists in Asia. How, then, could these people possibly come to a different conclusion, especially since all this "evidence" fits so well with their preconceptions that:

1. aggression is bad;
2. Communists tend to be aggressors; and
3. not to resist aggression could lead to World War III just as Munich had led to World War II.

For the Soviet people (and policy makers), as well as for others exposed to Soviet mass media, the picture presented was quite different. Given their perceptions (and certainly one does not get to be a senior reporter for Tass unless one has the "right" perceptions), the Tass reporter found evidence that SEATO was an attempt of the Americans to encircle the Soviet Union with bases and military allies. They were convinced that it was the United

---

[12] This example is taken from an unpublished study on communications problems in India, being edited by Ithiel De Sola Pool.

States—as a capitalist nation—that was behaving like an aggressor.
Thus, the Soviet people (even more than the American people,
because of the officially controlled press) could not possibly view
the American attempt to establish SEATO as anything but a
hostile and aggressive act, especially in view of their preconceptions that:

1. aggression is bad;
2. capitalists tend to be aggressors; and
3. not to resist aggression could lead to World War III.

The Indian people received an entirely different set of information, which coincided with and reinforced their perceptions. For
them the enemy was neither the Soviet Union nor the United
States, but Pakistan, with whom they were officially at war. For
their reporters, and ultimately for their decision makers and their
people, SEATO would be a danger to India because it would
involve the arming of Pakistan. American attempts to arm Pakistan
were seen as hostile acts aimed directly at India. American assurances that their arms would be used only against Communists
and not against Indians were not credible to the Indians since their
basic perception was that Pakistanis could not be trusted. And,
indeed, in each confrontation between India and Pakistan thereafter, it was American equipment that was brought into action
against the Indians, thus reinforcing their hostility to SEATO and
the United States.

Thus, the information received by both the decision makers and
the mass of the population in each of the three countries was completely different from the information the others received. Preconceived notions, values, and attitudes largely determined which information the news services selected for consumption at home. In
each case, this information reinforced already existing notions,
values, and attitudes.| And the same is true in almost every case of
international reporting.

Whether one considers wire services, radio, books, films, or
even the intenational exchange of persons—in short, any of the
nongovernmental channels that transmit information—the same
general pattern tends to emerge. Even on matters that may be of
vital importance to their countries, decision makers in weak states
tend to receive limited information, and the information they do
receive tends to be filtered first through the perceptual screens of
individuals in the mentor countries. Lacking the resources to attract a large quantity of information from diverse sources, and
lacking the resources to gather their own information, most of the
weaker countries are forced to rely heavily on the information

gathering and processing facilities of their mentor countries. They could conceivably switch mentors, but that would not give them more information. It would merely give them different information.

Governmental Sources of Information

Clearly the nongovernmental information weak countries receive tends to be highly biased. But governments seek to gather information through their own official channels. The question remains, however, to what extent these sources correct the biases.

Embassies and Consulates

Traditionally, one of the major tasks of foreign embassies has been the collection and interpretation of information about the country in which the embassy is located.[13] Indeed, because there is often so much to be reported, the more powerful countries often send out extensive staffs and divide the reporting assignments on a functional basis. It is not uncommon for an embassy to have separate political, military, commercial, and cultural sections, with at least one and sometimes many officers assigned to each. While there may be a number of other tasks these officials perform in their respective areas, the reporting function is usually considered extremely important.

Unfortunately, the poorer countries of the world cannot afford to have embassies in a large number of countries, or to attach large staffs to the embassies they do maintain. To illustrate the divergence in breadth of coverage, Table 5.2 gives the number of foreign embassies of a sampling of countries ranging from very powerful to very weak.

Even where a weak state has an embassy, it cannot send a large enough staff to provide information gathering and interpreting services on a par with the corresponding embassy of a powerful state. This is overwhelmingly evident, for example, in a comparison of the British and the Ceylonese diplomatic staffs in the United States in 1967. Britain had an embassy in Washington, D.C., staffed by at least seventy-three British diplomatic personnel, a United Nations mission in New York staffed by twenty-eight, a consulate in New York staffed by 22, and an information service in New York staffed by seven. It also had Consuls General in Atlanta, Boston, San Francisco, Chicago, Detroit, Cleveland, Houston, Los Angeles, New Orleans, Philadelphia, Seattle, and St.

---

[13] The primary political purpose of diplomatic representation will be discussed in Chapter 8 on political ties.

TABLE 5.2

Number of Embassies Abroad for Selected Countries

Country	Number of Embassies[a]
U.S.A.	111
France	111
United Kingdom	80
United Arab Republic	73
U.S.S.R.	59
Chile	41
Bulgaria	32
Ceylon	30
Burma	26
Liberia	21
Libya	19
Bolivia	15
Congo (Kinshasa)	10
Somali Republic	8

[a] Data are from the following sources: *Stateman's Year-Book, 1966–67; Information Please Almanac, 1968; Diplomatic Service List, 1967* (London: H.M. Stationery Office, 1967).

Louis, and lower level consuls in at least ten other cities.[14] Ceylon, on the other hand, had an embassy in Washington and a U.N. mission and consulate in New York staffed collectively by slightly more than a dozen people. Clearly, Britain's extensive diplomatic channels of communication can provide the kind of reporting that will maintain, stimulate, and strengthen all of its commercial, cultural, political, and military ties to the United States. Ceylon's paucity of diplomatic channels, though partly a reflection of Ceylon's much weaker U.S. ties (as well as its relative poverty), cannot help but reinforce the lack of ties, rather than expand them. The very information that might stimulate the development of Ceylonese commercial and other interests in the U.S. is simply not available to Ceylon.

Aside from the number and size of diplomatic missions, their location is of substantial interest from the perspective of channels of information available. Since the weaker states cannot afford to have world-wide diplomatic coverage, if they want international listening posts, one would expect them to place embassies in the countries they perceive to be especially important to their interests. Of course, they do just that. In terms of the perceptual biases of the information then available to them, the effect of having these diplomatic channels is a skewing of information that tends to reinforce their own predominant political biases. Table 5.3 illustrates this by rating on a pro-Soviet, pro-United States

[14] *Diplomatic Service List, 1968.*

continuum the diplomatic channels of information available to three weak countries—one pro-United States at the time (Bolivia), one pro-Soviet (Bulgaria), and one neutral (Burma).[15] The results, though only suggestive because of the small sample, are nonetheless striking.

The most striking thing about Table 5.3 from a communication point of view is that Bolivia, extremely pro-U.S. and anticommunist in foreign policy in 1966, had practically no official diplomatic communication channels over which anti-U.S., pro-Soviet information might flow. Bulgaria had a preponderance of diplomatic communication channels with essentially pro-Soviet countries, but it also maintained embassies in six very anti-U.S.S.R. countries (all European "neighbors"). One can only speculate about what bits of information get sent over these latter channels; it is likely that the messages are rather carefully screened —consciously or subconsciously—through rather intense anti-U.S. perceptual filters. The fact remains, however, that the channels for competing, conflicting information did at least exist in the Bulgarian case, while with the exception of a Bolivian embassy in Belgrade, the possibility of conflicting information reaching the Bolivian decision makers via diplomatic channels simply did not exist. As might be expected, the country most often neutral in international matters had a broad mixture of information channels and therefore received the most conflicting reports. The degree to which these official diplomatic communication channels reinforce the preconceived perceptions of decision makers in these countries can only be guessed, but on the basis of even this limited investigation it is evident that the embassies will not do a great deal to counter the biases of the nongovernmental sources of information on which these three states are dependent.

Aside from embassies and consulates, each of the associated states is tied through other kinds of diplomatic networks to the mentor Powers, which still further tend to reinforce intra-associational communication, while at the same time blocking nonassociated channels. The British have the Commonwealth of Nations, to which only historically associated states (that is, former British colonies) can belong;[16] the French have the French Community, made up exclusively of former French colonies in sub-Sahara Africa and Madagascar; the Russians have the Council for Mutual Eco-

---

[15] The placement of the countries derives primarily from their public voting positions in the U.N. The categories used are modified and updated versions of those applied in my earlier article with Barton Sensenig III, "Elections Within the United Nations," *International Organization*, Vol. XVII, No. 4 (1963), pp. 901–925.

[16] See S. A. de Smith, *The New Commonwealth and Its Constitutions*, (London: Stevens and Sons, 1964), p. 15.

TABLE 5.3

Location of Embassies[a] as Channels of Communication
(Three Countries, 1966)

Embassy	In Very Anti-U.S. Countries	In Moderately Anti-U.S. "Neutral" Countries	In Neutral Countries	In Moderately Anti-Soviet "Neutral" Countries	In Very Anti-U.S.S.R. Countries
Bolivian Embassies	(None)	Yugoslavia	(None)	(None)	Argentina Brazil Colombia Ecuador France West Germany Italy Mexico Paraguay Peru Spain United Kingdom United States Uruguay
Totals: 15 100%	0 0%	1 6.7%	0 0%	0 0%	14 93.3%
Bulgarian Embassies	Albania China (Mainland) Czechoslovakia East Germany Hungary North Korea	Algeria Ghana Guinea Iraq Syria	Ethiopia Finland India Indonesia Laos	Austria Dahomey Sweden	Belgium France Greece Italy Netherlands United Kingdom

Bulgarian Embassies (cont'd.)				
Mongolia Poland Rumania U.S.S.R. North Vietnam	U.A.R. Yugoslavia			Australia Canada France West Germany Italy Japan Thailand United Kingdom United States
11 34.3%	7 21.9%	5 15.6%	3 9.4%	6 18.7%

Totals: 32 100%

Burmese Embassies				
China (Mainland) Czechoslovakia Hungary Poland Rumania U.S.S.R.	Cambodia U.A.R. Yugoslavia	Afghanistan Ceylon India Indonesia Laos	Malaysia Pakistan Israel	Australia Canada France West Germany Italy Japan Thailand United Kingdom United States
6 23.4%	3 11.5%	5 19.2%	3 11.5%	9 34.6%

Totals: 26 100%

[a] Data on the locations of each country's embassies comes from *The Statesman's Year-Book*, 1966.

nomic Aid (COMECON) to which only Eastern European, pro-Moscow, communist states belong[17] (this organization can be considered to be, in some degree, the successor to the Comintern); while the Americans have a whole series of regional communication networks, largely (but not exclusively) associated with military alliances, like the Organization of American States (O.A.S.) and the North Atlantic Treaty Organization (NATO). Each of these international governmental organizations has periodic meetings of chief executives, foreign ministers, or other high-ranking government officials, which give the member governments an opportunity to communicate on matters of broad policy, to determine commonalities of interest, and to calibrate and reinforce perceptions of the world external to their association.

It has not been determined which of these associations is the more tightly knit communications network. Certainly the communist system consciously screens out external messages more completely than do any of the others. Certainly, too, there is a high degree of similarity of ideological perception among the leaders of the People's Republics (this was particularly true in Eastern Europe prior to the Sino-Soviet split), which facilitates intra-association communication. There is undoubtedly also a great deal of day-to-day consultation on a whole range of issues. But the French, too, have a closely intertwined (although slowly loosening) communications network with their former colonies in Africa. In part, language and identification with French culture account for the intensity of the use of this communications network. Even more, these states are enmeshed because of the many domestic matters on which French associated states are obliged to consult, and over which France continues to retain both formal and informal control. In addition, the continued presence of vast numbers of French administrators in many of these African states assures relatively open communication channels between ministries in France and ministries in these countries, and continuing reinforcement of similarities of perception.

The American communications network is far more extensive than that of any other Power. Not only do many of America's multiple associations tend to overlap, but regional, subregional and bilateral consultations are assured by a series of treaties and agreements, all of which tend to be mutually reinforcing. In addition, numerous communication channels exist via the functional advisers (that is, military, commercial, educational, et cetera) that the U.S. provides for many countries. Thus, while Americans do not fill ministerial posts in weaker countries (as the French formerly did),

[17] Plus Mongolia.

multiple commitments with many of these countries assure the presence of American advisers in a great many important ministries. And while being an adviser does not guarantee the influence that is possible when one holds the official position oneself, it does assure the existence of communication channels through which "preferred" messages can flow.

Of all the communication networks being considered here, the loosest is undoubtedly the Commonwealth of Nations. Still, S. A. de Smith is able to say of it:

> The normal channel of communications is through the medium of High Commissioners, who enjoy the immunities and precedence accorded to ambassadors but whose official contacts are not confined to Ministers of Foreign or External Affairs; they have direct right of access to the heads of other departments, and they are likely to have frequent consultations with Ministers in charge of economic affairs. In a Commonwealth capital they tend to form a distinct group; their personal relations with members of the government including the head of government to which they are accredited, are characteristically friendly and informal. In London, the Secretary of State for Commonwealth Relations has regular meetings with the assembled Commonwealth High Commissioners. From time to time there will be direct communications between Prime Ministers and Presidents, between departmental Ministers and between senior civil servants in the several Commonwealth countries. In a sense the Commonwealth is still a continuing conference of Cabinets, or of governments.[18]

What is more, members of the Commonwealth "have access to the stream of diplomatic information that issues from the Commonwealth Relations Office in London." [19] How much use they can make of the information they receive via these communications channels is difficult to assess. It is not really possible to determine the degree to which such communications can substitute for a member's own information gathering network in important matters. That India and Pakistan are both members of the Commonwealth, and their High Commissioners do sometimes communicate, in no way eliminated the need for their own intelligence gathering prior to the open hostilities between them. In short, the communications channels of these essentially political associations certainly link all the members to some extent, but they can be considered particularly strong only between the mentor and each associated state.

The argument that the weaker states receive an essentially one-sided view of world affairs is not significantly countered by the fact that they can and do receive conflicting information at least

[18] de Smith, *The New Commonwealth*, pp. 30–31.
[19] *Ibid.*, p. 28.

through United Nations diplomatic channels. One can only guess that the words spoken by diplomats from one country are heard quite differently by diplomats from another, whether at the United Nations in New York or at state functions in London, Paris, or Moscow. It is probably a fair generalization that governments reserve the "confusing" diplomatic positions for their more seasoned (read "socialized into the prevailing ideological orientation of the ruling elite") diplomats. Young diplomats, untrained in differentiating between information and propaganda—as defined by the decision makers in the home country—are, one suspects, generally sent first to assignments where they will not be exposed to much contradictory material. This practice has proven somewhat difficult for the newer states to follow because many simply do not have enough trained diplomats and therefore must send some poorly trained people on complex, important assignments. The result is sometimes a "loss of perspective" on the part of the inexperienced diplomat, who may overly identify with the values of the country to which he is assigned, to the possible detriment of the values of the country he represents. The fact remains that for the most part diplomatic communications channels do relatively little to contradict the major nongovernmental sources of information about the external world available to decision makers in the weaker states.

Intelligence Agencies

Not content with the prodigious coverage of world events by the wire services of their countries, or with the information relayed by the thousands of foreign service personnel they send throughout the world, the major Powers also have vast intelligence networks, which presumably supply information that would otherwise be unavailable. The question of how reliable this information may be need not concern us here. That question could be asked of every source of information. The point is that the wealthy countries invest staggering sums of money to acquire information secretly about trends, events, and people in almost every country of the world, and that this information—whether accurate or not—is an additional source of information for governmental decision makers. Precisely because this kind of information gathering is so expensive, only the very wealthy countries can afford it. To be certain, even less wealthy countries may try to develop international intelligence services, but sheer expense usually forces them to limit these efforts to acquiring information in neighboring "enemy" countries. Thus, there is little doubt that Egypt maintains an intelligence network in Israel and some countries within the Arab World, but it is not likely that the Egyptian government can afford much more. Similarly, the Israelis undoubtedly maintain intelligence efforts in the bordering Arab countries, plus some few additional countries it considers important.[20] (While the extent of the Israelis' intelligence effort was proved by the Eichmann affair to be greater than had previously been suspected, it is still not likely that its intelligence apparatus begins to compare to those of the major Powers.) The same can probably be said of the Indians, Cubans, Belgians, Swiss, Australians, Argentines, Brazilians, and most of the other weaker countries that have any intelligence network at all. For the most part, however, there is nothing to discuss with regard to international intelligence activities for most of the weaker countries. They may have an occasional informant in a particular country, but on the whole they simply cannot afford to acquire intelligence information, even in those countries that exert the most influence on them.

There are two ways in which some of these countries may be able to compensate for this vast information gap to some small degree. One is to use the intelligence services of the mentor country. That is, the Powers in many instances are willing to provide the governments of some of the weaker countries with some relevant information that their intelligence services have uncovered in the normal course of work. In relying on this kind of information, however, the weaker country must be fully aware that the information passed along is only that information the mentor decided the weaker state could or should have. There is little doubt that the intelligence services actually uncover far more information of relevance to decision makers in the weaker countries than the Powers are willing to pass along. In addition, the very decision as to what is relevant to the weaker country is not made by its decision makers, but by decision makers in the stronger country. There is always a strong probability that the information passed on to them has been "colored," at least by the unconscious value perceptions of the intelligence gatherer, and possibly consciously as well. Certainly, the decision makers in the weaker states must be constantly on guard as to the accuracy of the information they receive. But it is very difficult for them to check for accuracy and bias, or to determine whether the information is being supplied to serve the primary interests of the mentor. Decision makers in the powerful countries can always compare any specific information they receive with perhaps dozens of other sources of information. The decision maker in the weak country, on the other hand, may have available only that bit of information supplied, say, by the C.I.A. Thus,

[20] See Paul Jacobs, "Israel's Early Warning System in the Arab World," *New York Times Magazine* (Feb. 8, 1970), pp. 23–25, 85–90.

decision makers in all the Latin American countries were undoubtedly supplied by the C.I.A. with substantial "proof" that Castro,
Arbenz, and Bosch were, if not Communists themselves, completely
under the influence of communist advisers. Similarly, there is good
reason to believe that Soviet intelligence officers in May 1967 supplied Egyptian and Syrian decision makers with "proof" that Israel
was preparing an attack against them. If decision makers in these
weak countries ignore the information they receive from their
mentors, and it proves to be correct, the results could be disastrous
for them. Hence, decision makers in the weaker states have had no
alternative but to act as though the information from the mentor
were correct. But this source of intelligence information, although
in some cases, perhaps, better than no information whatever, may
often be of very dubious value.

The second source of intelligence information that may be available to decision makers in underdeveloped countries is freelance
international intelligence agencies, which exist in the real world
as well as on television (although undoubtedly with less efficiency
than their TV counterparts). While information obtained from this
source *may be* less biased than information obtained from official
intelligence sources of mentor Powers, it is also expensive. Presumably, freelance agencies would not be able to stay in business
if the information they supplied were frequently incorrect or too
biased. Neither could they stay in business, however, if they did
not charge substantial amounts for each piece of information supplied. This alone probably prevents their being used extensively.

It is very difficult to know in any scholarly way just how much
decision makers in the weaker countries rely on the services of
freelance intelligence agencies or the official intelligence agencies
of the Powers. Certainly there are many occasions when these
services, though far from ideal sources, can partially compensate
for an otherwise nearly complete lack of information about events
of vital concern to them. These may be relatively imperfect sources
of information, to be sure, but they are sources. Without them it is
entirely likely that many of the weaker countries would be forced
to make decisions based on no information whatever. Faced with
that reality, decision makers in the weaker countries probably use
these "outside" intelligence services, when available, far more
than they should.

Changing Communication Relationships

As in matters of perception and identity, so, too, regarding communications, prior to the Colonial period the weaker states and the

mentors had no meaningful relationship. They had little or no contact with each other and knew little of each other's existence. That is not to say that they were isolated from the entire world, only that, in terms of communications they were isolated from each other. There existed very well established channels of communications between what are now considered the weaker countries and other countries in the parts of the world traditionally most relevant to them. Before the arrival of the Europeans in Africa, for example, there were well defined and functioning caravan trails that spread news as well as goods from one part of the continent to the other. There were centers of culture and learning, particularly in North Africa and the Arabian Peninsula, that disseminated news of events through the Arab world and beyond. Arab shipping routes, which flourished prior to the defeat by the Europeans, spread Arab news and information as well as Arab culture and religion West to the Atlantic, East to Indonesia, North to Tashkent and Samarkand, and South to Northern Nigeria. As the slave trade developed in Africa, some Europeans began to know more and more about Africa and some Africans began to know more about Europeans. But until well into the nineteenth century, people living in Africa generally knew little or nothing of the people who lived in Europe, and as far as the Europeans were concerned, Africa was the "Dark Continent."

Much the same could be said of the various societies of Asia, which had developed highly effective channels of communication among themselves, but little or none with the Europeans prior to the fifteenth century. With the arrival of the Europeans, however, traditional channels were disrupted and new ones were established. The country that was made politically dependent very quickly became dependent in matters of communication as well. While some of the traditional channels of communication may have continued (in sharply curtailed form) even into the mid-twentieth century, they were dwarfed by the new channels of communication that emerged between mentor and dependent states.

What this meant, particularly in the early part of this century, was that nearly all information about the world at large—as well as much information about their own internal events—came to the weak states through communication filters of the mentors. British colonies received almost all of their news of the world through Reuters, French colonies through Agence France-Presse, while Eastern Europe and Latin American states were almost but not quite as dependent on Tass and the American wire services, respectively. Dependence upon these facilities meant that these countries received only news the mentor Power defined as important and, in language and symbols, most sympathetic to the mentor's interests. No dependence was ever total, but it was complete enough so that the values, attitudes, and perceptions of the mentor were overwhelmingly communicated.

The development of perceptual counterdependence usually brings a simultaneous development of communication counterdependence. And just as the intensity of perceptual counterdependence varies enormously from state to state, so, too, does the intensity of communication counterdependence. For a while it was almost axiomatic that in order to be "independent" a country needed a constitution, a flag, a national song, an airline, a newspaper, and a radio station. Some of the more affluent and more counterdependent elites of newly independent states have indeed set up their own communications networks. In practice, however, their airlines, newspapers, and radio stations have never really been able to compete with those of the Power. To be sure, there are notable exceptions; Radio Cairo and the Indian motion picture industry are just two examples of successful competition. But when it comes to collection of news for dissemination over their own wire service, they simply cannot compete.

Since these countries do not have the financial resources to compete effectively, communications counterdependence often takes a somewhat different form, particularly in those states where the ruling elite has experienced the most extreme perceptual counterdependence. There the elites simply refuse to believe what they read or hear on the communication channels of the former mentor and believe instead everything that comes over the communication network of the enemy of the former mentor. Thus, when Cuba, Egypt, Mali, and North Vietnam moved away perceptually from the Western Powers, they subscribed to the wire services of the Soviet Bloc countries and either cancelled their subscriptions to Western services, or went further and jammed their messages. Some countries may not be able to afford the cost of jamming, but psychologically they can refuse to believe the "propaganda" of the former mentor even though a year before they may have considered those same messages "information." Note that one of the acts of Dubcek's counterdependent Czech regime that most distressed the Soviet Union was to open Czechoslovakia to news from Western Europe. One of the first demands of the Soviets, after the invasion in August 1968, was that the Czechs again block out those Western messages. But while they could force the Dubcek regime to cut communication ties with the West, they could not force the counterdependent population to believe the Soviet messages.

In those countries that have achieved communication interdependence with the former mentor—and there are not many outside of Western Europe and Japan—the national news services often flourish side by side with the wire services of all major countries. Once a country has achieved a respectable communication network, the likelihood is that the former mentor will in some way tie into it, recognizing an advantage in getting its news about events in that country directly from that country's own correspondents and communications channels. Just as AP and UPI, which are both comparably strong, share certain facilities for their common good, so AP and Reuters or Tass and AFP may share certain facilities for their common advantage. The point is, of course, that interdependence in communications is a stage that can be reached only when both parties have much of importance to offer each other.

Chapter 6

Economic Ties

Economic ties (whether public or private) are perhaps the most discussed, and most controversial, of all the ties that exist between states. To the anticolonial extremist, foreign economic ties have the sole motivation of political domination for selfish economic gain.[1] Marxist theory places almost all such transactions in the category of "imperialism," the final stage of capitalism. To the Western free enterprise extremist, on the other hand, the sole motivation of foreign investment or trade is "the profit motive." Powerful governments, both capitalist and communist, insist alternately (depending on the audience) that foreign economic aid and trade ventures are conducted

1. for primarily altruistic reasons;
2. for primarily economic reasons;
3. for primarily political reasons;
4. to counter the other Powers' politically motivated ventures.

Much of the confusion about the subject stems from the different meanings different authors give to the term "economic dependence." In this age of ever-increasing specialization and division of labor, every country is to some degree economically dependent on some other country or countries. One need only take apart some complex mechanical device such as a radio and observe how many of the component parts were made in countries other than the one in which the final product was assembled, to see how interdependent the economic life of the industrial countries has actually become. But economic interdependence is not the same as economic dependence. For purposes of this work it is important to distin-

---

[1] For example, see R. A. Ulyanovsky, *The Dollar and Asia: U.S. Neo-Colonialist Policy in Action* (Moscow: Nauka Publishing House, 1965).

guish between the two, and to examine the reality of the various types and degrees of economic dependence that do exist among states. First, however, it is important to dispel some of the most prevalent myths on the subject.

Myths and Realities

Industrial Countries and Raw Materials

The first myth that must be cleared away is that the industrial countries of the world are dependent for their survival on the raw materials produced in the underdeveloped countries. It is true that rubber, tin, oil, copper, uranium, and a host of other raw materials are produced primarily—but not exclusively—in the weaker countries of the world, and are used mainly in the industrial countries. Industrialization, by definition, implies the ability to transform raw materials into finished products. Now, while it is also true that some raw materials are converted into finished products in some of the underdeveloped countries, generally the weaker countries have only limited facilities and limited demands for such transformations, while the industrialized countries have nearly unlimited facilities and demand. Even though some of the most industrialized countries of the world could (or do) produce many of the same raw materials themselves, because these materials can sometimes be obtained more cheaply from the primary producing states, it often pays for the industrial states to import them rather than divert labor and resources into the production of these primary products. But if these raw materials become unavailable from the usual sources —for whatever reason—it has generally been possible for the industrial states either to find alternative external sources of supply; or to find or develop substitutes or synthetic materials to use in their place; or to divert the necessary resources for domestic production of these materials. Indeed, there is some evidence that the industrial countries *export* as large quantities of *reprocessed* raw materials as they import from some primary producing countries. Industrialization, by its very nature, frees a country that is so organized from *dependence* on any specific product or raw material. One of the major lessons of World War II for the American economy was the realization that the country was not nearly as dependent for its survival on any of the raw materials upon which all industrial countries once thought they relied. Certainly, a sudden need for raw material substitution can cause inconveniences and dislocations in any economy that has come to rely heavily on specific primary products, but inconvenience is not the same as incapacity to function.

The Middle East crises of 1956 and 1967 showed that great dislocations could be caused by depriving the major industrial countries, particularly the ones in Europe, of the oil on which their industrial organizations had come to rely. But even the deprivation of a commodity as relatively scarce as oil did not cause economic collapse. Enough other sources existed so that the European economies were not without recourse to alternatives. (Ultimately, of course, the industrial countries will shift from the use of oil as their major source of energy to reliance on atomic and solar power, thus largely freeing themselves from their current degree of dependence on the oil producing countries.)

However, the case should not be oversimplified. Although the economies of larger industrial Powers would not be destroyed by the loss of some specific product, the problems of readjustment might be severe. The total blockage of oil to Europe now, or the denial of uranium to Europe in the future, would wreak considerable havoc on the economies of the European states. But industrial Powers have economies that are so well developed that, while they would certainly feel the effects of total denial of certain products from foreign countries, they would, given enough time, probably adjust fairly well. In terms of vulnerability to disturbances in the raw material user-supplier relationship, the dislocations an industrial state would suffer if deprived of a principal source of an important material are minor compared to the effects the underdeveloped state would suffer from the corresponding loss of a principal market.

The reality—in contrast to the myth—is that the primary producing countries of the world are dependent for their survival on the markets in the industrial countries. In many of the world's poorer countries a very large percentage of national income is derived from the sale of their primary products abroad. While most of the population in such a country may still be engaged in traditional consumption agriculture, significant segments are often employed in the production or extraction of the export commodities. Since the major market for these primary products is outside the country, the leaders of the country often have little or no control over many important decisions that affect their own economies. As Fidel Castro of Cuba and Mohammed Mossadegh of Iran both discovered, mere production is insufficient for economic wellbeing; someone must buy one's products. In Iran, even production was not possible without the foreign technical assistance required by modern extraction and refining methods. Although both these cases are extremes that occur infrequently in the modern world, less spectacular effects (but perhaps no less damaging over the long run) are caused by decisions made by private commercial interests every day in the market countries. These decisions may be no more significant than to decrease the proportion of real cocoa in chocolate bars, or to substitute a synthetic product for one previously purchased abroad, or to use up existing stock before importing more, but the impact can be devastating to the country that depends heavily on the sale of the product to maintain gross levels of national income.

As a generalization, it can be asserted that the more a country's economic well-being comes from one or two primary products, the more economically dependent upon decisions outside its own boundaries that country is likely to be. Almost by definition the more industrialized states produce a wide diversity of products. On the other hand the weaker states almost invariably rely heavily on one or two crops for export. Countries in this position have faced a particular difficulty in the steady decline of world prices on most primary products since World War II, at the very time that world prices on finished goods have steadily increased. If a country's one product is uranium or gold, then of course it will be in a much better economic bargaining position than if its one product is peanuts, but it will still be in a fairly vulnerable position. If a country has more than one primary product on which it relies, its economy will be less vulnerable to downward changes in world prices for that product, or to a bad harvest, or draught, or disease.

Unfortunately for the weak states, diversity of product is a concomitant of both development and wealth. In fact, one of the major indices of economic development is the degree of diversification of production. It is fair to generalize that the less economically developed the country, the more likely it is to rely on the production of only one or two primary products. The more a country must rely on the production of one or two primary products, the more economically dependent upon other countries—for both markets and finished products—it is likely to be.

Markets for Industrial Countries

The most persistent misconception, not only among left-wing and right-wing extremists, but also among many moderates of all political persuasions (particularly in the weaker states), is the notion that the industrial states need the markets in the economically underdeveloped states in order to survive and prosper. The myth goes even further to hold that private enterprise and government in the powerful states do, or should do (depending on political outlook) everything they can to keep these countries underdeveloped so that they will not become competitors to the Powers and will continue to be lucrative markets.

Merely because this myth is totally unfounded, as has been repeatedly demonstrated, does not mean that private firms and governments have not behaved as though it were reality. Much of the rationale for colonialism in the nineteenth century was based on this myth. J. A. Hobson, in his classic study of imperialism, quotes a self-avowed British imperialist, writing just after the turn of the twentieth century, as saying:

"We must have markets for our growing manufactures . . . such expansion is a necessity of life to a nation with our great and growing powers of production. . . . So long as England held a virtual monopoly of the world markets for certain important classes of manufactured goods, Imperialism was unnecessary. After 1870 this manufacturing and trading supremacy was greatly impaired: other nations . . . advanced with great rapidity, and while they have not crushed or even stayed the increase of our external trade, their competition made it more and more difficult to dispose of the full surplus of our manufactures at a profit. The encroachments made by these [industrializing] nations upon our old markets, even in our own possessions, made it most urgent that we should take energetic means to secure new markets. These new markets had to lie in hitherto undeveloped countries . . . where vast populations lived capable of growing economic needs which our manufacturers and merchants could supply." [2]

Hobson vigorously refuted this assumption by giving sufficient data to demonstrate that the weaker, underdeveloped countries (they were called "backward" in those days) provided only an insignificant fraction of Britain's markets. Britain's—and every industrial country's—prime market is its own domestic market.

While Hobson demonstrated that "backward" countries were not important markets for commercial products, he thought they were important markets for investment capital, and it was to this that he attributed the perpetuation and expansion of the colonial system in the late nineteenth century. Lenin seized on this idea, and quotes Hobson extensively in his *Imperialism, The Highest Stage of Capitalism*. Lenin says:

As long as capitalism remains what it is, surplus capital will be utilized . . . for the purpose of increasing profits and exporting capital abroad to the backward countries. In those backward countries profits are usually high, for capital is scarce, the price of land is relatively low, wages are low, raw materials are cheap. . . . The necessity

---

[2] Quoted in J. A. Hobson, *Imperialism: A Study*, 3rd ed. (London: George Allen & Unwin, 1938), pp. 71–72.

for exporting capital arises from the fact that in a few countries capitalism has become "overripe" and (owing to the backward stage of agriculture and the impoverished state of the masses) capital cannot find a field for "profitable" investment.[3]

But when Lenin asks where that surplus capital is invested, he answers his own question with some 1910 data that clearly show that the largest share of British, French, and German investment was in Europe and America. However, he dismisses French and German investment as being "different" from the British (despite the fact that France at that time had the second largest colonial empire in the world) and says:

> The principal spheres of investment of British capital are the British colonies, which are very large also in America (for example, Canada) not to mention Asia, etc. In this case, enormous exports of capital are bound up most closely with vast colonies, of the importance of which for imperialism we shall speak later.[4]

What Hobson, Lenin, and other extremists, particularly on the left, failed to recognize is that just as the less developed countries are poor markets for commercial products, so, too, are they poor markets for investment. Foreign export capital has always gone more to developed and rapidly developing countries than to "backward" or underdeveloped countries, for exactly the same reasons that commercial exports have done so. The poorer the country, the less it can be a good market, either for finished products or for foreign capital investments!

Despite repeated disproof, the myth persists. The "New Left" in particular has seized on it as one of the major explanations for why the capitalist system is able to survive. As Charles Perrow, in his collection of New Left writings, says:

> . . . the cry "imperialism" seems to be one of those absurd slogans and abstractions that ends all debate and inquiry with the new left. As enunciated, it is a single, sweeping explanation for wars, power politics, internal repression. In a somewhat different vein, it is the reason why the capitalist system has not long since torn itself apart through its contradictions. . . . the attack upon the business system reaches its culmination in the cry of imperialism; whatever that system has done to the non-affluent one-third of our nation is trivial compared to what it has supposedly done to two-thirds of the world.[5]

---

[3] V. I. Lenin, *Imperialism, The Highest Stage of Capitalism* (Peking: Foreign Language Press, 1965), pp. 73–74. (Originally published in 1916.)
[4] *Ibid.*, pp. 75–76.
[5] Charles Perrow, "The Radical Attack on Business," unpublished manuscript, Ch. 3.

In that same work, Perrow quotes Harry Magdoff, a leading American New Left authority on imperialism. Magdoff, like Hobson before him, quotes the misconceptions and overstatements of the Right to prove his point. If the American business establishment believes the myth to be true, then it must be so.

The interrelation between economic interests and foreign policy is seen more clearly by business-minded observers. Thus, the former president and chairman of the World Bank, Eugene R. Black, informs us that "our foreign aid programs constitute a distinct benefit to American business. The three major benefits are: (1) Foriegn aid provides a substantial and immediate market for U.S. goods and services. (2) Foreign aid stimulates the development of new overseas markets for U.S. companies. (3) Foreign aid orients national economies toward a free-enterprise system in which U.S. firms can prosper." [6]

Of course Black would emphasize the benefits of foreign aid to American business interests since a major part of his job was to "sell" foreign aid to suspicious and hostile business men. But Magdoff goes further and argues that between 20 and 50 percent of the production of "investment-type equipment" (often military-related) in America is for the export market, and sees this as proof that foreign markets are indispensable for the American business system. But again, what is overlooked is the fact that the vast majority of these exports (except for machinery, like oil rigs, for mineral extraction purposes) goes to the most developed countries in the world.

Andre G. Frank, another New Left writer, has written an interesting case study of American imperialism in Brazil in which he shows not only how American interests dominate the Brazilian economy, but how they do it largely with Brazilian capital.[7] Relatively, a very small American investment is involved. The mechanisms used by American capital are no different from those used in Europe and Canada. The big difference is that in the highly developed economy of Western Europe, American investment is only one among many, whereas in Brazil (as in the rest of Latin America) relatively small absolute sums of capital are able to dominate the economy.

Still worse than the New Left theorizing, some governments (both weak and powerful) continue to act as though the myth were reality. That it has cost governments billions of dollars, created

[6] Harry Magdoff, "Aspects of U.S. Imperialism," *Monthly Review,* Vol. 18, No. 6, Nov. 1966, quoted in Perrow, "Radical Attack on Business," Ch. 3.

[7] Andre G. Frank, "On the Mechanisms of Imperialism: The Case of Brazil," *Monthly Review,* September, 1964, pp. 285–297, cited in Perrow, "Radical Attack on Business," Ch. 3.

innumerable wars, and failed over the long run to sustain any of the empires created for the sake of "markets" in no way seems to deter those determined to believe that it is reality.

But the reality is quite different. To the small degree that the industrial countries depend on any external markets, it is the markets of other *industrial* countries that are most important. They alone have have sufficient resources to buy in large quantities what the industrial countries produce. The larger a country's population, the smaller the part foreign trade is likely to play in that country's Gross National Product.[8] For countries that are highly developed as well as populous, as much as 95 percent of all the goods and services they produce are consumed domestically, thus mitigating their need for foreign markets.

The United States and the Soviet Union, because they combine very highly developed economies with large populations, have such vast domestic markets within their own boundaries that they are considerably less dependent upon external markets than any other units in the world.[9] Japan, Britain, and France, while highly developed economically, must rely more on foreign markets than either of the Super Powers because of smaller domestic markets than the U.S. and the U.S.S.R. But the foreign markets on which they rely are not the markets of the weaker, underdeveloped countries of the world. Much more important to them are the richer, and therefore better, markets of the other developed countries. Upon investigation one finds that the strongest countries economically are among each other's best customers.

In 1967, the twenty-eight countries with the highest Per Capita Gross Domestic Product ($800 or above—a figure most economists would agree represented the highest levels of economic development) accounted for 71 percent of the total foreign trade of the United States, 70 percent of the foreign trade of France, 65 percent of the foreign trade of the United Kingdom, 60 percent of the foreign trade of the Soviet Union, and 50 percent of the foreign trade of Japan.[10] One might argue, of course, that 29 percent of the total foreign trade of the United States in 1967, was accounted for by the markets and raw materials of the weaker states, and to that degree the U.S. was economically dependent upon

[8] See K. W. Deutsch, C. I. Bliss, and A. Eckstein, "Population, Sovereignty, and the Share of Foreign Trade" in *Economic Development and Cultural Change,* Vol. X, No. 4 (July 1962), pp. 353–366.

[9] Mainland China and India also have potentially vast domestic markets within their own borders, but because they are not yet developed—i.e., because these vast populations are for the most part simply too poor to buy the products the industrial countries produce—they are not very good markets.

[10] See n. *a* to Table 6.1 for sources of economic data.

those countries. While that argument may have some validity, there
are three factors to keep in mind: total foreign trade of the United
States accounts for, at most, 5 to 6 percent of Gross Domestic
Product; the figure of 29 percent represents both imports and
exports, and thus only about half represented the export of American products into underdeveloped markets; the 29 percent of total
American foreign trade that was with the weaker countries was
divided among approximately one hundred different countries!
Thus the loss of any one of those smaller markets for American
products could in no way be viewed as a serious loss to the American economy.

Unfortunately for the underdeveloped, weaker states of the
world, the brutal truth is that they are simply too poor to be very
good or very important customers of the industrial Powers. For
countries like Sierra Leone or Dahomey, with 45 percent and 68
percent of their 1967 total trade accounted for by trade with
Britain and France respectively, it must indeed appear that their
markets are very important to those European Powers. But for the
British in 1967, Sierra Leone accounted for only .2 percent of the
U.K.'s total foreign trade, while for France in that year, Dahomey
accounted for only .1 percent of total trade.

What "imperialists" and "anti-imperialists" both fail to recognize is that so long as the demand for raw materials is greater in
the developed than in the underdeveloped countries, the underdeveloped countries will continue to be suppliers of raw materials.
(Where else shall they sell what they produce?) What is more,
until underdeveloped countries can produce in large quantities the
finished products demanded by their own and other countries'
populations, they will continue to buy those few finished products
they can afford from the industrial centers that manufacture them.
Only when, and if, these countries develop economically will they
become important markets for the more developed industrial
Powers.

It is precisely because of this that it is in the interests of both
powerful industrial states and weak underdeveloped states to see
to it that the latter develop as quickly as possible. It is in the interests of the weaker countries to become developed not only in
order to survive domestically, but also in order to lessen their international economic dependence. It is in the interests of the more
powerful countries to have the weaker countries develop because
the more developed they become, the better customers of the Powers they will become.

There is here a mutuality of interest rare in international affairs.
It would be a pity if both weak and powerful countries did not take
advantage of that opportunity.

Colonialism and Economic Development

The third myth that must be exposed as false is that colonialism (political dependence) prevented the economic development of the underdeveloped countries. Prior to the beginning of European colonial activities, the economies of most of the non-European world were sustenance agricultural economies. Indeed, one could rightly point out that despite the commercial activities going on in many of the European cities at the time, the economies of most of the states of Europe itself were also predominantly sustenance economies. Consumption agriculture was the occupation of the overwhelming majority of the people. Depending on the system of land tenure that prevailed, the surplus product of the land may have been given as payment for use of the land, or as payment for seed or for some of the handicraft products the peasant did not himself produce, but for the most part the peasant produced what he consumed and consumed what he produced.

Despite as much as 450 years of European colonial contact in some cases, the economies of many regions in the world are still predominantly of this character. But to the degree that there has been change in the economic structure of the non-European world, that change has been in the direction of increasing the production of commercial products (of course, these are usually primary products) for sale and/or reprocessing in the European and North American markets. What is more, while one portion of the population of these countries—usually the larger portion—is still engaged in consumption agriculture, another portion—the portion that very often contributes most to the country's Gross Domestic Product— is engaged in either the production, extraction, or manufacture of products meant to service the commercial/industrial centers of their own countries and of others.

That European, North American, and later Japanese and Russian economic interests exploited the weaker countries for their own economic advantage, there can be no doubt. There was often a relatively high return on investment in these weaker countries that was not reinvested in the weaker country but was usually exported to the mentor country for investment there. Colonial economic activity generally contributed more to the economic growth of the mentor than it did to the economic growth of the dependency. But nationalistic slogans from the underdeveloped countries nothwithstanding, there is little empirical evidence that the economies of these countries would be in as strong a position as they are today if Europe, North America, and Japan had not had an industrial/ commercial revolution, and if these industrializing countries had not come into direct colonial contact with the weaker states. There is no evidence to show that the industrial revolution would have occurred sooner, if at all, in any of the states that did come under big Power domination if that contact had not occurred. Of all the states that were not dominated by a colonial Power (Japan, Thailand, Ethiopia, and most of Africa prior to the 1870's), only Japan experienced an industrial revolution divorced from European political and economic penetration.

The reality is that those areas that experienced the longest and/or most direct colonial control tend to be among the most developed of the associated states. Startling as it may seem, if one examines the level of economic development of the associated states, one finds that—with some notable exceptions—it is usually those countries, or portions of countries, with which the Europeans, Americans, and Japanese had the most prolonged and extensive economic contact that are now among the most developed economically.[11] The countries or portions of countries, that for the longest periods came under the "Formal-Direct" colonial control of the British, French, or Japanese, tend to be considerably more economically developed than those areas that were under "Formal-Indirect," or "Non-Formal-Indirect" political influence. (Recall that the Americans and Russians both preferred direct incorporation or "Non-Formal-Indirect" influence to traditional colonial control.) The variations in current level of economic development that exist within each of the former dependencies verify this. For example, the Straits Settlements in what used to be Malaya, the Southern Regions of Nigeria, the directly ruled portions of India (as compared to the indirectly ruled "Princely States"), the coastal regions of what used to be called French West Africa, all are considerably more developed economically than are the other portions of the same dependencies that came under less direct political control.

This is not a paradox, nor is it a mystery: in order to "exploit" these countries to the fullest, it was necessary to invest large sums of development capital in them.[12] Not only were extraction and production facilities needed, but it was necessary to invest in what the economist terms "social overhead capital"—roads, railroads, schools, hospitals, et cetera. It paid the colonial Powers to invest in these prerequisites for economic development precisely because

[11] Excluded from this discussion are the "settler" colonies—all of which are now among the most highly developed areas in the world—that became in many respects merely extensions of the metropole Power itself.

[12] "Large" is a relative term. Those investments were large in relation to the Gross Domestic Product of the countries in which they were made, but they were often modest in comparison to the investments being made at the same time in the more developed countries.

the products of these non-European countries were so profitable, and it is precisely because these investments were made that the industries proved even more profitable and exploitable than they had been previously. Thus, a cycle of development was started in many of the underdeveloped countries that, while in no way complete in most of them, has been quite successful in some. This development was not undertaken for any altruistic motivation, but rather to enhance the economic interests of those who had most to gain. That others may also have gained at the same time was merely a side effect of the drive for greater profits. But, once the roads were built to exploit the lumber, or rubber, or tea, or copper, they also served many other economic purposes, as well. Once schools were built to teach some of the indigenous population the language, skills, and values of the metropole so that the expense of importing clerks and foremen could be avoided, the skills and values of development were available for other purposes. While the schools were limited to the few, it was these educated few who led the economic and political revolutionary movements that eventually brought political independence and have spearheaded the drive for economic development.

For the overwhelming portion of the colonial period, "possessions" were regarded by the metropole as contributing to its own economic advantage. That there were always political consequences, and that in most cases political considerations ultimately took precedence over economic considerations, should not obscure the fact that the relationships started as economic ventures and continued to be perceived predominantly in terms of economic advantage for the metropole to the end. During this period, any investment made in the colonies was made in the hope of securing greater economic return. Later, relationships changed and colonies were perceived in the metropole as primarily a political advantage, large-scale economic investments were still made, but predominantly in those territories over which the mentor had greatest political control.

By no stretch of either imagination or imperial rhetoric, can the colonial Powers be said to have developed the weaker countries for the sake of those countries. There can be no doubt, however, that the countries and portions of countries controlled most directly and/or longest by the Powers did receive considerable economic advantages. And in this sphere as in others, wealth tends to generate more wealth. Those areas that were the inadvertent beneficiaries of most of the initial colonial investments have tended to attract still more investment. The roads, electricity, sanitation, health facilities, and European-educated middle class resulting from the colonial presence, even though less than what is needed

220 THE TIES THAT BIND

by these countries, is usually more than what exists in areas where there was not direct colonial control. It is precisely the existence of such "social overhead capital" that tends to attract investors, both domestic and foreign, to make still greater investments. And while large-scale industry and export-oriented commercial production often remain owned mainly by Europeans and North Americans, in some countries, and for some export products, production is often in the hands of indigenous, relatively small-scale producers (as with cocoa in Ghana, rubber in Ceylon, and copra in the Philippines), thus increasing their economic standing in the country and helping to create an indigenous middle class.

Economic Development as a Western Value

The final myth that must be dispelled is that economic development is part of the Western materialist value system and is being forced upon reluctant peoples who value other, nonmaterial aspects of life more highly. Economic development is indeed highly materialist—it implies the production of all sorts of material items from bicycles to color television to office buildings, as well as the heavy equipment with which to produce these products for consumption. But economic development implies more than just material things. It also implies the elimination of disease,[13] the elimination of illiteracy, an enormous increase in life expectancy, a dramatic decrease in infant mortality, a decrease in the disparity between the richest and the poorest in the society, and an increase in the rights and personal freedom of women and young people. No wonder there is a "revolution of rising expectations" going on all over the world. Increasingly, the poor and the miserable are discovering that poverty, disease, and early death (both for themselves and for their children) are not inherent and unchangeable, as they have always been taught in the past. For the first time, they are coming to know that economic development can mean a longer life and a "better" life for millions of people, and they want it now.

Notice who it is who are most vocal in their perpetuation of the myth that economic development is a Western importation that will destroy all that is good in traditional societies. One group consists of the children of the affluent in the Western countries who, having discovered that affluence and happiness are not synonymous, are disillusioned with economic progress and believe that lack of material possessions will somehow help people achieve a utopian state of happiness and self-fulfillment. These are the people

[13] Certainly not all disease has been eliminated in the developed societies, but the fact is that cholera, plague, leprosy, malaria, and many similar diseases—which annually take millions of lives—are found today only in the underdeveloped countries.

who extol the virtues of the "happy natives" unspoiled by Western civilization and the desire for material possessions: twentieth century Rousseaus and Gauguins. Indeed, the big difference between the Old Left and the New Left in the Western world seems to be that the Old Left sought to achieve universal happiness by creating and distributing as much material wealth as possible ("to each according to his needs" meant material well-being). Correctly recognizing that creating material things is not a desirable end in and of itself, the New Left then incorrectly assumes that it is altogether undesirable, and must be avoided.

The other groups that are most vocal in perpetuating this myth are the defenders of the old order—the indigenous, conservative religious leaders, the "male chauvinists," the traditional aristocracies and oligarchies—who have most to lose if economic development occurs. Along with economic development comes an awareness that change and a better life—however defined—are possible. Hence it is imperative that the beneficiaries of the status quo perpetuate the notion that change is bad.

Most of the people in the underdeveloped countries want to avoid as much disruption of their traditional cultures and value systems as possible while at the same time achieving rapid economic development. In many instances this simply may not be possible. Some of the old values may have to give way. But because these countries don't want to become replicas of the West, doesn't mean that they can't develop along lines consistent with their own cultures. Some of their traditional values can certainly be preserved. Somehow, indigenous leaders are going to have to find ways to introduce change—even rapid change—while still preserving what they find best in the old order. Certainly this is no mean task. Most of the more highly developed societies—East and West—have found that change, once initiated, tends to generate a momentum that can, and sometimes does, get out of hand until it becomes so rapid that it is called "future shock." [13a] But that is a problem for which all of the overdeveloped societies will have to try to find solutions. For ever-increasing masses of the population in the economically underdeveloped countries, the reality is that they want as many of the material and nonmaterial benefits of development as quickly as they can get them.

The Nature of Economic Dependence

Having disposed of some of the myths concerning the economic relationships between the weaker states and the Powers, it now

[13a] See Alvin Toffler, *Future Shock* (New York: Random House, 1970).

remains to explore what in reality constitutes economic dependence, and how economically dependent the weak states actually are. To some degree, of course, every country is economically dependent upon some other state or states. The crucial matters are the degree to which decision makers—both public and private—in one country are in a position to make decisions that crucially affect the economy of another country; and the degree of reciprocity of dependence involved in the relationship.

For example, West German trade with the United Kingdom accounted for 4 percent of total West German foreign trade in 1967. In that same year, British trade with West Germany accounted for 5 percent of total British trade. In both countries, foreign trade accounted for approximately the same percent of the Gross Domestic Product. If, upon investigation, we were to discover that approximately the same relationship has continued to the present, and also holds true with regard to foreign investment and other international economic indicators, we would have to conclude that economically the two countries are reciprocally, or mutually, dependent. Decisions made in Germany—like a decision to revalue its currency, or a decision to impose an exorbitant tax on the import of British automobiles, or a decision to cut the price of the Volkswagen by 25 percent—could have a profound effect on the British economy. Similar decisions made in Britain could have an equally profound effect on the German economy. While decision makers in both countries can be counted on to make decisions they perceive to be most advantageous to themselves (as do decision makers in all countries), because of this mutuality of dependence they must take into account the possible effects of any decision on the other country and the responses—advantageous or retaliatory—it might elicit.

On the other hand, the economic relationships of Britain and Sierra Leone and France and Dahomey cited earlier are examples of "one-way" economic dependence. No economic decision made in either of those African countries could have more than the most minor effect on the economies of Britain or France. In contrast, any relevant economic decision made in those European countries would have the most profound effect on the economies of those African states.

As far as I know, no exact index of the degree of economic dependence of the world's countries currently exists. If such an index were to be constructed, it would have to include for each country:

1. total foreign trade as a percentage of gross domestic product;

2. total trade with each country as a percentage of total foreign trade;

3. total foreign aid received (if any) as a percentage of gross domestic product;

4. total aid received from each country as a percentage of total foreign aid received;

5. total foreign investment as a percentage of gross domestic product;

6. foreign investment from each country as a percentage of total foreign investment;

7. international "strength" of domestic currency;

8. diversity of customers for major exports of each country;

9. diversity of products produced in each country;

10. number of markets available for major products of country;

11. world demand for major products of country.

The exact weighting of each of these factors is a matter for the economists to decide. The important point is that such an index would reveal the nature of the economic equation between particular countries. Both sides of the equation must be approximately the same for a situation of reciprocal dependence to occur. To the degree that they are not—that is, that one country relies more for trade, investment, aid, et cetera, on the other than the other relies on it—a situation of economic dependence exists.

Because of the nature of the unequal distribution of economic wealth in the world, almost all of the weaker states are extremely dependent economically upon the Powers—much more so than the Powers are upon them. In considering this dependence, however, it is crucial to make a distinction between the degree of economic dependence of one state upon another, and the degree of economic dependence of significant segments of the decision-making elite of a particular state upon another state.

In many of the underdeveloped countries prior to the grant of political independence, primary commercial production was solely or almost solely in the hands of foreigners. Often it still is.[14] Many of the secondary and tertiary industries necessary to service the primary commercial interests, however, were not considered profitable enough to be handled by foreigners, and these needs were often filled by indigenous people. But what may not have seemed profitable enough to warrant foreign investment was often extremely profitable by indigenous standards. In other cases, certain products were more profitably raised on small,

[14] For a good case study of the degree to which this was so in Malaya and Singapore, see James Puthucheary, *Ownership and Control in the Malayan Economy* (Singapore: Donald Moore, for Eastern Universities Press, 1960).

indigenous farms, and the Europeans were content to act as mid-
dlemen in buying the product of the smallholders and selling it
on the European and American markets. Thus, for various reasons, in many of the underdeveloped countries an indigenous
commercial elite grew up whose interests were often tied to
markets or customers outside their own countries, if not directly
to the interests of a foreign-owned primary industry in their own
country. Such elites often have a vested interest in seeing to it that
their best customers remain customers. Indeed, their identification
with their own economic interest may be so strong that if their economic identity and their national identity come into conflict they
may well support the former over the latter. More often, however,
they will use their influence as members of an indigenous elite to
get the decision makers in their countries to view their personal
economic interest as a national interest worthy of government
support.[15]

Since the interests of this indigenous commercial elite are often
tied to the interests of the mentor Power, they sometimes exercise considerable influence to maintain the best of relations
with the mentor state. Even where the indigenous elite has bought
out the formerly foreign-owned economic interests, they are still
tied to the mentor state for processing, markets, et cetera. The
Ashanti cocoa farmer and the Ceylonese tea or coconut plan-
tation owner are as attuned to commodity price quotations on the
London exchange as any British entrepreneur raising the same
crops. Since these products are not as scarce or as profitable as
they once were, it is particularly important that their own countrymen do nothing that will make competition more difficult. Thus,
the indigenous owner may prove to be even more uncompro-
mising in negotiations with his country's labor union officials or
governmental decision-making elites than his foreign predecessor
was. And, because of family connections in other segments of the
elite, it is often easier for the indigenous owner to influence governmental decisions in ways favorable to his industry than it was
for his foreign predecessor, at least in the last generation or two
before political independence.

Consider two states, both equally dependent economically upon
a third (in terms of percent of G.D.P. accounted for by trade with
the third). If, in the first state, significant segments of the decision-
making elite happen to be personally tied to the foreign trade
sector of the economy, the likelihood is that national economic

[15] For a fascinating case study of how this was done in a specific instance
in the Philippines, see N. O. Berry, "Representation and Decision-Making:
A Case Study of Philippine—American War Claims," Ph.D. dissertation,
University of Pittsburgh, Pittsburgh, Pa., 1967.

decisions will tend to preserve and expand the foreign economic arrangements that already exist. If, in the second case, the decision-making elite is not personally tied to the foreign trade sector of the economy (as many of the military and ideological elites in the newer countries are not), their perceptions about national economic interest must be expected to be considerably different from the perceptions of an elite whose own personal fortune may be affected. Indeed, in the second case the foreign trade elite of the country may be viewed by the governmental decision-making elite as their competitors and as a potential threat to the enforcement of their definitions of national interest. To strengthen their own domestic power position, it is entirely possible that the governmental decision-making elite would attempt to enter into new economic arrangements that might help to weaken the foreign trade elite domestically. If the country itself is heavily dependent economically on a mentor Power, however, any decisions that might adversely affect that economic relationship will probably receive a great deal of considered judgment, regardless of the personal ties of the elite. No government, whatever the personal source of wealth of its decision makers, can lightly make decisions that might wreck the economy. The examples of Mossadegh and Nkrumah stand as glaring reminders of the consequences of such action.[16]

This is not to say that ruling elites may not change the economic trade patterns that have traditionally prevailed. Indeed, they may and they have. But those countries that have been economically most dependent on one product or one mentor have never done so successfully unless another Power was willing to play the role of economic benefactor. And they are much less likely to contemplate any change whatever if significant segments of their group are personally involved in the existing foreign trade patterns.

To move from the hypothetical to the actual, consider the case of Cuba between 1958 and 1963. In 1958 approximately 40.2 percent of Cuba's Gross Domestic Product was derived from trade with the United States. While exact figures are, of course, impos-

[16] I do not mean to imply that Mossadegh and Nkrumah were overthrown just because of the economic crises their countries faced. We now know that the American C.I.A. helped overturn Mossadegh, and there is strong evidence that other than purely economic considerations caused the overthrow of Nkrumah. But in both cases national leaders who were once exceedingly popular were able to be toppled with only the slightest push. It seems to me that in both cases this was so because the economies had deteriorated so badly that significant segments of the elite were feeling the economic "pinch" and agreed to work with the opposition to alleviate the situation.

sible to obtain, all objective information seems to indicate that very considerable segments of the elite surrounding Batista were profiting personally and directly from the economic relationship that prevailed between the two countries. In January of 1959, power was seized by Fidel Castro. The people most closely associated with his revolution, and the ones who ultimately occupied the decision-making positions, were in no way personally profiting, either directly or indirectly, from the trade with the United States. The share of Cuban G.D.P. accounted for by trade with the United States did not markedly change in the first months of the revolution, but the elite making the definitions of national interest did. For perhaps two years Castro and his new elite tried altering the traditional economic relationships between Cuba and the United States in order to pursue their definition of national interest—that is, the social revolution they envisioned for their country. Ultimately, they found that they could do so only at the cost of Cuba's United States sugar quota. Yet they were able to pursue these policies anyway because the Soviet Union was ready to step in and buy Cuba's sugar (whether it "needed it" or not).

While the case of Cuba, among others, proves that a sudden switch away from a traditional economic mentor is possible for a weak state, the costs to that state can be, and usually are, enormous. It may mean an almost total disruption of the economy, yet bring no real lessening of economic dependence. The country may merely become dependent upon a different mentor state. By 1963, more than 23 percent of Cuba's G.D.P. was accounted for by trade with the Soviet Bloc. Revolution by counter-elites, not personally tied to the foreign trade sector of the economy, is always possible, but upon coming to power the new decision makers will be forced to recognize that they may not be eliminating their country's economic dependence on a foreign Power by removing those elites that had personal interests in the traditional trade relationships. Rather they may simply be changing mentors. If a significant proportion of their country's G.D.P. is accounted for by trade with a foreign Power, they must be considerably more hesitant to do anything that might disrupt the traditional patterns of trade than they would be if that trade accounted for only an insignificant portion of G.D.P.

The likelihood, of course, is that the more any country economically depends upon another, the more the decision-making elite will also depend upon that trade for maintenance of its own personal economic interest. It is simply a reality of life that in almost every country of the world the decision-making elite tends to be recruited from (or closely related to) the country's major economic interest groups. And if a large share of the G.D.P. is derived by trade with one particular country, there is a very strong likelihood that the decision-making elite in the dependent country will in some way be economically bound to that foreign country.

In short, foreign economic contact with the underdeveloped countries has created a number of economic ties that both predate and postdate foreign political ties (and this is exclusive of those ties, like economic aid, that are primarily political in intent). This is especially true when the economic well-being of the society is based on one product or on investments from one source. When a very high percentage of a country's Gross Domestic Product is based on one commodity produced for a foreign market by perhaps one or two foreign-owned corporations—as in the oil industry in the Middle East, or the fruit produce business in Central America—those foreign firms are likely to have a major say in at least those political decisions they perceive as affecting their own economic interests. Unless the indigenous decision makers are prepared to undertake economic privation, at best, or economic suicide, at worst, they are very likely to accede to the definition of national interest imposed by the foreign firms.

Where the foreign firms or foreign markets are less important to the economic well-being of the state, the indigenous decision makers may, of course, have more leeway for maneuvering and bargaining. More than anything else, this helps to explain the strong desire on the part of many governmental elites to encourage diversification of both markets and products. It also helps to explain the pressure in many of these countries, particularly from the aware and often nationalistic segments of the indigenous population that are not part of either the governmental or business elites, to expropriate the foreign business firms.

To the degree that the interests of the governing elite are tied to foreign commercial interests—whether by interlocking elites or interlocking personal economic interests—there is less likely to be resentment and/or resistance on the part of the government to definitions of national interest made by the foreign business elite. Sophisticated foreign businessmen know this only too well and make a concerted effort to tie the personal economic interests of the indigenous decision makers to their firms' economic well-being. This has proved an extremely effective device throughout the world for encouraging favorable perceptions on the part of governmental elites. But it often has an adverse corollary effect: the economic interests of the governing elite sometimes become so tied to the foreign interests that antigovernmental movements within the country become dedicated to the overthrow not only of the government but also of the foreign economic interests. Indeed, nationalism is such a potent force in the second half of the twentieth century that antigovernmental movements find it advantageous to harness this sentiment by accusing the government of being antinational in their involvement with the foreign economic interest. Since almost every government finds that, for very pragmatic reasons, it must come to some kind of terms with foreign economic interests, almost every government is subject in greater or lesser degree to this accusation. Thus, there is hardly a nonelite antigovernmental movement in the world that is not also opposed to the influence of the foreign economic interests.[17] And this automatically involves foreign economic interests in the domestic politics of the host countries.

Foreign firms often become even more involved in the host's domestic politics when, and if, they are convinced by the indigenous decision makers that unless they actively support the government in its struggle with the opposition, the opposition might win and would then certainly take actions detrimental to the interests of the foreign firms. Faced with this prospect it is a rare, highly sophisticated, and uninvolved foreign business elite that would not come to the aid of their associates, friends, and, often, protectors. These are the "reasonable men" with whom the foreign firms have often spent years doing business. It would be almost unthinkable to desert them at the very time that their presence in office assures the foreign interests of continued opportunity in the country. Indeed, it is precisely because these foreign economic interests view the governmental decision makers with whom they had done business as the most "reasonable" group in the country, and because they view the antigovernmental movements as so hostile to their own economic interests (and by implication to the *political interests* of their own country) that they often seek to convince their home government that it has no choice but to support these reasonable decision makers. This message is often reinforced "independently" by the political representatives of the Power, who can honestly report that the antigovernmental movement is visibly and vociferously hostile to the Power's economic and, by implication, political interests. A vicious cycle is set in motion in which the mentor state comes to the aid of the "friendly" governmental elite in the weaker state,

[17] Most of the counterelite antigovernmental movements, such as the military or landowning counterelite movements typical of Latin America, do not wish to throw out the foreign economic interests, but rather wish for a share for themselves. For a very perceptive analysis of this, see Merle Kling, "Toward a Theory of Power and Political Instability in Latin America," in J. Kautsky, ed., *Political Change in Underdeveloped Countries: Nationalism and Communism* (New York: John Wiley & Sons, 1962).

thus confirming the worst suspicions of the leaders of the anti-governmental movement and reinforcing their own antiforeign, nationalist sentiment, which in turn reinforces and confirms the foreign elite's belief that the antigovernmental movement is anti-foreign. It is precisely this phenomenon that most often leads the major Powers to actively support the friendly governmental decision makers wherever they are in power, regardless of how broad a base of support they may command within their own countries. It is almost inevitable that the major Powers—and this includes the Soviet Union as well as Britain, France, Japan, and the United States—will support those governments that are friendly to their own economic interests abroad. It would take a high degree of long-range planning and of sophistication to do otherwise. And yet, it is precisely because the major Powers tend to support the economic status quo—wherever the status quo favors them—that indigenous antigovernmental movements are almost invariably against the mentor Power as well.

The Extent of the Weak States' Economic Dependence

Foreign Trade

What has come to be known as colonialism started out primarily as commercial ventures of private corporations looking for profit. The desire to spread Catholicism was one of the professed purposes of early Portuguese and Spanish colonial ventures, but this may have been something of an afterthought to placate ambivalent or antagonistic domestic forces. Regardless of the reasons given to support these early expeditions, there was little doubt at the time that their prime motive was profit; indeed, it was often to insure those profits that first private, and later public armies were sent to the areas in which the major European commercial interests were "doing business." Great private firms such as the British East India Company, the Dutch East India Company, and the French West India Company were chartered specifically to go beyond Europe's shores to mobilize both the products and the markets on which the wealth of European industry—and thus the power of Europe itself —was thought to rest. If in the course of their economic operations it became necessary for those giant companies to intervene polit-ically and militarily in the affairs of the areas in which they did business in order to maximize their profits, so be it. They had the full approval and support of the European governments. Ultimately, of course, these private trading corporations became so rich and so powerful that their home governments took over many of their functions, but there can be no doubt that modern colonialism started as primarily an economic, not a political, phenomenon.[18]

Since the profit motive was the driving force behind colonialism, even when the weaker countries were the political "possessions" of the metropole, rarely, if ever, was their foreign trade exclusively with the metropole Power. If higher profits could be had by trading with other countries, such trade usually took place—whether it was considered legal or not. But the lesson taught by the British loss of the American colonies (in no small measure because of British attempts to make the colonies trade exclusively or excessively with the metropole) was not lost on most colonial Powers, and although certain restrictions against trading with other countries persisted, and incentives for trade with the metropole were offered, other trade did exist, and was often very extensive.

While it is true that most (but not all) former colonies were better customers of the metropole before independence than they have been since, at least in the case of Britain and France this can be attributed as much to the decline of their "attractive" power (relative to the growth of competing Power centers) as it can to the grant of political independence. Grover Clark, in an unsophisticated, but intriguing statistical analysis of the colonial relationship to trade, originally published in 1936, reports that: "Britain's share of the trade of the overseas countries under the British flag was 49% in 1854–1863, 47% in 1894–1903, 42% in 1913, 36% in 1929–1933 and 39% in 1934." [19] Since that time Britain's share of trade with those same countries has continued to decline to approximately 38 percent in 1938, 30 percent in 1958, 25 percent in 1963 and 23 percent in 1967.[20] Contrary to Clark's contention that Britain's share of trade with the Dominions was on the increase, on the basis of more recent evidence it would appear that Britain's share in their trade has declined as much or more than it has with the weaker, more newly independent countries. In 1938, 66.3 percent of New Zealand's total trade, 48.1 percent of Australia's, and 30.2 percent of Canada's was with the United Kingdom. By 1967, the figures had dropped to 39.1 percent, 17.6 percent, and 8.2 percent respectively—despite the fact that the dollar value of the trade of both Australia and New Zealand with Britain had more than doubled, while that of Canada had increased more than three-

[18] See, among others, Stewart C. Easton, *The Rise and Fall of Western Colonialism* (New York: Frederick A. Praeger, 1964).

[19] Grover Clark, *The Balance Sheets of Imperialism: Facts and Figures on Colonies* (New York: Russell & Russell, reprinted in 1967), p. 78.

[20] See note *a* to Table 6.1 for sources of economic data.

fold. Similarly, Nigeria's trade with the United Kingdom dropped during the same period from 66 percent to 29.1 percent, while the dollar value increased more than four and a half times. In part, the explanation undoubtedly lies in the inflation not accounted for by the figures. Much more, however, the explanation rests on the fact that despite the enormous growth of the value of their trade with the United Kingdom, their trade with other countries has grown even faster. Recall the discussion above about the tendency for expanding economies to diversify their trading partners. That is exactly what has happened with the countries under consideration here. As their economies have grown, so has their trade with the United Kingdom in absolute terms, but relative to their total trade the British share has shrunk, and shrunk drastically in many cases.

Table 6.1 is a comparison of the trading relationships between the Powers and their associated states in 1938 and 1967. One of the advantages of calculating the trade figures as percentages of total trade is that the figures are thus relatively unaffected by inflation, devaluation, et cetera. The Absolute Percentage Change column tells how much trade has declined or increased over the thirty-year period, while the Relative Percentage Change column tells how much it had changed relative to what it was in 1938. Thus, for example, while Britain's share of Iraq's total foreign trade declined by only 13.8 percent, from 21.6 percent to 7.8 percent, this represents a *relative* decline of 63.9 percent. Similarly, because Bulgarian trade with the U.S.S.R. in 1938 was so minuscule (0.1 percent of total foreign trade), and because it was so high in 1967 (51.3 percent), the *relative* percentage change is astronomical.

Note that of the thirty-five U.K. associated states on which there is comparative data, thirty-one (89 percent) experienced a relative decline in trade with Britain; and French trade with twenty out of twenty-six (77 percent) of its associated states declined. Not only has British and French trade fallen off with proportionately more of their associated states than has the trade of the other Powers with theirs, but Britain in particular has experienced a greater decline in percentages of trade than the other Powers. In 1938 Britain accounted for at least one-third of the total foreign trade of twenty of the thirty-five countries on which we have data, and for six countries the U.K. accounted for approximately two-thirds of the weaker country's foreign trade. By 1967, however, Britain accounted for two-thirds of the foreign trade of no country (Ireland comes closest, but doesn't quite make it), and accounted for one-third or more of the foreign trade of only seven countries. France, in 1938, accounted for at least one-third of the total foreign trade of nineteen of its twenty-six associ-

TABLE 6.1
Trade with Major Powers as a Percent of Total Foreign Trade, 1938 and 1967[a]
(Grouped by Historical Association[b] and Ranked in Descending Order of 1967 Trade Figures)

Country[c]	1938	1967	Absolute Change[d] (in Percent)	Relative Change[e] (in Percent)
Trade of Associated States With United Kingdom				
Ireland	66.0	59.5	− 6.5	− 9.8
Malta	28.9	45.7	+16.8	+58.1
Sierra Leone	61.1	45.0	−16.1	−26.4
Barbados	43.1	40.6	− 2.5	− 5.8
New Zealand	66.3	39.1	−27.2	−41.0
Malawi	70.4	38.8	−31.6	−44.9
Cyprus	28.1	34.5	+ 6.4	+22.8
Zambia	40.3	31.4	− 8.9	−22.1
Kenya [f]	36.8	29.9	− 6.9	−18.8
Tanzania	30.2	29.5	− 0.7	− 2.3
Ghana	63.8	29.2	−34.6	−54.2
Nigeria	66.3	29.1	−37.2	−56.1
South Africa	40.9	27.7	−13.2	−32.3
Uganda [f]	36.8	27.7	− 9.1	−24.7
Guyana	37.9	23.1	−14.8	−39.1
Jamaica	43.7	22.7	−21.0	−48.1
Ceylon	36.6	22.2	−14.4	−39.3
Iran	21.1	18.7	− 2.4	−11.4
Australia	48.1	17.6	−30.5	−63.4
Israel	23.6	16.5	− 7.1	−30.1
Singapore [g]	16.2	15.5	− 0.7	− 4.3
Sudan	35.3	15.1	−20.2	−57.2
Trinidad & Tobago	43.3	13.6	−29.7	−68.6
Pakistan [h]	32.9	12.7	−20.2	−61.4
India [h]	32.9	12.4	−20.5	−62.3
Malaysia [g]	16.2	11.9	− 4.3	−26.5
Jordan	30.0	10.3	−19.7	−65.7
Burma	15.3	9.6	− 5.7	−37.3
Saudi Arabia	3.3	8.9	+ 5.6	+169.7
Canada	30.2	8.2	−22.0	−72.8
Iraq	21.6	7.8	−13.8	−63.9
United States of America	12.6	6.3	− 6.3	−50.0
China (Mainland)	16.5	4.3 [i]	−12.2	−73.9
United Arab Republic	27.5	3.4	−24.1	−87.6
Rhodesia	58.3	2.6	−55.7	−95.5

TABLE 6.1 (Cont'd.)

Country[e]	1938	1967	Absolute Change[d] (in Percent)	Relative Change[e] (in Percent)
Trade of Associated States With France				
Algeria	79.3	66.3	−13.0	−16.4
Senegal[j]	68.2	59.1	− 9.1	−13.3
Niger[j]	68.2	55.9	−12.3	−18.0
Malagasy	77.3	53.0	−24.3	−31.4
Central African Rep.[k]	50.6	52.9	+ 2.3	+ 4.5
Cameroon	42.1	51.0	+ 8.9	+21.1
Chad[k]	50.6	49.6	− 1.0	− 2.0
Dahomey[j]	68.2	49.1	−19.1	−28.0
Ivory Coast[j]	68.2	45.2	−23.0	−33.7
Gabon[k]	50.6	44.6	− 6.0	−11.9
Upper Volta[j]	68.2	39.6	−28.6	−41.9
Morocco	38.1	39.2	+ 1.1	+ 2.9
Congo (Brazzaville)[k]	50.6	39.1	−11.5	−22.7
Tunisia	59.1	30.4	−28.7	−48.6
Mauritania[j]	68.2	29.2	−39.0	−57.2
Mali[j]	68.2	24.7	−43.5	−63.8
Cambodia[l]	49.5	22.0	−27.5	−55.6
Guinea[j]	68.2	17.0	−51.2	−75.1
Belgium	8.2	16.3[n]	+ 8.1	+98.8
Lebanon[m]	14.2	9.1	− 5.1	−35.9
Laos[l]	49.5	9.0	−40.5	−81.8
Haiti	6.9	8.0	+ 1.1	+15.9
Syria[m]	14.2	7.5	− 6.7	−47.2
Vietnam (South)[l]	49.5	4.3	−45.2	−91.3
United Arab Republic	6.6	3.7	− 2.9	−43.9
Canada	1.0	1.0	0	0
Trade of Associated States With U.S.				
Dominican Republic	42.6	70.1	+27.5	+64.6
Canada	45.5	68.4	+22.9	+50.3
Mexico	57.0	59.6	+ 2.6	+ 4.6
Haiti	48.6	58.5	+ 9.9	+20.4
Panama	62.9	50.1	−12.8	−20.3
Honduras	72.8	46.0	−26.8	−36.8
Colombia	51.3	44.4	− 6.9	−13.5
Ecuador	36.3	43.2	+ 6.9	+19.0
Costa Rica	47.1	42.8	− 4.3	− 9.1
Bolivia	13.6	40.1	+26.5	+194.9
Peru	30.0	39.5	+ 9.5	+31.7
Venezuela	28.2	38.8	+10.6	+37.6
Philippines	75.9	37.9	−38.0	−50.1
Guatemala	56.7	36.5	−20.2	−35.6
Nicaragua	63.3	36.4	−26.9	−42.5

TABLE 6.1 (Cont'd.)

Country[c]	1938	1967	Absolute Change[d] (in Percent)	Relative Change[e] (in Percent)
Trade of Associated States With U.S. (cont'd)				
Brazil	29.2	33.7	+ 4.5	+15.4
Vietnam (South)[l]	7.3	31.5	+24.2	+331.5
El Salvador	54.5	29.0	−25.5	−46.8
Japan	25.0	28.3	+ 3.3	+13.2
Chile	20.8	27.7	+ 6.9	+33.2
Paraguay	10.4	22.0	+11.6	+111.5
Argentina	15.3	14.3	− 1.0	− 6.5
Liberia	40.4	12.4	−28.0	−69.3
Uruguay	7.8	10.7	+ 2.9	+37.2
Cuba	73.9	2.5[o]	−71.4	−96.6
Trade of Associated States With Soviet Union				
Bulgaria	0.1	51.3	+51.2	+51,200.0[p]
Germany (East)[q]	3.7	42.0	+38.3	+ 1,035.1[p]
Poland	1.9	35.3	+34.2	+ 1,800.0[p]
Czechoslovakia	6.8	35.1	+28.3	+ 416.2[p]
Hungary	0.1	34.7	+34.6	+34,600.0[p]
Rumania	0.1	28.2	+28.1	+28,100.0[p]
Finland	4.3	16.5	+12.2	+ 283.7[p]
Yugoslavia	0.1	12.9	+12.8	+12,800.0[p]
China (Mainland)	0.3[r]	11.8[i]	+11.5	+ 3,833.3[p]
Iran	77.4	1.9	−75.5	− 97.5
Trade of Associated States With Japan				
Korea (South)[s]	84.6	40.1	−44.3	− 52.5
China (Taiwan)	90.9	30.6	−60.3	−66.3
Philippines	8.1	30.4	+22.3	+275.3
Thailand	6.8	30.4	+23.6	+347.1
Vietnam (South)[l]	3.0	25.6	+22.6	+753.3
Indonesia	8.2	24.6	+16.4	+200.0
Malaysia[g]	5.8	23.4	+17.6	+303.4
Singapore[g]	5.8	21.0	+15.2	+262.1
China (Mainland)	45.5	13.8[i]	−31.7	−69.7
Laos[l]	3.0	11.7	+ 8.7	+290.0
Burma	3.3	8.8	+ 5.5	+166.7
Cambodia[l]	3.0	8.7	+ 5.7	+190.0

TABLE 6.1 (Cont'd.)

ᵃ Data for this table were compiled for the author by Steven Schecter and Cecil Ee. All data, unless otherwise noted, are for 1938 and 1967 and are taken from the following sources: United Nations Statistical Office, *Yearbooks of International Trade Statistics* (New York: U.N., 1953, 1958, 1964, 1966, 1967); International Monetary Fund and International Bank for Reconstruction and Development, *Direction of Trade Annual, 1960–1964* (Washington, D.C.: I.M.F. and I.B.R.D., 1965); International Monetary Fund and International Bank for Reconstruction and Development, *Direction of Trade Annual, 1963–1967* (Washington, D.C.: I.M.F. and I.B.R.D., 1968); *The Statesman's Yearbook*, 1938, 1949, 1953, 1968–69; Board of Trade, *Statistical Abstract for the British Commonwealth for each of the ten years 1936 to 1945* (London: H.M. Stationery Office, 1947).

ᵇ See Table 4.1 for a complete breakdown of which states were considered to have been historically associated with which Powers. Table 6.1 includes all of these states for which data could be found for both 1938 and 1967. Some countries appear more than once on this table because at different times they were associated with different Powers.

ᶜ Some countries that are now independent entities were a single unit in 1938 (such as India and Pakistan). Since it would be nearly impossible to determine the percentage of trade that came from each of the constituent parts, we have used the same figure for each of the parts as was listed for the whole. That is, in a case like prepartition India, where 32.9% of its 1938 trade was with the United Kingdom, we have artificially listed the 1938 percentage for *both* India and Pakistan as 32.9%. In many cases, this is an erroneous assumption, but for want of a better measuring instrument this procedure has been adopted throughout this table. In order to call the reader's attention to the questionable validity of those 1938 figures, the cases in which this procedure was adopted are footnoted.

ᵈ Absolute percentage change is the difference between the 1938 and 1967 figures.

ᵉ Relative percentage change equals the absolute percentage change, divided by the total 1938 percentages. Using this figure it is possible to ascertain something of the degree of importance of the change in trade to the country involved. The idea of expressing the changes in these relative terms comes from Paul London, "Ties Among Nations: A Case Study of Britain and Her Ex-dependencies," M.P.I.A. thesis, University of Pittsburgh, Pittsburgh, Pa., 1968.

ᶠ 1938 figures for Kenya and Uganda are for the joint entity.

ᵍ 1938 figures for Singapore and Malaysia are for the joint entity.

ʰ 1938 figures for India and Pakistan are for the joint entity.

ⁱ 1967 figures for China (Mainland) were not available; data shown are for 1965.

ʲ 1938 figures are for French West Africa, which included what are now Senegal, Niger, Dahomey, Ivory Coast, Upper Volta, Mauritania, Mali, and Guinea.

ᵏ 1938 figures are for French Equatorial Africa, which included what are now Central African Republic, Chad, Gabon, and Congo (Brazzaville).

ˡ 1938 figures are for Indochina, which included what are now Cambodia, Laos, and both North and South Vietnam.

ᵐ 1938 figures for Lebanon and Syria are for the joint entity.

ⁿ Belgium and Luxembourg are listed jointly in the data source for 1967, and thus the figure for Belgium alone should be somewhat lower than that shown here.

ᵒ Data are for 1963.

TABLE 6.1 (Cont'd.)

[p] The magnitude of the relative percentage change of trade for states associated with the Soviet Union deserves some comment. By 1938 the German economic offensive in Eastern Europe was well under way; as a result many of these countries' trade with the Soviet Union was so miniscule that even small absolute increases in trade by 1967 make for an astronomical relative increase. However, the 1938 figures are so low as to raise some suspicion about their accuracy, and the reader is warned to treat these figures with even more caution than the rest.

[q] 1938 figure is for all of Germany.

[r] Figure is for 1937.

[s] 1938 figure is for all of Korea.

ated states and for two-thirds of the trade of ten. By 1967 France still accounted for one-third or more of the foreign trade of thirteen countries and for approximately two-thirds of the trade with Algeria. While both Britain and France have experienced an increase of trade with a few associated states, relative to the number with which trade has declined the number of increases is insignificant. Still, the trade of Britain and France with their associated states should not be underrated. Britain in 1967 was the major foreign trading partner for only fourteen countries of the world, but all of them—without exception—were weaker associated states.[21] Similarly, in 1967 France was the major trading partner for only fifteen countries, but every one of them also was an associated state.

For the U.S., the U.S.S.R., and Japan, whose relative power has been on the rise since 1938, the picture is quite different of course. While it is true that each has experienced a decline in trade with at least some of its associated states, each has experienced an increase of trade with still more. U.S. trade with the Philippines and Japanese trade with Taiwan, China (Mainland), and Korea have declined sharply, for example, but note the increase of trade with countries that were not under "Formal-Direct" rule. U.S. trade with its associated states has declined in eleven cases, but it has increased in fourteen. Japanese trade declined with the three associated states it ruled directly, but increased with nine others. Soviet trade declined only in one case and increased astronomically in the seven other cases on which we have data. Even more important in some respects than the increase in trade of the newer Powers with their own associated states, is the increase in their trade with the associated states of the older Powers.

Observe that "Formal" political control does not seem to have been a prerequisite at all for economic trade domination. In 1938 neither Cuba, El Salvador, Nicaragua, Honduras, Guatemala, Panama, Colombia, nor Mexico were "Formal" ("Direct" or "In-

[21] See Table 6.2.

direct") associated states of the United States, yet each of them had more (and often considerably more) than 50 percent of their total foreign trade with the United States. Conversely, in that same year what are now Trinadad and Tobago, Jordan, India, Pakistan, Sudan, Jamaica, Ceylon, Guyana, Burma, Israel, Malaysia, Uganda, Zambia, Kenya, Singapore, Tanzania, Barbados, Cyprus, and Malta—all of which were at the time "Formal" associated states of Britain ("Direct" and "Indirect")—had less (and often considerably less) than 50 percent of their trade with what was then the metropole. In short, legal relationships aside, what this means in real economic (and, by implication, political) terms is that these Central American countries were far more dependent upon the United States, than the British "Formal" dependencies were upon Britain.

While Table 6.1 indicates the relative degree to which the Powers' foreign trade with their associated states has changed over a thirty-year period, it does not tell where that trade has gone. Further, the figures for trade as a percentage of total trade indicate who a country's major trading partners are, but they do not tell how important foreign trade is to the total economy of a given country. In order to determine those significant facts, Table 6.2 has been constructed. That table lists the trade of 116 countries for which both trade data and projections of 1967 Gross Domestic Product were available.[22] Total foreign trade with each of the major Powers, plus the European Economic Community, the Soviet Bloc, and the country's own region (Inter-Regional), has been listed as a percent of each country's G.D.P. The final column is the approximate percentage of Gross Domestic Product accounted for by the total of trade with these major Powers. While economic data are often less crude than other types that have been used in this work, these data are nonetheless still crude, and this table should be taken to indicate nothing more precise than orders of magnitude. (It was not possible to consider trade as a percent of G.D.P. on Table 6.1 because estimates of a country's G.D.P. for 1938 are so crude as to be nearly meaningless.[23]

[22] In some cases 1967 trade data and G.D.P. projections were not available and 1963 trade figures and G.D.P. projections were used instead. Wherever those earlier figures were used in the table, they have been so indicated by a footnote.

[23] We can place considerably more reliance on the relative accuracy of G.D.P. figures for 1958, 1963, and 1967, but even here some of the figures (particularly for the less developed countries) represent little more than guesses.

In order to determine the general statistical relationships between trade with the Powers as a percentage of total trade and trade with the Powers as a percentage of a country's G.D.P., a Spearman test of rank-order corre-

Table 6.2 establishes the degree to which the weaker states are dependent upon foreign trade for their economic prosperity. While there are no generally agreed upon cut-off points above or below which a country could be said to be "dependent" or not, it does not seem unreasonable to argue that if more than 20 percent of the G.D.P. of any country is accounted for by foreign trade (as was the case in more than two-thirds of all the countries in the world in 1967), at least the monetized sector of that country's economy can be considered dependent on foreign trade. Further, if more than one-third of that country's total trade is with just one Power (as was the case in more than one-third of the countries listed in Table 6.1), then clearly any decisions—public or private—made in the more powerful country that relate to the foreign trade of the weaker could have a profound effect on the economic well-being of the weaker; and thus the weaker could legitimately be considered economically dependent upon the stronger. Only the U.S. and the U.S.S.R. have less than 10 percent of their G.D.P. accounted for by foreign trade and hence are relatively invulnerable to outside foreign trade decisions. Interestingly, for almost one-third of the world's countries, total foreign trade accounts for between 10 and 20 percent of G.D.P. Some of these are among the most developed economically (like the U.K. and Japan) and some are among the most underdeveloped (like Yemen and Rwanda). It is a generalization that seems to hold with remarkable consistency that the more economically developed the country, the less likely it is to be dependent upon one major trading partner, regardless of what percent of G.D.P. is accounted for by foreign trade. On the other hand, some of the most underdeveloped countries are so little involved in production for world markets that foreign trade would appear to have little impact upon them one way or another.

If a country is economically dependent when 20 percent of its G.D.P. is accounted for by the total of its foreign trade, consider

lation coefficient was run, which showed a +.835 correlation coefficient between the two ranked sets of figures for the U.K. Associated States with n = 32. Now since a correlation of .478 for n = 30 is considered statistically significant at the .01 level of significance—which means, simply, that the likelihood of the two ranked sets of numbers correlating that highly merely by chance alone is one-in-one-hundred—the correlation we obtained means that the rankings being compared were extremely similar (if they were identical, the correlation coefficient would be +1). Interestingly enough, the similarity of rankings between trade as a percentage of total trade and trade as a percentage of G.D.P. were highest for the United Kingdom and its associated states. The French and Russian associated states also correlated considerably higher than would be expected at the .01 level of significance. Only the United States associated states correlated at the .05 level.

how dependent a country is when more than 20 percent of its
G.D.P. is accounted for by trade with *just one Power*. Yet almost
one-third of the countries listed in Table 6.2 are at least that dependent economically. All things are relative, to be sure. A country
like Gambia, which derives 53 percent of its Gross Domestic Product from trade with Britain alone, is certainly more dependent
economically than is a country like the Dominican Republic, whose
highest trade percentage of G.D.P. is 18 percent, with the United
States. But any state that derives even 10 percent of its Gross Domestic Product from trade with one country is tied to that Power.
If still another 10 percent or more of its Gross Domestic Product is
accounted for by trade with a different Power, that indicates the
degree to which the country is dependent upon foreign trade as
such, but it also indicates that the second country may be somewhat
less dependent economically upon each Power than it would be
if it were trading substantially only with one. As already noted, the
greater the diversity of trading partners, the less the dependence
upon one.

If Table 6.1 indicated the degree to which Britain's economic
power had declined in the thirty years between 1938 and 1967,
Table 6.2 indicates which other Power centers have emerged as being of equal or more economic importance to Britain's associated
states. By 1967, trade with the United States and the European
Economic Community accounted for a higher percentage of the
Gross Domestic Product of fourteen United Kingdom associated
states than did trade with Britain. In addition, trade with the Soviet
Bloc countries was higher for one U.K. associated state (Iraq),
trade with Japan was higher for another (Malaysia) and Inter-
Regional trade accounted for a higher percentage of G.D.P. for
five others. Thus twenty-one of the thirty-five U.K. associated states
on which data were available in 1967 (60 percent) were economically *more* dependent upon trade with other Power centers
than upon trade with the United Kingdom. What is more, in some
cases (such as the U.A.R., Yemen, India, and Saudi Arabia) the
U.K. ranked fourth in economic importance to each of those countries in 1967.

In 1960, in an effort to counter the economic pull of the E.E.C.,
Britain joined with Denmark, Norway, Sweden, Portugal, Switzerland, and Austria in an economic association called the European
Free Trade Association (E.F.T.A.)—commonly known as the
"Outer Seven." Finland became an associate member in March of
1961. While these countries have not been historically "associated"
with Britain in the same way that that term has been applied to
other states throughout this work, still they are weaker states now
economically associated with Britain and it is useful to include

TABLE 6.2

Trade[a] *with Major Powers as a Percent of Gross Domestic Product,*[b] *1967*[c]
(Grouped by Historical Association[d] and Ranked Within Group)

Country	Percent of G.D.P. Accounted For by Total Trade With:								Approximate Percent of G.D.P. Accounted For by Trade with all Major Powers[b]
	U.S.A.	U.K.	E.E.C.[e]	France	Soviet Bloc[f]	U.S.S.R.	Japan	Inter-Regional[g]	
United States and Associated States									
U.S.A.	—	0	1	0	0	0	1	2	4
Honduras	26	1	12	0	0	0	2	12	53
Costa Rica	21	2	7	1	0	N.D.	3	12	45
Panama	21	1	3	0	0	0	2	7	34
Nicaragua	20	1	9	0	0	N.D.	9	12	51
Bolivia	19	12	6	0	0	0	3	5	45
Dominican Republic	18	1	3	0	0	0	1	1	24
Venezuela	17	3	5	1	0	0	1	3	29
Ecuador	16	1	11	1	N.D.	N.D.	2	3	33
Peru	13	1	8	1	0	0	3	3	28
El Salvador	13	1	9	0	0	N.D.	3	15	41
Guatemala	10	1	5	0	0	0	2	7	25
Chile	8	3	8	1	N.D.	N.D.	3	5	27
Mexico	8	0	2	1	0	0	1	1	12
Colombia	8	1	3	0	0	0	0	1	13
Paraguay	5	2	5	1	0	0	0	6	18
Brazil	5	0	3	0	1	0	0	2	11
Philippines	5	0	1	0	0	0	4	1	11
Argentina	2	1	5	1	0	0	0	3	11
Uruguay	2	3	4	1	1	0	0	4	14
Cuba[e]	1	1	1	0	23	16	1	0	27

United Kingdom and Associated States									
United Kingdom	4	—	6	1	1	1	1	7	19
Gambia	3	**53**	28	0	N.D.	N.D.	9	2	95
Malta	4	**44**	30	3	3[i]	1[i]	3	5	89
Ireland	5	**38**	8	2	1	0	1	3	56
Barbados	20	**35**	0	0	0	0	1	20	76
Guyana	27	25	10	1	1	0	2	**31**	96
Malawi	2	23	4	0	0	0	3	12	44
Cyprus	2	19	15	2	5	2	2	6	49
Sierra Leone	3	19	9	2	1	0	3	1	36
Kenya	4	**16**	11	1	1	0	2	3	37
Trinidad—Tobago	**33**	15	5	0	0	0	2	14	69
Tanzania	3	**14**	10	1	1	0	2	3	33
Jamaica	**22**	13	3	1	0	0	1	10	49
New Zealand	4	**12**	3	1	0	0	3	4	26
South Africa	6	**12**	9	1	0	0	4	5	36
Uganda	6	**11**	7	1	1	0	3	1	29
Kuwait	7	**11**	**34**	6	1	1	15	3	71
Ceylon	3	9	5	1	3	2	2	5	27[n]
Nigeria	3	9	**10**	2	1	0	2	0	25
Saudi Arabia	10	8	**29**	4	N.D.	N.D.	21	2	70
Iran	4	8	**10**	2	2	1	9	2	35
Ghana	5	**8**	5	1	3	2	2	1	24
Malaysia	8	6	9	2	4[i]	3[i]	12	7	46[n]
Israel	7	5	**8**	1	1	0	0	0	21
Australia	**5**	5	4	8	0	0	4	1	19
Iraq	2	4	**22**	0	3	2	3	4	38
Jordan	3	3	7	1	2	1	1	9	25
Canada	**26**	3	2	1	0	0	2	1	34
Sudan	1	3	**5**	1	2	1	1	1	13
Pakistan	**4**	2	3	1	1	1	1	1	12[n]

TABLE 6.2 (Cont'd.)

Country	Percent of G.D.P. Accounted For by Total Trade With:								Approximate Percent of G.D.P. Accounted For by Trade with all Major Powers[h]
	U.S.A.	U.K.	E.E.C.[e]	France	Soviet Bloc[f]	U.S.S.R.	Japan	Inter-Regional[g]	
United Kingdom and Associated States (cont'd.)									
Burma	2	2	2	0	1	1	1	**5**	13
India	**3**	1	1	0	1	1	1	1	8[n]
United Arab Republic	2	1	4	1	10	6	1	2	20
Nepal	0	0	1	0	N.D.	N.D.	1	7	9[n]
Yemen	0	0	1	1	5[i]	3[i]	1	**3**	10
E.F.T.A. States[j] (ranked separately)									
Norway	4	9	14	2	2	1	3	**18**	50
Denmark	4	9	**15**	2	2	1	1	14	45
Portugal	3	6	**11**	2	1	0	0	7	28
Sweden	4	6	**14**	2	2	1	1	12	39
Finland	2	6	9	2	7	6	0	8	32
Switzerland	5	4	**25**	6	1	0	1	7	43
Austria	2	2	**21**	1	5	1	0	7	37
France and Associated States									
France	2	1	**10**	—	1	0	0	3	17
Congo (Brazzaville)	4	8	75	**42**	3	1	1	5	96
Gabon	14	3	55	**38**	0	N.D.	2	3	77
Algeria	1	1	36	**29**	N.D.	N.D.	0	1	39
Senegal	1	1	34	**29**	N.D.	N.D.	1	6	43

Mauritania	7	11	53	24	0	0	3	1	75
Cameroon	4	1	35	24	1	N.D.	1	2	44
Ivory Coast	5	1	34	23	0	0	1	3	44
Central African Rep.	5	1	26	20	0	N.D.	1	1	34
Malagasy	5	1	21	18	4	2	1	3	31
Morocco	3	2	24	17	1	0	0	1	35
Dahomey	3	1	22	16	1	N.D.	4	4	31
Togo	1	3	29	16	0	N.D.	1	4	42
Chad	2	1	18	13	4	1	1	3	26
Niger	1	0	14	12	0	0	0	4	20
Tunisia	7	1	20	12	4		0	1	33
Upper Volta	0	0	9	8	0		2	11	20
Lebanon	8	6	25	7	4[i]	1[i]	0	17	62
Mali	0	1	6	5	3	2	2	7	17
Cambodia	1	1	6	5	1	0	0	6	17[n]
Guinea	4	1	8	4	7[i]	5[i]	4	1	21
Laos	7	1	4	3	N.D.	N.D.	1	14	30[n]
Syria	1	1	7	2	8	3	1	6	24
Haiti	9	0	4	1	0	0	0	0	14
Vietnam (South)	9	0	4	1	0	0	7	6	26
E.E.C. States[k] *(ranked separately)*									
Belgium-Luxembourg[l]	6	5	44	12	2	1	1	6	64
Netherlands	6	5	41	6	2	1	1	8	63
Germany (West)	3	1	12	4	1	0	0	7	24
Italy	3	1	11	3	2	1	0	4	21
Greece	2	2	11	2	3	1	1	2	21
Turkey	2	1	4	1	2	1	0	1	10
Soviet Union and Associated States									
U.S.S.R.	0	0	1	0	3	—	0	3[m]	4
Bulgaria[e]	0	0	3	1	29	20	0	29[m]	32

TABLE 6.2 (Cont'd.)

Country	Percent of G.D.P. Accounted For by Total Trade With:								Approximate Percent of G.D.P. Accounted For by Trade with all Major Powers[h]
	U.S.A.	U.K.	E.E.C.[e]	France	Soviet Bloc[f]	U.S.S.R.	Japan	Inter-Regional[g]	
Soviet Union and Associated States (cont'd.)									
Germany (East)	0	0	3	0	21	**12**	0	21^m	24
Czechoslovakia	0	1	3	0	20	**10**	0	20^m	24
Hungary	0	1	4	1	22	**12**	0	22^m	27
Afghanistan	1	1	2	0	8	7	1	4	17
Rumania	0	1	6	5	11	**6**	0	11^m	18
Poland	1	1	2	1	12	**7**	0	12^m	16
Yugoslavia	3	2	**13**	1	11	5	0	11^m	29
Albania[e]	0	0	2	0	**13**	0	0	13^m	15
Japan and Associated States									
Japan	6	1	1	0	1	1	—	4	13
Korea (South)	14	0	2	1	0	0	**16**	5	37^n
China (Taiwan)	12	0	3	0	0	0	**13**	9	37^n
Thailand	6	2	6	1	0	0	12	9	35^n
Indonesia	3	0	5	0	N.D.	N.D.	**5**	3	16^n
Other Nonassociated States (not ranked)									
Burundi	**14**	2	5	0	N.D.	N.D.	1	2	24
Congo (Kinshasa)	7	4	**37**	5	N.D.	N.D.	1	1	50
Ethiopia	**5**	1	6	1	1	0	2	0	15
Iceland	9	9	**12**	1	8	5	1	16	55

Libya	8	16	87	14	3	0	0	2	116
Rwanda	0	0	7	1	N.D.	N.D.	1	2	10
Spain	3	2	7	2	1	0	0	2	15
Totals:									
Number of Countries with Highest Percentages	26	14	30	15	3	9	5	14	
Number of High Countries as Percent of 116 Countries	22.4	12.1	25.9	12.9	2.6	7.8	4.3	12.1	
			38.8		10.4				

A boldface figure indicates it is the highest of the G.D.P. percentages accounted for by foreign trade. While trade with the E.E.C. or the Soviet Bloc (both of which include trade with major Powers) may sometimes account for a higher percentage of a country's G.D.P. than does trade with the Power alone, if it is clear that the Power is responsible for the majority of the trade, the figures in the column of the Power have been boldfaced. Because figures were rounded, it sometimes happens that the percentage in one column appears to be identical with the percentage in another. Where one of those seemingly identical figures was set in boldface, it means that that percentage was actually higher prior to rounding.

[a] Foreign trade data for this table were compiled and computed for the author by Steven Schecter. Data are from the same sources cited in footnote a to Table 6.1.

[b] Gross Domestic Product estimates are projections based on E. E. Hagen's figures and estimated economic growth rates for 1960–1965, computed under the author's direction by Michael Jewel. Where economic projections of growth rate were unavailable, population growth rates were used. Since population growth rates tend to remain more stable than economic growth rates, it is uncertain which projections are more inaccurate. In either case, the reader is warned that the G.D.P. data upon which this table is based are extremely crude. I have used these figures only because I am interested in orders of magnitude, and in degrees of relative economic dependence on major Powers. It is to be hoped that as data become more refined, greater precision will be possible.

[c] All figures, unless otherwise indicated, are for 1967. No trade data for some countries were available to me for that year, but International Monetary Fund and International Bank for Reconstruction and De-

velopment figures were available for 1963. Although some noncomparability is involved, since the concern is with relative orders of magnitude, I have used the 1963 trade data for those countries, and taken them as a percentage of the estimated 1963 Gross Domestic Product of the countries involved. Countries for which this was done are footnoted c. Because G.D.P. estimates are so crude, figures have been rounded to the nearest full percentage. Hence, 0% may actually mean anything between no trade whatever and 44% of G.D.P.

[d] Countries have been grouped on the basis of Historical Association (see Table 4.1). No country has been listed twice on this table, and thus arbitrary decisions were made with regard to which Powers some weaker states should be listed with.

[e] Trade with the European Economic Community (E.E.C.) includes trade with France. Percentages were calculated by combining the trade figures of each country

TABLE 6.2 (Cont'd.)

with Belgium, Luxembourg, Netherlands, West Germany, Italy, and France and dividing the total by the estimated Gross Domestic Product of the country concerned.

f Trade with the Soviet Bloc includes trade with the Soviet Union, but excludes trade with China.

g Inter-Regional figures exclude the major Powers in the region. Thus, Inter-Regional trade for the Western Hemisphere excludes trade with the United States; for Western Europe it excludes trade with the U.K. and the E.E.C. countries; for Asia it excludes trade with Japan and (because of insufficient data) Mainland China.

h In theory (as well as in practice, for some of the smaller countries) total trade may exceed 100% of G.D.P. without implying unreliability of data. If a country exported everything it produced and imported everything it consumed (no country does), it would be theoretically possible for foreign trade to equal 200% of the Gross Domestic Product of that country. The figures listed in this column represent only the sum of the other columns (exclusive of France and the Soviet Union, since their percentages are included in the E.E.C. and Soviet Bloc figures, respectively). Even assuming G.D.P. estimates to be accurate, some error may nonetheless be involved because of rounding off percentages and because not all *all* foreign trade is included. The latter is particularly likely to affect the figures for the major Powers. For example, the figure listed in this column for Japan may be as much as 15% lower than it should be, because trade with countries like Canada, Australia, and the Scandinavian countries is left out. On the other hand, the figure for the United States would not be more than 1 or 2% higher even if all foreign trade were included.

i These figures represent rough estimates, based on 1963 data, projected for 1967 on the basis of known trends in the foreign trade of the countries involved.

j The states of the European Free Trade Association (E.F.T.A.) joined with Britain in 1960 in an economic association to counteract the adverse economic effects of the European Economic Community. Finland was given the status of an associated member in 1961, and is accordingly listed here. While none of these countries are associated states of the United Kingdom in the historical sense, because they are currently economically associated with Britain, they are listed here in a separate category.

k The states of the European Economic Community (E.E.C.—popularly known as the Common Market) joined with France in 1958 in an economic association aimed at ultimately achieving a complete customs union among member states. Greece and Turkey have special associated status (and are accordingly listed here), as do most of France's former sub-Saharan African colonies. While these European states (other than Belgium) are not associated states of France in the historical sense, because they are currently economically associated with France, they are listed here in a separate category.

l Trade data for Belgium and Luxembourg are normally combined in the sources, and thus the two countries are considered here as one economic unit.

m In this case, the region (Eastern Europe) was defined as synonymous with the Soviet Bloc, and thus the figures for the two are identical. Because of this, the Inter-Regional figure has not been added into the final column.

n The actual percent of G.D.P. accounted for by all foreign trade for these countries is probably considerably higher than what is listed here. That is because this figure omits trade with Australia and/or Mainland China, one or both of which are known to be important trading partners of the countries concerned.

N.D. = No data available.

their trade relationship in this analysis. As Table 6.2 shows, of the seven countries in the association exclusive of Britain, every one of them trades, more with the E.E.C. and also Inter-Regionally (which means, in effect, with each other) than they do with the U.K. Now these figures are somewhat misleading. If for each country the percentage of G.D.P. accounted for by Inter-Regional trade were combined with the percentage accounted for by the U.K., E.F.T.A. would in fact emerge as the major trading partner for all of the members except Switzerland and Austria.

Despite the creation of E.F.T.A., trade with Britain accounted for less of the G.D.P. of Denmark in 1967 than it did in 1958. Further, while trade with Britain in 1967 accounted for a somewhat higher percent of the G.D.P. of all the other association countries than it did a decade earlier, trade with other areas accounted for an even higher percentage increase. That is, for all of the countries concerned, except Switzerland and the United Kingdom itself, Inter-Regional trade accounted for a considerably higher increase in percentage of each country's G.D.P. than did trade with Britain. On the basis of these data, it would appear that although Britain is presumed to be the economic Power in the European Free Trade Association, the other countries collectively have gained more from the association than has Britain.

The data helps explain the imperative for Britain to join the European Economic Community. Not only has trade with Britain progressively become a smaller ingredient of the G.D.P. of most states, but more significant for Britain, it has become increasingly less important to the economies of those states at the very time that the E.E.C. and the United States are becoming more important. Whatever the rhetoric about Britain having deserted the Commonwealth when it made its bid to join the Common Market, the fact is that increasingly the associated states are economically deserting the United Kingdom. Unless Britain becomes a fully integrated member of the European Economic Community soon, then given current trends (and there is no reason to believe that they will be reversed) Britain will have only three alternatives economically: ultimately to accept any terms for admission to the E.E.C., regardless of how disadvantageous; or to attempt to join some sort of North Atlantic association with the United States and Canada (possibly including Australia and New Zealand); or to become little more than an economic dependency of the other major powers. None of these alternatives are particularly attractive to the British, to be certain. Perhaps the United Kingdom will come up with a better fourth alternative. But under present circumstances it would appear that the third alternative is inevitable, unless Britain takes some sort of major action to avert it.

Foreign Aid

The distinction between foreign aid and foreign trade is often highly artificial. For example: French industry buys the products of the French associated states at prices often considerably above world prices.[24] Is that aid or trade? Clearly, in intent it is an aid subsidy to the private producers in the producing countries, yet it appears in most official listings of foreign transactions under trade. The Soviet Union lends money on a "straight commercial" basis to certain underdeveloped countries, but the rate of interest charged may be considerably below private interest rates. This, too, would appear in official publications under a commercial heading, yet the difference between the rate the Soviets charge and the rates obtained on the world market are a form of economic aid. The United States government lends an underdeveloped country the money to buy products and services from the United States. Does this count as aid or trade? Note that countries that accumulate vast foreign reserves because of the favorable position in which they find themselves in regard to foreign trade obviously are in significantly less need of foreign "aid" than are countries that are in an unfavorable balance of payments position.

Questions and ambiguous cases could be cited ad infinitum. Rather than attempt a genuinely economic definition of the difference between trade and aid, I propose a definition based on intent. Thus, if the motivation for the foreign transaction is primarily economic—that is, to gain profit, or to fill a need for markets or products—it should be considered foreign trade. If, on the other hand, the transaction is undertaken for primarily political reasons—that is, to support the economy of a favorable regime, or to alleviate some natural disaster—it should be considered primarily foreign aid.[25] That there may be political implications in extensive trade relationships in no way lessens the fact that the primary motivation for most trade relationships is economic profit. Thus, it became very important politically to Cuba that almost all of its sugar production was purchased by companies in the United States prior to 1960, but the motivation behind those sugar trans-

[24] See Teresa Hayter, *French Aid* (London: Overseas Development Institute, 1966), especially pp. 71–84.

[25] While fully aware of the difficulties to be faced in using a definition based on intent, I am convinced they are no more insurmountable than those inherent in any other basis for definition. While for analytical purposes it is useful to make this distinction, unfortunately, because most of the data used in this work are drawn from sources using more traditional distinctions between trade and aid, all figures, unless otherwise specified, will reflect the more conventional definitions.

actions, since they were primarily economic in intent, should be considered foreign trade.

Under this definition, the investment of private or public capital in an underdeveloped country for the purposes of profit would clearly be foreign trade. If that capital were invested for political purposes it would be aid. In this context it is interesting to note that whereas investments of Soviet Bloc capital were in the past almost exclusively political in motivation, there is some evidence that more recent Soviet investments have been made (or offered) from primarily economic motivations. It would be difficult for anyone to argue that the trade that has occurred between the Soviet Union and the United States (although resulting from some political motivation, to be sure) has not been motivated primarily by economic needs. Certainly China has not bought Canadian wheat merely for political reasons, but because China had a real economic need for the wheat.

An interesting example of the fine line that exists between aid and trade was the bidding between a large American electronics corporation and the Soviet Union to handle the so-called "West Cairo Electrification Scheme." Egypt did not have the money to hire the American or Soviet engineers. One could easily argue that in this particular instance the Soviet intent was primarily political, and thus their offer of a loan was in fact an offer of a form of aid. The United States, for political reasons, also offered a loan to enable it to complete the transaction with the American corporation. The loan of money to the U.A.R. was aid, but the payment to the American electronics firm was trade.

It can, and often does, happen that relationships that began as primarily economic, undertaken for purely economic reasons, come to have a strong political impetus over the course of time. To the degree that the political motivation for maintaining the relationship comes to override the purely economic motivation, the relationship has changed from one primarily of trade to one primarily of aid.

Foreign aid is one of the prime ways in which the government of a powerful state helps the governmental decision makers of a less powerful state stay in office.[26] The motivations of this aid may differ: to protect their own foreign economic interests; to support an elite that is friendly to the political aspirations of the more

[26] There are, of course, exceptions, as when foreign military aid so strengthens the military elite as compared to other, competing elements within the elite structure of the country that the military elite is then in a position to seize power for itself; or when the quid pro quo for the foreign assistance is seen by significant segments of the society as so antinationalist that a coup is precipitated—as in the case of Nuri Al-Said of Iraq or King Farouk of Egypt. These are the exceptions, however, and not the rule.

powerful state; to make an antagonistic elite less hostile; or to aid the elite in power because the alternative to this elite is perceived as being detrimental to the interests of the mentor Power or more friendly to the interests of a competing Power. But the crucial point is that foreign aid, regardless of the form it may take, tends to help maintain in office the existing governmental elite of the recipient country. The Soviet Union, under Stalin's direction, very clearly recognized this, but because Stalin mistakenly saw "capitalism," rather than the United States, as Russia's major enemy, he refused to support any "bourgeois" regime.[27] After Stalin's death, his successors recognized that in a world struggle for power among the big states, the ideological sympathy of regimes in smaller nations was not as important as tying them to oneself—by whatever ties available. Indeed, if the lesson of China has taught the Soviet Union—and the other Powers—anything, it will have been that ideology is not nearly as binding as perceptual identity or economic interdependence.

Foreign aid may take many forms. It may be multilateral or bilateral. It may, if the latter, be overt or covert. It may be given for a number of very different stated reasons. Hans Morgenthau, in an outrageous but thought-provoking article, has classified these reasons into the following six categories: (1) humanitarian foreign aid; (2) subsistence foreign aid; (3) military foreign aid; (4) bribery; (5) prestige foreign aid; (6) foreign aid for economic development.[28] Morgenthau, rather unfairly, tends to see most of these categories—regardless of stated purpose—as having bribery as its basic intent—that is, the giving of money in return for favors either already granted or expected. He does see, however, that regardless of intent, the act of extending any economic aid (unless specifically given to a counterelite for subversive purposes) tends to have the effect of strengthening the regime in power.[29]

---

[27] Stalin's theory was that by denying aid to bourgeois regimes one would exacerbate the existing economic difficulties faced by the country (or at least not contribute to their alleviation) and, thus, increase the political discontent in the country, which would ultimately lead to proper conditions for the overthrow of the existing regime and the seizure of governmental authority by a communist counterelite. What Stalin failed to realize, however, was that there was no inevitability about an eventual overthrow of the bourgeois regime—particularly if that regime was supported by a competing Power.

[28] Hans Morgenthau, "A Political Theory of Foreign Aid," *American Political Science Review*, Vol. 56, No. 2, June 1962, pp. 301–309. It is interesting to note that despite his insightful analysis Morgenthau concludes that "foreign aid . . . is not a science but an art." It is precisely this contention, so prevalent among political scientists, that I wish to challenge here.

[29] Again, exceptions are possible, as in the case where the aid is clearly perceived by the population as a bribe that was taken in personal, anti-

In the same article Morgenthau also quite rightly points out how terribly misunderstood economic aid efforts are, particularly in the United States. The fact that the enemy Power gives economic aid primarily for political reasons is clearly understood, but the fact that "our" own intentions are also primarily political is considerably less well-understood. During the height of the cold war, when it was easiest to get appropriations for military aid, American policy makers were forced domestically to consider almost all types of aid as contributing to military security. The Mutual Security Program includes a great deal of "development aid" as well as "defense support," because American Congressmen so little understand the motivation for aid that it has been necessary to subsume most of it under the heading of "mutual security." Whether the other Powers' policy makers are equally as ignorant of the implications of foreign aid is a question that must, of course, remain unanswered. There is some evidence, however, to indicate that the French fully understand that extensive economic aid tends to 1. support the regime in power; 2. closely bind the receiving country economically to the donor country; and 3. produce a host of other ties that work toward tying the receiver more closely to the donor.

These principal ramifications of economic aid need to be examined in more detail.

Economic Aid Tends to Support the Regime in Power

It was noted earlier that the overwhelming majority of the world's weaker countries tend to have sustenance agriculture as their main mode of economic organization. To the degree this is the case, it follows that these countries would not have excess capital available either for the purchase of consumer goods from abroad or for the provision of welfare services, which many of the developed states are able to supply for their populations. There is no question that a country with a per capita income of $1,000 annually will be able to provide many more consumer goods and services for its populations than will a country with a $100 per capita annual income. But there are many more countries with a per capita income below $100 per year than there are with a per capita income above $1,000. Further, countries in the underdeveloped world have populations that desperately need more goods and services than their governments can supply. This is par-

---

national interest. The acceptance of aid under those circumstances might then be viewed as having weakened the existing regime. But on the basis of over 25 years of extensive foreign aid, one may point to very few examples where the acceptance of foreign aid can legitimately be viewed as the *major* cause of the downfall of a specific regime.

ticularly so in the face of the so-called "revolution of rising expectations." Thanks largely to the cheap transistor radio, there is hardly a villager in the world who is not aware that other villagers elsewhere may be enjoying a more comfortable, healthier, and longer life than he. If this is true for the villager, it is even more true for the urban dweller who is much more aware of the world around him. This puts tremendous pressure on the governments of these countries to "do something" to improve the daily life of their masses. Now it is almost axiomatic in the literature of economic development that the greatest bulk of resources for economic development will have to come from domestic sources. But it is just as axiomatic that none of the underdeveloped countries can, in fact, provide for any economic development without considerable help from external sources—unless they are willing to gather capital by reducing current consumption levels or by increasing production while holding consumption constant. In either case this means squeezing development capital out of one's own already dissatisfied population. This dissatisfaction is so compelling a factor, that it is necessary for every government to divert some resources away from what might be more productive investments into investments that are domestically visible and produce at least psychic satisfaction for some segments of the more articulate portions of the population. Clearly, the more adept a government is in winning external economic aid, the less it has to "squeeze" its own people and the more economic and/or psychic satisfactions it can offer them. The more satisfaction it can offer its population, the more secure its hold on governmental positions is likely to be.[30] Probably no government has ever been able to fully meet the aspirations of its own population for goods and services, but most governments would like to supply as many of them as is politically necessary to maintain at least the passive support of their populations. Thus, there is tremendous need on the part of the governments of underdeveloped countries for as much aid as they can get.

There is, on the other hand, a danger facing the government of every underdeveloped country that relies heavily on foreign sources of capital. That is the charge of being too dependent economically on a major Power. In order to mitigate or counter that charge and

[30] There is merit in the argument that some economic development tends to whet the appetite of most populations for accelerated economic development rather than appeasing it. However, there is evidence that this is a short-term, not a long-term phenomenon. To the degree that a government can begin to satisfy felt needs, and convince its population that it is likely to continue to do so, its chances of remaining in office over the long run are considerably better than those of a government that is associated with economic stagnation.

at the same time be in a position to provide the desired goods and services, many underdeveloped countries favor multilateral sources of economic aid such as the United Nations or various specialized agencies. The developed countries, on the other hand, fully recognizing that multilateral aid organizations tend to use different criteria to determine which governments will receive aid than do the Powers themselves, usually frown on this source of aid except for specific purposes.[31] And while, for any number of political reasons, the leaders of many underdeveloped countries might prefer to receive multilateral rather than bilateral aid, in the abesnce of the former they will usually accept the latter.[32]

Many other weaker countries prefer bilateral foreign aid to multilateral aid, however, because they often believe they can get more by direct negotiation with the Power than they could from a multilateral organization. But the aid usually must come only from a politically acceptable Power. For example, in many Latin American countries if the regime in office were to seek Soviet foreign aid, it would run the risk of being accused by the more conservative elements in the country of being procommunist, and might face the danger of a military coup. Similarly, one of the major factors contributing to the overthrow of the Dubcek regime in Czechoslovakia was its negotiations with West Germany for large economic credits, which led to the charge that the regime was "revisionist." Again, it is unlikely that any regime in North Vietnam could accept American economic aid, unless the population of that country could be made to believe that it was being offered as reparations for war damage. It is primarily because of such limitations on the sources of bilateral aid that the acceptance of foreign aid from specific Powers becomes so useful an indicator of the existence of informal political ties between weak and powerful states.

While the governments of most underdeveloped countries recognize that their regimes can be strengthened by foreign aid, there are few governments that will overtly accept aid expressly to put down an active opposition. Indeed, donor countries do not usually like to see their aid explicitly used for that purpose (in the event the opposition should win). But, because of the substitutability of resources, it is possible for foreign aid to be given for some generally acceptable purpose, thereby freeing the domestic funds that would otherwise be spent on that purpose for use in putting down

[31] For example, the debate and the vote on budgets for U.N. technical assistance agencies nearly always sees the developed countries—the United States, United Kingdom, U.S.S.R., and France—grouped on one side, against the developing countries on the other.

[32] Here, again, there are exceptions. Burma is the most notable, having at one time refused aid from both East and West, although willing to accept it from U.N. organizations.

the opposition. Thus, while it is unthinkable that an appropriation of millions of dollars to put down the Indonesian nationalist movement could have passed in the United States Congress, it was possible to appropriate millions for the rehabilitation of the Netherlands, and thus to free millions in the Netherlands to cover the expense of the Indonesian war. Similarly, U.S. development aid to France freed millions of francs in France for the suppression of the Algerian and Vietnamese nationalist movements. Because the latter movement was Communist as well as nationalist, it was, of course, ultimately possible to get billions of dollars appropriated by the U.S. Congress specifically to put down that movement. Where the opposition to the regime in power can be labeled Communist (or "revisionist" in communist countries) it is usually not difficult to get aid money to put it down. But where the opposition cannot be labeled Communist, aid often must be rendered either covertly for that purpose or overtly for other purposes that would permit the diversion of domestic funds.

Economic Aid Tends to Bind the Recipient to the Donor

Although this proposition, like the former, tends to be almost self-evident, the fact is that there are many who refuse to grant its validity. It is difficult to say why that is so, unless those who refuse to see the connection are simply blinded by the verbiage rather than the reality of economic aid.

In the first place, most donor countries today insist that their aid be spent within the donor country. For a number of reasons, most loans as well as most gifts are now specifically earmarked for spending within the country of origin. Thus a U.S. "grant" of $1 million to India really means that the vast majority of that money will be spent in the United States on American goods and services. Since the corporations and individuals who earn that million dollars will pay taxes to the U.S. government on the money they have earned, and since each of the people they pay with that million will presumably also pay taxes on what they have earned (what the economist calls the "multiplier effect"), the likelihood is that a very large portion of that million dollars will return in the form of taxes to the U.S. government and it may therefore be something of a misnomer to call it a "grant" in the first place. More to the point, however, are the effects on the recipient of spending that one million dollars in the donor country.

Once a country has purchased a million dollars' worth of goods and services in a donor country, it will be dependent on that country for spare parts, servicing, expansion, et cetera, and at least to that extent, will be bound economically to the donor. Suppose

India purchases a General Electric turbine system with the U.S. grant. Since General Electric has its own specifications for its products, presumably only G.E. technicians will be able to install and service the system. Now, it would be possible to teach Indians to become technicians for G.E. equipment, but once that is done, unless the Indian government is willing to invest the scarce time and resources to train these same or other Indians to be technicians for Seamans, Roots, Fiat, Mitsubishi, and a host of other corporations also, the Indian government is more or less committed to the continued buying of G.E. turbine systems. Spare parts present an equally obvious problem. A Soviet generator without an expensive adaptor attachment simply will not fit a G.E. system. What is more, innovations that update and streamline Soviet or Fiat systems may not be applicable to the original G.E. system. Thus, the Indian government on receiving the $1,000,000 grant may have the freedom to choose between tying itself to General Electric or to Westinghouse, but by the terms of the grant the companies of all other countries are excluded from the competition. From the time the initial decision is made to install the system of a specific American company, for the life of the system itself the Indians are bound to use the parts and technology of that company from that country, or to engage in considerable additional expense in retooling for use of a different company's product. Clearly, the latter choice can be made. If the United States ever cuts off economic aid to India and massive Soviet aid becomes available—as was the case in Cuba—India will of necessity switch to a Soviet-made system. But this would be at very considerable extra cost, which would be unnecessary as long as United States aid continued to be forthcoming. Of course, India might one day develop its own electric industry to the point where it would pay to make and use its own turbine system and eliminate the dependence on a foreign supply of parts, service, and technology. Until that time, however, India would in this regard be economically dependent on the donor country.

Aside from questions of supplies and technology, there is a still more critical question of degree of economic dependence upon foreign aid. For most countries, economic aid accounts for only a fraction of the receiving country's Gross Domestic Product. For other countries, however, the ratio to G.D.P. of aid supplied by a specific foreign country is extremely high. To mention a few cases, French aid to the Congo (Brazzaville) accounted for approximately 40 percent of that country's Gross National Product in 1966;[33] United States aid to Laos in 1963 accounted for 31 per-

[33] See Jon J. Kugelman, "The Dynamics of Franco-African Relations, 1957–1967," MPIA thesis, University of Pittsburgh, Pittsburgh, Pa., 1969, p. 70. Note that Kugelman's figures are based on percent of Gross National Product, rather than Gross Domestic Product.

cent of its G.D.P.; and British aid to Malta in the same year accounted for 16 percent of its G.D.P.[34] Note that this is foreign aid alone. When added to foreign trade, the figures often become truly staggering. Now, while there are no absolute measures of dependence, it seems fair to say that when as much as 10 percent of a country's G.D.P. depends on aid from a specific foreign Power, the receiving country is highly dependent economically on that donor. Theoretically the recipient country may be free to refuse the economic aid and, therefore, free itself of dependence on the donor country, but practically, the cost to its economy of such action would probably be prohibitive. Any country that has been so economically dependent on another country will probably continue to need some major country on which to depend economically. That is, should Vietnam for purely political reasons refuse to accept any additional United States aid, or the United States refuse to offer any additional aid, South Vietnam would have to find another Power to take over the former economic role of the United States, or its economy would crumble—and along with it almost inevitably would go the regime responsible for the debacle.

Economic Aid Tends to Produce Other Ties

As observed before, there is a mutually reinforcing quality to the ties between donor and recipient. The more economic aid is extended by one country to another, the more foreign trade there is likely to be. The more foreign aid and trade exists, the more economically dependent the weaker state may become on the more powerful. The more economically dependent a weaker state, the more likely it is to support the political interests of the more powerful (other things being equal). The more it tends to support the political interests of the more powerful state, the more likely it is to receive more foreign aid. And so it goes.

One could no more argue that economic aid, alone, is sufficient to get the recipient state to do what the donor wants than one could argue that air power alone is sufficient to ensure the military victory of one state over another. Obviously it is not. But it is true that economic aid is considerably more sensitive to political pressures than, for example, economic trade. Indeed, perhaps it is precisely because it is so politically sensitive that it is so useful a tool in tying the interests of the receiving regime to the interests of the donor state.

While extensive foreign trade tends to strengthen both the

[34] Soviet aid figures for communist countries were not available in comparable terms, but there is reason to assume that in cases like Mongolia and North Vietnam, they are as high, or higher than the U.S./Laos figures.

foreign and indigenous portions of the commercial segment of a country's elite structure, and foreign military aid tends to strengthen the military segments of the elite, foreign economic aid tends to strengthen the governmental decision makers vis-à-vis the other segments of the elite, as well as vis-à-vis counterelites. There are a number of reasons for this. First, of course, the governmental decision makers can use this economic aid in politically rewarding ways domestically. That is, foreign aid is very often used either for general welfare or for prestige projects, both of which—if success-ful—bring political credit to the ruling regime.[35] Second, to the degree that foreign assisted projects prove politically successful, they tend to strengthen the hand of the governmental decision makers vis-à-vis the other segments of the elite, sometimes to the point where they feel strong enough to take some actions—such as enforcing tax collection or perhaps land reform—they may not have previously felt secure enough to undertake. Third, foreign aid projects often have the secondary (if not primary) effect of strengthening the structure of the government's decision-making apparatus. Sometimes a project does so merely by providing trained indigenous inspectors or administrators. Sometimes it does so by facilitating a governmental reorganization that makes planning and implementation of governmental socio-economic actions more ef-fective. The more a governing elite has been strengthened by foreign economic aid, the more it is likely to do what it can to keep and increase the flow of aid.

There are still other concomitants of economic aid that lead to mutually reinforcing ties. When economic aid is extended to a country, there is likely to be an influx of foreign technicians to administer the aid and to offer development assistance. The more of these foreign nationals there are in a country, and the longer they are there, presumably the more they will be able to inculcate their value system in the host country. Whether consciously or not, even a member of a group as altruistically committed to "doing good" as the American Friends Service Committee cannot help but inculcate American cultural values and assumptions as he goes about "his business." The more sophisticated American govern-ment adviser and his Russian, British, and French equivalents are only too aware that it is not just development they are trying to encourage, but development along the lines proven suc-cessful in their own countries.[36] To some degree, of course, as the

---

[35] Unsuccessful projects can of course often generate enormous hostility toward the regime in that they raise aspirations when announced and create sometimes violent frustrations when they fail.

[36] The same, of course, holds true for Chinese, German, Israeli, and other advisers from other states.

adviser becomes more familiar with the country in which he is serving, he can influence (by his feedback) the direction his country's aid will take. If he has been a particularly sensitive observer and if his voice has been heard in his home capital, his country's aid may more directly reflect the actual needs of the country in which he is serving. It appears that for the most part, however, foreign advisers view their role as "getting the natives to do things our way." Of course, to the degree that he is sensitive to the needs and values of his host nationals, and adapts his technology to their local conditions, he will be more successful in getting them to modify their behavior and adopt his country's way. Thus in getting his technology adopted, he will be aiding in tying the host nationals perceptually to his country.

Further, massive amounts of foreign aid to a country usually mean a massive flow of people from that country to the donor for study. As was explained in the section on educational ties, the more foreign nationals study in the donor country, and the longer they do, the stronger the perceptual bonds that are likely to develop between the two states.

If nothing else, this exchange of articulate portions of both populations causes a marked increase in the communication links between the two countries. It may be fairly easy to write off as propaganda what one sees in the movies of life in the United States or the Soviet Union, but the testimony of someone who has visited the country—someone who "saw it with my own eyes"—is another matter. But this flow of communication established by extensive foreign aid is two-way. Perhaps equally as important as the impact of the donor country on the visitor from the recipient country, is the impact of the receiving country on the donor national working or visiting there. It is very easy to have totally misguided aspirations for a country when one knows little about it. As many donor nationals return home with eyewitness reports on the recipient country, donor policy toward that country will become more effective because it will be more realistic. And there is nothing that strengthens the bonds between states as effectively as a mutual perception of each one's ability to influence the policy of the other.

The Givers and the Receivers

That there are political as well as economic disadvantages against which the poorer countries must guard in accepting foreign economic aid goes without saying. But it is overwhelmingly in the interests of the governments and the people of the underdeveloped world to accept, and use productively, as much development aid as they can possibly get—from as many sources as they possibly can.

The United States has clearly been, since the end of World War II, the major supplier of foreign aid to the world. Exclusive of direct military aid, the United States obligated $86 billion in grants and loans between 1946 and 1966.[37] In absolute dollar terms, the United States alone has given more economic aid each year than all of the other Powers combined. But relative to national income, the United States is behind France, and probably Japan. Teresa Hayter gives the following figures for the net official aid disbursements of the main donors in 1962, 1963, and 1964:[38]

TABLE 6.3

Official Aid of Main Donors

(Net Disbursements)

Country	Totals ($m.)			As Percentage of National Income		
	1962	*1963*	*1964*	*1962*	*1963*	*1964*
France	977	843	841	1.76	1.38	1.26
[West] Germany	427	421	459	0.62	0.58	0.58
U.S.	3,713	3,842	3,534	0.82	0.81	0.70
U.K.	418	414	490	0.64	0.61	0.67

Since 1964 the absolute amount of U.S. economic assistance has declined, while national income has risen, thus reducing still further the relative percentage figure for U.S. aid.

With regard to magnitude of big Power aid, some comparisons are in order. The British claim to have given nearly $426 million in capital and technical assistance in 1962.[39] By comparison, in that same year American economic aid to India alone accounted for $763 million.[40] Miss Hayter cites another comparison, this time between French and British aid: "Oddly, Algeria with a population of 10 million and the 14 ex-French African and Malagasy States, with a population the size of Nigeria's, get more aid from

[37] Agency for International Development, *U.S. Overseas Loans and Grants and Assistance from International Organizations: Obligations and Loan Authorizations, July 1, 1945–June 30, 1966* (Washington, D.C., 1967), p. 4.

[38] Hayter, *French Aid*, p. 45.

[39] Central Office of Information, *Consultation and Cooperation in the Commonwealth*, Ref. Pamphlet 25 (London: H.M. Stationery Office, 1963), p. 19. Note that this figure is somewhat higher than the figure quoted by Miss Hayter. When dealing with foreign aid data these inconsistencies are inevitable since every one considers somewhat different things when calculating totals. The important thing, for this study, is the order of magnitude.

[40] *U.S. Overseas Loans and Grants*, p. 11.

France than the whole of the Commonwealth, with a population of 700 million, gets from Britain." [41] Considering grants and loans (exclusive of those for defense and with repayments subtracted) *actually dispersed or expended* (a figure often considerably lower than that for commitments and obligations) Steven Schecter has come up with these comparative figures for the 1963–64 fiscal year: [42]

Power	$ Millions
United States	3,238
Soviet Union	409 (exclusive of intra-Bloc aid, which is presumed to be extensive)
France	529
E.E.C. (exclusive of France)	463
United Kingdom	323
Japan	117
China (Mainland)	110 (exclusive of intra-Bloc aid, which may be extensive)

In all likelihood, if the Soviet Union's intra-Bloc aid were included, the figure for the Soviet Union would surpass that for France. Also, if Soviet Bloc figures (exclusive of the Soviet Union and China) were available, the likelihood is that those figures would surpass the 1963–64 figure for Japan.

Which weaker countries receive this aid? About 90 percent of all British aid goes to Commonwealth countries, [43] while an even higher share of French aid goes to French associated states. Similarly, much of the E.E.C. aid goes to countries historically associated with Belgium (Congo Kinshasa, et cetera), Holland (Indonesia), Germany (Tanzania, Cameroons, et cetera), and Italy (Libya, Somali, et cetera), while most Japanese aid goes to Asian countries formerly associated with it. United States and Soviet aid, on the other hand, are much more directly related to the cold war. War-devastated, noncommunist Europe was the prime recipient of U.S. economic aid prior to its economic recovery, receiving almost one-third of all American economic aid since World War II. Simi-

[41] Hayter, *French Aid,* p. 9.

[42] Figures compiled by Steven Schecter for the author from the following sources: *Geographical Distribution of Financial Flows to Less-Developed Countries: Disbursement 1960–1964* (London: Organization for Economic Cooperation and Development, H.M. Stationery Office, 1967); Kurt Miller, *The Foreign Aid Programs of the Soviet Bloc and Communist China* (New York: Walker, 1967). Communist aid figures are not quite compatible, as they represent loans committed and are yearly averages of the five year period 1960–1964.

[43] *Consultation and Cooperation in the Commonwealth,* p. 19.

larly, to the degree that the Russians gave any aid prior to Stalin's death, primarily Eastern Europe, and later China, received that aid. After 1950 (and the Korean War) American attention turned to the underdeveloped world—particularly in Asia—to bolster anticommunist regimes in Korea, Taiwan, and Vietnam, and to compete for influence with the Soviet Union in India. Actually, popular impressions notwithstanding, India is the only "neutral" country that has received massive economic aid from both the U.S. and the U.S.S.R. Like the United States, the Soviet Union tends to support those regimes most hostile to its enemies—Cuba, the United Arab Republic, and other anti-American leftwing governments in the Middle East, Asia, and Africa. Whereas British and French aid tends to go to a country regardless of the regime in power (with the notable exception of Guinea after it voted "Non" in 1958 [43a]), U.S. and Soviet aid is generally tied to governments rather than countries. With the overthrow of Nkrumah, Russian aid to Ghana all but ceased and American aid, which had ceased during Nkrumah's regime, was resumed. The U.S. often expresses its displeasure with a regime by refusing to extend aid, and only begins sending aid again when the offending government has been replaced by one more to its liking. This is not to say that the United States does not give aid to its historically associated states. It does, but not nearly to the extent to which it gives aid to anticommunist governments on the periphery of the Soviet Union and China.

The entrance of China into the field of economic aid is interesting. China itself could use all of the economic aid it could get. But the Chinese, like the Israelis, are seeking to counteract political isolation, and have used their aid as a first step toward the establishment of diplomatic relations in a number of African and Asian countries. While Chinese aid is small in absolute amounts, it has great symbolic value for countries choosing to consider themselves nonaligned.

Other smaller countries like Canada, Australia, Sweden, and Switzerland also give economic aid to underdeveloped countries, but in order of magnitude it is insignificant compared to the aid of the Powers and Super Powers. What is more, there is every indication that these countries use their aid primarily as an opening wedge for foreign trade.

[43a] In 1958 Charles de Gaulle gave the French colonies of sub-Sahara Africa the choice of limited autonomy within the French Community and the promise of massive economic aid if they voted "Oui" to his proposed Constitution, or complete independence without any economic assistance if they voted "Non." When Guinea opted for complete independence the French went so far as to remove the boots of local policemen and to return to France all pencils, paper, and paperclips they had formerly supplied it.

Foreign Investment

Even more important to the economies of some of the countries of the world than foreign aid or foreign trade is private foreign investment.

The total direct foreign investment is currently estimated by the OECD to be about $85 billion. An overwhelming share of that is American, but surprisingly Europe and Japan account for $31 billion. "If, to use a shorthand calculation made by the National Industrial Conference Board, $1 of investment generates $2 in sales, the $85 billion of international direct investment contributes to roughly $170 billion in world commerce." [44]

Now, while most United States investment is in Canada, Japan, and Western Europe, and most European and Japanese investment is in the United States, foreign investment in the weaker countries still accounts for 50 percent or more of some weak countries' Gross Domestic Product. There is no question but that foreign investment produces profound political and economic effects on those weaker countries. J. J. Servan-Schreiber says:

It is a historical rule that politically and economically powerful countries make direct investments (and gain control) in less-developed countries. Thus, European capital used to flow into Africa—[and he might have added Asia and Latin America] not for simple investment, but to gain economic power and exploit local resources.[45]

The situation within the weaker countries is made worse, argues Servan-Schreiber, because indigenous property-owning classes in these countries do not balance this foreign inflow of capital by investing their own resources domestically. Rather, they tend to invest their earnings in the more developed countries. Thus their own countries tend to be overwhelmed by foreign investment.

There is, of course, nothing intrinsically evil about foreign investment. In fact it can be highly valuable and useful to the countries that can attract it. Russia prior to the 1917 Revolution experienced one of its most rapid economic growth periods thanks to the influx of huge sums of French capital. The industrialization of the United States between 1865 and 1914 has been attributed in no small measure to the influx of European and especially

[44] Sanford Ross, "The Rewarding Strategies of Multinationalism," *Fortune,* September 15, 1968, p. 100.
[45] J. J. Servan-Schreiber, *The American Challenge,* Trans. Roland Steel (New York: Atheneum, 1968), p. 12.

British capital. Since 1945, Canada, Mexico, and several other Latin American countries have experienced the influx of literally billions of dollars of U.S. capital. That these countries have begun to become concerned lest the bulk of their economy soon be foreign-owned will be discussed subsequently. The fact is, however, that with the influx of foreign capital there is often a simultaneous boom in the economy of these countries to the point where they may achieve what W. W. Rostow has called "self-sustained economic growth." [46] Disproportionate foreign investment can mean disproportionate foreign influence in the domestic affairs of a country, but it can also mean the difference between economic stagnation and economic growth.

Even Servan-Schreiber, in his concern about American domination of the European economy—which, compared to the economies of most of the rest of the world, is extremely strong—recognizes the advantages of this foreign investment. He says:

In the short run, dependence is beneficial. American investment [and he could very easily say the same for European and Japanese investment in the weaker African and Asian countries], although it is presently an instrument of domination, is also the principal vehicle of technological progress for our economies. It introduces manufacturing processes and management techniques that are new to us. Indirectly, it forces European manufacturers to a rationalization and modernization they would never have accepted without such competition. The immediate economic effect of American investment is, therefore, quite positive. If we continue to permit American investment in its present form, Europe will share in the profits that foreign investors make from their high productivity. These profits spread throughout the economy raising the general standard of living.[47]

He does point out, however, that in the long run, unless Europe can become as "developed" as the United States it will lose control over its economic destiny and become little more than a satellite to American industry. But nationalization of foreign interests, or restrictions of those investments are not the answers he suggests. Quite rightly he sees those as highly destructive responses. The only constructive alternative he sees is for Europe to copy American managerial and technological skills in order to be in a position to compete with the U.S.

Although in many of the newly independent countries the foreign economic interests are being bought out by indigenous economic interests or expropriated, direct foreign investment in the weaker

---

[46] W. W. Rostow, *The Stages of Economic Growth: A Non-Communist Manifesto* (Cambridge, Eng.: Cambridge University Press, 1960).

[47] Servan-Schreiber, *American Challenge*, p. 38.

countries continues to increase. As economic development schemes
are launched in the underdeveloped world, giving the promise
of a more prosperous population, many more private foreign firms
will be encouraged to invest in these countries than ever before.
In some of the underdeveloped countries, there is recognition that
neither domestic private investment nor foreign economic aid will
supply sufficient quantities of capital to develop their economies
rapidly, and they have turned to private foreign capital to speed
the process. It is, of course, too early to say whether these schemes
will succeed or not, but there can be no denying that foreign
private capital can be a major stimulus to the economic growth of
an underdeveloped country. Foreign firms are often willing to
take economic risks that indigenous investors may consider excessive, and foreign capital is often willing to create industries that
indigenous capitalists consider inappropriate for men of high status.
Further, the foreign capitalist often brings with him highly advanced technologies and sophisticated managerial skills lacking in
primarily agricultural economies. In return, he asks two things: a
high return on investment, and investments relatively safe from expropriation. Nationalistic propaganda notwithstanding, the foreign
capitalist is often quite willing to take the initial profits of his investment and reinvest them in expansion of his facilities. This is
particularly true where the investment shows promise of becoming
extremely profitable in the long run. Often, he is willing to settle
for a lower rate of return over the long run, rather than insisting
on massive returns on a "one shot" investment.[48] Also, the more

[48] Some years ago, when there was a great deal of talk in Venezuela of
nationalizing American oil interests there, one of the larger U.S. oil companies, which had considerable investments in that country, is reported to
have held a confidential seminar with a large number of American economists. The company reportedly told the economists that it was then
annually repatriating more than 100% profit on its total investment in
Venezuela. The question it put to the economists was this: Should the
company step up the extraction of oil and repatriation of its profits to
300% annually (which, apparently, was technologically feasible) on the
assumption that it would be nationalized within 3 to 5 years anyway, or
should the firm reinvest a larger portion of its profits in the Venezuelan
development effort, and thus, perhaps, stave off nationalization entirely
and hence realize a larger total profit in the long run. It was reported to
me by one of the economists present that the majority of the economists
assembled suggested that the company adopt the first alternative, while
only a minority suggested that it adopt the latter policy. The company is
reported to have accepted and implemented the minority report. Now, more
than a dozen years after that conference was held, Venezuelan development progress is among the most rapid in Latin America, and there no
longer appears to be any talk of nationalizing American oil interests. Both
Venezuela and the American oil company seem to be profiting greatly
from the arrangement.

sophisticated foreign investor today knows that perhaps the best way to avoid expropriation is to staff his firm with indigenous personnel who then have a vested interest in its future.

Not only does the foreign investor help initiate much needed capital investment, he supplies a great many employment opportunities in societies where unemployment is often a major problem. Since it is far too expensive to import large numbers of skilled laborers from his home country, he often finds it cheaper to train unskilled natives in the skills needed by the industry. The host country, benefiting by the creation of capital and jobs, and social overhead capital in the form of a more skilled labor force, finds it to its interest to encourage and protect the foreign firm.[49]

What starts out as a mutually advantageous economic relationship also often takes on, because of its very success, highly political overtones. When an investment or industry is first started, the prime, and perhaps exclusive motivation of the foreign corporation is usually economic profits. After the industry or investment has proven financially successful, however, the managers of the firm (whether foreign or indigenous) find it in their financial interest to protect what they have started. The more successful the foreign investment in terms of growth and employment of indigenous population, the more politically dependent the country becomes on its continued success. This gives the foreign investors (and perhaps their indigenous managers) a certain leverage in making demands on the government for what they perceive as vital to their corporation's continued success. Thus, the more economically successful the foreign investment, the more likely that political resentment will build up against it, particularly on the part of those nationals who are not directly sharing the benefits of its success.

Ideally, of course, in a circumstance where the perceived interests of the foreign corporation come into conflict with the perceived interests of the host state, a solution would be found that would prove to be in the perceived interests of both. If the ideal solution cannot be found, however, the managers of the foreign firm—particularly when they are foreign but often even when they are indigenous—are likely to take the solution favoring the perceived interests of the firm. Often, if the foreign corporation is well enough entrenched in the host country, it will be able to convince the indigenous governmental decision makers that the interests of the firm are in the interests of the state (again the "What's good for General Motors . . ." phenomenon). This is particularly true where the managers of the foreign firm are in-

---

[49] See Leon Weintraub, *International Manpower Development: A Role for Private Enterprise in Foreign Assistance* (New York: Frederick A. Praeger, 1969).

digenous. We know enough about the elite structure of many of the countries of the world (both developed and developing) to know that interlocking commercial and governmental elites contribute substantially to a similarity of perception about what is and is not good for both country and foreign firm.

It is perhaps inevitable that some differing perceptions will arise. Not only are the principal goals of the commercial elite (profit) and the principal goals of the governmental elite (the state's welfare) likely to be different, but the clientele of both—particularly in the underdeveloped world—are also likely to be different. The clientele of the governmental elite is clearly the population (or at least the informed, articulate portions of the population) of its own country. The clientele of the business elite, particularly of the segment involved with foreign investment, is very likely to be foreign markets and perhaps foreign boards of directors. Thus there is a tendency on the part of the management of foreign-owned companies to look to a foreign constituency and peer group for both goals and criteria of effectiveness. The governmental elite, to a much larger extent, must take its goals and its criteria of effectiveness from a domestic constituency. Conflict, or at least potential conflict seems inherent, in such a situation. But, since in many countries of the world the foreign economic interests are profoundly important to the economic life of the country, the governmental elite may have no alternative but to give in to the perceived interests of the foreign investors.

Though foreign domination growing out of foreign economic interests is always a danger for weaker countries, the case should not be overdrawn. As we shall see in the final chapter, there are ways in which weaker states can, at least to some degree, protect themselves from this danger.

Currency Ties

Just as many of the languages of the world are simply too "weak" to become a medium of international communication, so, too, many currencies are too weak for international financial transaction. Thus, just as many weaker countries tie themselves to the language of a major Power, so, too, many of the weaker countries tie themselves to the currency of a major Power.

The dollar, the ruble, the yen, the mark, and to a lesser degree in recent years, the pound sterling, and the franc are among the most stable and strong currencies in the world—the "dollar crisis" of 1971 notwithstanding. This is still another of the basic distinctions separating the Powers, economically, from the weaker states.[50] No matter how shaky these principal currencies may be at times, relative to the currencies of most of the weaker states they are impregnable. Often the only reasons the currencies of the weaker states have any international worth at all is because they are backed by dollars, rubles, pounds, or francs. Indeed, one of the most important ways in which the weaker states are economically dependent upon the Powers is this "pegging" of their currencies to the currencies of the Powers. Yet without that pegging a great many of the currencies simply could not survive.

As a result of the United Kingdom's leading position in international trade, and as a center of finance, during the 19th century, many countries tended to use sterling as the most convenient medium for international transactions and to maintain central currency reserves in London. In some cases they also used British currency for their domestic needs. When the United Kingdom abandoned the gold standard in 1931, the members of the sterling Commonwealth, plus certain other countries who were already operating a sterling exchange standard, did likewise, and maintained unchanged the relationship between the exchange rate for their own currency and the pound sterling; these countries become known as the "sterling bloc." In 1939, with the outbreak of war, the pound sterling was no longer freely convertible into other currencies, and the group, *now somewhat contracted in numbers,* became legally defined for exchange control purposes as "the sterling area." Within this area the United Kingdom imposed virtually no restrictions on payments for current or capital transactions.[51]

Burma, Iceland, the Irish Republic, Jordan, Kuwait, Libya, South Africa, Western Samoa, and all Commonwealth countries except Canada were members of the Sterling Area in 1963.[52] Over a third of total world trade was estimated to be financed in sterling. While there are no legal or formal agreements pertaining to membership in the area:

> Because their external banking is in sterling, any margin of foreign currency that accrues to them is turned into sterling or any margin that they may need is purchased with sterling; much of the gold produced within the sterling area is also sold in the London market for sterling. The transactions of the sterling area with the rest of the world

[50] Obviously, Switzerland is a weak state with a strong currency, as are the Scandinavian countries, South Africa, Australia, and Canada, among others. But while these countries may be weak in many respects, they are certainly not weak economically.

[51] *Consultation and Cooperation in the Commonwealth,* p. 16. (Emphasis added.)

[52] *Ibid.,* p. 16.

are thus cleared through London, and the Exchange Equalization Account, which holds the British reserves, buys and sells exchange as appropriate.[53]

In this respect it is interesting to note that when Britain devalued the pound in November 1967, the countries that also devalued tended to be those countries whose G.D.P. was most dependent upon trade with the United Kingdom. Of the twenty-nine countries studied by Paul London, eleven also devalued their currency. They were Malta, Malawi, Barbados, Guyana, Sierra Leone, Trinadad, Cyprus, New Zealand, Jamaica, Ceylon and Israel.[54] Note that nine of the eleven countries were dependent for more than 12 percent of the G.D.P. on trade with the United Kingdom.

The situation with regard to membership in the Franc Zone is similar:

The Franc Zone was elaborated mainly after the Second World War, in a period of monetary instability and balance of payments difficulties, as a defensive organization intended to serve the interests of the Metropolis. It was authoritarian and centralized, and it involved a greater degree of protectionism than had been known since the middle of the nineteenth century. Its elaboration coincided roughly with that of the Sterling Area; but its organization was, and remains, tighter and more integrated than that of the Sterling Area—in much the same way as the administration and political organization of the French territories was more centralized and more integrated than that of the British. . . . Some of France's overseas territories—Laos, Cambodia, Vietnam and Guinea—have left the Franc Zone. . . ; others—Morocco, Tunisia, Algeria and Mali—have looser links than in the past. But for most of the members of the Franc Zone at least the monetary aspects of the system have not fundamentally changed as a result of independence.[55]

Being a member of the Sterling Area or the Franc Zone considerably facilitates trade among members. No exchange control is necessary within the area, and the accumulated sterling or francs can be used on the international market as a "hard" currency to purchase from nonsterling or nonfranc countries.

While the United States and the Soviet Union do not have "areas" or "zones" in the more formal way in which the British and French do, many of the weaker countries are as bound to the dollar and the ruble as others are bound to sterling or francs.

[53] *Ibid.,* p. 17.
[54] London, "Ties Among Nations," pp. 62–63. Ireland was not included in his study, although it and several other countries not considered by him may also have devalued at the same time.
[55] Hayter, *French Aid,* p. 61.

Within the Soviet Bloc in Eastern Europe, the marketing, pricing, and monetary system that prevailed from the 1940's until the early 1960's was different from the system found elsewhere. It was a completely controlled system in which market forces of supply and demand simply were not allowed to operate. Most trade was intra-Bloc trade, particularly with the U.S.S.R.; prices were fixed on the basis of economic planning goals; and exchange rates were officially fixed by the Soviet Union. These rates often discriminated against the weaker associated states, but without the backing of the ruble, the currencies of many of these countries would have been worthless in trade with the outside world.[56]

Particularly for the first ten or fifteen years after World War II, the United States dollar assumed the position once held only by gold. Many currencies had purchasing power only to the extent that they were backed by U.S. dollars. In effect, for many years the economy of the entire noncommunist world was directly or indirectly tied to the dollar. As the domestic economies of many European countries and Japan revived, their own currencies gradually came to be accepted in international trade, thus reducing their dependence upon the dollar. But because of the continued relative strength of the dollar, many weaker currencies are still tied to it.

As with economic dependence generally, so, too, with currency dependence. A weak country with a currency that is not acceptable in international trade must rely on some other stronger currency. It can shift its dependence from the franc to the ruble, or from the £ sterling to the dollar, but it must in some way be pegged to a stronger currency in order to survive. If no Power will back the currency of the weaker country, no one will accept that currency in international trade, and the foreign trade segment of that country's economy simply will not survive.

Changing Economic Relationships

Central to a situation of dependence is the *feeling* of dependence. In an economic context, this takes the form of feeling that the mentor Power's economic assistance (regardless of the type) is essential to the economic well-being of the individual, group, or state. In a sense, everything said thus far in this chapter has been a discussion of the degrees and types of economic dependence experienced by states and elites of states. This must be added, how-

[56] See Frederic L. Pryor, *The Communist Foreign Trade System* (Cambridge: Massachusetts Institute of Technology Press, 1963), particularly pp. 150–151.

ever: to the degree that the elite of a weak country gains a sense of satisfaction ("psychic reward") from the material transactions involved in the economic dependence relationship, that relationship is likely to persist. To the degree that the relationship is, or comes to be, perceived as disadvantageous—and some alternative seems possible—economic counterdependence is likely to start.

Counterdependence is a state of mind in which one wants to strike out at the individual, group, or state one formerly felt dependent on. What forms, then, do economic counterdependence take?

It may take the form of a complete refusal to buy from or (less likely) to sell to the formerly dominant Power; or, at a minimum, it may take the form of a reduction in buying and selling. The angry refusal of several Arab countries to sell oil to Britain after each Middle East crisis is a classic example of an economic manifestation of counterdependent feelings. In strict economic terms, the Arab countries were more hurt by the loss of sales than were the British who could buy elsewhere, but the psychic satisfaction that accrued to the Arab states by virtue of that counterdependent action more than compensated, in the short run, for the material loss. Ultimately, of course, the Arab countries realized that they were being hurt more than the British by their actions and the decision was reversed.

Ghandi's campaign to produce more homespun cloth may have been symbolic of many things, but one of them was certainly economic counterdependence. The boycott of South African products by Americans opposed to that country's apartheid policy could *not* be described as economic counterdependence because Americans were never economically dependent on South Africa. But the boycott of South African products by South African Bantus would certainly be an economic manifestation of counterdependence.

If over a period of time a weak country becomes economically less dependent upon one Power in terms of percent of G.D.P. accounted for by trade with that Power, and more dependent upon another, does that necessarily mean that the weaker is displaying counterdependent economic behavior? It may. But it may instead mean merely that the economic strength of the first Power has declined relative to the economic strength of the second, and that the second Power may be in a better position economically to satisfy the needs of the weaker. Indeed, this latter explanation is probably a far more accurate description of what has generally been happening in British and French former dependencies than any other single explanation. But the conscious effort on the part of the leadership in Tanzania, for example, to break what they had perceived to be Britain's "strangle-hold" over the Tanzanian economy is certainly an example of economic counterdependence. Thus, while all of formerly British East Africa is becoming economically less dependent upon Britain, one might predict that because of Tanzania's counterdependent attitude the process of transferring trade ties may be more rapid there than it will be for the rest of East Africa.

Economic counterdependence does not necessarily have international overtones. The expropriation of the property of a formerly dominant class or group by a government regime representing those who were formerly dominated is an expression of economic counterdependence regardless of whether the previously dominant group was foreign or indigenous. The nationalization of foreign investments often means not only that the state takes over the ownership of foreign property, but also that foreign managers are replaced by "nationals." Economic counterdependence need not mean acquiring ownership at all, but merely the denial of managerial positions in the indigenous economy to foreigners. A growing number of large international firms are finding that one of the most successful ways of either avoiding or mitigating economic counterdependence aimed at them is to staff the subsidiary in each country with nationals of that country.

Given the enormous economic disparities that exist among states, is international economic interdependence possible? If so, what forms can it take? Just as dependence and counterdependence are largely states of mind, so, too, interdependence can be viewed as a state of mind. In private industry in America there are enormous disparities in the relative wealth and power of firms in the same or related fields, but this does not prevent them from becoming economically interdependent. Sometimes a relatively small firm will develop and hold an exclusive patent on a product that becomes a component in a product put out by a larger firm. The smaller firm may need the market of the larger firm or firms, but to the degree that the product of the smaller firm becomes crucial to the product of the larger firm, the larger is also dependent on the smaller. Once there is a *perceived mutual economic dependence* between individuals, groups, or states, they can be said to have become economically interdependent. Usually, however, the more equal the power relationship, the more possible it is for interdependence to develop. Just as the larger firms (in similar or related fields) tend to become each other's best customers, the most powerful countries tend to become each other's best customers. Thus the advantages to be gained by economic interdependence (which are more often perceived by private firms than by governments) make it very much in the mutual economic interest of both weak and powerful countries that the weak countries become economically strong as quickly as possible.

Pessimism about the possibilities of eventual economic interdependence between the weak and powerful states is often based on the widening economic disparity that has occurred since 1945, but that pessimism overlooks many positive signs. American economic penetration of Europe may worry some, but the American economy is being substantially penetrated by foreign interests, too. It is projected that by 1975, 20 percent of American Gross National Product will be tied to European or Japanese interests.[57] What is more, with the increasing development of multinational firms there are signs that capital technology and managerial skill will flow more and more freely across national boundaries. States that are trying to become nations may slow down these trends toward interdependence somewhat not only because of their fear of foreign domination but because of a general economic counterdependence expressive of intense nationalism. (Often this takes the form of "protection of infant industries" or of the demand—solely for the sake of national pride—to produce the whole product domestically, despite advantages that could be gained by specializing in specific components.) But this may be nothing more than a short-term phenomenon, which will pass (as it has passed in other, more developed, countries) when private entrepreneurs and governments of the weaker states come to realize the advantages of economic interdependence.

While economic dependence is usually dangerous in that it limits a country's control over its own economic future, and economic counterdependence is often costly in terms of both efficiency and real cost to consumers, economic interdependence is a situation in which both parties profit. It is precisely because of the mutual economic advantage, and because businessmen, wherever they happen to reside, are interested in maximization of profit, that I believe eventual economic interdependence between weak and powerful states to be not only possible, but even highly probable.

---

[57] Estimate made by National Industrial Conference Board and cited by Ross, "Multinationalism," p. 100.

Chapter 7

Military Ties

Motivations for Military Ties

The Needs of Weak States

The protection of the inhabitants of a state from attack by the military of another state is and always has been universally perceived as one of the major functions of every government. No matter what other functions a government may perceive as legitimate, protection of its own population always has priority. Thus, with but few and isolated exceptions, every government, in every culture, in every historical era has maintained, even if only on a temporary basis, some sort of military establishment whose primary stated purpose has been protection of the population from external attack.[1] Just as universally, however, there has always existed an inequality among countries as to their ability to provide this protection. Weak states simply have never had the power to protect themselves from the military onslaught of stronger states. Sometimes geographic location or topography has been of major assistance, but even given those natural defenses, weak states have traditionally been forced to seek assistance from more powerful states for their protection. This, in turn, has always presented the dilemma for weak states that was so well-expressed by Rogers and Hammerstein in the lines of the King of Siam:

> Shall I join with other nations in alliance?
> If allies are weak, am I not best alone?

---

[1] Costa Rica is one of the more notable exceptions in the Western Hemisphere.

If allies are strong with power to protect me,
Might they not protect me out of all I own? [2]

In every period of history there have been some states that have
attempted to avoid this dilemma by pleading neutrality, but as the
Belgians learned in 1939, and as the Laotians and Cambodians
learned in the late 1960's and early 1970's, neutrality works only
so long as more powerful neighbors are willing to respect it, and/
or are not interested in taking what the neutral state may have to
offer. In addition, neutrality in some disputes offers no protection
from involvement in others. While some weaker countries were
maintaining neutrality and nonalignment in the cold war (seeing
no benefit to themselves in getting involved in big Power con-
frontations), they were simultaneously involved in disputes with
their neighbors that necessitated their building military establishments with big Power assistance.

Protection against external military threat is not the only reason
weak states seek military ties with Powers. In fact, it might not
even be the major reason. It is not unthinkable, and in some cases
may even be likely, that some weaker countries seek military
assistance not for defensive but for offensive reasons. Certainly
the Israelis consider this the motivation for the Arabs' military
ties to the Powers. Conversely, most Arab governments are convinced that the only reason Israel seeks and receives military support is because of aggressive designs on Arab lands, which are
perceived to fit the interest of certain Powers in keeping the Middle
East under their own domination. Like the Arabs and Israelis, each
side in a dispute usually views its own efforts to obtain big Power
support as purely defensive (the protection of its population),
while it views similar efforts on the other side as purely aggressive
and expansionist. To assume there is no element of truth in both
sides of the argument would be naive. But, except in rare instances,
it would be difficult in the extreme to document expansionist
motivation on the part of any country.

Another, and probably much more frequent reason why the
governments of weaker countries seek military support from the
Powers is undoubtedly to maintain themselves in office. Not every
ruling elite is sanguine about the possibilities of staying in office
without the use of coercion against disaffected segments of its
own population. Indeed, if one examines the record since 1945,
one finds that the only major instances of non-cold war open
hostilities *between* weaker states have been the Arab/Israeli wars,

[2] Richard Rogers and Oscar Hammerstein, "A Puzzlement," *The King
And I*. Copyright © 1951 by Williamson Music, Inc. Used by permission of
Williamson Music, Inc.

the Indian/Pakistani fighting, and the Malaysian/Indonesian conflict during the period of Sukarno's "confrontation" policy.[3] On the other hand, there have been many cases of the ruling elite in weaker countries using the military assistance they obtained from the Powers to maintain themselves in office (such as in Gabon, Kenya, the Philippines, Guatemala, et cetera). In addition, there have been a number of cases in which weaker countries have used foreign military assistance to quell secessionist movements on the part of large segments of their own population (as in Nigeria, Sudan, and East Pakistan, to mention only three). There are dangers to the political elite inherent in strengthening its own military establishment, as will be seen in a later section. But the ruling elites in most of the weaker countries obviously feel that there are even greater dangers to their continued rule in *not* strengthening their military, and, therefore, almost all do.

Just as a flag and a national anthem are considered essential accoutrements of statehood, for many countries so, too, are modern military establishments. Jet planes, battleships, the latest rockets, all seem to have become important prestige symbols to many of the leaders of the weak countries. Whether it is the political elites themselves who want this paraphernalia, or the military elites who demand it as the price for continued support, may vary from country to country. In any case, none of the weak countries (and only a few of the medium-level countries) are capable of producing the equipment themselves; therefore, they have to procure it from one or another of the major Powers.

Whatever the reasons, and despite the dangers, both internal and external, of becoming very dependent militarily on a major Power, nearly every one of the weaker countries is in some way tied militarily to at least one of the major Powers. Just as with economic ties, some of the weaker countries have come to recognize that they can in some measure lessen their dependence on a particular mentor by tying themselves militarily to more than one Power. Weak countries bought weapons from many more countries in the 1960's than they did in the 1950's,[4] 'and they are acquiring more aid from medium-level states than was previously possible. But it is not always easy for a country to diversify its military suppliers. If one attempts to tie one's military too closely to some state that one's major supplier disapproves of, there is

---

[3] One might also include the hostilities between the Indonesians and the Dutch, and the Indians and the Portuguese (in Goa) in this category, but those were essentially violent manifestations of anticolonial conflicts.

[4] See Jack L. Sutton, and Geoffrey Kemp, "Arms to Developing Countries: 1945–1965," *Adelphi Papers*, No. 28 (London: Institute for Strategic Studies, Oct. 1966).

always the danger that the major Power will retaliate by cutting off support.

The Interests of Powerful States

Why are Powers interested in having the weaker countries militarily tied to them? The motivations for requesting military protection and/or assistance are rarely the same as the motivations for granting it. In the broadest sense one might argue that they are the same when both countries perceive a common enemy against whom they recognize a mutual need for protection. This may occasionally be the case. During the 1950's, the leaders of many communist countries genuinely perceived "international capitalism" or "capitalist imperialism" as a direct threat to the continued existence of their regimes and "naturally" turned to the Soviet Union for military support. Similarly, many of the leaders of the anti-communist countries genuinely perceived the "international communist conspiracy" as a direct threat to the continued existence of their regimes, and equally as "naturally" turned to the United States for military protection. The leaders of the Soviet Union and the United States, for their parts, genuinely perceived an international threat from the other Power, directed at them and all like-minded governments everywhere. Thus, military treaties with and military assistance to the weaker countries in the "Free World" or the "Socialist Camp" were perceived by both sides as measures of mutual self-defense.

There were other reasons besides mutual perception of a common enemy, however, motivating much of the military assistance given by the Powers, just as there were other reasons besides "protection from external attack" for the aid having been requested. Catherine McArdle says of this:

> The extension of military assistance, to be sure, is hardly a new development. One need only glance over the diplomatic history of the 19th and early 20th centuries to find instances in which powerful nations have provided arms, equipment, training and economic subsidies to other nations or groups fighting or fearing a foreign invasion or domestic insurgency. . . .
>
> A major change in emphasis seems to have taken place with respect to the goals of assistance efforts. Few of the developing states are sought as present or potential military allies capable of adding significantly to the armed strength of donor nations against an actual or expected enemy. *The prime purpose now seems rather to develop military client states, to build up military-political strongholds through*

which to preserve or upset regional balances, or to maintain favored regimes against internal subversion or revolt.[5]

During the days of colonialism, most of the major Powers did not have to engage in the development of military ties to bolster regimes or to prevent penetration by competing Powers. They simply conquered an area, or by some other means made it a political dependency, and then sent their own troops into the area to protect their political interests. None of the Powers ever sent vast numbers of troops; they sent small groups who, in turn, trained native armies (often of mercenaries from different regions or of minority peoples who would feel no sense of identity with the local political elite) that the colonial Power commanded, armed, and paid. With the demise of the old colonial system and the emergence of some seventy independent new states, the power struggles on a world-wide scale among the major Powers did not cease, but rather required new modes of operation. One could no longer legally proclaim an area a "protectorate" or a "sphere of influence" and thereby be assured that competing Powers would stay out. It was necessary to use other means among them the establishment of military ties. In the place of spheres of influence have come "mutual security agreements" and multilateral and bilateral defense treaties. In the place of a small number of troops to train native armies have come military advisers to train independent indigenous armies. Instead of arms supplied free-of-charge, there are arms sales, loans, and grants; instead of salaries to the native armies, have come defense support, budget support, and economic aid. And, in many areas of the world, in the place of the old Powers who once ruled much of the land mass of the globe have come new Powers.

The major difference is that the "colonies" had no choice but to become the military dependency of whichever Power had won the last war among the Powers, but the new weak states can choose—within certain limits—which Power they would like to tie themselves to militarily. But military dependency remains so long as they are weak.

In their Institute for Strategic Studies report, "Arms to Developing Countries," Jack L. Sutton and Geoffrey Kemp discuss each of the Powers' motives for the sale of arms to the developing countries. The United States publicly gives the following reasons:

[5] Catherine McArdle, *The Role of Military Assistance in the Problem of Arms Control: The Middle East, Latin America and Africa,* C/64–24 (Cambridge: Massachusetts Institute of Technology, Center for International Studies, Aug. 10, 1964), pp. 1–2. (Emphasis added.)

(1) to strengthen the defense forces of the free world in accordance with American political and military objectives by selling military material [sic]; (2) to preserve and extend American military influence in accordance with American national objectives; (3) to assist in offsetting the foreign exchange costs of maintaining the American military position abroad; and (4) to reap the additional benefits that a successful American military sales effort will bring to such aims as standardization of equipment and joint acceptance of strategic and tactical concepts and doctrine through use of common hardware.[6]

While they find British policy toward arms sales less explicit than American, they cite a six-point British policy statement made public in 1959:

1. The Provision of British Service equipment to Commonwealth and allied governments is of direct military advantage through the benefits that follow standardization of equipment between forces that may have to fight side by side.
2. Overseas sales often help to recover the cost of past research and development . . . and reduce the cost of production to HM government.
3. . . . . the Royal Ordinance Factories. . . . have to be maintained in the interest of defense, and overseas orders help to ensure that fuller use is made of them than would otherwise be possible.
4. Overseas sales often provide outlets for equipment which has been rendered surplus by changes in British defense programmes.
5. The supply of arms to overseas governments may help strengthen political as well as military ties.
6. The sale of arms brings into the country considerable earnings of foreign currency. In selling arms to other countries, departments must, of course, have regard to political and security considerations as well as to the economic advantages of the trade. . . .[7]

The Soviets, as one might expect, do not publish explanations of this sort. The authors, however, say of Soviet motivations:

There are military advantages to be gained from having access to airfields and ports in friendly countries outside the Soviet hinterland, and nearly all the recipients of Soviet aid are situated in areas considered to be of strategic and economic importance to the West—the Middle East, South-East Asia, Central Africa and the Caribbean. The Cuban crisis of 1962 was proof of Soviet willingness to threaten the United States from an overseas base. . . . These motives can be termed *strategic-offensive*. Military programmes to India, Afghanistan and Iraq can be termed *strategic-defensive*. . . .
On the political side, there has been a wish to preserve the neutral status of countries that might otherwise turn to the West for military

[6] Sutton and Kemp, "Arms to Developing Countries," p. 6.
[7] *Ibid.,* p. 7.

assistance—Egypt, Syria and Indonesia. . . . in nearly all cases, the main adversaries of the recipient countries were favoured by the West (Israel, Pakistan, Malaysia). . . .

Though the immediate motives of Soviet policy seem to be political and strategic rather than commercial, it can be argued that in the long run there are considerable economic benefits to be gained by establishing friendly political relations with developing countries. After all, the Middle East, India and South-East Asia are all areas rich in natural resources and, given time, are likely to be a lucrative market for a whole range of consumer products.[8]

Finally, with regard to France, the authors of the report have this to say:

If the Soviet Union has been reluctant to outline her official policies towards military aid programmes, so have the governments of France, Italy and Switzerland. It would seem that the motives of the major West European countries (excluding Britain) have been almost entirely economic, though in the case of France there have been strong political undertones with respect to military aid to her former African territories. In addition, there has been a resolute French desire to create an armaments industry independent of the United States. This, in itself, is an essentially political move, though one that must have a sound economic basis. For this reason alone, the search for export markets has been pursued with vigor.[9]

These rather lengthy quotations have been cited here because they illustrate well the diverse motives of the Powers in engaging in military assistance. But regardless of which Power one considers, they all seem to have certain common motivations:

1. the political motive of furthering their own interests in their own struggles;
2. the economic motive of reducing their military expenses by selling surplus (usually outmoded) military hardware abroad;
3. the expectation that military ties will enhance both political and economic ties with the recipient.

Types of Military Ties

Multilateral "Collective Security" Agreements

Multilateral defense treaties against mutually perceived enemies probably predate the Peloponnesian wars. What is new about them

[8] *Ibid.*, pp. 7–8.
[9] *Ibid.*, p. 8.

is the degree of integration of the armed forces of different countries that many of these treaties now theoretically entail, and their proliferation, particularly since the end of World War II. The North Atlantic Treaty Organization (NATO), the Warsaw Pact, the Central Treaty Organization (CENTO—formerly called the Baghdad Pact), the Treaty of Rio, the South-East Asia Treaty Organization (SEATO), ANZUS (Australia, New Zealand, United States), the Arab League, the French Community, and the Commonwealth of Nations are just the more famous of these. Of these organizations, only the latter three are not specifically cold war alliances, and only the Arab League does not contain a major Power as a member.

The British Commonwealth and the French Community, while not specifically military organizations, presumably can function that way. Despite the lack of a formal multilateral military treaty among Commonwealth members, there is every indication that they conduct their affairs as though one did exist. While none of the Commonwealth members sent troops in support of the British participation in the Suez fiasco of 1956, when Britain entered World War II, in 1939, so did all the other already independent members of the Commonwealth.[10] A pamphlet put out by the British Central Office of Information says about current Commonwealth defense:

Each Commonwealth nation is entirely responsible for the organization of its own defenses and for determining the extent and nature of its commitments at all times. But although there is no central coordinating agency for the defense of the Commonwealth, there is close liaison between the Governments and valuable practical cooperation by the Services. Defense problems are frequently discussed at the meetings of Prime Ministers. . . .

There are frequent exchanges of visits between British and Commonwealth Ministers concerned with defense and between senior officers of the British and Commonwealth Services. The process of cooperation is materially assisted by the attachment of Service officers as advisors to the staffs of all British High Commissioners in Commonwealth capitals and at those of most Commonwealth High Commissioners in London.[11]

The French Community is a post World War II creation and France has not since been faced with military attack, so there is

[10] All except Ireland, which had already left the Commonwealth.

[11] Central Office of Information, *Consultation and Cooperation in the Commonwealth*, Ref. Pamphlet 25 (London: H. M. Stationery Office, 1963), pp. 14–15.

no way of knowing how that grouping would operate in such an event, although there are some indications that it would act similarly to the Commonwealth.

Agreements for cooperation between France and the newly-independent States were signed immediately after the various proclamations of independence. These agreements contained important provisions for mutual military aid. . . . The defence agreements with the Central African Republic, Chad, the Congo Republic, and Gabon were supplemented in 1961, when these 4 States joined to form, with French cooperation, the "Defence Council of Equatorial Africa."
France also has defence agreements with African countries outside the Community, namely Cameroon, Dahomey, Ivory Coast, Mauritania, Niger, and Togo.[12]

Ostensibly, multilateral alliances are concluded among states that perceive a common enemy and recognize the advantages to themselves of "collective security." Many, but not all, of these mutual defense treaties contain a phrase or a clause to the effect that an attack on one will be regarded as an attack on all, presumably making the response to the attack as nearly automatic as national regulations will allow. In actual practice, however, where a Power predominates, that Power is usually the one making the decision as to whether an attack has occurred and whether the attacker is worthy of repulsion. When India seized Goa, Portugal claimed to have been attacked and demanded a NATO response. Similarly, when war broke out between India and Pakistan, Pakistan perceived it as a direct attack and demanded a SEATO response. In neither case, however, was the collective security agreement activated. It is unlikely that Czechoslovakia or Hungary demanded a Warsaw Pact response to the invasion of their countries by Warsaw Pact troops for exactly the same reasons that it is unlikely that the Dominican Republic or Cuba demanded an OAS response to the American or American-supported invasions of their countries. When there is a major Power in a multilateral military organization, it, and it alone, has the power to define when an attack is of the nature to warrant an organizational military response. On the other hand, as the experience of the Arab League and the Commonwealth of Nations demonstrates, in the final analysis every country decides for itself whether, and how, it will respond, even if a Power calls for organizational action.

[12] *Treaties and Alliances of the World: A Survey of International Treaties in Force and Communities of States* (Keynsham, Bristol: Keesing's Publications, 1968), p. 103.

Bilateral Military Treaties

Far more numerous than the multilateral military treaties, and far more important to both the weak and the powerful countries (in the sense that they are utilized more extensively and frequently), are the bilateral military treaties that almost every weaker country of the world has with at least one major Power. Bilateral treaties can range from the sale, loan, or grant of small amounts of outmoded military equipment; through arrangements for advising, training, supplying, and/or commanding the military in question; to sending troops in support of the regime in office against both internal and external threats. Bilateral treaties provide for the establishment of mentor bases and the stationing of mentor troops on the soil of the weaker country; for the equipping of indigenous military with specific kinds of weapons; for the training of an indigenous officer corps in the mentor country; for "special assistance" or "budget support" or "defense support" for a host of military-related functions; and so on. It was under the terms of such bilateral treaties that, on the request of individuals whom the mentors chose to recognize as the legitimate governments of the countries, British troops were sent to Jordan, French troops were sent to Gabon, Belgian troops were sent to the Congo, American troops were sent to South Vietnam, and Russian troops were sent to Hungary. In each of the cases cited, it is almost certain that the regimes requesting the intervention would not have been able to remain in office without the assistance of the Power.

These treaties—whatever their contents—do not necessarily stem from a sinister neocolonial plot by the Powers to maintain control over the weaker countries. The governments of the weaker countries often simply are not in a position to protect themselves from either internal or external attack. Without the existence of these bilateral treaties, some of them would have no means of self-defense at all, while others would have only the most rudimentary and inefficient of military capabilities.[13] Without the existence of some sort of effective military arm, many of these weaker countries could very well be faced with chaos and anarchy. What is more, these states often genuinely do feel threatened by their neighbors. They must have some means of preserving internal order and preventing external attack. While it may be true that these treaties tend to keep the weak countries militarily dependent

[13] See H. Roberts Coward, *Military Technology in Developing Countries,* C/64–5 (Cambridge: Massachusetts Institute of Technology, Center for International Studies, April 15, 1964).

upon the major Powers, and in large measure help to perpetuate big Power spheres of influence, it is equally true that without them many of the states would not be able to provide even the most elementary functions of government.

Initially, as might be expected, most of the former colonies chose their former metropoles as their source of assistance. To the degree that they had any military establishment whatever, it had been trained, equipped, and conditioned by the former metropole. Many of the former metropoles already had military bases or troops stationed on their territory. It was only natural to turn to them for military support. Those weaker countries governed by highly counterdependent elites, of course, demanded that the military of the former metropole leave the country as a symbolic demonstration of their independence. But since they could not protect themselves, they immediately found it necessary to turn to another Power for military assistance. Almost all of the former colonies were sufficiently counterdependent to insist that their military establishments be commanded by their own nationals, but having achieved that symbol of independence, they then usually asked the former metropole to remain in an advisory capacity.

Military assistance to the weaker countries is expensive, however. France to some degree, and Britain to a great degree, are finding that they cannot afford to continue military assistance to weak countries around the world. As Britain has withdrawn, the weaker countries formerly militarily dependent upon the United Kingdom have had to look to other Powers to provide the military services they need. The United States and the Soviet Union have both displayed a willingness, if not eagerness, to step in and provide these services.

Egypt, Iraq, Syria, Algeria, Southern Yemen, Libya, and Guinea are only some of the noncommunist states previously dependent upon Britain and France that are now becoming equally as dependent militarily upon the Soviet Union. Jordan, Israel, Iran, Pakistan, and South Vietnam are some of the former British and French dependencies that are now militarily dependent upon the United States. But for the elites of many of the weaker countries, an invitation to one of the Super Powers means becoming embroiled in cold war politics, which they might prefer to avoid. Accordingly, some countries have entered into limited military agreements with both the United States and the Soviet Union, thus attempting to avoid taking sides. India is one country that has long followed this policy. But what these weaker countries have often found is that a request for military assistance from both protagonists produces little more than token response. If one wants or needs massive military assistance, both sides in the cold war seem to set as a condition that the recipient rely on them primarily, if not exclusively.

Another approach followed by some of the weak countries has been to seek military protection and/or assistance not from the major Powers, but from the medium-level countries. Thus Burma, Ghana, the Central African Republic, and Dahomey have turned, at least in part, to Israel for military support. Others have turned to West Germany, Czechoslovakia, and Sweden for various types of military assistance. While this approach may avoid direct involvement in the cold war, it cannot bring the kind of massive support some governments feel they need. These medium-level countries can supply military equipment of the smaller variety, and technical and managerial training, but little else. They do not have, or cannot send, combat troops to defend the weak country.

An interesting case of the replacement of the British by medium-level states occurred in 1971. Lacking an adequate defensive military capability of their own, Malaysia and Singapore have since their independence relied upon their former metropole, the United Kingdom. Not only have the Malaysian and Singaporean military been trained either at Sandhurst or by Sandhurst graduates in British techniques, equipment, values, and modes of behavior, but British troops have been physically present in these countries to defend them from external attack. Militarily, Malaysia and Singapore were both tied to and dependent upon the United Kingdom. Now, a military culture as such certainly transcends national boundaries (as does a commercial, artistic, or scientific culture), but there are enough differences in emphasis, nuances, techniques, and equipment in each Power's military culture that for Malaysia and Singapore to have switched to a totally different military mentor, like the United States or Japan or (most difficult) the Soviet Union, would have produced a major "shock" to the Malaysian and Singaporean military establishments. Thus, it is not at all surprising that the Malaysians and Singaporeans chose to establish military ties with Australia and New Zealand in place of Britain.[13a]

Protective Umbrella

There is a third type of military tie that deserves mention, even if it is somewhat less important than the other two. That is the "protective umbrella" or "shield" under which some states are

[13a] In addition to a military guarantee by Australian and New Zealand troops, Singapore is increasingly coming to rely on British trained Israeli advisors to train its armed forces.

placed by a major Power, whether they request it or not. Militarily, this is analogous to the sphere of influence. A major Power by this device announces to the world that it would consider penetration by another Power as a hostile act and would respond militarily. Cambodia, Laos, and South Vietnam were placed under such an umbrella by SEATO after the French withdrew. Originally, the area was supposed to have been neutralized, but as the United States came to support the governments of President Ngo Dinh Diem and his successors in South Vietnam and of Prince Souvanna Phoumna in Laos, the protective umbrella notion was invoked to justify military assistance to those friendly regimes. Only later did Diem sign a bilateral military agreement with the U.S. To this author's knowledge, no such bilateral military agreement was ever signed with Laos and thus our military assistance to the anticommunist forces there presumably flowed under the terms of that protective shield. The "Truman Doctrine," which preceded NATO and bilateral treaties with Greece and Turkey, was another such umbrella, as was the "Eisenhower Doctrine" in the Middle East. Again in the latter case, to this author's knowledge there was no bilateral or multilateral military treaty by which Lebanon was tied to the United States, and thus American troops were dispatched under the notion of the protective umbrella.

In a sense, the Chinese had a similar arrangement with North Korea during the Korean War, and announced to the world a number of times that if the United Nations forces advanced too close to the Yalu River (the Chinese border with North Korea), they would be forced to intervene. General MacArthur did not believe they meant it and found to his dismay that they did. When the Chinese announced a similar protective cover of North Vietnam against an American and/or South Vietnamese invasion, it was apparently more credible.

The Extent of Military Assistance

One encounters great difficulty in attempting to measure accurately the degree of military dependence of specific weak countries on major Powers. Military assistance can take so many different forms that some may appear on a country's books as nothing more than economic aid of one sort or another. Whether certain kinds of assistance are termed military or not may depend more on domestic political considerations at any given moment than on which sector of the society will actually be most served by the assistance. What is more, there have been a number of cases where the major Power has refused to supply a weaker country with military assistance because it disapproved of the purposes for which that assistance would be used, but has—for any number of reasons—granted economic assistance, which was promptly used by the weaker to make up the deficiencies within its economy created by the diversion of its own funds to those military purposes. It was because the Dutch were doing this during their war with Indonesia that the United States threatened in 1949 to cut *all* aid to the Netherlands. And, indeed, it is the use of economic aid in this way in much of the world that makes it so very difficult to determine precisely what is or is not military assistance.

There is another problem that is even more frustrating: secrecy. Not only do most countries prefer not to disclose the exact nature and extent of the military assistance they allocate to friendly weaker states, but there is even a reluctance on the part of many Powers to admit that certain of their associated states are receiving any military assistance at all. Occasionally, covert deals do come to light however, supplying us with evidence that covert military ties are not merely the figment of some fanatic's imagination. But because precise information is not available, imagination is sometimes allowed greater reign in this matter than it deserves. It is a fact that covert military assistance of various sorts, from all major Powers to many weaker states, does exist. This makes it very difficult to determine the precise extent of a country's military dependence.

The picture is not totally clouded, however. In the first place, some of the major Powers do report some, and probably most, of the military assistance they offer. Second, while the Soviet Union reports practically none of the military assistance it provides, various U.S. agencies, public and private, publish figures on Soviet military aid that may be fairly reliable. In addition, there is a private institution in London, the Institute for Strategic Studies, that sometimes publishes amazingly detailed analyses of military aid to and from all countries. The reason this information is available, despite official secrecy, is because it is often impossible to hide massive military assistance. A country may possibly receive several million dollars worth of military support of one sort or another without the fact becoming public knowledge, but it is unlikely in the extreme that any country could receive tens of millions of dollars worth of military support without the public —at least in the recipient country—finding out about it. This is precisely what leads most observers to agree that those military ties that are covert are probably quite insignificant compared to the military support that is overt.

While it is true that even a few million dollars worth of very selective covert military support, given at precisely the right moment, may be crucial to the receiving country in certain situations, in the long run it may do very little to alter the basic relations between the donor and the recipient. In those cases where that small amount of covert aid was sufficient to change or to maintain the regime in power, the aid may indeed have basically altered the relations between the two states. In such situations, the likelihood is that the initial minimal covert aid would be followed by more massive overt aid, in which case the changed relationship would be reflected in the available data.

Sales and Grants

The United States in the post World War II period has, of course, been the major supplier of all sorts of aid to the world. In the twenty years between 1946 and 1966, the United States reports having obligated or authorized a total of $122 billion of economic and military assistance in overseas loans and grants. Although specifically military programs comprised only $36 billion, to this can be added the loans used for purchasing U.S. arms. "The total for weapons transfers can be broken down into loans and grants, with the former resulting in arms sales by the U.S. Government." Thus, from 1949 to mid-1966:

United States arms sales amounted to nearly one-half of the value of arms transferred by grants. That is, the United States provided military assistance through grants in the amount of $30.2 billion and sold arms worth $16.1 billion for a total of $46.3 billion. The total is reported to be $4 billion greater than the amount of economic aid extended through grants and loans in the same period. Current sales of military weapons are reported to exceed grants by approximately two to one with sales and grants totalling $3 billion per year.[14]

While the United States is the major supplier of an assortment of aid, some specifically military, some military-related, and some presumably economic (but which can be used to free the recipient's domestic resources to buy military hardware), its aid is not as widespread as the dollar figures might suggest. The greatest bulk of American economic and military aid in the first decade after World

[14] "The Impact of U.S. Military Assistance on Selected Recipient Countries," project proposal prepared under the direction of Daniel S. Cheever, University of Pittsburgh, for submission to the Department of Defense, July 28, 1967, pp. 1–2. Figures are from *U.S. Overseas Loans and Grants and Assistance from International Organizations—Obligations and Loan Authorization, July 1, 1945–June 30, 1966,* Special Report, House Foreign Affairs Committee.

War II went to Western Europe. During the Korean conflict and thereafter, American assistance efforts—particularly military assistance—shifted to South Korea, Taiwan, and South Vietnam, which received the lion's share. The United States actually accounts for less of the military assistance that goes to the so-called developing world than would at first appear. In fact, from 1945 to the mid-1950's, Britain was more responsible for the *sale* of arms to the developing world than was the United States.

British arms export figures in 1965 were reliably reported to be about $400 million annually, of which about half was in army equipment. Comparable totals for other years have not been obtained, but statistics are available which show that the export of arms from 1951 to 1961 (excluding naval vessels) averaged about $300 million yearly and was increasing. Although the value of naval exports during the past years has been relatively small, if this total is added to the total of other arms exports, and the increasing price of weapons is taken into consideration, this would explain the current figure of $400 million for all arms exports. Thus, Britain's arms export figure has increased slowly, though her share of the market has declined. . . . It is more difficult to estimate what part of the total is going to the developing areas, although the known movement of British arms to foreign countries indicates that it is much greater than the 10 per cent estimated for American arms exports. The figure probably lies between one-quarter and one-half of the total and may be estimated roughly as $150 million annually.[15]

Up to 1955 Britain supplied 95 percent of all jet aircraft delivered to the Middle East, and almost all of the jets to India, Pakistan, Australia, New Zealand, South Africa, and Rhodesia. But it was not just Commonwealth countries that Britain supplied; Britain was also the second supplier of jet aircraft to Latin America.[16] Indeed, Sutton and Kemp report that until 1955 "there was a virtual Anglo-American monopoly on the supply side, and a gentleman's agreement between the two countries not to upset local balances by large inputs of weapons." [17]

Since that time, however, the Soviet Union and France have entered the field and, although the absolute amount supplied by Britain has not markedly decreased, it no longer supplies the percentage of the market it once did. In an attempt to place monetary value on the military goods delivered to the developing world since 1955, Sutton and Kemp estimate that the Soviet Union now sells an average of $400 million worth of armaments

[15] Sutton and Kemp, "Arms to Developing Countries," p. 28.
[16] *Ibid.*, pp. 9–11.
[17] *Ibid.*, p. 5.

per year; the United States $150 million (which is exclusive of the approximately $300 million in military armaments it *gives* as grant aid); and France $200 million.[18]

In short, all of the major Powers are now suppliers, on a large scale, of military hardware to the weaker countries. But the dollar figures may be somewhat misleading. Since one of the prime motives behind equipment sales is political, the price paid for a particular piece of military hardware may vary considerably, depending on the eagerness of the Power to have the weak country buy from it. In many cases the Power has to lend the weak country the money for the sale anyway, so the price actually paid is somewhat irrelevant. What counts is that the military of the weaker state become equipped with and trained to handle the hardware of the Power, creating a high degree of dependence on the supplier for training, parts, and replacements. This is exactly what the Powers mean when, in seeking to sell military equipment to weak countries, they speak of "standardization of equipment" and "joint acceptance of strategic and tactical concepts and doctrine through use of common hardware." It is no different from the concept underlying the supply of capital goods to weak countries discussed in Chapter 6 on economic ties. Once a country has bought your weapons system they can buy another's only at great cost to themselves.

Table 7.1 is a revision of a table compiled by Sutton and Kemp on the delivery of jet aircraft to the developing countries between 1945 and 1965. It is presented in an effort to supply the reader with at least some indication of the degree to which some of the weaker countries are dependent on the Powers for major military hardware. Not all countries are included—notably absent are the Soviet associated states and South Vietnam, South Korea, and Taiwan (which presumably received many times more jets than all other U.S. associated states combined). In many cases the situation has changed markedly since 1965. Also, in considering Table 7.1, the reader should bear in mind that the less developed the country, the less likely it would be to be able to use jet aircraft. Propellor-driven craft may constitute a much higher proportion of a weak country's air force than jet planes, and many of these older types of aircraft may have come from countries other than those that supplied the jets. Further, aircraft are hardly the only equipment the military of developing countries use. Tanks, jeeps, and ordinary rifles may very well be more important to some of the more underdeveloped countries.

Despite all these limitations, however, Table 7.1 reveals some

[18] *Ibid.,* p. 29.

TABLE 7.1

Military Jet Aircraft Delivered to Developing Countries, 1945–65[a]

Breakdown of Aircraft by Countries of Origin

Recipient Country	1945–1955				1955–1965				On Hand 1965				
	U.S.S.R.	U.K.	U.S.A.	France	U.S.S.R.	U.K.	U.S.A.	France	U.S.S.R.	U.K.	U.S.A.	France	Other
U.K. Associated States (ranked by number on hand from U.K.)													
India	—	50	—	70	12	387	—	159	12	378	—	110	—
Australia[b]	—	258	—	—	—	48	90	20	—	110	80	20	—
Rhodesia	—	15	—	—	—	47	—	—	—	52	—	—	—
South Africa	—	45	—	—	—	17	—	16	—	50	—	16	36[c]
New Zealand[b]	—	50	—	—	—	10	—	—	—	46	—	—	—
Iraq	—	28	—	—	64	55	5	—	46	34	—	—	—
Jordan	—	20	—	—	—	21	—	—	—	30	—	—	—
Ceylon	—	—	—	—	—	12	—	—	—	12	—	—	—
Kuwait	—	—	—	—	—	10	—	—	—	10	—	—	—
Sudan	—	—	—	—	—	9	—	—	—	9	—	—	—
Burma	—	8	—	—	—	—	10	—	—	6	10	—	—
Ghana	—	—	—	—	—	—	—	—	—	—	—	—	8[d]
Saudi Arabia	—	—	—	—	—	—	20	—	—	—	16	—	—
Afghanistan	—	—	—	—	100	—	—	—	90	—	—	—	—
Iran	—	—	—	—	—	—	170	—	—	—	110	—	—
Pakistan	—	36	—	—	—	—	192	—	—	—	122	—	—
Israel	—	20	—	12	—	3	—	286	—	—	—	270	—
United Arab Republic	—	100	—	—	450	—	—	—	370	—	—	—	—

French Associated States
(ranked by number on
hand from France)

Country												
Cambodia	—	—	—	7	—	—	—	7	—	—	—	—
Lebanon	6	—	—	—	10	—	—	—	14	—	14	—
Morocco	—	—	—	20	—	—	—	20	—	—	—	—
North Vietnam	—	—	—	40	—	—	—	40	—	—	—	—
Algeria	—	—	—	60	—	—	—	60	—	—	—	—
Syria	20	—	—	119	7	—	—	94	—	—	—	—

U.S.A. Associated States
(ranked by number on
hand from U.S.A.)

Country												
Philippines	100	—	—	—	—	70	—	—	—	70	—	—
Argentina	—	—	—	—	—	55	50	—	40	45	45	—
Chile	5	—	—	—	—	55	30	—	40	45	30	—
Brazil	—	—	—	—	—	50	—	—	—	30	—	—
Peru	70	20	—	—	24	24	—	—	21	30	—	—
Ecuador	18	—	—	—	—	27	—	—	12	23	—	—
Venezuela	12	6	—	—	52	22	—	—	50	18	—	—
Colombia	—	6	—	—	—	26	—	—	—	15	—	5°
Mexico	—	—	—	—	15	20	—	—	15	15	—	—
Uruguay	—	—	—	—	—	20	—	—	—	14	—	—
Nicaragua	—	—	—	—	—	4	—	—	—	4	—	—
Dominican Republic	50	—	—	—	17	—	—	—	50	—	—	—
Cuba	—	—	—	220	—	—	—	220	—	—	—	—

TABLE 7.1 (Cont'd.)

Breakdown of Aircraft by Countries of Origin

Recipient Country (not ranked)	1945–1955				1955–1965				On Hand 1965				
	U.S.S.R.	U.K.	U.S.A.	France	U.S.S.R.	U.K.	U.S.A.	France	U.S.S.R.	U.K.	U.S.A.	France	Other
Other													
Congo^e	—	—	—	—	—	—	—	3	—	—	—	3	—
Ethiopia	—	—	—	—	—	—	20	—	—	—	20	—	—
Indonesia	—	—	—	—	115	—	—	—	100	—	—	—	—
Libya	—	—	—	—	—	—	2	—	—	—	2	—	—
Somalia	—	—	—	—	6	—	—	—	6	—	—	—	—
Thailand	—	—	—	—	—	—	112	—	—	—	70	—	—

a Taken from Sutton and Kemp, "Arms to Developing Countries," pp. 36–37. Figures include jet fighters, jet trainers, and light jet bombers acquired by purchase, grant, or licensed production.

b The inclusion of Australia and New Zealand as "developing" countries is something of a surprise, but since they were included by Sutton and Kemp, I have also included them here.

c Supplied by Canada.
d Supplied by Italy.
e Unspecified as to whether Kinshasa or Brazzaville.

interesting data. Particularly noteworthy is the picture it gives of the degree to which the U.S. and the U.S.S.R. have become suppliers of jets to states formerly associated with Britain and France. As of 1965, the U.S. and the U.S.S.R. had supplied the majority of jet aircraft in almost 50 percent of the countries previously considered associated states of Britain and France. Thus, while in no way complete, this table does suggest the degree to which these weaker countries are becoming increasingly dependent for modern military hardware—with all that implies—on the two Super Powers. Despite increased costs involved, many of the weaker countries are consciously seeking a multiplicity of supply sources precisely because they fear too great a military dependence on one Power. They recognize the consequences of total military dependence and many of them are trying to escape these consequences by diversifying their sources of supply. Of course, if all the major Powers agree not to compete in supplying arms, then there is nothing the weaker countries can do. But except in very limited circumstances the likelihood of such an agreement is remote. Hence the weak countries are using big Power competition as their opportunity to develop their military policy free from dependence on single Powers.

Military-related Economic Assistance

Military hardware is only one of the types of military assistance possible, and perhaps not the most important type. The major Powers collectively give, or loan on favorable terms, somewhere on the order of $3 to $4 billion in aid anunally, and perhaps as much as half that amount has to be considered defense-related.

As H. Roberts Coward observes:

The pattern of economic support for the military in the underdeveloped world is far from uniform. In many cases these countries have been able to unload much of this burden upon military aid programs or upon former metropolitan powers. . . . France, for example, is believed to provide about four times the amount of Malagasy's current defense budget, about $9 million, to that country in aid. Thus, the budgetary data represent an indicator of the burden of the defense effort on the Malagasy economy, but it does not reflect the size of the military effort. In other cases, a trade-off occurs where substantial economic aid permits a country to divert more of its own resources to military effort than would otherwise be possible.[19]

Are harbors, paved roads, and airports primarily military or are they part of the economic infrastructure of a country? What

[19] Coward, "Military Technology," pp. 22–23.

about the economic development activities undertaken by the military of a country? An even more difficult type of aid to categorize neatly is one called "special assistance." As far as the American Congress is concerned, all of these are usually considered military aid, and appropriations are made each year on that account. When the only way to get aid through an economy-minded Congress is to label it military assistance, almost everything is so labeled. Whenever there is an overreaction in Congress to military spending, however, such assistance normally gets reclassified as primarily economic aid. Actually, it is both.

Catherine McArdle summarizes the arguments for including capital development aid in military assistance appropriations:

According to official statements aid of this kind is provided for three purposes: first, to maintain economic and political stability in countries where the donor nation has strategic political interests; second, to secure access to overseas bases; and third, 'to provide an alternative to excessive dependence on Sino-Soviet aid.' [20]

The rationale is clear:

. . . in the long run a country's capacity to defend itself against external attack or internal subversion is inherently related to the state and level of its economic and social overhead capital base.[21]

When viewed from this perspective, a great deal of the economic assistance that goes to the weaker states from the major Powers can be considered military assistance.

Far more important than the amount of military-related aid the Powers lend or give to the weaker countries may be the amount of military and military-related support they provide that is not included in their aid budgets, but in their own Defense budgets. I. F. Stone cites some rather startling revelations that came out of a recent study done by the National Urban Coalition. In fiscal year 1971, of the $74.5 billion Pentagon budget, only a little more than one-fifth ($16.3 billion) went for the "pure defense of the United States," that is, for the so-called ". . . strategic forces—both offensive and defensive—with required backup supporting components including intelligence and research" that are necessary for the actual defense of America. An almost equal amount went spe-

---

[20] McArdle, *Role of Military Assistance,* p. 7. McArdle quotes from U.S. International Development Agency (*sic.*) (A.I.D.), *Proposed Mutual Defense and Assistance Programs* for FY 1964, p. 64.
[21] McArdle, p. 8.

cifically for the war in Vietnam ($14.2 billion). But the lion's
share went for what are called "General Purpose forces." As Stone
explains:

Our conventional or General Purpose forces are almost entirely
geared to the defense (or control) of other nations. As McNamara
put it, in a summation quoted by the Coalition from his final posture
statement, "the overall requirement for General Purpose forces is not
related so much to the defense of our own territory as it is to the support of our commitments to other nations." These General Purpose
forces are costing more than $44 billion in the current fiscal year, or
almost three times as much as the $16.3 billion cost of our strategic
offensive and defensive forces. The Coalition points out that this $44
billion goes to implement commitments of various kinds to 45 nations
—21 in the Western hemisphere, 13 in Western Europe, two in Central
Asia, six in Southeast Asia and the Pacific, and three in the Far East.
The Pentagon does not customarily display the allocation of these
General Purpose forces to various regional contingencies. But Wm W.
Kaufman, a Pentagon consultant under McNamara, author of "The
McNamara Strategy" provided the first overview of these allocations
last year in testimony to the Joint Economic Committee. The Coalition
utilizes this to show that the $44 billion spent on General Purpose
forces this fiscal year (excluding the incremental cost of the Vietnam
war), was allocated—

Europe	$19.6 billion
Asia	$15.8 billion
Latin America	$ 1.3 billion
Strategic Reserve	$ 4.3 billion
R[esearch] and D[evelopment]	$ 3.0 billion[22]

While there are no comparable figures available for the Soviet
Union, one can only guess that it probably allocates a similar proportion of its own defense budget for exactly the same General
Purpose forces, only these are probably deployed overwhelmingly
in Eastern Europe. Although the British are cutting down on this
component of their own defense budget, they and the French have
traditionally used such forces as their principal military assistance
to associated states. Thus, the magnitude of military assistance from
the Powers to their associated states may actually exceed by a
very great deal the figures contained in all standard estimates.
Everything that was said about the economic ties between weak

[22] "How Much The Pax Americana Costs," *I. F. Stone's Bi-Weekly*, Vol.
XIX, No. 12 (June 14, 1971), pp. 1, 2. Stone cites: National Urban Coalition, Robert S. Benson and Harold Wolman, eds., *Counterbudget: A Blue-
print for Changing National Priorities* (New York: Praeger paperback,
1971).

and powerful countries in the previous chapter could be repeated here with regard to military ties. Military assistance does tend to support the regime in power. Military assistance does tend to make the recipient country militarily dependent upon the mentor. Military assistance does tend to produce a host of other ties that still further bind the weaker to the stronger. And, as in the consideration of economic assistance, it is important here to distinguish between the degree to which a weak country is militarily dependent upon a mentor, and the degree to which the military elite of that country is tied to the Power.

To the degree that the assistance involves the supply of military equipment, training of the military elite, or any specifically military assistance, the military elite of the country is likely to perceive itself as personally tied to the mentor. On the other hand, to the degree that the assistance takes the form of defense-related aid, or straight economic aid that gives the political regime the freedom to allocate domestic resources to direct military spending, the military elite may consider itself less dependent upon the mentor and more dependent upon the good graces of its own political elite. In so far as the assistance from the mentor is nonspecific, it may be possible for the political elite of the country to determine which branch of its own military establishment will be strengthened relative to which other branch. When the assistance is specifically military, that discretion may be removed from the political elite.

If the assistance from a foreign Power is not specifically military, the political elite may have the flexibility to strengthen the society as a whole rather than the military elite in particular. It may be in a position to unify the country through the building of roads or the construction of communication networks. It may be able to build a sufficient infrastructure to allow for the establishment of its own small-scale armaments industry. It may use the aid to establish a military that, like the military in Israel, Singapore, and several other rapidly developing countries, is a principal means of teaching a heterogeneous population a common language, literacy, and modern (as opposed to traditional) values. In some countries, indeed, through use of these funds the military has been employed as the major modernizing instrument in the country, whether by actually building the roads, schools, or other public works, or by engaging in various so-called "civic action" programs. In the early days of the communist regime in North China, for example, it was the Red Army that actually undertook the constructive programs of building dams, irrigating fields, and teaching literacy, which made the regime so acceptable to the mass of the population.

Training of the Indigenous Military

Perhaps the most effective military tie, from the perspective of the Powers, is the training of the indigenous military establishment by a mentor. That is because training, more than any other single type of military assistance, directly affects the perceptions, values, and attitudes of the military. Hence, training of the military seems to be the aid big Powers are most willing to provide. And since training is what many of the weaker military establishments need most, there is a more or less mutual interest on the part of both weak and strong to see that the military in the weaker gets trained by the stronger.

For many of the weaker countries, whatever modern military establishments they have are due to the efforts of the colonial Powers. In establishing military forces in their colonies, the metropoles invariably patterned them on the model of the military "back home." Indeed, prior to independence the top command was exclusively in the hands of military officers from the metropole. If any indigenous officers were allowed into the upper echelons at all, the people chosen were invariably those who had best learned the values, attitudes, and modes of behavior expected of an officer of the metropole Power. For example, one finds in the colonies that there was a much higher percentage of Christians among the indigenous military officers than among the population at large.[23] These officers spoke the language of the metropole, often as their first language; often had wives who were born in the metropole; and held political views strikingly similar to those of the officers in the metropole country. In short, they were among the most "acculturated" segments of the entire population.

When formal independence came, one of the first acts of most countries was to put the military under the command of their own nationals. But a number of countries did not do that, either because they had none of their own people who were sufficiently trained, or because the political elite trusted the nationals of the mentor more than they trusted their own military people. While the Jordanian and Polish cases are the best known, they were not the only countries that retained mentor commanders for a time. In those countries that had to fight for political independence—such as Algeria, Indonesia, and North Vietnam—of course the military

[23] This was true, at least, in those cases where the mentor was Christian. In the case of Eastern European countries, of course, belief in the omnipotence of the Communist party was a more important value than belief in a Supreme Being.

elite broke their ties with the former metropole. But those countries
are the exceptions to a general rule. In most of the weaker countries, the military had become so close to carbon copies of the
military "back home" that even after independence the military
elite often continued to reflect the values, attitudes, and modes of
behavior of the mentor Power learned in pre-independence days—
whether or not they retained any mentor commanders.

While for many of the weaker countries it was a symbol of independence and prestige to have their own nationals commanding
their armed forces, the fact often was (and in many cases still is)
that their own commanders lacked the technical skills necessary to
run relatively large complex organizations such as military establishments. Thus, while the persons officially in command were nationals, in many cases the former mentor commanders were retained as advisers to the newly established independent armed
forces. In those cases where the political elite was sufficiently
counterdependent to demand that the mentor advisers be sent
home, or where the former mentor could not afford to maintain
advisers, the advisers of different Powers were called in to replace
them.

Most of the weaker states do not have armed forces that are
capable of functioning at the level desired without assistance from
some major Power. The operative factor here is "the level desired."
It seems that no matter how efficient or modern a military establishment is, it seeks to be more so. The military in some of the
weakest states may actually depend for survival upon technical
assistance from more powerful countries, but the military establishments in other countries are extremely sophisticated and com-
petent on their own. Yet even in those cases they seem to feel a
need to surpass themselves—to compete with the military establishment of neighbors, enemies, or peer groups. Whatever the reason,
almost every one of the countries considered in this study—with
the exception of some of the middle-level states like Australia,
Canada, and Sweden—seem to feel the need to be more advanced
militarily than they are, and accordingly have teams of advisers
from the mentor Powers to assist them in one way or another. As
of 1967, the United States had "military advisory units" in no
fewer than thirty-eight countries, of which almost 50 percent were
in Latin America.[24] Similarly, the British maintained military advisers in most of the Commonwealth countries, while France and
the Soviet Union provided military advisers primarily for their
associated states. As Britain and France, in cutting back their

[24] *New York Times Magazine,* Part I (Sept. 17, 1967), p. 30.

foreign commitments, have more and more withdrawn their military advisers, American and Soviet advisers have, of course, moved in.[25] While accurate comparative figures were not available for this study, what data there were suggest that an excellent indicator of degree of military dependence may be the ratio of foreign military advisers to indigenous military officers in a country. There is some indication that the ratio may be considerably higher than one might expect. We know, for example, that in the thirty-eight countries advised by the United States, there were approximately 12,300 American servicemen and civilians serving as members of Military Assistance Groups (MAGS).[26] While undoubtedly the bulk of those were in South Korea, Taiwan, and South Vietnam, given the relatively small number of officers that many of the weaker countries have, these figures still suggest a very high ratio of foreign military advisers to indigenous officers.

One of the major tasks of these military advisory teams seems to be the actual training of the indigenous military personnel. Now, whether that training is in use of the latest weapons systems or in counterinsurgency, military advisers, like educational advisers in general, are going to teach that their own approach is the best, precisely because they genuinely believe that it is. While they are teaching how to fire bazookas or how to organize one's logistics, they will simultaneously be teaching the values, attitudes, and perceptions of the military establishment in their own country.

A way of life, a preferred value system, and a preferred set of reference groups are transmitted even more effectively, of course, when the indigenous personnel take some of their military training in the mentor country. While studying at Sandhurst, or St. Cyr, or Fort Levenworth, one learns more than the technicalities of how to be a good officer. Everything that was said in Chapter 4 on perceptual/identity ties about how education abroad molds and reinforces the perceptions of the scientist and the humanist applies equally well to military officers who study abroad. One Pentagon official, quoted in *Congressional Quarterly,* described the value to the United States of this training as follows:

While military equipment and hardware may deteriorate in time, an understanding of American techniques, and most importantly, *of American culture,* carries over long after the foreign national returns to his

[25] For the extent to which this has been so in Africa, see David Wood, "The Armed Forces of African States," *Adelphi Papers,* No. 27 (London: Institute for Strategic Studies, Apr. 1966).

[26] Don Oberdorfer, "Nonintervention, 1967 Style," *New York Times Magazine,* Part I (Sept. 17, 1967), p. 30.

own country. . . . Such an understanding and appreciation of the United States may be worth far more in the long run than outright grants or sales of military equipment.[27]

It may be suspected that if an officer of a weak country has learned modern military techniques and values at Levenworth or Sandhurst, he may experience considerable embarrassment at the thought of the existing military system in his own underdeveloped country being judged by those whom he perceives to be his reference group in the United States or the United Kingdom. When he goes back to his country, one may presume that he would devote much effort to making his own military over into the image he learned to value abroad. Considerable evidence exists to support this hypothesis. With but few exceptions, in the past two decades, each time the military of a weaker state has taken the government into its own hands, it has claimed that it was doing so to prevent the spread of communism or to put an end to corruption in high places. But where did the military learn that communism and corruption were "bad"? Admittedly, they did not have to go abroad to the United Kingdom, France, or the United States to learn these values—values often travel with military advisers just as do products with traveling salesmen. But the definition of communism and corruption as "evil" forces comes from the West— and particularly Western military institutions.[28]

There can be no doubt that the Powers recognize the significance of training officers of the weaker countries in their own countries. While comparative figures are simply not available on where and for how long military personnel are trained in each mentor country, some indication of the magnitude of these programs may be seen in the fact that between 1950 and 1968 the United States alone brought approximately 287,221 foreign military personnel either to the U.S. or to special centers overseas to be trained. Table 7.2 is an adaptation of a table that appeared in the *Congressional Quarterly* "Fact Sheet" of October 21, 1969. It lists the number of foreign military personnel trained under the American Military Assistance Program (MAP) from 1950 through 1968. While some

[27] U.S. Military Commitments Face Closer Scrutiny," *Congressional Quarterly*, "Fact Sheet" (Washington, D.C.: Congressional Quarterly, Oct. 21, 1969), p. 9.

[28] That one of the values also taught in the West is subordination of military to civilian leaders does not contradict this hypothesis. First, there is always a rank ordering of values whenever any two values come into conflict. Second, the military leaders seem to have learned this subordinate value as well, for they almost always announce at the time of the coup that their action is "temporary" and that power will be restored to civilian authorities again as soon as the communism and/or corruption are eliminated.

TABLE 7.2
Foreign Military Personnel Trained under United States Military Assistance Programs, 1950–68[a]
(*Grouped by Historical Association and Ranked within Groups by Total Trained*)

Country	Trained FY 50–63	Trained FY 64–68	Total Trained
U.K. and Associated States			
Iran	6,228	2,782	9,010
Pakistan	3,498	642	4,140
United Kingdom	3,853	14	3,867
Saudi Arabia	621	496	1,117
India	6	465	471
Iraq	241	163	404
Jordan	142	203	345
Nigeria	18	298	316
Malaysia	18	123	141
Sudan	34	92	126
Ghana	33	13	46
Nepal	—	15	15
Ceylon	—	7	7
Yemen	—	5	5
France and Associated States			
France	14,312	30	14,342
Vietnam (South)	10,756	3,242	13,998
Belgium	4,809	389	5,198
Lebanon	60	1,280	1,340
Morocco	4	1,002	1,006
Indo-China[b]	434	—	434
Cambodia	334	3	337
Tunisia	20	206	226
Mali	7	49	56
Syria	3	20	23
Upper Volta	4	8	12
Senegal	3	5	8
United States Associated States			
Japan	13,790	1,490	15,280
Philippines	9,141	3,076	12,217
Brazil	3,416	2,255	5,671
Peru	2,820	1,624	4,444
Colombia	2,516	1,378	3,894
Ecuador	2,246	1,549	3,795
Chile	2,219	1,448	3,667
Nicaragua	2,366	1,204	3,570
Venezuela	724	2,382	3,106
Panama	768	2,106	2,874

THE TIES THAT BIND

TABLE 7.2 (Cont'd.)

Country	Trained FY 50–63	Trained FY 64–68	Total Trained
United States Associated States (cont'd.)			
Argentina	1,190	1,216	2,406
Dominican Republic	955	1,419	2,374
Bolivia	764	1,432	2,196
Guatemala	903	1,117	2,020
Uruguay	807	607	1,414
Honduras	746	602	1,348
El Salvador	304	528	832
Paraguay	204	564	768
Mexico	240	306	546
Costa Rica	208	321	529
Cuba	521	—	521
Haiti	504	—	504
Liberia	94	241	335
Others			
Korea (South)	21,160	7,365	28,525
China (Taiwan)	19,508	3,604	23,172
Turkey	12,894	4,000	16,894
Greece	9,399	3,351	12,750
Thailand	7,340	2,796	10,136
Italy	9,215	148	9,363
Spain	6,049	1,426	7,475
Netherlands	6,085	212	6,297
Norway	5,229	303	5,532
Denmark	4,129	581	4,710
Indonesia	2,379	485	2,864
Ethiopia	1,555	968	2,523
Portugal	2,288	205	2,493
Germany (West)	1,251	373	1,624
Yugoslavia	844	—	844
Libya	58	321	379
Afghanistan	164	88	252
Luxembourg	158	18	176
Congo (Kinshasa)	—	165	165
Classified Countries	6,310	13,031	19,341
NATO Agency	465	—	465
Total	209,364	77,857	287,221

[a] Table is based on figures released by the U.S. Defense Department and published in "Fact Sheet," *Congressional Quarterly* (Oct. 21, 1969), p. 8. Figures include personnel trained abroad and in the United States.

[b] Since South Vietnam and Cambodian figures are given separately, it is presumed that "Indo-China" figures refer to Laos.

of these military people were trained at American training centers outside of the U.S., the vast bulk of them seem to have received their training directly in the United States. It is not clear what proportion of those trained were officers, but one can assume that where only relatively few individuals were involved, officers were trained exclusively. Where very large numbers were involved relative to the size of the country's armed forces—as in the case of China (Taiwan), Korea, and even Pakistan and the Dominican Republic—one can assume that training included most of the officer corps of those countries, and also substantial numbers of rank and file military personnel. Considering the rather limited size of the military establishments in many of the weaker countries (to say nothing of the relatively limited size of the military elite in those countries), the U.S. appears to train an extremely high percentage of the military of the weaker countries *in the United States.* Note that the largest numbers of personnel trained are from countries tied by military treaty to the United States. Without implying which is cause and which is effect, this clearly indicates the reciprocal reinforcement of military ties. The more closely a country is tied to the U.S. militarily, the more military personnel tend to be trained in the States. The more personnel trained in the States, the more closely tied (militarily and perceptually) the weaker country is likely to become. And so the mutual reinforcement of ties is perpetuated.

While there are no precise figures available for other mentor Powers, there is strong evidence that the French train in France an even higher percentage of the military of some of their associated African states than the percentage of military personnel from American associated states trained in the U.S.[29] The Russians also train in the Soviet Union large numbers of military personnel of their associated states, (and of weaker states more recently tied to them militarily), although no exact figures are available. And while the British have in recent years markedly cut back on this type of training, the top officers in most of the former British colonies were probably trained, at least in part, in Britain.

Military Ties and Military Coups

It has already been observed that one of the major reasons Powers give military assistance is because they want to support particular existing regimes. But if the assistance given to a country is

---

[29] David Wood, "Armed Forces of African States," p. 6.

such that it strengthens the military elite vis-à-vis other elites, and particularly relative to the political elite, the likelihood is that in the event of a dispute among the country's power groups, the military elite will emerge victorious.

A number of attempts have been made (mostly by military experts of the powerful countries) to deny the existence of any relationship between military assistance and military coups, but the arguments always seem to be rather spurious. For example, an article in the *Military Review* of December 1967 listed all the military coups that occurred between 1961 and April 1966 in comparison with a list of countries that had U.S. Military Assistance Programs and concluded that "Actually, coups occurred in more countries receiving little or no MAP deliveries than in countries receiving substantial assistance." Countries receiving only small assistance programs were counted with those receiving no MAPs at all on the basis that "a two-week orientation tour in the United States by four military officers from a country—which is the extent of one of the 'small MAP's'—hardly constitutes a major influence." [30] But if these countries had been grouped with those that received more substantial assistance, the figures would show twenty coups in recipient countries against eleven in those that received no MAPs, necessitating a different conclusion. The argument was based only on the existence of American Military Assistance Programs and the incidence of coups. Nothing at all was said about the plethora of other possible military ties with the U.S., or about the relationship of coups to military aid from other Powers. The author was merely trying to prove that *American* military assistance does not necessarily contribute to the incidence of military coups, and even there he had to "bend" the data to reach the conclusion he wanted.

The fact is that the ratio between foreign military assistance from one of the Powers and the incidence of military takeovers in the weaker countries is extremely high. And it is high precisely because the military receiving assistance—even if the aid is only modest—emerges, as H. Roberts Coward has pointed out, as "a highly organized interest group in a situation with few countervailing centers of power." Coward goes on to say, "This gives the armed forces considerable leverage in acquiring a sizeable share of a young nation's economic resources." [31] To this, Morris Janowitz adds: "The ability of the military to act as a political coalition partner often depends upon the extent of its own economic base.

[30] David R. Hughes, "The Myths of Military Coups and Military Assistance," *Military Review*, Vol. 47, No. 12 (Dec. 1967), p. 7.
[31] Coward, "Military Technology," p. 22.

The more economic resources it has at its command the greater is its scope for domestic politics." [32]

Clearly, foreign military ties tend to strengthen the military elite in the weaker countries. Since other elites are often not being similarly strengthened by other kinds of foreign assistance, even relatively minor amounts (in monetary terms) can produce major imbalances within the recipient countries. Thus, despite all of the disclaimers by the major Powers, there is a high correlation between military coups and foreign military assistance.

Indeed, there is some evidence that the Powers may not be unhappy about that correlation. Scholars like Guy Parker have argued for some time that the Powers should encourage military takeovers in the weaker states to assure both the economic development of those countries and the protection of "Free World" interests. The major Powers seem to favor those kinds of assistance that most tie the military elite of the weaker to the mentor precisely so that in the event the political elite becomes "untrustworthy" or attempts to shift mentors, the military elite may intervene in the domestic political process to prevent such a shift.

Sukarno, Nkrumah, Ben Bella, and Keita may have attempted to tie their countries militarily to Powers other than the one with which they were then associated specifically to end what they undoubtedly considered excessive military dependence on one Power. But that very attempt to seek other ties may have precipitated their overthrow by the military. It was, after all, a largely American-assisted army in Indonesia, a British-assisted military in Ghana, a Soviet-assisted military in Algeria, and a French-trained (if not assisted) military in Mali that overthrew their respective governments. The military took action in no small measure because they perceived the political leadership to be moving too far in attempting to supplement the ties to the former mentor with ties to a new Power. In those cases, it was at least to some extent a matter of the military elite being perceptually so tied to the values of the old mentor that they merely did what they perceived to be "best" for their countries.

No doubt (although no hard empirical evidence has yet come to light) the military elites in those instances were also protecting their jobs. There is every likelihood that as the political elites of these countries became more tied to new Powers, they would view the old military elites with increasing suspicion and gradually begin to replace them with new recruits to the military elite who

---

[32] Morris Janowitz, *The Military in the Political Development of New Nations: An Essay in Comparative Analysis* (Chicago: University of Chicago Press, 1964), p. 77.

could be counted on to be more loyal to the government's political disposition and more receptive to training from the new mentor's military advisers. Not only were the old military elites being asked to learn to fly new aircraft and to learn to shoot new types of weapons, but the instructions often came in verbal and ideological languages alien to their background. They would have to undertake the difficult tasks of learning the new languages if they wanted to keep up with the latest technological, managerial, and ideological advances, which new members of the elite would do with ease. Thus, in ousting the political regime and reestablishing old military ties, the military were, in effect, protecting their own positions within the general elite, as well as preventing changes in the ideological orientations of their countries.

There have been military takeovers in approximately one quarter of the weaker countries since 1945, indicating the delicate position in which the political elites find themselves. Without foreign military ties, a regime may not have sufficient coercive power to assert its authority throughout the country and to protect its inhabitants from external attack. On the other hand, unless it is extremely cautious in the way it handles the amount and type of military assistance it allows, it runs the constant risk of being overthrown by its own military. This is not a problem faced only by political elites in the weaker countries. The balance between military and political power is delicate everywhere. But in the weak countries the problem is particularly acute because the political institutions and traditions of the state are fragile. Because of that fragility, military establishments that are weak when compared to the military in powerful countries may actually be strong in comparison to the other institutions or elites in their own states.

Changing Military Relationships

Military dependence is perhaps the most threatening form of dependence. To be militarily dependent upon another country means that a government is not capable of defending its own population in matters, literally, of life and death. If the Power on which one is militarily dependent conveys the impression that it will always be there when it is needed, anxiety on this account may not be very high. But several things have happened in recent times to increase—not decrease—the anxiety of weak states about their military defense. For one, World War II proved to the weaker countries of Asia and North Africa that the Powers are not always *capable* of defending themselves from other enemy Powers, let alone of defending weaker countries dependent on them.[33] For another, development of nuclear and hydrogen weaponry has made it possible for the Super Powers to destroy not only each other, but also the weaker countries, which may have no interest whatever in the quarrels of the Powers. Most of the weaker countries recognize that they would probably be devastated if the Powers ever come to open warfare with each other, and there would be nothing they could do to prevent that from happening. The weaker countries also recognize that defense, as the Powers define it (and have always defined it) means defending the interests of the Powers—as the governments of the Powers define that interest—and not defending the interests of the people in the weaker countries. Recent events have brought home the practical effects of this definition of the weaker countries' defense: often a Power will refuse to defend a weaker country against external enemies the weaker finds threatening, but the stronger does not; often a Power is incapable of or unwilling to defend the elite of a weaker country against certain internal enemies; and—above all—the Powers seem perfectly prepared to destroy a weaker country while in the process of "defending" it.

Given these realities, it is not at all surprising that so many of the weaker countries want to become as militarily independent of the Powers as they can. But they know that they can never become totally independent militarily, simply because few will ever have the technological and industrial base necessary to support an ever changing and more deadly military technology. They also know that they will probably never become strong enough to achieve a genuine military interdependence with the Super Powers.[34] The only rational choice for the weaker countries has appeared to be to attempt to reduce their military dependence on the Powers as much as possible. To do so, however, often requires the expenditure of vast amounts of scarce resources, which many would prefer to see diverted into the industrial development of their countries.

[33] In all fairness, it must be admitted that this is not merely a post World War II phenomena. Weak countries from time immemorial have learned that bitter fact. But for most of the countries with which this study deals, the military vulnerability of the European Powers in World War II was the most relevant experience.

[34] Even the French since de Gaulle have been forced to recognize that unpleasant reality. While officially the concept of NATO has always been a North Atlantic military interdependence, unofficially all of the weaker countries in that alliance have always recognized their position of military dependence upon the United States. Those, like de Gaulle, who pushed for a more united Europe, did so at least in part to free themselves of this military dependence.

Further, the political elites of some of these countries are only too conscious of the possible consequences to civilian government if they strengthen their military establishments extensively. Thus, they are caught in the King of Siam's dilemma. No wonder that counterdependence—particularly over defense matters—has been so common in the weaker states!

Most military counterdependence is directly related to, and probably stems from perceptual and/or political counterdependence. That is, if the governing political elite of a country comes, for whatever reason, to be highly counterdependent toward a Power on which it was formerly dependent, the likelihood is that this counterdependence will express itself in the military sphere as well as in all others. The installation of a Peoples' Republic in Southern Yemen (following the withdrawal of the British from what was then Aden and South Arabia) was followed by the expulsion of all British military personnel and advisers, as well as the severing of diplomatic relations and most other ties to the U.K. But since no weak state can completely "go-it-alone" in any sphere, military counterdependence often takes the form of inviting the major enemy of the Power upon which one was formerly dependent to replace the former mentor. In the Southern Yemen case, Soviet and Chinese military personnel and advisers were asked to replace the British.

Sometimes military counterdependence precedes the counterdependence of the political elite. For example, when there has been a high degree of military dependence on just one Power in the past, and that Power has failed to "come through" as the military of the weaker country had hoped it would in a time of crisis, a high degree of counterdependence has developed among the military elite of the weaker country, who in turn have put enormous pressure on the political elite of that country to change mentors.

It has also sometimes happened that lower echelon military leaders have become counterdependent toward their superiors, who may have been dependent militarily on a particular Power. If the upper echelon military are closely tied to the political elite of their country (as they often are) and thus the political elite, too, is seen as overly dependent on a particular foreign Power, then this counterdependence is often expressed by what has come to be called a "Colonel's coup." Egypt, Iraq, and Libya are only a few of the countries in which the ruling political and military elites were replaced by groups of younger counterdependent military officers who promptly cut military ties with the Power they perceived to be oppressing them, and established military and political ties with the enemy of that Power. There is some evidence that the Powers —particularly the United States—now recognize the danger of encouraging dependence only of the upper echelon military elites and now attempt to tie as many of a country's military elite—of all levels—to themselves as possible. (See Table 7.2.)

In the military sphere, as in other areas, it is simply not possible for weak countries to be totally independent. They may become militarily independent of their former mentor, but what the more counterdependent elites—whether political or military—seem to learn only after the fact is that their extreme counterdependence toward their former mentor often makes them equally as dependent militarily upon their new mentor. Just as with economic ties and communication ties, so too with military ties; until the time that the weaker countries become equal (or nearly equal) in military strength with the Powers (which most of them will never achieve) the best chance they have for maintaining some degree of military flexibility is to diversify the Powers upon which they are militarily dependent and/or to develop some military quality the Powers might need from them. In the past, the most effective "military quality" some weaker countries had to offer the Powers was geography—whether propinquity to an enemy of a Power; strategic location on international waterways; or simply ports or airfields that the Power could use for bases. But in the age of the intercontinental ballistic missile, geography is becoming an increasingly insignificant military factor.

There are alternatives for the weaker countries to perpetual military dependence on the major Powers, and these will be discussed in Chapter 10 on Policy Recommendations.

Chapter 8

Political Ties

What are political ties? Is it really possible to distinguish between political ties and all the others that have been considered? Certainly the signing of a treaty of mutual friendship (or the breaking of such a treaty) is a political act, but the act itself may be far less significant politically than the entire range of perceptions and events which led up to it, and that may not have been, in and of themselves, political. Professor Alex Weilenmann has very rightly observed:

. . . there are very few things that are political, in and of themselves. If the act of voting is essentially political, it is because the entire situation surrounding it makes it so; but the act of dropping a piece of paper into a box or of pulling a lever in and by itself is not. If we want to define "political" in the same way in which we define "economic" or "educational" (the latter in a narrow sense) or "military," etc., we are likely to limit ourselves too much. As a Belgian theorist . . . said, the political system cannot (conceptually) stand on its own, but spills over into all kinds of other systems, and in reverse, there is not an individual or group or activity that is not potentially a member of the political system.[1]

In a case like the signing of a treaty of friendship, it is entirely possible that such a treaty would be signed not for exclusively or even primarily political reasons, but rather to encourage economic ties, or as a *quid pro quo* for receiving economic aid, or for reasons of military strategy. Conversely, all of the ties discussed in the chapters above have obvious political connotations, whether implicit or explicit. Certainly, if significant segments of the elite of any country alter their general perceptions of another country after extensive study or travel there, they would be simultaneously,

[1] Alex Weilenmann, personal communication, Mar. 25, 1970.

even if imperceptibly, altering their political perceptions. Having consular officers in a foreign country or subscribing to the international news services of another country may serve a communication function, but they certainly have major political ramifications as well. Could anyone really demonstrate that the signing of a military or an economic treaty is more a military or an economic act than a political one? The decision to tie one's country militarily to this Power or that—or not to do so—is unquestionably a political act. It *may* relate most to the military aspects of that relationship, but the decision is essentially political. Similarly, the decision to tie oneself economically to another country by accepting economic aid, or foreign investment, or increased trade from that country is also very often as much political as it is economic.

All of this makes any attempt to steady political ties *per se* extremely difficult. Weilenmann, in the passage quoted above, is arguing that it is more useful to consider political ties as *consequences* of other ties than as a separate category. Certainly they are often consequences, but political ties often produce a host of other ties as well. Therefore, despite the difficulties, for a more complete understanding of the ties that bind states together it is necessary to analyze both political ties as such, and political implications of the other ties that exist among states.

In former times the predominant form of political tie between weak and powerful states, at least in the case of Britain and France in relations with their associated states, was one of direct political control, although many weaker countries were politically tied to stronger states in more subtle ways. Those more direct forms of legal political domination have now been sufficiently discredited to force the big Powers to seek other types of political ties. Political *control* has very largely given way to political *influence*. This is not meant to imply that the two are actually the same. As a general rule, it is probably fair to say that a weak state has considerably more latitude operating under the political influence of a major Power than it had while under the direct political control of that Power. But this is a relative matter, and depends largely on the context of the relationship. Nor is it meant to imply that there were not significant instances of influence relationships between weak and powerful states in former times. In the late nineteenth and early twentieth centuries, like today, the United States did not usually exercise direct political control over Latin America (particularly Central America), but rather exercised considerable political influence. It intervened militarily often enough to establish that it would and could take control if the weaker countries did not go along with major U.S. desires, but it did not find direct political control necessary for any length of time. Even where close formal ties existed, the *de facto* political relationship was sometimes a matter of influence rather than direct control. Though much of Eastern Europe was an integral part of the Russian Empire, and some of the colonies of Britain and France were considered integral parts of their countries, there is considerable evidence that many of these areas experienced more influence than control from the Power, legal arrangements not withstanding.

Political ties can take many forms, both formal and informal. In recent times, formal political ties have more and more taken the form of treaties, of one sort or another. Every major Power has a host of bilateral and multilateral treaty commitments with its historically associated states, and has joined with these states in complex multilateral organizations (like the British Commonwealth and the French Community). The United States since 1945 and the Soviet Union since the death of Stalin have concluded a full range of treaties not only with states historically associated with them, but also with states historically associated with other Powers. Just as it was possible to determine the degree to which one state was economically tied to another by considering what percentage of a country's total economic trade was with that other country, so, too, it should be possible to determine the degree to which one state is politically tied to another by considering what percentage of a country's total formal political ties are with that other country. The analogy is not quite that simple, of course. Not every treaty is of equal importance. Merely to count the number of treaties a country has signed and to ask what percentage of those treaties is with a particular Power would be roughly equivalent to counting the number of boatloads of goods exchanged between countries without inquiring into the relative value of the goods being shipped. A treaty in which one of the signers agrees to supply the other with limited amounts of surplus military equipment is no more equivalent to a treaty in which both countries agree that an attack on one will be considered an attack on both, than is one boatload of cement equivalent to a boatload of uranium. Still, at least theoretically it should be possible to construct a weighted index of formal treaty obligations that could measure fairly accurately the degree to which two countries are formally tied politically. But treaty ties are only one of the formal political ties that exist among states.

Diplomatic recognition and the exchange of diplomats are another such formal tie. It may seem that diplomatic recognition is more a sign of the existence of political ties rather than a political tie itself. But if a country does not grant diplomatic recognition to another it could be said to have no formal political ties to that country. If that is true, then the existence of diplomats from one country in the capital of another must represent a formal political tie. In that diplomats are the formal channel for official political communication between countries, the exchange of diplomats between countries in and of itself constitutes a formal political tie. So does the acceptance of economic aid, or the pegging of one's currency to the currency of a major Power. Before any aid can flow or currency can be exchanged there must usually be a formal agreement between the two countries stating the precise terms under which the exchanges are to take place. That agreement can be considered in exactly the same light as can any other treaty between two countries. Certainly the decision about whether or not to establish economic ties to one or another Power is essentially a political decision.

Aside from the formal political ties between states, there exist a host of informal political ties that are much more important in determining the political behavior of states. Indeed, one could make a very strong case that the formal political ties are often the *result* of informal ties. Therefore the first step in investigating the nature of political ties must be to examine what constitutes the informal ties, and what the relationship is between those ties and international political behavior.

Informal Political Ties and International Political Behavior

Actual and Perceived Political Influence

Mentor Powers often actually do exercise significant influence in the domestic decision-making process of most weaker countries. Richard Cottam has written a book devoted almost entirely to a discussion of the types of influence—he calls it "intervention"— that all states, weak as well as strong, attempt to utilize in their relations with other states.[2] Obviously, because strong states have more power they are usually able to exercise the greater influence. One of the most significant aspects of Cottam's book is his matter of fact demonstration that every state—but particularly the weaker ones—*expects and accepts* at least some outside interference in domestic decision making; different states, at different times, merely have different "tolerance levels of interference." Cottam's book is filled with so many specific, documented instances of actual influence being exerted by one state on another that the point need not be labored here.

[2] Richard Cottam, *Competitive Interference and 20th Century Diplomacy* (Pittsburgh, Pa.: University of Pittsburgh Press, 1967).

The most normal channel of influence, of course, has always been the regular diplomatic channel. An official of country A merely informs the proper authority in country B that his government would "look with favor" upon a particular action. If the official of government B is so disposed, he accepts the recommendation of country A. In many cases in the weaker countries, because of deficiencies in information-gathering or technical know-how, the advice of the stronger government not only is usually accepted when offered, but often is actually sought. In those cases where the official in the weaker country is not immediately disposed to accept the recommendation, there are various means of "persuasion" available. The persuasion might take the form of a bribe, or a threat to take the matter to a higher level. If the higher level official is known to be a golf playing or poker playing intimate of the ambassador of the stronger country, the likelihood is that the lower ranking official will accept the advice. Bribes need not take the form of cash to the official concerned (although cash has never been ruled out). Often a recommendation for promotion, or the selection of the official for an extended trip to the stronger country is a more acceptable version of diplomatic bribery.

In those countries that rely heavily on advisers from the major Powers in almost every branch of their public services, more direct but subtle influence is exercised. The adviser, in his day-to-day working relationship with his indigenous counterpart, is in some degree exercising influence on the decision-making process of the country he is advising. Indeed, he is there precisely to exercise influence. If the weaker country did not intend to accept any of his recommendations, either it would not have invited him in the first place, or would have sent him home after he arrived. But these countries ask for advisers because they want and need the influence—advice—the adviser can supply.

Perceived political influence differs from actual political influence only insofar as the more powerful country does not really have the ability, or does not have the interest, to influence decision making on a particular issue, but the decision makers in the weaker country *think* that it does and therefore behave as though it did—thus giving to the Power influence it did not actually have in the first place. Very often Powers are perceived in weaker countries as nearly omnipotent. If they can explode hydrogen bombs, go to the moon, have cities with two or three times the population of the entire weak country, and spend more on golf balls each year than the entire budget of the weak country, what is it that they could not do if they really wanted to?

Many decision makers in the weaker countries take domestic

political positions or behave internationally in the way in which they think the Power wants them to behave, even though the Power may not care what position is taken on that particular issue. I was once told by a representative of one of the Powers at the United Nations that he wished the delegates of his country's associated states would not always vote with his country on every minor issue because it exposed those delegates to charges of being "satellites" of the Power, and created the impression that the Power was forcing them to vote as they did. He cited a number of instances in which he was approached by delegates from weaker associated states asking him how his country intended to vote on an issue before they would decide how their delegation would vote. These delegates presumably did so because they *thought* that the Power wanted them to vote the way the Power was going to vote.

Similarly, there have been instances where a Power would have liked certain individuals or types of individuals appointed to particular positions in the weaker associated country, but would not have requested the appointment—that is, exercised actual influence—for fear of being accused of undue interference in the weaker country's internal affairs, or because the Power felt that it would "use up" on a relatively unimportant matter, the political favors it could normally expect to have honored, or because the Power assumed that if its request was granted it would have to reciprocate with some favor it would rather withhold. To the surprise of the Power, however, just the individual it wanted was appointed. The Power had not actively exercised influence, but the weaker country thought the Power would exercise its influence if someone were appointed who did not meet the Power's approval.

In countries experiencing any degree of counterdependence, of course, this kind of situation is much less likely to occur. Counterdependent countries will often test the Power by doing precisely the opposite of what they think the Power wants, just to see how far they can go before the Power will actually intervene.

Similarity of Political Perceptions

Is the fact that two countries have a similar political system sufficient motivation for the political decision makers of one state to support the international political decisions of the other? Certainly, to the degree that the decision makers share common political perceptions—called "ideology" when those perceptions have been clearly articulated and are reasonably well-defined, or *Weltanschauung* (world outlook) when they are more vague and diffuse—they will have a disposition to define issues in a similar manner. But no one would seriously maintain that Fourth Republic France supported the international political positions of the United States more than Fifth Republic France because the Fourth Republic was more "democratic" than the Fifth. Nor would anyone maintain that the British Commonwealth is an association held together primarily by similar political systems. Similarly, no serious scholar or practitioner would still argue that the so-called communist bloc is monolithic in ideology and values.

There is no question but that the political ideology of individual leaders can and does bring countries together politically or keep them apart. In large part it was the political *Weltanschauung* of Nkrumah and Tshombe that drove the former toward the Soviet Bloc and the latter toward the West. The political reality world of General de Gaulle explained the foreign policy stance of the Fifth French Republic until 1969 more than any other single factor. The specific political perceptions of their decision-making elites may be a major factor in determining how similarly countries define the international reality world. In other words, it is the similarity of political perceptions on the part of the foreign policy decision-making elites—*not the name of the political system under which they operate*—that is most important in determining whether any two states will define a specific policy as being in the best interest of both.

Consider the political perceptions of the decision-making elite in the two hypothetical countries presented in Diagrams 1 and 2 below:

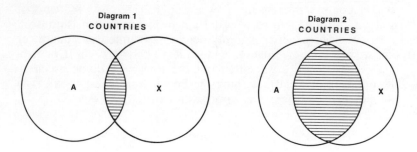

Diagram 1
COUNTRIES

Diagram 2
COUNTRIES

The circles in each diagram represent those international political positions that the decision makers of both A (the weaker) and X (the stronger) perceive as being in their own best interest. The lined areas represent the congruence of perception on international matters. Clearly, the decision-making elites in Diagram

2 will be politically "closer" than will the decision-making elites in Diagram 1. Each may be motivated by what it perceives to be the best interests of its own country, but because of the greater congruence of international perception, the elites of Diagram 2 are more likely to define international matters more similarly than are the elites in Diagram 1. Thus, other things being equal, the likelihood of countries A and X *behaving* similarly in international matters is greater in Diagram 2 than in Diagram 1.

As was said in Chapter 2 on perceptions, similarity of perception tends to breed even greater similarity of perception. It is only to be expected that as other perceptual ties are strengthened, political perceptions will also become more similar. Thus, the stronger the identity, communication, economic, or military ties between the elites of states, the more likely that there will be a greater similarity of political perception between the elites of those states. The greater the similarity of political perception, the stronger the informal political ties between the states are likely to be. And, the stronger the informal ties, the more any formal political ties are likely to be strengthened and the more both countries are likely to behave similarly on international political issues. The spirals are mutually reinforcing.

Conversely, the fewer identity, communication, economic, or military ties between the elites of states, the less likely that there will be significant degrees of similarity of political perceptions between the elites of those states. The less similarity of political perception, the fewer informal political ties there are likely to be between the states. The fewer the informal political ties, the less likely are there to be formal political ties, and the more both countries are likely to behave *differently* on international political issues. Thus, these negative spirals, too, are mutually reinforcing.

What this means in practical terms is that the strengthening of any ties—identity, communication, economic, military, or political —between countries is likely to lead to an increase in the degree of similarity of political perception and, thus, to an increase in the likelihood of similar political behavior and closer informal political ties between the two countries. Consider, for example, Guinea's political relations to the West after the removal of de Gaulle's restrictions on Western countries entering into relations with Guinea. As Guinea established economic, communication, and formal political ties with the West, there was a marked shift in Guinean political perception and international political behavior. Conversely, a weakening of any of the ties between countries is likely to lead to a decrease in similarity of political perceptions and, concomitantly, to a decrease in international ties. Observe, in this instance, Cuba. When Castro came to power he brought with him markedly different political perceptions from those of his predecessor. Concomitant with the decline in similarity of political perceptions between the United States and Cuban elites came a decline in identity, communication, economic, and military ties, which further decreased similarities of political perceptions, which in turn led to a decrease in number of political ties, which led to further decrease of all other ties. And so the spiral continued and reinforced itself, until the two countries stand almost at a state of war, with only the fewest ties existing between them. But as United States-Cuba ties decreased, Cuban-U.S.S.R. ties increased until today Castro's Cuba is tied—perceptually, communicationally, economically, militarily, and politically—to the Soviet Union in approximately the same degree as Batista's Cuba was formerly tied to the United States.

In terms of measurable indices of behavior such as economic, communication, military, or formal political ties, two weak countries (A and B) may be equally dependent upon a strong third (X). But if, for some reasons, there is a higher degree of similarity of political perception between the elites of A and X than there is between the elites of B and X, the likelihood is that the international political behavior of A will more closely approximate (and support) the political behavior of X than will the political behavior of B. It is precisely this matter of degree of similarity of political perception that may explain why Guinea, which was perhaps as tied to France as any of the other French Community countries, withdrew from the French Union while the others remained. The same could be said of Yugoslavia under Tito, Czechoslovakia under Dubcek, and Hungary under Nagy in their relations with the Soviet Union.

Actual and/or Perceived Aid Dependence

If there is a high degree of similarity of political perception among the decision-making elites of two states, then the fact that the weaker and the stronger act in a similar way internationally should be expected. But even if this high degree of similarity of political perception does not exist, the weaker may see little or no alternative to supporting the international political positions of the stronger. This may be particularly true if the weaker country's decision makers feel—correctly or incorrectly—that the decision-making elite of the stronger can take actions (whether economic, military, or other) that could adversely affect the weaker; and that the stronger is likely to take those actions unless the weaker goes along with its international position.

Every year the Congress of the United States scrutinizes the foreign aid appropriation bills to see how much it can cut. Decision makers in every one of the hundred-odd weaker countries receiving aid know that the appropriation must pass Congress before they can get their assistance. If a country's economic development plans are geared to the expectation of receiving a significant portion of the financing from the United States (as many are) it is not likely to do anything internationally that it thinks might upset enough congressmen to have their appropriation cut.[3a] The same is even more true of those weaker French associated states that rely on France to supply as much as one-half of their entire annual budgets. All of the Powers (and some of the other developed states) use the lure of foreign economic or military assistance, and the threat of cancelling that assistance, to achieve their international political goals.

The so-called "Hickenlooper Amendment" to the Foreign Assistance Act is an explicit threat to the weaker countries that they face automatic and instant cancellation of all foreign assistance if they nationalize American private firms without proper compensation. While this amendment is not resorted to often, it has been used sufficiently to establish the credibility of the threat. Similarly, in 1958 when General de Gaulle gave the French colonies in Africa the choice between continued association with France or total independence, he was very explicit that any country opting for the latter would instantly be cut off from all economic assistance. Only Guinea dared take the risk, and the economic cost to that country was staggering. Israel and China both offer fairly extensive economic, technical, and military aid to those countries that will grant them diplomatic recognition, and withhold that aid from countries that refuse. West Germany has in the past cancelled all economic assistance to countries that recognized East Germany. Since 1952 the Soviet Union has extended a considerable amount of economic and military assistance but—like every other Power—at a political price.

Decision makers in the weaker countries are well aware that rhetoric to the contrary, every economic or military aid package is tied in political strings. If they are really convinced that they need the assistance they are not likely to untie those strings before the package has arrived. Sometimes, of course, Powers demand more than weak countries are willing to give. In those cases in which the two countries are unable to work out an agreement ac-

[3a] When these countries forget how economically dependent they actually are on the U.S., the Congress is quick to remind them. The angry refusal of Congress to appropriate *any* foreign assistance after the vote to seat the Peoples Republic of China in the U.N., in late 1971, was just such a reminder.

ceptable to both—and it is often literally a bargaining process that goes on—no "deal" occurs. But in most of those bargaining sessions, unless the weaker country knows that another Power is ready to offer a more advantageous agreement (as did Nasser in his dickering with Dulles over the Aswam Dam), the Power has the advantage because it knows that the weaker needs what it has to offer.

Perceived Vested Interests

Specific elites in both weak and powerful countries with personal, nonpolitical ties of one sort or another to the other country, may be able to influence decision making within their own countries to conform to definitions of national interest growing out of their personal vested interests. The perceived vested interest may be a narrow one ("What's good for General Motors . . ."), or it may be defined more broadly on the basis of racial, religious, cultural, class, or other such ties. When elites in both the weak and the powerful state have ties in the other, there is likely to be much more mutual salience and much more feeling of interdependence than if only the elites in the weaker have nonpolitical ties to the stronger. Of course, the existence of those ties tends to affect political perceptions as well.

Bruce Russett explored this phenomena in some depth in his analysis of relations between elites in the United States and Britain. In examining speeches of British Members of Parliament he found that "MP's with ties of any sort to the United States are more likely to speak up on matters affecting Anglo-American relations than are MP's without ties. And when they speak, they are more likely to be responsive [to the U.S.]." He summarized some of his findings as follows:

1. Legislators with economic or personal ties to the other country are more likely to be responsive to the needs of that country than are legislators lacking those ties.
2. This holds true when party affiliation is controlled though party is itself an important variable.
3. It makes little difference whether a legislator has a number of ties to the other country, or only one.
4. There is some evidence, though not enough to be conclusive, that economic ties are more likely to be effective than personal ones.
5. The importance of a constituency tie is directly proportioned to the weight of economic interest in the constituency.[3]

[3] Bruce M. Russett, *Community and Contention: Britain and America in the Twentieth Century* (Cambridge: Massachusetts Institute of Technology Press, 1963), pp. 147, 161.

While there are apparently no precise measures of the degree to which political perceptions of elites are altered by specific nonpolitical ties, the fact that they are so altered has been demonstrated not only by Russett but by a number of other scholars as well.[4]

Perceived Political Interdependence

As in nonpolitical matters, it often happens that elites in two countries perceive their political interests to be interdependent. That is, decision makers in two countries may well recognize a common external threat and recognize still further that the only way to deal with it is by joint efforts. This occurs most commonly perhaps, among countries of relatively equal power but it is not uncommon even when there are enormous disparities in the power relationship. Thus, the decision makers in Western Europe and the United States perceived a commonality of political self-interest in opposing "international communism," and each felt it needed the other (and that the other needed it) in order to succeed. Similarly, the decision makers in Eastern Europe and the Soviet Union undoubtedly perceived a commonality of political self-interest in opposing "capitalist, imperialist encirclement," and each felt it needed the other (and that the other needed it) in order to succeed.

On a somewhat different power level, faced with the British withdrawal from Malaysia and Singapore in 1971 and the possibility of U.S. withdrawal from Vietnam and perhaps Laos and Thailand soon after, the countries of South East Asia are aware that a power vacuum may be created—that is, the current leaders feel that they may lose the protection and support they have received from the Powers that are withdrawing. With China and Japan both eager to move back into an area each has dominated at some time in the past, the leaders of the South East Asian countries (and Australia and New Zealand) recognize a mutual political interest in resisting this very real, potential threat. No one country could successfully resist the influence of any one of the region's major Powers, and decision makers in the weaker countries recognize their interdependence. Whether this perceived political interdependence will be sufficient to enable them to overcome some of the existing local animosities and fears so that they can effectively cooperate to resist the threat, remains to be seen. But there is no doubt that the commonly perceived threat of big

[4] See, for example, Raymond A. Bauer, Ithiel de Sola Pool, and Lewis Anthony Dexter, *American Business and Public Policy: The Politics of Foreign Trade* (New York: Atherton Press, 1963).

Power intervention is the one factor that gets the countries to work together as closely as they now do.

Indicators of Informal Political Ties

Regardless of the mix of factors that may be operating at any given moment in the international decision-making process of both weaker and strong countries, some or all of these various informal factors at one time or another influence the international political behavior of elites in all countries. Now, the difficulty this raises for the student of international affairs is that it is easier to measure the more formal international political ties than it is to measure the informal ties—despite the fact that these informal ties may be largely responsible for the existence of some of the formal ties. But that is an indication of the inadequacy of the current state of social science measuring devices, and does not take away from the fact that these informal ties exist and are crucially important in determining the relations between states.

If empirical social science research in this and related areas is to move forward significantly in the next decade, what is desperately needed are comparative data on the perceptions, attitudes, and values of elites in every country of the world. Standardized attitudinal and perceptual scales will have to be developed with maximum cultural flexibility and minimum cultural bias to make them meaningful measures in all societies.[5] What is more, they will have to be administered not only to the political elites currently in power, but to secondary and tertiary elites likely to come to power within the near future. Also, since so many crucial decisions in every society are made by groups other than governing elites, these tests will have to be given to economic, military, bureaucratic, intellectual, religious, labor, rural, urban, and particularistic[6] elites in every society as well. Only after all of these comparative attitudinal data are available will it really be possible to determine, with fairly high degrees of accuracy, the informal political ties that actually exist among states. Until such time as those data are available, however, the social scientist working in this area must recognize the limitations of his findings.

Still, the social scientist is not totally incapable of pursuing meaningful research despite the lack of knowledge about crucial

[5] While this is admittedly a difficult task, it is by no means conceptually impossible.

[6] By "particularistic" I mean groups unique to a society, such as caste and language groups in India, various tribes in each of the African countries, blacks in America, etc.

variables. If he cannot, at this time, accurately measure all of the informal factors that influence the international political behavior of elites of states, he can measure the behavior itself, and on that basis draw inferences with regard to informal political ties. That is, while he may not now know precisely which informal political ties motivated some weaker states to actively support the military intervention of the United States or the Soviet Union in their weaker associated states, or why they voted in intcrnational organizations the way they did, he can determine just how much support each of the weaker states gave, and on the basis of that observable international behavior, it may be possible to make some inferences concerning the informal political ties between states.

Indeed, one can hypothesize that (all other things being equal) the stronger the informal political ties between a weak and a powerful state, the more likely it is that the weaker state will support the international political behavior of the mentor. What is more, one can argue that the degree of informal political support will vary in direct relationship to the strength of other ties that exist between the countries. This does not mean that the weaker state will automatically support every action of the mentor in exactly the same degree, or that it will always support the mentor in at least some degree. It does mean, however, that over relatively long periods of time, on a wide range of issues, those states most strongly informally tied will tend to support the mentor most strongly and most consistently. Indeed, it is precisely this mutuality of informal political identities which comprises political interdependence.[7]

Voting in International Organizations

A good index of informal political ties between countries is the way a country votes in international organizations on political issues of major concern to the mentor Powers. By analyzing the voting behavior of the weaker countries over long periods of time on a large number of issues, it appears possible to make inferences about informal political ties that may exist (or not exist) between states.

Nothing disturbs some political scientists more than the assertion that voting behavior (or for that matter any international political behavior) can be predicted with a fairly high degree of accuracy on the basis of a statistical analysis of past voting behavior and of other intervening variables. Somehow it is seen by these scholars as a denial of free will that one can predict more or less accurately on the basis of a person's religion, place of residence, and socio-economic group, how he will vote in the next election—before the candidates are even nominated, and before the issues have been stated. Yet that is precisely what the domestic voting studies have done.[8] So, too, in international politics, one can predict with a fairly high degree of accuracy how the government of a state will ïnstruct its representatives to vote in an international organization if one knows the nature of the state's international relationships—that is, if one knows:

1. the degree of economic dependence (or interdependence) on one or more Powers of the state, and of the elite of the state;
2. the degree of military dependence (or interdependence) of the state;
3. the degree of communication dependence (or interdependence) of the state;
4. the degree of similarity of political perceptions between decision makers in the weak and the powerful states.[9]

With this knowledge one should be able to determine better whether the relationships can be considered more dependent or more interdependent, and on that basis to make fairly accurate predictions.

This is not to say that one can predict the exact vote on every specific issue. But one can predict how a country will generally vote, on certain kinds of issues. "Ah ha!" says the critic, "Just as I thought; you are implying cause and effect. What you are saying is that their political behavior is *determined* by the extent of their economic, military, perceptual, and communication ties to their mentors. But would it not be equally valid to argue that the reason they are tied in all those other ways is because of their political

[8] See, for example, Bernard Berelson, Paul F. Lazarsfeld, and Hazel Gaudet, *The Peoples Choice* (New York: Columbia University Press, 1948); *Voting,* and all other domestic voting studies conducted in the United States between 1940–1968.
[9] Obviously, if we could easily measure degree of similarity of political perception, our predictions would be that much more accurate. Since we cannot, we must content ourselves with an examination of the more easily quantifiable indices and a lower degree of accuracy.

perceptions?" The answer to this charge, of course, is "Yes, it would be as valid to argue that the other ties may indeed have all followed from the political." But that is just the point. The basic argument of this whole study is that all of the variables tend to co-vary in the same direction, and to reinforce each other; changes in *any* variable should produce changes, in the same direction, in the other variables. What the critic does not seem to realize is that it is he who is arguing for only one type of cause—namely, that political change must precede all other change. What I am arguing here, instead, is that perhaps the way to induce political change is to induce change in the other variables. More will be said of this in Section III on policy implications.

Suffice it here to note that in examining international organization voting records over long periods of time, it becomes evident that some weaker associated states tend to support their mentors more than others in those organizations.[10] By rank ordering the countries according to how much they tend to support particular Powers, an index of international political behavior is then available with which to compare the indices for the other variables. From this comparison it should be possible to show that informal political ties—as expressed by such measures as voting in the U.N. (or any other international organization that votes on political issues and makes public those votes)—tend to vary in the same direction as other ties. That being so, then on the basis of examining the other ties alone, it should be possible to predict, not necessarily how a country will vote on a specific issue, but rather, how a country is likely to vote on a specific range of issues over time.

Similarly, by examining a country's voting behavior in international organizations, it should be possible to make predictions about what other sorts of international action the same political regime is likely to take on issues of importance to its mentor Power. While no very detailed or widespread analysis of voting behavior in international organizations has been attempted here, an examination of some samples of United Nations General Assembly voting data proved to be extremely revealing.

For example, a number of years ago, Barton Sensenig and I, did a study on elections in the United Nations that attempted to establish the relationships between election to U.N. offices and a

---

[10] A number of studies on voting behavior in international organizations have been done. For example, see Hayward R. Alker, and Bruce M. Russett, *World Politics in the General Assembly* (New Haven, Conn.: Yale University Press, 1965); Thomas Hovet, Jr., *Africa in the United Nations* (Evanston, Ill.: Northwestern University Press, 1963); and my article with Barton Sensenig, III, "Elections within the United Nations: An Experimental Study Utilizing Statistical Analysis," *International Organizations,* Vol. XVII, No. 4 (1960).

number of other variables.[11] In the course of preparing that article, a voting index on cold war issues was constructed for three time periods, each covering five sessions of the General Assembly: 1946–49, 1950–54, and 1955–59. Each country was ranked on the basis of how often it voted with the U.S., with the U.S.S.R., or abstained on major issues on which the U.S. and U.S.S.R. voted opposite. Voting with the United States on every single recorded vote studied produced a voting index of +1. Voting with the Soviet Union on every single recorded vote studied produced a voting index of −1. Between these two extremes all the countries were ranked. The "Most Pro-U.S." states were considered to be only those states that voted with the U.S. at least seven times as often as they voted against it. The "Pro-U.S." states were those that voted with the U.S. at least three times as often as they voted against. The "Neutral" states often abstained, but when they did vote they tended to vote with the U.S.S.R. as often as they voted with the U.S. The "Most Pro-Soviet" states were those that voted with the U.S.S.R. at least seven times as often as they voted against.

When we examined, for each period, the states in the "most Pro-Soviet" category, we found that without exception they were the states that were least tied economically, militarily, perceptually, and in terms of communications to the United States, and were most tied in each of those ways to the Soviet Union. Conversely, the states in the "Most Pro-U.S." category were those that were most tied economically, militarily, perceptually, and in terms of communications to the United States, and were among the least tied in each of those ways to the Soviet Union.

Table 8.1 is a rank order of the index obtained by each country in the 1955–1959 period (the tenth through fourteenth sessions of the General Assembly) in voting on twenty-eight important cold war issues. The hypothesis the table was meant to demonstrate was that the countries most dependent—in all ways discussed thus far—upon the U.S. tended to be the countries that voted most closely with it on matters the U.S. considered most important. More careful examination of the data in the table revealed, however, that the countries that voted most closely with the United States during that period were not necessarily the ones most dependent on it, but rather those countries that were most *interdependent* with it. On careful consideration, this should not be very surprising, since one would expect to find the greatest informal political ties among interdependent countries. But so much has been made of the dependent countries behaving internationally as the mentors want

[11] Singer and Sensenig, "Elections within the United Nations," pp. 901–925.

TABLE 8.1
*Voting on Cold War Issues in the
United Nations General
Assembly, 1955–59
(Ranked by Degree of Support
for U.S. Position)*[a]

Country	Voting Index
"Most Pro-U.S."	
United States	+1.
United Kingdom	+1.
Australia	+1.
Belgium	+1.
Canada	+1.
Netherlands	+1.
New Zealand	+1.
Brazil	.964
Luxembourg	.964
France	.963
Italy	.956
South Africa	.917
Spain	.917
Colombia	.893
Nicaragua	.889
Japan	.867
Portugal	.864
Dominican Republic	.857
Peru	.857
Turkey	.852
Venezuela	.821
Laos	.818
Iceland	.815
Honduras	.808
China (Taiwan)	.786
Cuba	.786
Malaya	.786
Austria	.783
Argentina	.750
"Pro-U.S."	
Pakistan	.741
Ireland	.739
Chile	.714
Panama	.714
Paraguay	.714
Haiti	.704
Thailand	.678
Costa Rica	.667
El Salvador	.667
Philippines	.667

TABLE 8.1 (Cont'd.)

Country	Voting Index
Bolivia	.643
Denmark	.643
Liberia	.643
Norway	.643
Uruguay	.643
Ecuador	.640
Israel	.630
Sweden	.607
Iran	.592
Greece	.571
Tunisia	.565
Ethiopia	.536
Guatemala	.536
Mexico	.500
"Neutral"	
Jordan	.391
Lebanon	.385
Libya	.261
Nepal	.227
Cambodia	.217
Ceylon	.217
Iraq	.214
Finland	.174
Ghana	.133
Burma	.107
Morocco	.045
Indonesia	−.071
Sudan	−.091
India	−.107
Afghanistan	−.143
Saudi Arabia	−.143
United Arab Republic	−.227
Yemen	−.280
Yugoslavia	−.308
"Most Pro-U.S.S.R."	
Albania	−1.
Bulgaria	−1.
Byelorussia	−1.
Czechoslovakia	−1.
Hungary	−1.
Poland	−1.
Rumania	−1.
Ukraine	−1.
U.S.S.R.	−1.

TABLE 8.1 (Cont'd.)

ᵃ This table is based on data collected and
used by Singer and Sensenig in "Elections
within the United Nations." Categories
were arbitrarily created by the authors on
the following basis: Voting with the U.S. on
all votes studied gave an index of $+1$; voting with the U.S.S.R. on all votes studied
gave an index of -1. Between the two extremes, countries were categorized "Most
Pro-U.S." if they voted at least 7 times as
often with the U.S. as against it; "Pro-U.S."
if they voted at least 3 times as often with
the U.S. as against it; "Neutral" when they
voted as often with the U.S.S.R. as with the
U.S.; and "Most Pro-Soviet" when they
voted at least 7 times as often with the
U.S.S.R. as against it.

them to (each side calls the other's associated states "Satellites")
that logic is sometimes obscured.

Of the ten countries that voted most closely with the U.S., all
but Luxembourg would have to be described as countries with
which the United States is most interdependent. To be certain, the
Batistas, Trujillos, and other petty dictators whom the U.S. supported during that period (under the delusion that they were indispensable in the fight to oppose international communism) also
voted very closely with the U.S. But with the overthrow of those
overly-dependent regimes in those countries, the governments that
replaced them, perhaps inevitably, expressed their antipathy toward
the U.S. for having supported their oppressive predecessors by
sharply reducing their international support for the United States.
Cuba is only an extreme case, going from a $+.786$ index in the
1955–59 period to a $-.939$ index in the following five-year period.
In contrast, while the voting index of France during the years of
General de Gaulle fell to a $+.455$ from a high of $+.963$ in the
last years of the Fourth Republic because of his own personal animosity toward (or counterdependence with) the United States,
because France, as a country, is highly interdependent with the
U.S., upon his retirement that index seems to have steadily risen.

It should also be noted that although there was some disparity
in voting records during the period covered by Table 8.1, every one
of the states historically associated with the United States (see
Table 4.1) that were in the United Nations were at least in the
"Pro U.S." category. As with the other variables examined, long
historic association tends to breed informal political ties.

The voting on matters of importance to the Soviet Union is
clear. Throughout the history of the United Nations—and not just

in the period covered by Table 8.1—the communist countries have voted 100 percent with the Soviet Union on cold war questions. There have been other issues on which they have abstained, or voted in opposition to the U.S.S.R., but not on cold war issues. Note that Yugoslavia is the major exception to that rule. In the first four sessions of the General Assembly it, too, tended to vote exactly as did the U.S.S.R. on cold war questions. But after Tito's break with Stalin, Yugoslavia moved to a more neutral cold war position (obtaining a $-.056$ voting index in the 1950–54 period) and has only gradually become more pro-Soviet in its voting behavior as Yugoslav-Soviet relations have improved. Despite all the improvement that has occurred in those relations, however, Yugoslavia still maintains what might be called a "mildly Pro-Soviet neutrality" in its U.N. voting on cold war issues.

I know of no published study that analyzes the U.N. voting behavior of states formerly associated with Britain and France on matters of most concern to those Powers.[12] The only study I know of that is specifically concerned with how closely former British dependencies vote with the U.K. on matters of concern to Britain is an unpublished Master's thesis by Hershey Leaman, a former student of mine.[13] While the statistical techniques used were not very sophisticated, the findings, even if only tentative, are rather interesting and tend to confirm findings presented elsewhere in this book. The paper starts with the hypothesis that voting in the U.N. on issues of importance to Britain would correlate highly with the degree to which the country was economically dependent on Britain. Voting was analyzed for General Assembly meetings between 1955 and 1965 (with the exception of 1964, a year in which no votes were taken). Between nine and thirteen issues were chosen for each General Assembly session. If a country voted exactly as

[12] In *World Politics in the General Assembly,* Alker and Russett point out the degree to which there is greater voting coherence among various subgroups of the Commonwealth than there is among the Commonwealth as a whole, but the focus of their work is on major issues before the General Assembly and not on issues of specific concern to Britain. Russett in his *International Regions and the International System: A Study in Political Ecology* (Chicago: Rand McNally, 1967) comes to the same conclusion. Indeed, in his breakdown of major groups within the U.N. in 1963, the Commonwealth, as such, is not even considered. While Hovet in *Africa in the United Nations,* does consider the cohesion of voting of the African members of the Commonwealth, again the issues discussed are not those primarily of concern to the U.K.

[13] M. Hershey Leaman, "The Correlation Between the Economic and Political Ties of Commonwealth Countries and the United Kingdom in terms of Trade and Aid and Voting Patterns in the United Nations," Master's thesis, Graduate School of Public and International Affairs, University of Pittsburgh, Pittsburgh, Pa., 1968.

did the U.K., that vote was considered an "identity" vote with the U.K. Where the country abstained rather than voting with or against the U.K. the vote was called a "solidarity" vote. Where the country voted opposite the United Kingdom, the vote was labelled "divided." [14]

At first glance, Figure 8.1 looks like a very impressive show of political support for the United Kingdom within the U.N. Only two countries have an "identity" voting record of 50 percent or below with the U.K., and that figure is based on votes on so few issues as to warrant those countries not being considered at all. Most obviously missing, however, is a comparison with how the membership of the United Nations as a whole voted on those same issues. If the average vote of the world organization as a whole was 90 percent identity with the U.K. (a proposition that is unlikely in the extreme) then this chart would indicate that most associated states support Britain in the U.N. *less* than does the total membership of that organization. If, on the other hand, the average vote on those same issues came closer to 50 percent or less identity with the U.K. (a much more likely proposition) then indeed this chart would indicate greater support of the U.K. by associated states in the U.N. than by the general membership. I simply do not know the answer, as of this writing, but I would not be very surprised if on investigation of total voting, the latter proposition were upheld. Indeed, Mr. Leaman offers some support for this conclusion when he says: ". . . with the exception of Zambia and Tanzania. . . . the newly independent countries [associated with the U.K.] voted more in line with the United Kingdom than the other Afro-Asian countries." [15]

Considering only "identity" votes with the U.K., Mr. Leaman divided the countries into four groups as follows: Group I, 80–100 percent identity; Group II, 69–79 percent identity; Group III, 60–69 percent identity; Group IV, 45–59 percent identity.[16] His attempt to relate this voting behavior to economic dependence on the United Kingdom ran into some difficulty. He discovered that the four countries in Group I, Australia, New Zealand, South Africa and Canada, were not at all the countries economically most dependent. Indeed, of all the countries considered, these are the four that must be considered economically most *interdependent* with the United Kingdom. While Mr. Leaman found this damaging to his basic hypothesis, I find it highly significant. It seems yet another confirmation that countries that prove to be the most reliable allies over long periods of time are not the weaker coun-

[14] *Ibid.*, p. 3.
[15] *Ibid.*, p. 13.
[16] *Ibid.*, p. 12.

Figure 8.1   Votes Cast by Associated States on Issues of Importance to the United
             Kingdom, 1955-65[a]

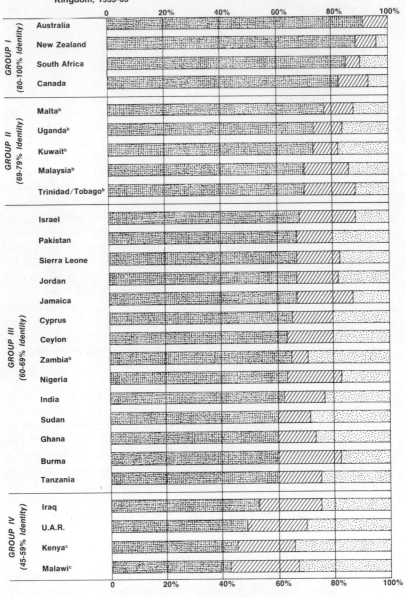

Key: ▦ Identity   ▨ Solidarity   ▒ Divided

[a]Taken from Leaman, *op. cit.*, p. 18.   [b]Voted first in UN in 1963.   [c]Voted only in part of 1965.

tries most dependent upon the Powers, but rather are those countries with which the Powers are most interdependent.

Formal Political Ties

Diplomatic Relations

Traditionally, the index of international political behavior that has been most sensitive to changes in political relationships between states has been formal diplomatic relationships. It is standard, expected, and accepted behavior for the ambassador of country A to express his country's displeasure with a particular policy of country B by not attending a banquet given by a high-ranking official of B. If the displeasure of A is somewhat stronger, the ambassador of A might send an appropriately strong communication to the government of B. Still stronger protest could be expressed by withdrawing the ambassador from B entirely and leaving the embassy in the charge of a lesser official. Country A could register even stronger protest by requesting that B's ambassador be sent home. Ultimately, of course, one state might break diplomatic relations altogether.

In short, in the diplomatic world there exists a language, understood by all familiar with that "culture," in which it is possible to register even very slight nuances of agreement or disagreement with the policies of other states. Presumably, if "normal" relations between two countries are the goals of the policy makers in both, and A was so offended by a particular policy of B that its decision makers were willing to disrupt those normal relations, the decision makers in B would be moved to reexamine that policy, and perhaps to change it, in order to reestablish normal relations. Whether B will change that policy, however, is a function of how important B's decision makers perceive that particular policy to be for the well-being of B, relative to the importance of good relations with A. This, in turn, may well be determined by B's perceptions of how important A is to it.

All of this implies, of course, that every state will have diplomatic relations with those states it perceives as important to its own well-being. This tendency is limited, by the simple fact that most states cannot afford to have diplomatic relations with many other states. One of the signs of big Power status is the ability to afford diplomatic relations with most of the countries in the world. But, most states must be highly selective in judging which other states are important enough to warrant the considerable expense involved. It is precisely because, for each country with limited resources, exchanging ambassadors involves decisions as to which foreign countries are most important to its interests, that this is such a good index of each country's perceptions of its relationships with the other countries of the world.

In Chapter 5 the communication implications of the location of embassies was discussed. Here the location of embassies serves as an index of formal international political ties.

Many of the smaller countries must maximize their international representation by locating embassies in the major world capitals and at the United Nations. If a country can afford to have only ten to fifteen embassies abroad, the likelihood is that the United States, the United Kingdom, France, Japan, and the Soviet Union will account for three or four of them, and the others will be located in countries with which it has had historical, religious, or commercial ties. A large portion of these are likely to be regional neighbors. What is most interesting for this study, however, is that if for political reasons the mentor Power does not have diplomatic relations with an immediate neighbor of the weaker state, the likelihood is that the weaker state also will not have diplomatic relations with that state.

Whether because the leaders of most of the former French political dependencies in Africa perceived Chinese communism to be "bad," or because few of the decision makers in those countries were willing to do anything intentionally to offend France, prior to France's recognition of the People's Republic of China in 1964 only four of the sixteen African states associated with France (Guinea, Mali, Morocco, and Algeria) recognized Communist China. Immediately following France's recognition, however, four others (Congo-Brazzaville, Central African Republic, Dahomey, and Tunisia) also recognized the People's Republic of China. While it is impossible to prove motivation for behavior, my own guess would be that those countries waited for the French lead because they perceived France to be more important to their interests than any possible gain that might accrue from recognition of the Communist Chinese regime. As for those countries that did not recognize the People's Republic of China even after France did, I would be tempted to argue that they probably perceived Communist China either adversely or as unimportant to their national interest, and continue to do so. Whatever the motivations, however, the significant point is that one-quarter of the francophone countries in Africa immediately altered an international diplomatic position to concur with a new French position.

Similarly, before the United States broke diplomatic relations with Castro's government, nearly every other Latin American country recognized Cuba.[17] Since then, only Mexico has maintained formal diplomatic relations with Havana. Whether Latin American countries broke relations because they perceived Castro in much the same light as did policy makers in the United States, or because of compliance with actual or perceived U.S. wishes, it is impossible at this time to determine.

Aside from the question of which countries recognize which other countries—in itself a highly sensitive index of political ties— there is a related question that may provide an equally valid index: What proportions of the weaker countries' relatively scarce diplomats are sent to particular countries? Steven J. Brams, who analyzed diplomatic exchanges (along with foreign trade and shared membership in intergovernmental organizations) in order to determine the "transaction flow" of messages in the international system and, from that, to establish the political salience of one country for another, says in an article based on those studies: "the number of diplomats which country A sends to country B is an indicator of the salience of B to A's decision-makers. If B were a large country, we would expect A to send to B a higher proportion of its diplomats than if B were a small country."[18] As was observed in Chapter 5, exchange of diplomats is indeed a good index of saliency and degree of communication ties between countries, but it should be an equally valid index of intensity of political ties. Hopefully Brams, or other scholars, will attempt to construct a political index for a relatively long time period on this basis. Without having that data available in a form in which it could be used here, I would hypothesize that there would be a direct correlation between the intensity of political ties as measured by percentage of diplomats sent, and all the other ties discussed in this work. That is, the more a weaker country becomes tied in any way to a mentor Power, the stronger one would expect the formal political ties to become; and a good index of the intensity of those political ties would be the percent of a weak country's total diplomats sent to a particular Power.

The complementary data—the percent of big Power diplomats sent to the weaker country—should be equally revealing about the intensity of formal political ties between countries. Certainly, the size (both physical and in terms of population) of the country, and the political saliency of that country at a given time would be

[17] It should be noted that Venezuela and several other Latin American countries broke diplomatic relations with Castro prior to the United States.
[18] Steven J. Brams, "Transaction Flows in the International System" in *American Political Science Review*, Vol. LX, No. 4 (Dec. 1966), p. 882.

major factors in determining the number of diplomats sent,[19] but those could be accounted for in a carefully constructed index. Steven Schecter has suggested that diplomatic exchanges could be viewed similarly to foreign trade: diplomats sent corresponding to exports; diplomats received corresponding to imports; total diplomats exchanged corresponding to total foreign trade. Preliminary evidence suggests that while the big Powers tend to trade diplomats more among each other than they do with weaker countries—just as they trade more goods and services among each other than they do with weaker countries—those weaker countries that are politically most tied in other ways to a specific Power tend to trade most of their diplomats with that Power. The exchange of diplomats itself can be viewed as a political tie in exactly the same way that trade of goods and services can be viewed as an economic tie. The higher the percentage exchanged—relative to the total for each—the stronger the tie.[20]

Political Associations

There are many regional organizations from which the big Powers are intentionally excluded for fear of their domination or interference. These include, among others, the Organization of African Unity and the Asian-African Legal Consultative Committee. There are others, essentially representing economic interests, such as the Cocoa Producers' Alliance and the Organization of Petroleum Exporting Countries (OPEC), from which the big Powers are also excluded. Still other international organizations or associations strive to be universal in membership and nonpolitical

[19] For example, in 1963–64, despite its relatively small size, Vietnam received a higher percentage of U.S. diplomats—exclusive of A.I.D. and military personnel (both of which were there in large numbers)—than any countries except Italy, India, United Kingdom, Brazil, U.S.S.R., Japan, West Germany, Indonesia, and Spain. Figures are from data cards prepared by Steven J. Brams, which he kindly made available to me and Steven Schecter. See Bram's *Flow and Form in the International System,* Ph.D. thesis, Northwestern University, Evanston, Ill., 1966.

[20] It is possible that in considering the number of diplomats exchanged, raw figures may have to be adjusted, just as raw economic figures sometimes have to be adjusted. For example, according to the printout of Brams' data, Gabon in 1963 exported a total of 10 diplomats to other world capitals. Four of them were in Washington, four were in Bonn, one was in Paris, and one was in a neighboring capital. Because of the small numbers involved, a switch of just one or two individuals would make a major difference in percentages. France, however, exports enough diplomats to Gabon so that the "total trade of diplomats" figures are not much different from what one would expect them to be. Hence, scholars who use these figures will have to do so with extreme caution.

in character, although they do not always succeed. Among these one might list the International Postal Union, the International Red Cross, and most of the specialized agencies of the United Nations. For purposes of this study, however, the organizations of interest are the more clearly political associations under the leadership, tacit or otherwise, of the big Powers.

As we have seen, these formal political associations need not be explicitly political in content. Military alliances are, after all, merely a special type of international *political* association. By signing such an agreement, one state is publicly proclaiming that it *politically* supports the other state, in some cases even to the point of going to war. Similarly, many economic associations also have distinct political overtones. To deny the political significance of membership in the Alliance for Progress, the Colombo Plan, the European Free Trade Association, and other such associations that have economic goals as their stated purpose, would be to overlook the realities of world politics. Consider the political ramifications of one of the most famous economic associations, the Marshall Plan. While the Soviet Union and other Eastern European countries were invited to join, in reality they could not have done so without making the kind of political compromises that would have been unthinkable for them. In fact, the Soviet Union applied considerable political pressure to get some European states not to accept the American economic assistance, and organized the Eastern European states into a competing economic organization, the Council for Mutual Economic Aid (COMECON or CMEA).

The political relationships embodied in many of these associations have deep historic roots. Both the Commonwealth of Nations and the French Community are historical successors to the British and French Empires, respectively. In a sense, the Organization of American States, the Rio Pact, and the Alliance for Progress can be viewed as the successor organizations to indirect U.S. imperial interest in Latin America. By similar extension, it is perhaps possible to view the Council for Mutual Economic Aid and the Warsaw Pact as the successor organizations to the traditional interests of imperial Russia in Eastern Europe. Each of these organizations officially is a voluntary association in recognition of a continuing commonality of interest among a group of states. Yet membership constitutes a set of formal political ties to a particular mentor state. No state in any of these organizations is formally bound to follow the international political lead of the mentor Power. Yet (except for the "new members" of the Commonwealth), there is a high degree of similarity of international political behavior—either because there is a high degree of similarity among the members as to definition of political self-interest in international matters, or because the weaker states feel obliged to go along with the definition of international self-interest supplied by the mentor Power.

Great Britain

Without question, the major political association of the United Kingdom associated states is the Commonwealth of Nations.[21] As of 1968, twenty-seven countries were members.[22] The U.K., Australia, New Zealand, and Canada, plus Ireland and South Africa (which have both withdrawn) are often referred to as the Old or First Commonwealth. The present membership is often called the New or Second Commonwealth.

It is interesting to note which countries have chosen to join the Commonwealth of all that were eligible. Officially only "Her Majesty's dominions" (presumably meaning territories at one time "Formal-Direct" colonies) are eligible for membership upon receiving *de jure* independence.

> Protectorates and trust territories are not technically part of Her Majesty's dominions [and thus presumably not eligible for membership]. . . . Consequently on the date of independence the Northern Territories and Togoland in Ghana, the greater part of Nigeria and Sierra Leone, and the whole of Tanganyika and Uganda had to be "annexed" to Her Majesty's dominions for the first time.[23]

That being the case, why did Burma, which was clearly eligible for membership, and some of the protectorates and trust territories, which could have been "annexed," choose not to join? Presumably, either they lacked a sufficiently strong perception of a commonality of political interest with the United Kingdom, or local and/or regional political considerations interfered. Whatever the cause, the fact is that no Arab country is or has been a member. On the other hand, of the non-Arab states only Israel, Burma, and the Maldive Islands chose not to make themselves eligible to join.

Politically, the New Commonwealth is probably the least coherent grouping of any being considered in this study. Two of its

---

[21] See Frank H. Underhill, *The British Commonwealth: An Experiment in Cooperation Among Nations* (Durham, N.C.: Duke University Press, 1956).

[22] U.K., Australia, New Zealand, Canada, Pakistan, Malaysia, Singapore, Kenya, Uganda, Cyprus, Malta, Mauritius, Sierra Leone, India, Ceylon, Barbados, Botswana, Gambia, Ghana, Guyana, Jamaica, Lesotho, Malawi, Nigeria, Trinidad & Tobago, Zambia, Tanzania.

[23] S. A. de Smith, *The New Commonwealth and Its Constitutions* (London: Stevens and Sons, 1964), p. 15.

members, India and Pakistan, have officially been at war with each
other since the time of their entry. Many members publicly condemned Britain during the Suez crisis, and one, Tanzania, actually
broke diplomatic relations with Britain temporarily because Britain
refused to use force in the Rhodesian crisis. Nonetheless, there
can be no question that the Commonwealth is a going concern.

In the older Dominions there is a powerful sense of affinity with
Britain and with one another—loyalty to a common Crown, a somewhat ambivalent affection for what some people still call the old
country, memories of comradeship in two world wars, a widespread
feeling that they are all essentially one people, a broad measure of
agreement as to the appropriate form and ends of government. But
self-interest is no less significant a unifying factor. . . .

In discussing world issues with its fellow-members [a newer mem-
ber] may not convert them [the older members] to its own way of
thinking, but its point of view will be listened to and taken into
account and it will obtain a clearer appreciation of other points of
view in these exchanges. . . . it can expect a sympathetic hearing
when it is in trouble. When it is in serious trouble it can reasonably
hope for practical help from other Commonwealth countries. And as
a Member of the Commonwealth it will be better able, if it so wishes,
to resist the gravitational pull of neighboring great powers or closely-
knit regional groupings.[24]

As noted in Chapter 7 on military ties, the Commonwealth is not
specifically a military organization. Yet twice, newly independent
members (Kenya and Uganda) called upon the U.K. for military
assistance to prevent anarchy, and the troops were sent forthwith
(before bilateral military agreements were signed). What is more,
Britain does have special bilateral military treaties with at least
eight of the members (and, as far as can be determined, with only
three nonmembers—Nepal, Maldive Islands and Libya). While
some of these treaties only call for the provision of limited amounts
of military equipment, some guarantee the weaker countries' military security.

Aside from the economic aid to the poorer countries supplied
through regular Commonwealth channels, participation in the
Commonwealth entitles members to a system of tariff preferences.
These allow goods from Commonwealth countries into the United
Kingdom and other Commonwealth countries either duty-free, or
at lower rates than those imposed on non-Commonwealth countries. These so-called "Commonwealth Preferences" are the successors to the "Imperial Preferences" and also apply to Ireland

[24] de Smith, The New Commonwealth, pp. 26, 28.

and South Africa, even though they are no longer members of the Commonwealth.[25]

Membership in the Commonwealth also implies membership in a host of Commonwealth-related functional organizations. These Inter-governmental Organizations (IGO's) range all the way from such nonpolitical associations as the Commonwealth Forestry Association and the Commonwealth Telecommunications Board ("an advisory body on matters related to external telecommunications systems"), to organizations with a high degree of political content such as the Commonwealth Parliamentary Association, the Federation of Commonwealth Chambers of Commerce, and the Royal Commonwealth Society (whose explicit aim is to "promote understanding among the peoples of the Commonwealth").[26]

Another British-oriented association, the Colombo Plan, was originally established to foster the economic development of South and Southeast Asian Commonwealth Countries. It has now been opened to non-Commonwealth countries as well. The United States and Japan have joined as donor members, while Afghanistan, Bhutan, Burma, Cambodia, Indonesia, Iran, South Korea, Laos, Maldive Islands, Nepal, Philippines, Thailand, and South Vietnam have joined the Asian Commonwealth members (Ceylon, India, Malaysia, Pakistan, and Singapore) as recipients.[27]

Although its members are not associated states of the United Kingdom in the sense used in this study, the European Free Trade Association (E.F.T.A.) is primarily a British-oriented economic association. Membership may constitute as much of a formal political tie as does membership in the Colombo Plan or in the Commonwealth itself.

France

There is a formal international organization known as the French Community composed officially of France and six African states that were formerly colonies (Central African Republic, Congo (Brazzaville), Gabon, and Chad—all of which comprised French Equatorial Africa prior to 1958—and Senegal and Malagasy). But in considering formal political ties between France and its

[25] See *Treaties and Alliances of the World: A Survey of International Treaties in Force and Communities of States* (Keynsham, Bristol: Keesing's Publications, 1968), p. 97.

[26] *Ibid.,* p. 98.

[27] *Ibid.* Of the 13 non-Commonwealth recipients, only seven are not historically associated with Britain, but every one of those seven has been associated in one way or another with the two non-Commonwealth donor members. It appears that the U.S. and Japan were willing to join provided that their Asian associated states could be included among the beneficiaries.

former colonies in sub-Sahara Africa and Madagascar, one really must refer to a broader community. All of France's former colonies in sub-Sahara Africa save Guinea are associated with France in this broader community. In order to distinguish the two more clearly, the first group will be referred to in this discussion as the *Communauté*. The *Communauté* members are officially more closely tied to France than the others are, but *de facto* the differences are a matter of degree rather than of kind.

In . . . political matters—the coordination of foreign policy and defence—the agreements with Senegal, Madagascar and the four States of Equatorial Africa contain broader undertakings than the others. These states remain in the Community and are supposed to have certain common political institutions with France, including the Presidency. But the Community institutions provided for have not met, and the Community no longer has much practical significance. The agreements with the other States contain political provisions which are hardly less important; . . . The most interesting part of the political provisions is the undertaking to consult together frequently on foreign policy matters.[28]

These agreements to consult on foreign policy matters appear to be considerably more important than similar agreements among Commonwealth countries, because the French community tends to behave internationally with considerably more cohesion than does the Commonwealth. This greater cohesion is probably not the result of stronger *formal* political ties between France and the community than between Britain and the Commonwealth, but the result of stronger *informal* political ties which find formal expression in the Cooperation Agreements signed by each of the former sub-Sahara colonies at the time of independence (or shortly thereafter). Every conceivable field is covered by these Agreements: "foreign policy, defense, monetary affairs, the common aspects of economic and financial policy, policies for primary commodities and strategic materials, justice, higher education, the organization of international transport and telecommunications"[29] to mention only the more obvious. In all fields the "Cooperation Agreements" seem to bind the community more closely together than any other international association binds its members, except perhaps the Council for Mutual Economic Assistance. But the Soviet Union does not directly underwrite the budgets of the East European states, as France literally does for the countries of the community.

[28] Teresa Hayter, *French Aid* (London: Overseas Development Institute, 1966), p. 143.

[29] Hayter, *French Aid,* p. 142.

In a book on the Cooperation Agreements published by the French government, Maurice Ligot says:

> Franco-African cooperation thus appears as the preservation of close, multiple and fundamental links. . . . It can thus be defined as a new type of relations between sovereign states. [These Agreements made it] possible for the African and Malagasy States to achieve independence, inside or even outside the Community, without profoundly modifying either the juridical links or the links of friendship, with the ex-metropolis.[30]

This "new type of relations between sovereign states" is so close, in fact, that there are many people, particularly in the more anticolonial parts of Africa, who insist that the Agreements do not constitute "independence" at all. In light of the premise underlying this study that independence is not an either/or proposition, but rather is best seen as relative points on a continuum, the view of the critics seems extreme. But certainly one could make a very strong case that these formal political ties (which after all are what the Cooperation Agreements are) bind the community countries to France as closely as any independent states could be bound and still be considered "independent."

Being associated with France in the community implies membership in a large number of French-led Inter-governmental Organizations. The direct tie to the economy of France is reinforced by the formal agreements making these countries members of the Franc Zone. Membership in the French Community also entitles these countries (by special formal agreements sponsored by France) to be Associated Members of the European Economic Community, thus further tying them formally to an intricate network of European-dominated international organizations. The economic benefits to these countries from these ties are óbvious; the political implications are more subtle. Access to a protected European market for their raw materials is an enormous economic advantage, to be certain, but at the same time their trade relations with countries outside the European Economic Community are severely limited. Outside economic penetration is thus inhibited, if not prevented, and by extension, so is penetration of any kind.

Maurice Ligot, in the book quoted earlier, says that the Cooperation Agreement on cultural matters is "extremely important: it conditions the preservation and expansion of the French language and culture in Black Africa, as well as the development—

---

[30] Maurice Ligot, *Les Accords de Coopération entre la France et les Etats Africains et Malgache d'Expression Française,* series Le Monde Contemporain (La Documentation Française, 1964), quoted in Hayter, *French Aid,* p. 142.

since it is notably concerned with cooperation in the field of higher education—of the African intellectual and political elite in the French cultural tradition." [30a] This passage clearly illustrates the interrelationship between all of the various ties between states. Here are formal political treaties (the Cooperation Agreements) that stipulate that the French language and culture are to be preserved and strengthened (linguistic, educational, and cultural ties) in order to strengthen the *informal* political ties between France and the community, which in all likelihood will lead to further formal political ties. What is perhaps most significant about the formal ties of the French community is the relative lack of ties between those countries and Powers other than France.

The United States

The Organization of American States was formed only in 1948, but its heritage can be traced back to the Monroe Doctrine of 1823. Keesing's *Treaties and Alliances of the World* says:

The idea of the unity of interests of the countries of the American continents, or of Pan-Americanism, received its first impetus from the so-called Monroe Doctrine which rejected all interferences in American affairs by outside Powers. . . .

An "International Union of American Republics" was set up at a First International Conference of American States in Washington in 1889–90. The fourth conference of this organization decided in Washington in 1910 to change its name to "Union of American Republics," and at the fifth conference in Santiago de Chile in 1923 it was decided to adopt the name "Union of the Republics of the American Continents" and to establish the Pan-American Union as its permanent organ. [31]

In 1948, the Pan-American Union became the "central and permanent organ" of the newly reconstituted Organization of American States. Like the Commonwealth and the French Community, membership in the O.A.S. implies membership in various functional organizations associated with it. The O.A.S. itself is not a military organization, but all its members are signatories of the 1947 Rio Pact, a multilateral military alliance pledged to mutual cooperation in the event of aggression from outside the Americas.

Originally, the intention of the Monroe Doctrine was to warn European Powers that "the American Continents . . . are henceforth not to be considered as subjects for future colonization by

[30a] Quoted in Hayter, *French Aid*, p. 143.
[31] *Treaties and Alliances of the World*, p. 104.

any European Power." [32] It was meant to prevent France and Russia in particular from meddling in the disintegration of Spain's American Empire. The United States at that time did not have the power to prevent such meddling by itself, and had to rely on the congruence of British political interest and the British Navy to enforce the Doctrine.

By the start of the twentieth century, American power had increased sufficiently so that President Theodore Roosevelt could issue his famous "Big Stick" Corollary: "In the Western Hemisphere the adherence of the United States to the Monroe Doctrine may force the United States . . . to the exercise of an international police power." [33] Bemis describes this as "benevolent United States intervention to prevent non-American intervention." [34] And the United States has intervened on any number of occasions to prevent what it—and it alone—defines as "non-American" intervention.

Since the end of World War II, of course, the major enemy of the United States has been perceived by American policy makers to be "international communism." The O.A.S. has taken stands against communism since its inception and in 1954 it adopted the "Declaration of Solidarity for Preservation of the Political Integrity of the American States Against International Communist Intervention." [35] It is that aim to which most of the attention of the O.A.S. is directed. Even the Alliance for Progress, which is presumed to have as its primary goal the more rapid economic development of Latin America, has the underlying political motivation of preventing the appeal and spread of communism.

Precisely what mix of informal political ties prompts the elaborate network of formal international organizations and treaties that exists in the Americas is, of course, impossible to say at this time. There is little doubt, however, that anticommunism is an issue on which there is a high degree of similarity of perception among governments of the American states. The United States continues to intervene in the internal affairs of these states to put down what it considers to be communist infiltration or intervention, and it receives the approval, support, and sometimes the active cooperation of many of the weaker states in the hemisphere when it does so.

Ronald Steel has described this modern-day policy as the Johnson Doctrine and says that it is

[32] From the Monroe Doctrine, quoted in Samuel Flagg Bemis, *The Latin American Policy of the United States: An Historical Interpretation* (New York: Harcourt, Brace & World, 1943), p. 63.

[33] *Treaties and Alliances of the World*, p. 104.

[34] Bemis, *Latin American Policy of the United States*, p. 157.

[35] *Treaties and Alliances of the World*, p. 109.

. . . a formula that would justify the dispatch of United States troops to any country in the hemisphere threatened by a communist take-over. Harking back to the Monroe Doctrine and the Theodore Roosevelt corollary, it asserts the right of the United States to provide order in and exclude unfriendly influences from the Americas.[36]

On the basis of American action in Vietnam, Laos, and Cambodia, it would appear that this doctrine is not confined either to the Americas or to President Lyndon B. Johnson. Indeed, the number of bilateral and multilateral military treaties concluded by the United States with countries around the globe, and the number of actual interventions that have occurred, with or without treaties, seems to indicate an extension of the Monroe Doctrine and the Roosevelt Corollary to include the entire "Free World." But this seems to be the pattern of great states at the height of their power (compare Table 4.1 and Table 8.1). When Britain and France were at their pinnacle, they established formal and informal political ties in all corners of the world to protect what they perceived to be their vital national interests. As their power has declined—relative to the rise of other Powers—their formal and informal political ties with their historically associated states have been loosened, and the number of states with which they have such ties has been reduced. Since World War II, when the United States has been at the pinnacle of its power, its political ties with its historically associated states have increased and it has established formal and informal political ties far beyond the Western Hemisphere to protect what it perceives to be in its national interest everywhere in the world.

The Soviet Union

In considering the Soviet Bloc countries, what is most striking is the historical continuity of Russian imperial interests. Eastern Europe, Mongolia, North Korea, and parts of China were the outer limits of the old Russian Empire in the late nineteenth and early twentieth centuries. The Treaty of Brest-Litovsk, which the Bolsheviks signed with the Germans in 1918 (at the nadir of Russian power), surrendered most of Russia's holdings in Eastern Europe. With the defeat of Germany in World War II, what had been Russia's empire in Eastern Europe, and more, was returned to it. This time, however, these countries were not directly incorporated, but were controlled indirectly through the institutions of the Red Army and the Communist Parties. In those countries that were

[36] Ronald Steel, *Pax Americana* (New York: Viking Press, 1967), p. 232.

never occupied by the Russian Army (Yugoslavia, Albania, and China) the Russians had to rely on the Communist Party as their sole political tie, and that tie has proved considerably less binding than the military presence.[37]

In a fascinating article on the Communist Bloc, originally published in 1961, Zbigniew Brzezinski said:

> In some ways, if one for a minute overlooks the ideological elements, it [the Communist Bloc during Stalin's day] was much like the Roman or French or English empire in their earlier days. Precisely because of that it did not require elaborate machinery. The present development within the camp is increasingy transforming it into an international Communist empire, dominated by various Communist elites, bound together, to be sure, by Soviet power, but also by common interests and aspirations. . . . they increasingly find it necessary to express their unity through various organizational devices.[38]

The major organizational devices for tying the Eastern European associated states to the Soviet Union politically have been the Council for Mutual Economic Assistance, established in 1949, and the Warsaw Pact, established in 1955.

Officially, the Council for Mutual Economic Assistance is an economic organization to promote "the exchange of experience in the economic field, and mutual assistance in regard to raw materials, foodstuffs, machinery, equipment, etc." [39] But, as Frederic Pryor points out:

> It is easy to detect both economic and political strands in the striving toward autarky in the Bloc. One political goal is quite clear: economic independence from any nation which is believed to be unfriendly. For instance, the DDR [German Democratic Republic] Prime Minister declared: "We will make ourselves very quickly independent from the arbitrary measures of the American imperialists; the industry of the DDR will produce out of its own means the important products which we now import from the capitalist countries, or else we will import these goods from the countries of the camp of peace. . . . we do not need or will not allow ourselves dependence (on the west)." [40]

[37] Recall that it was partisan groups in Yugoslavia and Albania that ousted the Germans, and not the Russian army.

[38] Zbigniew K. Brzezinski, "The Organization of the Communist Camp," originally published in *World Politics*, Vol. XIII (Jan. 1961) reprinted in Zbigniew K. Brzezinski, *The Soviet Bloc: Unity and Conflict*, Rev. Ed. (New York: Frederick A. Praeger, 1961), p. 478.

[39] *Treaties and Alliances of the World*, p. 92.

[40] Frederic L. Pryor, *The Communist Foreign Trade System* (Cambridge: Massachusetts Institute of Technology Press, 1963), pp. 23–24.

Brzezinski is equally specific on the subject:

> The two most important multilateral organs binding some of the Communist states together are the Warsaw Treaty Organization (WTO) and the Council for Economic Mutual Assistance (CEMA) [*sic*]. There is, however, no organ officially including all the Communist states. . . . The WTO is both a political and a military organization. . . . It is . . . primarily a European organization, serving externally as a counter to NATO, internally as the formal device for the perpetuation of close ties between the Soviet Union and its European satellites. In fact, to this day it constitutes the single most important formal commitment binding the European Communist states to the U.S.S.R., officially limiting their scope for independent action by precluding their participation in other alliance systems.[41]

Of the Council for Mutual Economic Assistance he says: "At the present time, CEMA is doubtless the single most important organ for actively shaping policies designed to promote the camp's unity." [42]

As with each of the other Power's major international organizations, membership in CMEA implies membership in associated functional commissions as well. Also, as with the other Powers, these multilateral formal political ties are buttressed by a series of bilateral defense and economic treaties. And, as with the other Powers, these bilateral treaties usually include provisions for "extensive exchange of scientific knowledge and scientific cadres, and numerous bilateral arrangements between the various national institutes and academies as well as the bilateral commissions for scientific-technical collaboration established not only between the Soviet Union and the other Communist states, but among the People's Democracies as well." [43] Thus there is provision for reinforcing general perceptual ties, which can be counted to reinforce the informal political ties. As in the inter-American system, in the Soviet system defection by counterelites attempting to loosen ties or to pull their countries out of the system altogether is generally not tolerated where political conditions are right for preventing them from doing so (as in Poland, East Germany, and Hungary in 1956 and Czechoslovakia in 1968). Where political conditions are not right, of course, some of the weaker countries can get away with pulling out of the system—but again notice only with the help of some other big Power.

---

[41] Brzezinski, *The Soviet Bloc,* pp. 446–447. Note that Comecon is referred to by different writers as CMEA or CEMA.

[42] *Ibid.,* p. 450.

[43] *Ibid.,* p. 458.

China

China, while an associated state of the Soviet Union, is in a distinctive position. While it is not quite as powerful as Russia, neither is it nearly as weak as the other associated states. What is more, China has never been as politically tied formally or informally to the U.S.S.R. as were the East European states. Stalin opted for a narrowly defined national interest over ideological ties in 1928 when he supported the Kuomintang at the expense of the Chinese Communist Party, and despite the short honeymoon between 1949 and 1960, both the U.S.S.R. and China have been perfectly willing to split the communist camp over questions of national hegemony in their respective regions. To be certain, there are genuine differences in ideological approach between the two communist giants, but these seem to be far less significant in their dispute than their conflicting interpretations of national interest.

As Chinese power has increased since 1949, China has demanded all the perquisites to which it feels entitled—including nuclear weapons, space rockets, and associated states of its own. There is no question that it is China's increasing power that permits it to acquire its own associated states. If and when China can fully consolidate its domestic power, those weaker communist states on its periphery will surely abandon their neutrality in the Sino-Soviet dispute (they will have no choice) and will become formally tied to China in much the same way that Eastern Europe is tied to the Soviet Union.

Japan

At the time of this writing, Japan has no states politically associated with it, despite its enormous economic power. This is largely because, since World War II, Japan has been formally associated politically with the United States. Indeed, despite Japan's phenomenal economic development, it has been much more politically tied to the U.S. than China ever was to the Soviet Union. (The U.S. military was, and still is, in Japan; Russian troops never occupied China.) But just as the increase in Chinese power permitted China to break the "gravitational pull" of Russian power, so the rise in Japanese power, can be expected ultimately to allow Japan to break the even stronger pull of U.S. power. And when it does, it can be expected to politically "attract" a number of the weaker states of Southeast Asia to it.

At the beginning of the 1970's, Japan's increased political saliency in the region was already evident. Early in 1970 Indonesia's foreign minister publicly said that the Power the countries of Southeast Asia had most to fear in the immediate future was Japan, not China. Nonetheless Japan was invited to a conference called by Indonesia to discuss the spread of the war into Cambodia, and was the only Asian Power to attend.[44] The visit early in 1970 of Crown Prince Akihito to many of the countries occupied by Japan in the 1940's was another indication of Japan's growing political presence in the region. If the hypotheses put forth thus far are valid, there is every reason to expect that many of the states of Southeast Asia, now only economically tied to Japan, will increasingly become politically tied as well.

Indicators of Formal Political Ties

In an attempt to illustrate visually which weaker countries have formal political ties to particular Powers, Table 8.2 has been constructed. It is not a weighted index, which obviously would be much more meaningful. Unfortunately, it was not feasible to construct such an index for a work of this scope. Rather, the table simply shows the existence of diplomatic relations, military defense treaties, currency or economic aid ties, and membership in a number of international organizations, the latter selected on the basis that they seem to be among the most indicative of weak state relations with the Powers. Where possible, the level of the diplomatic representation has been indicated in the notes. It was said earlier that since some treaties are so much more important than others, merely counting the number of treaties between two countries is inadequate for determining the intensity of the political relationship. Here again a weighted index is what is needed. In lieu of such an index, the table shows which Powers each of the weaker countries has military defense treaties with, on the assumption that defense treaties are politically among the most important any country can sign. No attempt has been made to show how many such treaties each weaker country has signed, or how extensive each was, but multilateral defense treaties have been considered somewhat more important than bilateral defense treaties (although that often is not the case).

For Britain, the Sterling Bloc, the Colombo Plan, and the E.F.T.A. were chosen as the politically significant economic indicators, and for France the Franc Zone and the E.E.C. were chosen. In lieu of such groupings for the U.S., U.S.S.R., China, and Japan, the table shows which countries have accepted economic aid from

[44] China and India were invited, but refused to attend.

TABLE 8.2[a]

Formal Political Ties (Circa 1967)

Country	With U.K.						With France						With U.S.A.					With U.S.S.R.					With China			With Japan		
	Commonwealth[b]	Multilateral Defense	Bilateral Treaties[c]	Sterling Bloc	Colombo Plan/EFTA	Diplomatic Relations[d]	French Community	Multilateral Defense	Bilateral Treaties[c]	Franc Zone	E.E.C. or Associated States	Diplomatic Relations[d]	O.A.S.	Multilateral Defense	Bilateral Treaties[c]	Economic Aid[e]	Diplomatic Relations[d]	C.M.E.A.	Warsaw Pact	Bilateral Defense[e]	Economic Aid[e]	Diplomatic Relations[d]	Bilateral Treaties[f]	Economic Aid[e]	Diplomatic Relations[d]	Bilateral Treaties[f]	Economic Aid[e]	Diplomatic Relations[d]
U.K. and Associated States (crudely ranked)[g]																												
Old Commonwealth																												
United Kingdom	X	—	—	X	X	—		X				X		X	X	P	X					X			X		X	X
Australia	X	X	X	X	X	X						X		X	X		X					X					X	X
New Zealand	X	X		X	X	X						X		X	X		X					X						X
Canada	X	X			X	X						X		X	X		X					X			X			X
New Commonwealth																												
Pakistan	X		X	X	X	X						X		X	X	P	X				X	X		P	X		X	X
Malaysia	X	X	X	X	X	X						X				X	X											X
Singapore	X	X		X	X	X						?				X	X								X			?
Kenya	X		X	X		X						X				X	X				P			P	X		X	
Uganda	X		X	X		X						X				X	X				P	X		P	X		P	

Cyprus
Malta
Mauritius
Sierra Leone
India

Ceylon
Barbados
Botswana
Gambia
Ghana

Guyana
Jamaica
Lesotho
Malawi
Nigeria

Trinidad & Tobago
Zambia
Tanzania

Other U.K. Associated States

Iran
Maldive Islands
Nepal
Ireland
Jordan

Kuwait
South Africa
Burma

TABLE 8.2 (Cont'd.)

Country	With U.K.						With France						With U.S.A.					With U.S.S.R.						With China			With Japan		
	Commonwealth[b]	Multilateral/Bilateral Defense/Treaties[e]	Sterling Bloc	Colombo Plan/EFTA	Diplomatic Relations[d]		French Community	Multilateral/Bilateral Defense/Treaties[e]	Franc Zone	E.E.C. or Associated States	Diplomatic Relations[d]		O.A.S.	Multilateral/Bilateral Defense/Treaties[e]	Economic Aid	Diplomatic Relations[d]		C.M.E.A.	Warsaw Pact	Bilateral Defense[e]	Economic Aid	Diplomatic Relations[d]		Bilateral Treaties[f]	Economic Aid	Diplomatic Relations[d]	Bilateral Treaties[f]	Economic Aid	Diplomatic Relations[d]
Other U.K. Associated States (cont'd.)																													
Israel					X						X			X X	X	X						X							X
Saudi Arabia					X						X			X X	P	X						X[h]							X
Southern Yemen					X[j]						?					X[j]						X			?				
Iraq					X						X				P	X					?	X			X				X
Sudan					X						X				X	X					P	X			X				X
U.A.R.					X						X				X						P	X		X	P				X
Yemen																						X		P	P				
Rhodesia																													
France and Associated States (crudely ranked)[g]																													
French Communauté																													
France	X				X		X	X	X	X	X			X	P	X					P	X		P	P	X			X
Central African Rep.					X[h]		X	X	X	X	X			X		X						X							

Chad
Congo (Brazzaville)
Gabon
Senegal
Malagasy

French Community

Cameroon
Dahomey
Ivory Coast
Mauritania
Niger

Upper Volta
Togo
Mali

Other French
Associated States

Belgium[l]
Tunisia
Morocco
Algeria
Cambodia

Laos
Vietnam (N)
Syria
Lebanon
Vietnam (S)
Guinea

TABLE 8.2 (Cont'd.)

Country	With U.K. — Commonwealth[b]	Multilateral Defense	Bilateral Treaties[e]	Sterling Bloc	Colombo Plan/EFTA	Diplomatic Relations[d]	With France — French Community	Multilateral Defense	Bilateral Treaties[e]	Franc Zone	E.E.C. or Associated States	Diplomatic Relations[d]	With U.S.A. — O.A.S.	Multilateral Defense	Bilateral Treaties[e]	Economic Aid[c]	Diplomatic Relations[d]	With U.S.S.R. — C.M.E.A.	Warsaw Pact	Bilateral Defense[e]	Economic Aid[c]	Diplomatic Relations[d]	With China — Bilateral Treaties[f]	Economic Aid[c]	Diplomatic Relations[d]	With Japan — Bilateral Treaties[f]	Economic Aid[c]	Diplomatic Relations[d]
United States and Associated States (crudely ranked)[m]																												
Organization of American States																												
U.S.A.		X	X			X		X	X			X	X	—	—	—	—				X	X					P	X
Brazil						X						X	X	X	X	X	X					X					P	X
Colombia						X						X	X	X	X	X	X											X
Bolivia						X[i]						X	X	X	X	X	X					X[h]						X[i]
Guatemala													X	X	X	X	X					X[h]						X[i]
Honduras						X						X	X	X	X	X	X											X[i]
Panama						X						X	X	X	X	X	X											X
Peru						X						X	X	X	X	X	X					X						X
Chile						X						X	X	X	X	X	X					X[h]					P	X[i]
Costa Rica													X	X	X	X	X											

Dominican Republic
El Salvador
Paraguay
Uruguay
Haiti

Argentina
Mexico
Venezuela
Ecuador
Nicaragua

Other U.S.
Associated States

Philippines
Liberia
Cuba

Soviet Union and
Associated States
(crudely ranked)[c]

Council of Mutual
Economic Assistance

U.S.S.R.
Germany (East)
Hungary
Poland
Bulgaria
Czechoslovakia
Rumania
Mongolia

TABLE 8.2 (Cont'd)

Country	With U.K. Commonwealth[b]	With U.K. Multilateral Defense	With U.K. Bilateral Treaties[c]	With U.K. Sterling Bloc	With U.K. Colombo Plan/EFTA	With U.K. Diplomatic Relations[d]	With France French Community	With France Multilateral Defense	With France Bilateral Treaties[c]	With France Franc Zone	With France E.E.C. or Associated States	With France Diplomatic Relations[d]	With U.S.A. O.A.S.	With U.S.A. Multilateral Defense	With U.S.A. Bilateral Treaties[c]	With U.S.A. Economic Aid[e]	With U.S.A. Diplomatic Relations[d]	With U.S.S.R. C.M.E.A.	With U.S.S.R. Warsaw Pact	With U.S.S.R. Bilateral Defense[c]	With U.S.S.R. Economic Aid	With U.S.S.R. Diplomatic Relations[d]	With China Bilateral Treaties[f]	With China Economic Aid[e]	With China Diplomatic Relations[d]	With Japan Bilateral Treaties[f]	With Japan Economic Aid[e]	With Japan Diplomatic Relations[d]
Soviet Union and Associated States (cont'd.)																												
Other U.S.S.R. Associated States																												
Afghanistan					X	X						X				X	X			X	X	X	X	P	X			X
Finland					X	X						X				P	X			X	?	X		P	X		X	X
Yugoslavia												X					X					X			?			X
Albania[p]						X																?	X	X	X			
China (Mainland)[p]																					?	?						
Japan and Associated States (crudely ranked)[g]																												
Japan					X	X						X		X	X	P	X					X			?	X		X
Korea (South)					X	X						X		X	X	X	X					X	?		?	X	X	X
Thailand					X	X								X	X	X	X										X	X
Taiwan					X^i	X						X		X	X	X	X									X	X	X
Indonesia					X										X	X	X			X	P	X	?	P	P		X	X
Korea (North)															X	X	X			X	?	X	X	X	X	X	X	X

Other European Countries (not ranked)

Country									
Austria	X	X			X X	P X		X X		X X
Denmark	X	X			X X	P X		X X		X X
Germany (West)	X	X	X		X X	P X		X		X X
Greece		X			X	P X				X Xⁱ
Iceland	X				X	P X		X		X Xⁱ
Italy	X	X			X X	P X		X X		X X
Luxembourg	X	X			X X	P X		X X		X Xⁱ
Netherlands	X	X	X		X X	P X		X		X X
Norway	X	X			X X	P X		X X		X X
Portugal	X	X			X	P X		X X		X
Spain	X				X	P X		X		X X
Sweden	X	X			X X	P X		X X		X X
Switzerland	X	X			X X	P X		X X		X X
Turkey	X				X X X	P X		P X		X X

Other Non-European Countries (not ranked)

Country									
Burundi	Xʰ				X X	P X		P X		X
Congo (K)	X				X X	X X		X X		X Xⁱ
Ethiopia	X				X	X X		X		
Libya	Xᵍ X				X	Xᵍ P		P X		Xⁱ
Rwanda	Xʰ				X X	X X		X		
Somalia	Xʰ				X X	X X		X Xʰ	P X	

For meaning of X and P see note e below.

a This table is a first attempt to establish such a world-wide listing. I know of no siderably more sophisticated rankings for military ties (see, for example, Martin C. Needler, *Latin American Politics in Perspective* (Princeton, N.J.: Van Nostrand, 1963), economic ties (see Bruce M. Russett, *International Regions and the International System,* Chicago: Rand McNally, 1967), etc., but I know of no combined ranking for all ties for all countries. No attempt at precise quantification or weighting has been attempted here. See footnote "g" below.

TABLE 8.2 (Cont'd.)

ᵇ Only those countries that were formally independent and members of the Commonwealth in 1967 receive an X in this column.

ᶜ Data on defense treaties are from *Treaties and Alliances of the World*; David Wood, "Armed Forces of African States," *Adelphi Papers*, No. 27 (London: Institute for Strategic Studies, Apr. 1966); and Agency for International Development, *U.S. Overseas Loans and Grants and Assistance from International Organizations: Obligations and Loan Authorizations, July 1, 1945–June 30, 1966* (Washington, D.C.: 1967). Other treaties may very well exist, about which I have no information.

ᵈ Diplomatic representation has been culled from the following sources: U.S. Department of State, *Foreign Service List January 1970; The Diplomatic Service List 1968* (London: H.M. Stationery Office, 1968); *Whitaker's Almanack, 1969; Statesman's Year-Book 1968-69*.

ᵉ Not all countries receive economic aid from specific Powers every year. The Communist countries, particularly, tend to give aid to most non-Communist developing countries on a "one-shot" basis. To consider figures for one year only would, therefore, miss some of the major recipients of economic assistance. The decisions to grant or withhold aid are highly political, and a change of regime in any country in a given year could mean the discontinuation or start of aid. In order to partially account for those shifts, countries to which economic assistance obligations, authorizations, or expenditures of $500,000 or over—either in loans or grants—were made in 1967 (1966 for aid from the U.S.S.R. and China) have received an X in the appropriate column. If the country has received economic aid from that same source in previous years, but not in 1967 (or 1966 in the Soviet and Chinese cases) that fact is designated by a P in the appropriate column. A more sensitive index, of course, would include the magnitude of the aid received in all years, but this table makes no pretense of being highly sensitive. Economic aid data are from the following sources: Agency for International Development, *U.S. Economic Assistance Programs Administered by the Agency for International Development and Predecessor Agencies* (Mar. 28, 1969); Thomas L. Hughes, "Communist Governments and Developing Nations: Economic Aid and Trade," U.S. Department of State, RSB-80 (July 21, 1967); Organization for Economic Co-Operation and Development, *Geographical Distribution of Financial Flows to Less Developed Countries (Disbursement) 1966–1967* (Paris: Publications de l'O.C.D.E., 1969).

ᶠ China's bilateral treaties are not necessarily military treaties, and none of Japan's are military. The treaties shown here are merely those known to exist, and they are not meant to imply comparability to military treaties. They are shown here as evidence of the existence of some formal political ties.

ᵍ The rankings in this table are meant to indicate degree of formal political ties to the Powers, but they are extremely crude at best. Some weighting of ties has been employed insofar as multilateral defense treaties have been considered more important than bilateral defense treaties (a perhaps unwarranted assumption in some cases) and defense treaties have been considered more important than economic treaties. What makes these rankings most crude, however, is that little attempt has been made to consider the relative importance of specific bilateral treaties, or the exact number of treaties of a particular kind between states. The rankings are not always linear, but sometimes represent clusters. Also see "m" and "o" below.

[h] Diplomatic relations but no exchange of diplomatic representatives.

[i] Diplomatic representation below embassy rank.

[j] Diplomatic relations were severed after 1967.

[k] Mali left the Franc Zone in 1962 and rejoined in 1967.

[l] Because Belgium and France are immediate neighbors and are both members of the E.E.C. and a host of other inter-European organizations, they are probably more formally tied politically than any of the other French associated states listed here. The only reason Belgium was not put at the top of the list was to avoid breaking up the listing of the *Communauté*.

[m] The ranking among members of the Organization of American States (in which there are X's in all columns) is based on the number of bilateral defense treaties with the United States in force in 1967. This ranking does *not* take account of the magnitude of those treaties.

[n] The only formal political tie existing between Cuba and the United States in 1967 was the treaty (originally signed in 1903) giving the U.S. control over what has since become Guantanamo Bay. The U.S. has not allowed Cuba to abrogate that treaty.

[o] The ranking among Council of Mutual Economic Assistance members (in which there are X's in each column) is based on whether the U.S.S.R. had troops stationed in that country in 1967.

[p] Although there were a number of treaties still officially in force between Albania and the Soviet Union, and China and the Soviet Union in 1967, since neither side seems prepared to honor any of them, Keesing's suggests that they are now meaningless. *Treaties and Alliances of the World*, p. 89.

[q] A Treaty of Friendship and Alliance between Libya and Britain (signed in 1953) has been rendered worthless by Libya's 1967 request that the U.K. withdraw all forces from the country and liquidate all of its military bases. U.S. military assistance agreements have, since 1967, also become meaningless.

? Question marks throughout the table indicate uncertainty as to the existence of particular ties.

each. Clearly, these indicators are not totally compatible. Membership in the Colombo Plan is certainly not equivalent to membership in the European Free Trade Association or the European Economic Community. Nor is the receipt of economic aid nearly as formally binding as membership in any of those economic associations. But the political decisions involved in each were similar enough to warrant their parallel use.

No claim of comprehensiveness is made for this table. Some important formal political ties may have been omitted while some that have been selected may prove to have been insignificant. What the table attempts to do, is to establish in a very crude manner the degree of formal political ties between states. It is hoped that if other scholars see merit in this approach, they will refine and improve upon what is presented here.

Changing Political Relationships

Policy makers, taking a short-term view, no doubt perceive the immediate benefits of having weak, compliant client states, whose regimes are dependent for their continued existence on the patronage of the mentor. This gives the mentor enormous leverage for getting the weaker associated states to behave internationally in a way preferred by the mentor. The thrust of this book's argument, however, is that in the long run the mentor can achieve more by encouraging and nurturing interdependence than it can by perpetuating dependence. Sketchy though it may be, the empirical evidence seems to indicate that dependence, consciously perpetuated, tends to breed counterdependence, while interdependence, consciously and genuinely striven toward, tends to breed still greater interdependence.

The Middle Eastern countries over which Britain attempted to maintain informal dominance, and the other historically associated states over which Britain tried hardest to perpetuate formal dependence, are today among the most counterdependent toward the U.K. The North African and Indo-Chinese states over which France tried hardest to perpetuate dominance and dependence (particularly Algeria and Vietnam) are among the most counterdependent toward France. It is not at all an accident that Cuba, the Dominican Republic, and some of the other Central American and Carribean states in which the U.S. has most often intervened militarily to perpetuate dependence (formal or informal) are among the most hostile and counterdependent toward it today. Similarly, should Soviet troops withdraw from Czechoslovakia, Hungary, Poland, and East Germany—and remain withdrawn—

it would surely not take long for latent hostility and counterdependence toward the U.S.S.R. to surface.

Of all Britain's associated states, the Old Commonwealth countries were and are the ones most interdependent with the U.K. Certainly the historic, linguistic, religious, racial, and educational ties—in short, all of the perceptual links discussed in Chapter 4—are greatest with these "settler" countries. Also, the power relationships between some of them and Britain are much less unequal than are the power relationships between Britain and most of the other associated states, thus facilitating interdependence. But Britain also treated these countries more nearly as equals, having granted them the greatest degree of local self-government, and granting them *de facto* independence long before the other associated states. The bonds of interdependence have paid off politically. These countries are certainly among Britain's closest and most faithful allies, supporting it more internationally than any other of the associated states.[45] They do not always agree with Britain, but they rarely censure it publicly. In the United Nations and in Commonwealth meetings they are among Britain's staunchest supporters. Britain learned from the American Revolution that it did not pay to attempt to perpetuate dependence (at least in regard to the settler countries) and it has nurtured interdependence with those countries ever since. Had the U.K. attempted to keep these countries dependent, there is no doubt that it would have lost them, too.

Of all France's associated states, those of Black Africa have had the closest ties to France. The *elites* of these states were encouraged to become most interdependent with France (even to the point of being allowed to sit in the French Parliament). However, the *states* could not by any stretch of the imagination be described as interdependent with France. Indeed, France dominated them and exploited them "in a fashion comparable only to that in the Portuguese African territories," says Waldemar Nielsen in a recent book on Africa. But, he continues:

. . . African leaders generally respected France, took pride in their French culture, and profoundly admired the non-racial feelings of the French intellectual and political elite. Such feelings [on the part of the African elite] help explain the phenomenon of African colonial support for France during World War II. . . . when, in the name of Free

---

[45] Note that Ireland, which received independence later and more violently than the other Old Commonwealth states (and not complete independence since Britain still retains direct control of the North) is highly counterdependent—despite continued economic dependence. In 1939 it was the only Old Commonwealth country not to declare war on Germany.

France, de Gaulle appealed for support, [French] . . . Africa became the territorial base for the Free French movement, and thousands of Africans rallied to its cause. At one time nearly half of de Gaulle's forces were Africans from the colonies, and black African troops took part in General La Clerc's historic desert crossing and in the liberation of France itself.[46]

Certainly the power relationship between the units is such that true interdependence is unlikely as long as black francophone Africa remains divided. But their current extreme dependence upon France (and increasingly upon Europe) could "pay off" for them economically, in the sense that they now have the opportunity for rapid development of their societies to the point where perhaps one day they will be able to achieve some measure of interdependence. With the exception of Vietnam and Algeria, France has not used coercive power in recent times but rather is using all of the *attractive powers* at its disposal to assist its associated states to develop. At the present time the result is greater dependence of these countries upon France than any other weak states upon their mentors. But because the stated aim, and the attitude, is one of building interdependence and not maintaining dependence, there is some likelihood of success in achieving that goal in the long run.

There are no states with which the Soviet Union is truly interdependent. China has the power potential to become so, but because the U.S.S.R. chose to perpetuate Chinese dependence instead of interdependence the result—very quickly—was counterdependence. Perhaps with new political leadership in both countries, an awareness could grow that attractive power is more effective an instrument than coercive power, and Russia may again make an attempt to help China develop as an equal (or at least as a potential equal). Czechoslovakia and Hungary aside, in recent years the U.S.S.R. seems to have recognized the importance of building interdependence in Eastern Europe, at least to some extent, and has certainly gained more support there, among most segments of the population, than it had during the days when it was consciously perpetuating continued dependence.

For the first forty years of the twentieth century—but particularly in the 1930's and 40's—Japan attempted to establish militarily an "East Asian Co-prosperity Sphere." Because of superior American power, that scheme failed, but within twenty-five years after the end of World War II, Japan had achieved through noncoercive instruments (particularly through the use of reparations

---

[46] Waldemar A. Nielson, *The Great Powers and Africa,* Council on Foreign Relations (New York: Frederick A. Praeger 1969), p. 82.

payments) most of the economic goals of that scheme. The bitter memories of the military adventure prevent it from establishing closer political ties to countries in the region for the present, but because of the existence of the many economic ties, political ties probably will not be long in developing.

Japan is, of course, far more interdependent with the U.S. than it is with the weaker countries of South and Southeast Asia. Given the level of development of most of them, it is suspected that their prospect for the foreseeable future is increasing dependence on Japan. The major unknown in Asia, as of this writing, is the future relationship of the U.S. to Japan. If the U.S. continues to nurture its own interdependence with Japan, the likelihood is that Japanese-Chinese relations will improve only slightly over what they currently are. If Japanese-American relations should for any reason deteriorate however, allowing an existing element of counter-dependence to grow, the likelihood is that China and Japan will become increasingly interdependent. There is no better potential market for Japanese heavy industry in Asia than China, and their is no better market in Asia for China's fast-growing light industry than Japan. We have already seen how economic interdependence can produce political interdependence. There is no reason to assume that the same mechanism will not operate in the relations between China and Japan, should anything happen to disturb current Japanese-American interdependence.

Western Europe and Britain have not been treated here as historically associated with the United States, but they certainly could have been, particularly regarding the period since World War II. Canada and Japan have been. Yet all of these countries are among the states most interdependent with the U.S. These countries are also among the most powerful in the world, outside of the U.S.S.R., and it has therefore been relatively easier for them to become interdependent with the U.S. than it would be for most weaker countries. But aside from the relatively short occupation that followed Japan's defeat in 1945, historically none of these countries (except Canada) have been dominated by the U.S. either formally or informally,[47] and the U.S. has done more to foster the interdependence of them all than it has done for any other countries. Surely, it is not merely accidental that today these countries are the ones that support the international political positions of the U.S. most

[47] Of course, U.S. troops have been and still are stationed in most of the European countries. Not coincidentally, those countries (and parts of countries) in which troops were so stationed after World War II "opted" for the free enterprise, democratic model. Since that time, however, the troops are retained with the support of almost all political parties in those countries save the Communist parties.

consistently. To be certain, it is the more dependent countries that send the troops when the U.S. says "Send troops!" and it is the most dependent countries that refuse to recognize the states the U.S. refuses to recognize, but regarding long-term basic support on matters of most significance to the U.S., there is no doubt in any policy maker's mind about what position Britain, Western Europe, Canada, and Japan would take. All of these countries and the U.S. are so very interdependent that an attack on any one would be perceived to be an attack on all. That is the long-term significance of interdependence—and the security it affords each of the parties. Weak states that are consciously kept dependent cannot be relied upon in time of crisis. They are simply too weak to provide much assistance; and their governments, having permitted the perpetuation of dependence, cannot be counted on as securely in office. There may be more deviation in terms of day-to-day support among interdependent states than there is when states are completely dependent, but interdependent states can generally be relied upon to provide meaningful support over the long haul.

SECTION III

Conclusions and Policy Recommendations

Chapter 9

Themes for Policy Makers

Several themes seem to run throughout this work. One is that the power of strong states tends to "attract" weaker states. Regardless of which specific tie was examined, the same pattern emerged. When Britain and France were most powerful, they tended to attract most states strongly to themselves. To be sure, they often used coercive power—or the threat of coercive power—to achieve their goals, but the attractive power of their education, economy, communications, and the rest, did the most to perpetuate the relationship between them and the weaker states. As the power of these nineteenth century giants has waned (relative to the power of the United States, the Soviet Union, the E.E.C., Japan, and, to a lesser extent, China) the weaker countries have increasingly been attracted—in one way or another—to these new power centers. Admittedly, Soviet influence in Eastern Europe and American influence in Western Europe and Asia coincides remarkably with the extent to which those areas were "liberated" by the troops of the Super Powers at the end of World War II, but as with Britain and France in the nineteenth century, it has been the attractive qualities of those Powers that, more than anything else, have perpetuated the relationships, with but few exceptions.

A second theme, closely related to the first, is that the ties between weak and powerful states tend to reinforce each other and create additional ties. In some areas it was the perceptual ties that came first (as in settler areas), in others it was military (where the area was conquered), in others it was economic. Regardless of which came first, other ties almost invariably followed and tended to reinforce existing ties. Note, that this is not a one-way process. The relative decline of British and French power has been accompanied by a weakening in almost all the ties that once existed with those Powers, while new ties have been created and reinforced with the newer Powers. This being so, a conscious change in any one tie by policy makers in either weak or powerful states is likely to produce a host of changes in other ties as well. More than anything else, this may explain why some policy makers in some weaker countries are so reluctant to create ties where none have previously existed, and while other policy makers—sometimes in the same country—are so anxious to create new ties.

A third theme, related to the other two, is the tremendous disparity in power that exists among states. Recall from Chapter 3 that the major components of power were considered to be wealth, organization, and status. Which came first, which was cause and which effect, is not terribly relevant to this discussion. What is important is that all three components of power are mutually reinforcing and thus power tends to generate still more power. Equally as important, impotence—lack of wealth, organization, and status—tends to breed still further impotence. Hence, the tendency is for the more powerful countries (with some notable exceptions) to get still more powerful, while the weaker countries (also with some notable exceptions) get *relatively* weaker. This is roughly equivalent to what Hans Singer has described as "the vicious cycle of underdevelopment." [1] And while it is certainly a self-reinforcing cycle, it is by no means inevitable. Once weaker states learn that by altering any one of the variables, they stand a chance of altering them all—and once powerful states learn that it is in their own best interest to help weak states break that cycle —it may be possible for the weaker underdeveloped countries to begin to acquire sufficient power to achieve some degree of interdependence with the Powers.

This is not to suggest that the Maldive Islands is capable of becoming the new Super Power of the twenty-first century. No amount of wealth, organization, or status will enable it to do so by itself. The 1959 film "The Mouse That Roared" was a fantasy about a tiny mythical kingdom that declared war on the United States expecting to lose and then receive all of the material benefits Germany, Italy, and Japan received after their defeat. By a quirk of the script writer's imagination, when this little country invaded the United States it succeeded in capturing and bringing home a newly invented super bomb (something scarce and sought after), and suddenly it had the means of getting the big Powers to do what it wanted. Unfortunately, reality is not quite that simple. Even if the Maldive Islands did manage to capture a super bomb, without a sophisticated "delivery system"—catamarans

---

[1] Hans W. Singer, *International Development: Growth and Change* (New York: McGraw-Hill, 1964), p. 12.

simply will not do—it would be unable to use it against anyone save itself. On the other hand, if the Maldive Islands were to unite with all of the other countries of South and Southeast Asia into one massive political unit, and if this new political unit were to organize in such a way as to be able to mobilize all of its resources effectively (two fantasies on approximately the same order of magnitude as the one in "The Mouse That Roared") it would indeed become a Power to reckon with.

But achieving Super Power status need not be the goal of the weaker countries. There is hardly a country in the world that does not have the potential to so organize itself as to maximize its resources (of whatever kind) and "attract" the big Powers to make concessions in order to share those resources. Therefore, a more realistic and attainable goal for the weaker countries would be to maximize this potential in order to achieve "the good life" domestically (however they choose to define that term, but certainly including adequate food, shelter, clothing, healthcare, and security for the whole population) and a significant degree of real international interdependence.

From the perspective of the weaker states this is certainly a reasonable goal. But, as the themes of this book make clear, the realities of the relationship between weak and powerful states can lead the Powers to seek very different goals with regard to the world's weaker countries. There are undoubtedly those who see one major policy conclusion for the Powers: to tie as many of the weaker states as they can to them, by as many different ties as they can create. In a sense this is not an incorrect goal. But, unfortunately, some will conclude that the most efficient way of doing that is to make as much of the world dependent upon them as they can. They will pursue a twentieth century neo-imperialism in which the big Powers do not necessarily annex weaker states, but rather install regimes most favorable to the mentor, station troops in the country to maintain the friendly regime in office, and proceed to build the ties and remake the countries in the fashion most favorable to the Power's interests. This kind of relationship with the weaker states, has a great deal of appeal for those who have little patience with dissent, who are convinced that "we" are the "good guys," and that our enemies are evil; and that anyone supporting evil should be punished—or at least prevented from coming to power. But if the evidence presented in this book means anything, it is that the Powers that are wisest will use their attractive powers to help the weaker countries achieve interdependence with them as quickly as possible and in as many ways as possible.

Does this mean the Powers should build ties—of all sorts—with the weaker countries? Of course it does! Is it in the interest of the Powers to build these ties? Of course it is. But it means building ties that are perceived in the weaker countries as needed and desirable—that is, building ties on the basis of *mutual perceived interest*. In this way the ties would have a wide base of support and the likelihood of enduring beyond the change of regimes or the defeat or death of favored politicians. The building of ties with weaker countries that the weaker countries themselves want and need (and only those they want and need) are less likely to be perceived in either the weaker or the more powerful country as demeaning or immoral, or an infringement of highly cherished sovereignty, and therefore would be less likely to cause resentment.

There can be no question that there are objective needs the weaker states must have fulfilled somewhere. The dangers of tying one's country too closely to only one major Power are all too clear from past history. But the needs of the weaker states are real and there is no reason why they should or would feel demeaned by making efforts to fulfill those needs from whichever Powers will cooperate on the basis of reciprocal mutual interest. The Powers must make clear precisely what it is they are doing when they seek to fulfill those needs for specific weaker countries, and the weaker states must make clear precisely what they are doing when they seek to fulfill those needs from as many different Powers as possible. Ties undertaken from the realistic perspective of mutual self-interest, honestly admitted and honestly executed, are much less open to misinterpretation than projects undertaken under the guise of altruism. Thus, on the basis of enlightened mutual self-interest, current relationships of dependence can be channelled away from counterdependence toward the construction of interdependence.

Coercive vs. Attractive Instruments of Power

There are, no doubt, those "big stick" advocates (called "hawks" in the contemporary world) who will argue that in all matters the national interest of the Power is best served by a show of force— particularly in relation to weaker states. Certainly, the reasoning of the hawks seems to have prevailed in the Dominican, Vietnamese, Cambodian, Hungarian, and Czechoslovakian cases, to mention only the more spectacular. But while their reasoning may have prevailed, what kind of results have they produced, and at what cost, both to the Powers and the weaker states concerned?

Finding indigenous people in the weak states who are anxious to take the reins of government themselves, and are willing to follow the policies advocated by the mentor in order to do so has rarely been an impossible task.[2] In fact, these people are the ones who often call in the outside Power because they know that they have insufficient support and/or strength domestically to seize or hold the government themselves. But putting people into office is not the same as keeping them there. To do that often requires enormous expenditures by the Power, and no small amount of repression of opposition. As of this writing, the anticommunist or anticapitalist governments the Powers put into office in each of the cases mentioned above are still in office. But how much support these regimes have within their own countries, and whether they will be able to remain in office without the physical presence of the Powers' troops remains to be seen. What is more, the bitterness of the people opposed to these "puppet" governments is readily extended to the mentor. In each of the cases cited, there are counterelites and underground movements either biding their time or actually making overt attempts to overthrow the "puppet." Without permanent, direct intervention by the mentors, the likelihood is that these governments will fall and that their successors will be staunchly anti-mentor.

There is another, less coercive, approach that is far less costly, and that has proved successful. Yet policy makers in the big Powers are reluctant to try it because of their conviction that power means force (and probably also because of their own personal predilection for authoritarian solutions). That different approach involves the use of the "attractive" instruments of power.

The Truman administration used attractive rather than coercive instruments of power in Yugoslavia to prevent that country from being reabsorbed by the Soviet Bloc. Truman could not have used a coercive solution there without risking the precipitation of a direct and major conflict with the Soviet Union. Therefore his alternatives were either to allow the Stalinists to topple the Tito government, or to provide Tito with the kind of assistance he needed in order to survive: markets for his products, supply of finished goods, technical, economic, and even military assistance. How much it has actually cost the U.S. to help Tito remain inde-

[2] There is some indication that there have been a few instances where this was not so. Apparently, after the demise of Nuri al Said and his followers in Iraq, the United States would have been willing to recognize almost anyone who could claim to be the legitimate successor to that regime and who would have been willing to call in U.S. troops to oppose Kassim. Not being able to find anyone in Iraq who would or could do that, the U.S. apparently settled for sending troops into Lebanon to prevent a similar coup there.

pendent and neutral in the cold war is difficult to know.[3] Agency for International Development figures on the subject are highly contradictory. Taking the figures available for economic assistance administered by A.I.D. through June 30, 1968 (and leaving out economic aid administered by other international organizations, which was substantial) the amount comes to $573 million.[4] If we add to that the $694 odd million in military aid that A.I.D. says Yugoslavia had received as of June 30, 1966,[5] that comes to a total of $1.3 billion altogether. Because of the way in which economic and military assistance actually works, we know that a sizeable portion of that money actually returned to the U.S. government in the form of taxes on the profits of the corporations that supplied the material assistance to Yugoslavia. But even leaving that aside, the total cost (in dollars) for keeping Yugoslavia a neutral country in the cold war for 22 years has averaged approximately $59 million a year. In human lives and suffering, the total cost to both Yugoslavia and the U.S. has been zero (although most assuredly Tito has imprisoned and perhaps executed any number of his own political enemies within Yugoslavia).

Compare that figure to the cost of keeping Diem and his successors in office in Vietnam since 1954. Admittedly the regimes in Saigon have been much more pro-American and anticommunist in foreign policy than Tito, but given our uncertain ability to keep that kind of government in office in Saigon, and the distinct possibility that the country may eventually become totally anti-U.S. (whether communist or not) once the American presence is removed, one could make a strong case that in the long run Vietnam's neutrality would be more advantageous to the U.S. In addition, it would be legitimate to ask how much more valuable these pro-U.S. governments in Vietnam have been to U.S. foreign policy than a neutralist regime would have been. But we will come to that in a moment. For now, let us just compare the costs of the coercive instrument in Vietnam with the cost of the attractive instruments in Yugoslavia.

[3] There are those who will take issue with the statement that Yugoslavia has been neutral in the cold war, but no matter what index one checks— voting in the United Nations, diplomatic representation, or any others— Yugoslavia comes out neutral, despite its continuation as a communist country.

[4] Agency for International Development, *U.S. Economic Assistance Programs Administered by the Agency for International Development and Predecessor Agencies: April 3, 1948—June 30, 1968* (Washington, D.C.: Mar. 28, 1969), p. 76.

[5] Agency for International Development, *U.S. Overseas Loans and Grants and Assistance from International Organizations: Obligations and Loan Authorizations: July 1, 1945—June 30, 1966* (Washington, D.C.: 1967), p. 25.

A.I.D. admits to having committed $3.4 billion in economic aid to Vietnam as of June 30, 1968 (again, this is exclusive of assistance from other international organizations).[6] A modest estimate is that between 1965 and 1970 the war in Vietnam cost the U.S. an average of $30 billion a year, and for the prior 10 years an average of $1 billion per year, for a grand total of approximately $190 billion. Add to that the $3.4 billion in economic assistance and the total for 16 years comes to $193.4 billion *at a minimum,* for an average of approximately *$12 billion per year.* These are merely dollar figures for the U.S. and in no way show the incredible cost in human lives and property in Vietnam.

Now, the idea that the United States might have instead spent $12 billion a year to help develop a country like Vietnam *economically* is absurd. We allocate only a few hundred thousand dollars a year for the economic development of India with a population of 500 million. We certainly would never allocate anything approaching that order of magnitude to a country of about 17 million people. Even an appropriation of only $1 billion a year in economic assistance exclusively would probably never pass Congress. Yet $1 billion a year *since 1954* would add up to little more than *half* of what we now appropriate *per year* for a policy that relies almost exclusively on the coercive instruments of power. How much more effective would it have been to have spent a fraction of that amount on the attractive instruments of power?

Admittedly, the situations in Yugoslavia and Vietnam were and are very different. Tito was a communist leader who had defected from Moscow. He was the best we could have hoped for in Yugoslavia. If he fell, the next regime would certainly have been more pro-Soviet and more anti-American. In Vietnam in 1954, the North was ruled by a pro-Soviet atheist Communist whose avowed intention was the reunification of the country under his authority. In the South was a pro-American Catholic, anticommunist who believed that with U.S. assistance he could keep South Vietnam from being "lost" to the Communists. That was more than we could resist, even though the Geneva Accords stipulated an election (which even President Eisenhower says Diem would have lost, if it had been allowed to take place). What was not anticipated, or was ignored, was the likelihood that the Viet Minh would fight if they could not unify the country under their control via an election.

But suppose the United States had chosen a different course? Suppose, at Geneva, the U.S. had said, "Since Vietnam will be united under Ho Chi Minh if an election occurs, let us avoid the humiliation of losing an election to the Communists and recognize

⁶ *A.I.D., U.S. Economic Assistance Programs,* p. 42.

a unified country under Ho from the start. In addition, let us offer
to assist this unified Vietnam with a billion dollars worth of economic assistance a year to help the recovery from the devastation
resulting from [what was then] almost fifteen years of continuous
warfare (first against the Japanese and then against the French)."
Since Ho in particular and Vietnam in general were suspicious of
China's power, it is likely that Ho would have accepted such an
offer and that Vietnam today would be a rapidly developing *neutralist* country, far more tied to Washington than to Peking or
Moscow.

"But that would have been an impossible risk," says the skeptic.
"How do we know that after having poured a billion dollars worth
of economic assistance a year into Vietnam for sixteen years that
we would have a neutralist regime there? Might it not instead be a
rapidly developing anti-American regime?"

The answer is that, of course, it would be a risk. But do we not
(after more than $190 billion worth of military spending, more
than 50,000 American dead, and perhaps 1 million Vietnamese
dead) run the even greater risk that *any* government that comes
to power in Saigon after the American troops leave will be anti-
American? Since all ties tend to reinforce or create other ties, it is
unlikely in the extreme that there would not have been a host of
perceptual, communication, economic, military, and political ties
between Vietnam and America after sixteen years of economic aid.
Indeed, when one contemplates how tied to a Power any country
would be if it received economic development aid of the magnitude
suggested, a totally different question arises: Might not China
have felt so threatened by the presence on its border of a country
so closely tied to the U.S. that it might have attempted to overthrow
the Ho regime? The question is a valid one, but it changes the
subject from Vietnam-U.S. relations to Vietnam-Chinese relations.
What is more, China need not have felt threatened if we were not
using our "neutralist ally" to imperil China. Suppose that while we
were giving Vietnam a billion dollars worth of development assistance each year, that we spent $10 billion each year on the
economic development of China? What would that do to China's
relationship to the U.S.? "The United States Congress appropriate
$10 billion a year for the economic development of China! Singer
is either an impossible dreamer or else this is a misprint. It is
unthinkable that Congress—or the American people—would ever
allow any U.S. government to spend $10 billion a year to help
develop Communist China."

But is it unthinkable? President Nixon asked the United States
Congress—and indirectly the American people—to allow him to
spend what would ultimately amount to at least $10 billion a year

to develop an Anti-Ballistic Missile (ABM) system—which no one is certain would actually work—specifically to preserve the security of the U.S. in the event of an attack by Chinese missiles. The United States Congress approved that request. In addition, it is estimated that the U.S. is spending approximately $8 billion a year maintaining troops and bases around the periphery of China, merely to "contain" that country militarily.[7]

If the budget of the United States can include an annual appropriation of $80 billion for armaments and other military spending to strengthen the coercive instruments of power—most of which wind up unused or obsolete—why is it unthinkable for the budget to contain instead an annual appropriation of $80 billion to help eliminate poverty, hunger, unemployment, and disease everywhere in the world (including the United States)? *It is unthinkable only because when we think of power we think primarily of coercive power and not of the power to attract.* This is not to deny that there are times and situations when it is essential to have strong military capabilities. But military capability rests, in the last analysis, not on the military hardware in one's stockpile, but on the level of development of one's economy. Government spending on defense is a major boost to the American economy to be sure, but there is no reason to assume that spending $80 billion annually assisting the economic development of the currently underdeveloped countries (and areas of our own country) would not boost the American economy equally as much, if not more. What is more, there is absolutely no evidence whatever that $10 billion worth of economic assistance to China a year would be a less sure defense against Chinese attack than the ABM. On the contrary, the evidence suggests that it would be a better defense. We have become so completely conditioned to thinking of power solely in terms of the ability to coerce that we have totally ignored the fact that people are most influenced not by force, but by persuasion. Scholars and practitioners alike—particularly in the field of international affairs—have tended to ask only Stalin's question, "How many troops does he have?" instead of asking, "What are the most effective instruments at my disposal to achieve my policy goals?" or even more visionary, perhaps, "What is the most effective way of achieving the kind of world in which we would want to live?"

There are those who argue that it is our enemies who force us to use coercive instruments temporarily, since they are opposed to our building long-term positive relationships with the weaker coun-

[7] See I. F. Stone's analysis of Senator Mike Mansfield's report on his 1969 trip to Southeast Asia, "The China Menace is America's Most Costly Hallucination," in *I. F. Stone's Weekly,* Vol. XVII, No. 18 (Oct. 6, 1969), p. 2.

tries, and they will not hesitate to use violence to stop us. They say that once our enemies desist from *their* coercive efforts to disrupt our peaceful assistance to these weaker countries, or once their coercive efforts can be effectively suppressed, then it will be possible for us to utilize primarily the attractive instruments of power. This argument should be rejected on two counts:

1. There will always be enemies (of both the Power and the weaker country's governing regime) who will attempt violent disruption of peaceful efforts to assist the government in office.
2. The best defense against indigenous coercive disruption (insurgency) is for the regime itself to honestly determine the cause of the discontent and opposition (not the coercive manifestation of that opposition) and attempt to dissipate it, not through counter-insurgency, but rather, as Charles Merriam suggested, by "allurement."

Hindsight and speculation are always easy and rarely scientific. Still, I ask the reader to speculate for a moment on what kind of world we might be living in today if, over the past twenty-five years, the United States, the Soviet Union, Britain, France, China, and Japan,[8] having collectively spent perhaps $2 trillion on military preparedness, had instead spent the same amount on economic development of the underdeveloped countries? For one thing, collectively this would be a much richer world. Military spending is essentially consumption. It adds little to the capital producing capability of the world. Had significant portions of that amount been spent on capital development projects (with the built-in multiplier effect such investments have) uncalculable trillions worth of new wealth would have been created. Remember that we are talking here exclusively of governmental spending. In some of those countries, even if the initial investments were government sponsored, they might eventually have been sold to private enterprise, thus freeing still more billions of governmental money for further development investment. Experience has demonstrated that government investment, rather than discouraging private investment, tends to stimulate it. Thus, it seems fair to speculate that at least an equal amount (and probably several times more) of private investment would also have occurred.

From the viewpoint of world security, a far more significant result of this investment in development than mere creation of new wealth would have been the creation of interdependence

---

[8] Japan is officially barred by its constitution from military spending, but has nonetheless built a sizeable "Self-Defense Force."

among states. It is a basic premise of this study that an interdependent world is more secure than one in which there exist hostile competing systems. And there can be little doubt that massive development assistance of the magnitude suggested here—if given on the basis of need rather than on the basis of the name of the political system—would have produced a world so completely interdependent as to render war itself unthinkable. That is indeed a utopian dream worthy of contemplation.

The Question of Intervention

At the opposite extreme from those who advocate a show of force in all matters are those who believe that a Power should not interfere in any way in the internal affairs of a weaker country. While the former have misread reality and so chosen the less effective instrument of power over the more effective one, the latter have not recognized reality at all. As the various analyses in Section II of this book make clear, Powers intervene—directly or indirectly—in the internal affairs of every weaker country *no matter what they do or do not do.* If a Power buys the products that a weaker state produces, or if it refuses to buy those products, it is interfering in the internal affairs of the weaker. If it offers students from the weaker state scholarships to come to it for study, or does not offer those students scholarships, it is interfering. If it offers military assistance or refuses to offer military assistance, it is interfering. Because of the vast disproportion in the power relationships between states today, there is almost nothing that a Power can do or not do that could not be considered intervention. That reality must be recognized for what it is and dealt with.

Those who call for a halt to intervention in the internal affairs of weaker states are merely calling for a halt to intervention as currently practiced; or else they are calling for a halt to "their intervention," while they see nothing wrong with "our assistance." A complete reversal of the policy of any of these Powers would still mean intervention, but it would be of a different kind. The Powers often have to make the difficult choice between "direct" intervention and "indirect" intervention, but that is the only choice they have. Nonintervention is simply not an option. For example, the American decision to remain "neutral" in the Nigerian civil war was as much intervention in that conflict (indirect intervention to be sure, but intervention nonetheless) as aid to one side or another would have been. The American indirect intervention in that civil war assured the Nigerian Federal Government of a victory that would have been improbable if the U.S. had chosen direct intervention on the side of Biafra. On another level, the British decision to sell equipment to Cuba was as much intervention in that country's internal affairs as was the American decision not to. This is a very difficult reality for both weak and powerful countries to face.

The only questions really open to discussion, then, are the types and degree of intervention that are more or less proper under different circumstances. Although no firm rules are possible in matters as complex as these, I would argue that particularly in situations involving coercion of any sort, indirect intervention is probably more beneficial to both weak and powerful states than direct. Far fewer people tend to get killed in the weaker country when the big Powers practice indirect intervention in a weaker country's civil strife than when the Powers intervene directly. And regardless of which side wins in these disputes, the Power can always intervene directly with noncoercive instruments after the fighting is over.

The point, then, is not to suggest that the Powers follow a policy of nonintervention. The purpose of this work is to explore realities, and policies of the possible, not dreams of the ideal. Rather, the hope is that the logic of this book's argument, if not the volume of empirical evidence (which has yet to be collected) will convince at least some policy makers and scholars in both weak and powerful states that in the course of the inevitable interventions in the affairs of others they ought to pay more attention to the instruments of attraction and less to the instruments of coercion—building toward interdependence, not dependence—than they have in the past.

Chapter 10

Policy Recommendations
for Weak and Powerful States

Most scholarly studies try to avoid the realm of the ought, and attempt merely to describe what is. Too often, scholars hide behind the facade that the only proper area of scholarly endeavor is the *is,* and thus unwittingly they become the handmaidens of the status quo. It is not surprising that universities all over the world have become the battleground between a younger generation impatient for change and their professors who tell them that they can teach nothing about change but only what is, or has been. This book is an effort to break out of that mold. Having taught at a professional graduate school for a number of years, training practitioners in international affairs from both weak and powerful states, I know that understanding what currently exists, and what has gone before, while crucially important, is often insufficient as a guide for action. Practitioners cannot merely understand, they must act, and act with a view to future outcomes. What they do must be based on understanding if it is to have any hope of success. But equally as important, a practitioner needs guidelines for action.

Obviously, different goals require different guidelines. Before specific policy recommendations can be made, it is therefore important to make explicit the goals that one hopes to achieve, and the assumptions about the world order that underlie those goals.

1. It should be a truism today that war and fantastic expenditures on preparations for war are highly wasteful of life, resources (human and material), and energy. Few, if any, benefit, while many suffer. Yet man seems so conditioned to think of power in coercive terms that he largely ignores the other attributes and instruments of power, and, often sheerly out of habit, concentrates instead on a course that is largely self-destructive. I believe that this habit must be broken—and that it could be if scholars could

amass enough empirical evidence on the effectiveness of the attractive qualities of power to convince the policy makers.

2. Decision makers in all states seek to maximize the power of their state. But very often, instead of expending their state's major energies and talents on constructively mobilizing power, they waste resources and dissipate energy battling groups within their own state or other states that appear to them (at any given moment in time) to be a major threat to the values they hold dear, or even just to their continuation in office. This is as true for weak states as it is for Powers. In part, at least, this is surely due to the short-term policy orientation of most decision makers, whose view rarely extends much beyond their expected tenure in office. The goal of realizing one's power potential is sound, but short-term policy orientations generally fail to serve this goal.

3. Since the big Powers currently feel more threatened by some other big Powers than by the weaker states, they are likely to view their relations with the weaker states primarily in terms of the comparative advantages they can gain in their struggle with the other Powers. This means there is a likelihood that in regard to the weaker countries each of the Powers will be primarily concerned with bringing to office (or preserving in office) regimes favorable to their international political positions. It implies that the Powers are more concerned with short-term considerations of big Power conflict than with long-term positive relationships with the weaker states. This is a major mistake.

4. The disparity of power that exists in the world today between weak and powerful states is a danger for all states. The powerful states, recognizing this disparity, are going to be tempted to seize the advantage while they have it and are likely to try to impose an order that is to their liking on the weaker states. The weaker states, by one means or another, are ultimately going to try to alter that disparity in their own favor. They may attempt to utilize the conflict among the Powers for their own purposes. The danger is that in attempting to manipulate the Powers to serve their own power objectives—as in the Middle East—they could trigger a major war between the Powers, or a smaller war fought on their territory —as in Indochina—in which the weaker states themselves turn out to be the major losers.

5. For both weak and powerful states, interdependence is preferable to dependence of the weaker. Dependent states are in reality of little advantage to the Power in either peace or war, while interdependent states are a major advantage at all times. Dependence tends to breed counterdependence. Interdependence tends to breed further interdependence. The goal of both weak and powerful

states should be the building of interdependence. The policy recommendations that follow are geared toward achieving that goal.

Perceptual / Identity Perspectives

Historical Perspectives

The efficacy of a history of trust and confidence and mutually rewarding ties is beyond dispute. Relations between the Powers and all weaker countries have not always been based on those essentials of interdependence. Often there have been years of hostility. But history begins today. If the U.S., for example, were to begin today to change the basis of its relationship with Indochina from one of reliance on coercive power to reliance on attractive power, in a generation, the enmity of the past decade would be largely forgotten and the memory of a sweeter relationship would remain. If the U.S. persists in using exclusively, or even primarily, coercive means to achieve its objectives, with the connivance and support of transparently "client" regimes, the result will almost inevitably be enmity, hostility, and distrust for a very long time.

One of the unexpected findings of this study is the amazing tenacity of historical ties. The power of Britain and France may have declined relative to the new Power centers, but to the degree that any weaker states are still associated with them, it is their formerly dependent states that are. The Russian Empire has come and gone, but the states that were once dependent upon it are now dependent upon its Soviet successor. If history is to provide any guide for current policy it would be that the Powers could only gain by associating themselves with as many weaker states as they possibly could. From the perspective of each Power, it is in its interest to build these relationships irrespective of what the other Powers do. But the lesson history also teaches is that such association should not be based on the dominance of the weak by the powerful, but rather on building mutual dependence.

From the perspective of the weaker states, historical association has had both positive and negative effects. Where the association has been one of unmitigated subordination, the negative probably outweigh the positive. But the dichotomy is not nearly as clear as one might expect. For certain countries like China, subordination to the Powers was probably quite inhibiting of social, economic, and political growth. But for others, the relative peace and unification provided by the metropole may very well have been quite positive. It was certainly the major force uniting modern India. For the small countries, it may have provided their only or primary contact with the modern world. Is Thailand or Ethopia really that much better off than its neighbors for not having been associated with one major Power until the late 1930's or early 1940's? I think not.

Association with one Power usually meant a lack of association with others (most weaker states have had a succession of associations with different Powers over the course of the centuries, but usually association with only one Power at a time). If the lesson of history teaches these countries anything, it is that simultaneous association with several Powers is preferable to exclusive association with one. But unfortunately for the weaker states, they often have no choice in the matter. If one Power marches in (figuratively or literally) and no other Power is prepared to oppose it, there is little the weaker can do. If, on the other hand (and this has always been so) another Power is there to oppose the first, the likelihood is that the weaker state will be the battleground for a struggle between the two Powers, without regard to the life, property, or welfare of the inhabitants of the weaker country. After almost forty years Spain has still not recovered from the wounds inflicted upon it during the 1936–39 civil war, and one can only wonder how many decades it will take Vietnam to recover from the incalculable damage done to it by conflicting Power interests.

One of the most disadvantageous aspects of past historical association with the Powers has been the splitting up of more or less "natural" units into many different states. The state boundaries in Africa and much of Asia bear little relationship to the people who inhabit the region. In some cases a "people" were artificially divided into three or four different states, merely because different colonial Powers ruled the regions, and once separated, the elites were taught different languages, different religions, and different cultures. These differences intensified to such a point that reunification (or unification if they were never previously united) has become nearly impossible.

Certainly the perpetuation of some 120 weaker states, most of them created by accidents of colonial history, helps perpetuate the weakness of these countries. If organization is a major component of power, how much more powerful would many of these ministates be if they could unite (organize) with other small states to form larger units? But despite the rhetoric and the widespread sentiment among intellectuals in favor of various "Pan" movements, the likelihood of these states coming together is slight at best. Once a unit like a state has been created, there is a strong tendency for it to perpetuate itself. After all, 120 weak states mean 120 prime ministers, 120 deputy prime ministers, 120 foreign ministers, 120 deputy foreign ministers, 120 ministers of agriculture, et cetera. If they were to unite into even 20 larger units, that would mean that several hundred ministers, secretaries, ambassadors, and so on, would be out of jobs—or at least would have less prestigious jobs. There are other problems (which will be discussed shortly) that make amalgamations into larger political units even more difficult.

Although the weak states could in reality rectify the power imbalance somewhat by mergers into larger units, all the evidence indicates that it will not happen. The British did unite India, Nigeria, and Malaysia, yet India split in two upon independence, Biafra tried to secede, and Singapore and Malaysia could not coexist in one unit for more than two years. France gave independence to the Mali Federation, which immediately split into Senegal and Mali. The only post-independence merger that seems to have worked, out of all that were tried or talked about, is the merger of Tanganyika and Zanzibar into Tanzania. All others have failed, or never even got beyond the talking stage.[1] This is an historical reality that is likely to severely inhibit future attempts at union. Nonetheless, efforts to reverse the colonial legacy of division should —must—be made.

Language Perspectives

Traditional students of international affairs rarely think of language as an instrument of power, yet it is perhaps one of the more effective instruments any Power could employ. To build similarities of perception one needs communication. To facilitate communication, one needs a common language. By helping people in the weaker countries to learn the languages spoken in the powerful countries, the Powers are helping to expose these people to the ideas and world views current in the powerful countries. It is a major step in the direction of building lasting relationships. People in every one of the weaker countries have no choice but to learn the language of one of the major Powers if they are to move their countries into the twentieth century. The Powers could assist them in a need they themselves perceive and desperately want to satisfy.

But language ties work both ways. The Power that has many citizens who can speak the languages of the weaker states has a decided advantage over those Powers where the languages of the

---

[1] For example, Egypt and Syria in the United Arab Republic; Malaysia, Philippines, and Indonesia in Maphilindo: Guinea-Mali-Ghana; the East African Federation; and the Central American Federation.

weaker states are unknown. Any representative—official or private —from the Power who goes to a weaker country speaking the language of that country is in a much better position to build more similarities of perception than his counterpart who does not. The person who understands the weaker country's language—or languages—is in a position to communicate with broad segments of that country's population, and thus can better interpret the desires, needs, and aspirations of the people in the weaker country to policy makers (both public and private) in his home country, as well as communicate the desires, needs, and aspirations of people in the powerful country to masses of people in the weaker country.

Perhaps it is because France faces the distinct prospect of seeing its language become second rate as an international medium that it is so active in encouraging people the world over to study French. Indeed, there is hardly a country that does not have an "Alliance Français" at which French is taught. In France's African associated states, French is being taught to many more millions of people than it was when these countries were colonies. The reason is obvious. Without the language, people are barred from study in France and from direct exposure to French ideas. Hence the enormous effort since World War II, but particularly after General de Gaulle took office, to teach French to as many people as possible.

The Americans seem not to have had a conscious or consistent policy on language training. At one time United States Information Services (U.S.I.S.) around the world taught English at each of their centers. Later, in what was intended as an economy move, that was discontinued. As noted earlier, however, Peace Corps volunteers, wherever they are, have been teaching English even if that has not been their primary assignment. There is no question but that English is the international *lingua franca* of the late twentieth century, and all the exclusively English-speaking countries benefit from that. But since so many more people in the world want to speak English than currently do, the United States would be well advised to start a major program of teaching English (at a nominal charge)[2] to as many people as are willing to learn— not just in the capital cities of the weaker countries, but in the provinces as well. By doing this America would be helping itself as well as helping people in the weaker countries.

Russia, China, and Japan all face a comparative disadvantage

[2] It is a curious fact that something that is free is less sought after and is more suspect than something for which people have to pay. On the other hand, any Power offering to teach its language at prices most people could not afford to pay would face the accusation of setting up services that catered only to the rich.

in the area of linguistic ties to the weaker states. In the first place, the script of each is forbidding and tends to frighten people away. Second, each is a complex language that requires several years of intensive study to be mastered. These are major handicaps, but with enough extra effort they could be overcome. As the power of each of these countries has increased, more and more people in the weaker states (as well as in the other Powers) have begun learning those languages.[3] Russia and Japan do some teaching of their language for those students who come to them for study, but they have yet to begin campaigns to teach their languages in the weaker countries. China seems to rely on the "overseas Chinese" to teach the language to their offspring privately, and appears to do little to promote the study of Chinese abroad. One can predict, however, that within the next decade Russia and Japan in particular will have as many centers in weaker countries for the study of their languages as the French currently have. Indeed, it is highly advisable for them to do so.

With regard to learning the languages of the weaker countries, Japan, Russia, China, and to a lesser extent, France, have something of an advantage over the U.S. and Britain. Their languages are so little known in the weaker countries (outside of a few associated states) that the people they send abroad are forced to learn the indigenous languages. English is so widely spoken in so many places that most Americans and British can "get by" on English, and may never learn the language of the weaker, even if they live in the country for some years.

The weaker states clearly have a problem with regard to language. On the one hand, there is strong domestic political pressure in former colonial areas to push the indigenous language (or languages, where there are more than one spoken by large numbers of people) in place of the language of the former metropole. On the other hand, there is a recognition that their languages (with some exceptions) are not major world languages, and are often not even spoken outside the borders of their country. In many countries, the situation is even worse—not all of the population speaks one language. Certainly, if they are going to modernize and move into the mainstream of twentieth-century life they have no choice but to teach large numbers of their population major world

---

[3] Just how effective the "attractive" qualities of power are, can easily be illustrated. Prior to 1958, although Russian was taught in some American universities, it was often difficult to convince enough students to study the language to get sufficient appropriations to hire one teacher. "Sputnik" seems to have convinced many Americans that the U.S.S.R. really was a Power, however, and within a decade, thousands of American students were studying Russian in universities throughout the United States. In addition, many more thousands had begun to study Russian in high schools.

languages. But they do not have a completely free hand on this. For one thing, they are rightly reluctant to abandon the language (and by implication, the culture) that makes them distinct. There are very strong political pressures in each of these countries to teach more, not less, of the indigenous language, and in some, the pressures are to teach *only* the indigenous language. At the same time, the leaders know that it is precisely those people in each of their countries who speak only the indigenous language who are most resistant to modernization and change. These people want all of the advantages of modernity but are among the most reluctant to adopt the modernizing values, attitudes, and modes of behavior that could make it possible. Where there is only one indigenous language spoken in the country, and almost all the inhabitants speak it (as in much of Latin America and the Arab world, for example) the problem is very much simpler. An effort to learn a world language in those countries is not seen as a great threat to their already well-established cultural identity. But in those societies in which no one indigenous language is spoken by everyone, the learning of the language of a Power (usually the former metropole) is often seen as a threat to national identity, and as such it is resisted.

Rationally, it is precisely in those countries where many languages are spoken, and no one indigenous language is spoken by everyone, where it makes most sense to adopt a world language as the official language, and give equal subordinate status to the various indigenous languages. In that way people from each language group in the country would (theoretically) be on the equal footing of having to learn an international language, while no one local language would be given precedence over others. This is being attempted in some countries, particularly those with hundreds of different indigenous languages and where the international language is a major unifying factor. But in many other countries such a solution is politically out of the question. Voters are notoriously emotional, not rational. For better or worse, one of the indigenous languages (the one with the strongest political support) is being and will continue to be chosen as the official language, and all the inhabitants who do not know it are simply going to have to learn that language. In those countries, the elites are (and will continue) sending their children to private schools where they can learn an international language, but in the short run, the mass of the population will have no choice but to learn the official indigenous language. As those languages become more entrenched and as the supporters of those languages become more secure, then—and only then—will the governments in those countries be able to turn their attention to teaching world languages.

Now it is precisely here that the Powers can help the governments of the weaker states. There is strong evidence that weaker
governments would welcome efforts by the Powers to teach large
numbers of the population their languages. The need to learn the
languages is clearly recognized by these governments, but for
internal political reasons they cannot themselves push the teaching
of those languages. Governments in this position are accordingly
well-advised to negotiate with as many different Powers as they
can to have the languages of those Powers taught—at Power expense and, if at all possible, by Power instructors—as widely as
possible.

Religious Perspectives

Religion is an area the Powers clearly should avoid. During the
colonial period many of the Powers pushed religious conversion
so hard and so brutally that in the eyes of most nationalists any
attempt to proselytize now would be viewed with open hostility.
In most cases, however, since there are already large Christian
populations in many former colonial countries, there would be no
harm done if ties between the various church groups and the Christian populations of those countries were maintained through such
activities as conferences and church-sponsored scholarships for
Christians to study abroad. In many of the weaker countries a large
share of the country's social services (hospitals, schools, et cetera)
are provided by church groups. Therefore, the governments of the
Powers might be well advised to encourage churches in their own
country to perform still more and better social services in the
weaker countries—but the governments themselves ought not to
be associated with these endeavors.

The two major exceptions ought to be the E.E.C. countries
(particularly if Spain is ever admitted) in relation to Catholic
weaker countries, and Japan and China in relation to Buddhist
countries. In the former instance, since the countries of the E.E.C.
are largely Catholic, there would be advantages to be gained by
strengthening religious ties. But even here caution must be exercised. Many of the weaker Catholic countries resent what they
perceive to be European domination of their local churches. The
Catholic Church in Europe, if it wants to build interdependence,
will have to follow the lead set by Pope John XXIII in appointing
greater numbers of cardinals from the weaker countries and in
generating a feeling of interdependence, rather than follow the
more traditional approach, which implied that all religious wisdom
emanates from Rome or Madrid, and that the inhabitants of the

weaker Catholic countries, while not actually heathens, are somehow less authentic or less knowledgeable or less pious Catholics.

In the Japanese case, Japan would be well advised to strengthen its religious identity with the predominantly Buddhist countries of South and Southeast Asia. Granted that Japanese Buddhism is somewhat different from the variety practiced in much of the region, still Japan could do a great deal to strengthen its own Buddhist identity in those countries. Because the current government of mainland China is antireligious, it is likely to make the same mistake the Russians originally made with regard to religious identity. As the vanguard of the revolution, first Russia and now China have scorned the opportunity of building on the religious identity of people in their own country as well as in others. Should Chinese communism change, as Russian communism has, and become less antireligious, the Chinese may recognize that they could do a great deal to strengthen the religious bonds between themselves and Buddhist countries in Asia.

As for the weaker countries themselves, religious ties are one of the ties that do transcend most of the boundaries of these states, and to some degree do help to create a sense of identity among them. This is one instrument of power that many weaker states do have and should cultivate among themselves. The strong religious identity among Muslim states has already been noted, as has the Buddhist identity among some of the South and Southeast Asian states. Governments of these weaker states would do very well to strengthen these bonds at every chance they get.

Of course, one of the dangers inherent in strengthening religious ties with coreligionists in other states, is the possibility that they may separate themselves from neighbors of a different religion with whom they should also be building ties. For example, as some of the sub-Sahara Muslim countries strengthen their ties to their North African neighbors they may be weakening their ties with the other countries of sub-Sahara Africa. Properly handled, however, this strategy need not succumb to this danger. Some Muslim countries have found ways of strengthening religious ties with other Muslim countries without having to take sides with Pakistan against India, or with the Arabs against Israel.

Weaker countries that are predominantly Christian may be able to use their religious identity to their advantage. Not only can they build ties with other Christian weaker countries, but they can count on at least some degree of "most favored nation" treatment, so to speak, from powerful Christian countries. As religion has come to play a less central role in the West, this is one tie that has become weaker, but it is one that should not be totally ignored.

Race Perspectives

It is in the area of race relations that the major European Powers and America are most vulnerable. Being overwhelmingly "European" while the majority of the world identifies itself as "non-European," race is more of a barrier for most of the Powers than an asset. No doubt in some measure it is the similarity of racial identity among the Europeans and Americans that assists them in building their interdependence with each other, but racial identity is of little value to them in building ties with most of the weaker states. As already noted, France is in a somewhat better position on this count than most other European Powers, but it is still identified as "European," with all the racial connotations that implies.

Even the Chinese and the Japanese are accused by other Asians of displaying attitudes of racial superiority, and of looking down on other races as inferior. If the Chinese and the Japanese continue to allow that attitude to prevail, certainly they too will find that it forms as much a barrier to close relations as do the Europeans.

The Americans are being watched very closely on this score by much of the world. If they should succeed in becoming a truly multiracial (or at least biracial) country, chances are good that the American model would be copied (or at least attempts would be made to copy it) in multiracial societies around the world. Should the so-called backlash gain the upper hand, however, and the U.S. begin repressing Americans of African, Asian, and Latin American origin, the barrier to closer relations with most of the weaker states may well become insuperable. No single domestic issue—save perhaps the total collapse of the American economy— could possibly have more far reaching repercussions in America's relations with the weaker states.

Racial identities are dangerous precisely because they are immutable. But dangerous or not they are a reality, and states with a homogenous racial population tend to use that identity as a means of tying themselves to other states with the same racial identity. The feeling of *Négritude,* which is most prevalent in francophone black Africa, is a feeling of "we-ness" that could be used among all black states. The perception of self as Black could be one of the major unifying forces of sub-Sahara Africa and in that unity there could be strength. Black identity itself, if sufficiently nurtured, could be an instrument of power. Where a state is racially homogenous but tribally diverse—as many of the states of middle Africa are—racial identity could be a major factor in forging a stronger identity with, and loyalty to, the larger unit.

The danger of heightened racial identity is greatest, of course, in multiracial societies. In those states, if racial identity is allowed to thrive, the state could be irrevocably torn apart. Once racial identity is activated it is terribly difficult to contain. That is precisely the danger for any state using racial identity as a conscious instrument of policy. States that are racially homogenous may utilize these identities for their own domestic purposes, but there is no guaranteeing that the process can be contained within given territorial boundaries. The Asian in East Africa today is experiencing the negative effects of heightened racial identity in that part of the continent. The Asians there form a small enough minority so that disaffection of that group does not endanger the very existence of any state. But the suffering imposed on the minority population is sufficiently serious to give rise to questions about the value of using this policy instrument anywhere. What is more, if this heightened African-Asian racial animosity should spread to the Caribbean area, for example, it could destroy half a dozen states in its wake, and wreak untold human suffering. Thus, while there is a strong tendency to use racial identity as a conscious instrument of policy in many states, decision makers in all states are well advised to be cautious about starting something that they may not be able to control.

Class Perspectives

Major social revolutions are almost invariably led by middle class individuals, but rarely, if ever are they led or encouraged by middle class societies. Mao Tse-tung's harsher rhetoric notwithstanding, Russia has in fact become a middle class society in the fifty years since its revolution, and now has a stake in peace and evolutionary change rather than violence and revolution. Despite the increasing violence in the developed middle class societies of Western Europe, America, and elsewhere in the 1960's and early 1970's, only the extremists of the far right and far left would describe those countries as "revolutionary." Rather, there seems to be violent discontent among those segments of the population that have not yet become middle class, supported by younger sympathizers from the middle class who are disillusioned and dissatisfied by the slowness in extending the benefits of affluence to all segments of the population.

There is a lesson in this for all proponents of stability and evolution rather than violence and revolution. When black Americans rioted in more than 100 cities in the United States after the assassination of Martin Luther King, the response of those who think of power only in coercive terms was to spend millions equipping police forces and riot squads across the country with the hardware, paraphernalia, and training necessary to suppress riots. Domestically, as internationally, in the short run coercion can no doubt work. But in the long run, the most effective means for suppressing riots and discontent is to remove the poverty, disease, and racial barriers that produced the frustration and anger that produced the violence.

On the international scene, leaders in all the developed countries are concerned about the "revolution of rising expectations" occurring in the poorer countries of the world, and fear that these "revolutions" will become violent. Once again, those who think of power primarily in coercive terms are immediately inclined to strengthen the coercive forces of the poorer countries in order to assist them to suppress whatever violence might occur. But here, too, the most effective long-term solution would be to convert the bulk of the population from "have-nots" into "haves"—to help transform these societies, not necessarily into middle class replicas of the already developed world (with all the pollution and congestion that implies) but rather into middle class societies of their own design.

Paul Rosenstein-Rodan of the Massachusetts Institute of Technology has argued that it is not merely accident that those countries that earliest and most effectively introduced the graduated income tax (thereby assisting in a more equitable distribution of wealth) are the countries with the smallest and most ineffective revolutionary political parties.[4] In societies in which a fairly even and equitable distribution of wealth exists, revolutionary parties simply have no base of support. On the other hand, in societies where the disparities between rich and poor are glaring, and in which the disparity has a tendency to widen rather than narrow, the potential constituency for violent revolution is ever increasing.

If, then, the goal of the big Powers is to avoid violence—in both their own countries and abroad—it would appear that the most meaningful and effective method of preventing violence would be to work toward a world-wide equitable distribution of wealth. This is not a utopian suggestion. As can be seen in each of the developed countries, the graduated income tax and the development of genuinely middle class societies have not hurt the rich. Quite the contrary. As the bulk of the population became more comfortable materially, two favorable things happened: once the masses perceived that the rich were willing to share their wealth, demands for total expropriation of the rich subsided; and as the masses be-

[4] In a personal communication.

came better consumers, the rich discovered that they could become even richer selling to the segments of their own society who could, for the first time, afford to buy the products the rich produced.[5] In Russia, China, and Cuba, where the rich, refused to allow themselves to be meaningfully taxed or to allow land reform, they lost all their wealth, and in many cases their lives as well. Today in much of Latin America, Asia, and Africa, the rich are following the same short-sighted course, and they, too, stand to lose their wealth and possibly their lives.

Because the weaker states tend to have a wider disparity between rich and poor than do the more developed states, the potential for violence, dissention, and instability is greatest in those countries. From the point of view of the leaders of the underdeveloped countries there are two approaches they can take to this problem. One is to stockpile huge accumulations of personal wealth in foreign banks while they strengthen the forces of repression domestically to maintain the status quo and to delay the day when they will have to make a "quick getaway." This is the policy many of the oligarchies in Latin America and many of the oil-rich sheiks of the Middle East follow. From their personal perspective, this strategy has much to recommend it. They often have very comfortable homes waiting for them abroad, their children are often already in schools outside their own countries, and their personal planes are always kept ready for a rapid withdrawal. The major problem with this approach is that they don't always make it. King Idris of Libya, King Farouk of Egypt, Battista of Cuba, and certain others did, but Nuri al-Said in Iraq, Trujillo in the Dominican Republic, and Tzar Nicholas in Russia did not. As increasing numbers of people in the underdeveloped countries become aware of the possibilities of a better life, the chances for their rulers to successfully follow this approach becomes increasingly slim.

The second approach is one that more and more leaders of the underdeveloped countries have been attempting. That is to make every effort to develop their countries while simultaneously trying to redistribute the existing wealth in such a way as to gradually reduce the disparity between the very rich and the very poor. That

---

[5] Now obviously this has not applied in every case. Many of the traditionally rich derive their wealth from land, or from noncommercial occupations that do not benefit directly from the increasing wealth of the masses. But it is true that demands to expropriate their wealth—however derived—have in many cases ceased. On the whole, the process has tended to function as described above. See, for example, Joseph A. Schumpeter, *Capitalism, Socialism, and Democracy,* 3rd ed. (New York: Harper & Bros., 1950), and F. L. Allen, *The Big Change: America Transforms Itself 1900–1950* (New York: Bantam Books, 1961).

is an extremely difficult task, however. Most of the modern developed states industrialized at the expense of the masses of their own populations.[6] They kept wages low (and thus consumption down) to allow huge profits to accrue to the industrialists, who in turn reinvested their profits for further capital growth. In the developed communist countries, where the state replaced the private industrialists, the restrictive political order made it possible to raise production while keeping wages low, and to accrue profits for reinvestment purposes by the state. In democratic societies—indeed, in any societies with less restrictive political orders—some of the increase in production simply must be passed on to the mass of the population in order to maintain their support. But the poorer states are incapable of passing on as much of the increased wealth as the population wants, and thus inevitably some discontent and social unrest will arise in the states that begin the process of development.

To survive that discontent and social unrest, the poorer countries are going to have to develop institutional mechanisms that give the state sufficient power to maintain stability and at the same time make some strides toward eliminating poverty so that it can convey a feeling of progress. This is no mean task. Most of the underdeveloped states are today groping for such institutional arrangements. Some have tried the strong one-party system, some have tried modernizing military dictatorships, some have tried modifications of the communist model, some have tried modifications of various democratic models, but all are attempts to maintain strong enough central leadership to initiate and guide economic development and *simultaneous* redistribution of wealth. There are no easy-to-copy models available to them. They are going to have to experiment with many models before they discover the one that works most effectively in their society. But unless they opt for the first self-defeating strategy of maintaining the status quo while their rulers seek personal gain, they have no choice but to find a system that will enable them to develop economically at the same time that they set about attempting to build essentially middle class societies.

Ideological Perspectives

A young politician from one of the developing countries once said that two revolutions have fired the imagination of people in the underdeveloped world. One was the American revolution, which

---

[6] See Zbigniew Brzezinski, "Politics in Underdevelopment" *World Politics,* Vol. 9 (Oct. 1956); and A. F. K. Organski, *The Stages of Political Development* (New York: Alfred A. Knopf, 1965).

taught that each nation ought to be free to determine its own political destiny. The other was the Russian revolution, which taught how a nation, once free, could develop rapidly so as to determine its own economic destiny.[7]

The ideology of national self-determination that started with the American revolution reached its culmination in the two decades following World War II when more than seventy countries obtained their political independence. Nationalism is still one of the most important ideologies current in the world, but although it started in the West, the Western Powers do not seem to have used that ideology very effectively as instruments of their own foreign policy. Many of them opposed the nationalism of their own colonial holdings. Although the United States never publically opposed nationalist movements as such, it often openly supported other states, like France, Britain, Spain, Portugal, Holland, and Belgium, that had colonies and were more or less reluctant to let them go. In addition, although most Americans have never perceived their actions in Indochina or the Caribbean as essentially colonial operations, many people all over the world have. Thus, while the United States can be said to have initiated the ideology of national self-determination, and while most of the nationalists learned this ideology when studying in the West, the U.S. has been perceived in the last two decades as resisting the nationalist aspirations of the weaker states. This is truly a pity, for historically it has almost always projected an image of favoring national self-determination (particularly after World War I). It could have gained a great advantage from this ideological image if it had given more visible and consistent support to nationalists in the weaker states in their struggle with the colonial Powers after World War II.

The Soviet Union, and to a lesser extent China, have had an enormous advantage over the other Powers on the score of nationalist ideology. Since neither had any formal colonies of its own, nor allies with formal colonies, it was very easy for them to give complete support to nationalism whenever it appeared (except in Eastern Europe).

Ideology has proven to be an extremely effective "attractive" instrument of power for the Soviet Union and China. The communist ideology itself has wide appeal among intellectuals and "have-nots" throughout the weaker underdeveloped countries of the world. People become adherents merely by hearing about this ideology that, if adopted, can supposedly work miracles and transform the weaker countries into major world Powers within a matter of decades, enabling those formerly backward states to

[7] From a speech given by Nirmal Karunatillike at the New School for Social Research in 1958.

send rockets into outer space, develop atomic bombs, and redress their grievances against the former colonial rulers. It is certainly true that Russia has transformed itself within half a century from an essentially peasant society to a modern industrial one. It is also true that China, after the disruptions of the 1960's, may be making progress in the same direction. But note that prior to the communist revolution, Russia had already made enormous strides toward the development of its economy; and that West Germany, which followed a completely different model of recovery from East Germany, developed at a much more rapid rate than its communist counterpart; and that neither East Germany, Poland, Czechoslovakia, Bulgaria, Rumania, Albania, Yugoslovia, North Korea, North Vietnam, nor Mongolia have launched any rockets, exploded any atomic bombs, or redressed any national grievances, even though they have followed the communist model longer than has China. But the communist ideology, as such, has tremendous appeal, whether or not it actually "works."

While communist ideology is essentially development oriented and ignores—or at least the myths surrounding it ignore—the human costs of adopting such a system, Western "liberal democratic" ideology, to the degree that it exists, focuses on the presumed political equality of each individual, and tends to ignore the development aspects. Somehow, development is just supposed to occur. But development has not occurred in most of the underdeveloped states, and thus a disenchantment with liberal democracy has set in, despite the appeal of its political tenets. Particularly in the states that were formerly British colonies, there is widespread admiration of the Westminster model, and while many of the former colonies have abandoned democratic institutions, they cling tenaciously to the ideology of liberal democracy. Indeed, the appeal of this ideology, coupled with a fear of communism, has done a great deal to strengthen the ties between those weaker states and the Western Powers.

From the standpoint of the weaker states themselves, the most useful ideology to emphasize may be neither communism nor liberal democracy, but nationalism. As was noted earlier in this study, most of the weak states are not yet nations. Accordingly, the ideology of nationalism could be one of the major instruments for uniting and developing the weaker states. Once people come to identify with the symbols of nationhood they will often be willing to sacrifice a great deal for the sake of the nation. That is a force the weaker, underdeveloped states should harness. The difficulty, of course, is to get diverse people living in a common territory to identify with these newly created units. But the state is in an advantageous position to do so because it controls or regulates so many of the major communication media in the country and because it can generate policies that could foster feelings of national identity. Those underdeveloped states in which national identity already exists are in a considerably more fortunate position than those that have first to create it. Where it already exists it can be, and often is, put to immediate use in the service of the development effort. Israel and Singapore are but two of the states in which nationalist ideology has produced a concomitant "development ideology" whose major tenet is develop or perish. Despite rather heterogeneous populations, both these states are outstanding examples of the constructive ends to which ideology can be put.

There are dangers inherent in the use of nationalism as an instrument of policy, to be sure. Nationalism can rather easily deteriorate into xenophobia, which in turn can lead countries into foreign adventures in the name of the nation that are in reality extremely detrimental to the well-being of the state. Nazi Germany and pre-World War II Japan are two extreme examples. Modern-day Israel and the several states of the Arab nation come perilously close to falling into a similar trap. But carefully controlled, nationalist ideology can be an extremely constructive force in the service of the weaker states.

Educational Perspectives

It is doubtful if the major Powers have ever consciously thought of their universities as effective instruments of foreign policy, yet they are probably far more effective than any military weapon yet devised. Outstanding universities are like magnets: they attract students from all over the world. The profound effect that study in the powerful countries can have on students from the weaker countries has already been discussed. The question is how the Powers could make more effective use of this instrument.

Literally tens of thousands of young men and women around the globe would like to receive the best university education they can possibly get. As the mass education programs that were started in many of the weaker countries after independence gain momentum, and populations of these countries begin to produce millions of high school graduates, the pressure to get into the better universities will increase. In most of the weaker countries university systems have already started and are growing rapidly. Some of them offer educations of the highest quality. Most do not, however. Most of the weaker countries simply do not have the material or human resources necessary to produce first rate universities and technical schools. But the demand is there. This is where the Powers could do most to satisfy the needs of the weaker states and at the same time help mold the perceptions of the future elites and middle classes of these countries.

To send all the young men and women who want a university education abroad to acquire it is far too expensive a proposition to contemplate. Nor is it necessarily wise. Once abroad many of these youngsters become so "detribalized" that they are reluctant to go home, and if and when they do return, they are often discontent and alienated from their native culture. In addition, the education they get at universities abroad is not always applicable to the situation in their home environment. A far more efficient, and cheaper, solution would be for the governments of the powerful states to financially assist universities in their own countries to assist universities in the weaker countries.

The universities in the powerful states are in a much better position to assist universities in the weaker states than any government would ever be. But this assistance would require governmental financing. There is no reason why a system could not be devised whereby universities in the weaker countries would be encouraged to contract with universities of their choice in the powerful countries to help start or strengthen departments or schools. If the powerful governments were to make sufficient resources available to universities in their own countries, those universities could induce appropriate professors to go to the weaker countries to teach and help develop educational programs. At the same time, the most qualified students from the weaker countries could be trained at universities in the powerful countries with the specific purpose of eventually returning to their own countries and replacing the foreign professors.[8] The departments and schools in the weaker countries could contract with different universities (presumably the ones that were strongest in the needed fields) to provide the assistance, but the governments of the Powers would

[8] This is exactly the kind of program in which I was engaged at the beginning of the 1970's. Despite obvious and desperate need, in the mid-60's there was no place in Malaysia where anyone could be trained in Development Administration. Under Ford Foundation auspices, the University of Malaya and the University of Pittsburgh entered into an agreement whereby Pittsburgh would supply professors for a period of five years to teach and help develop a program in Public Administration. It was agreed that in each of those five years, five Malaysians would be selected to get graduate degrees in various aspects of Public and Development Administration at various universities in the U.S. and Europe. By the end of the five-year period enough Malaysians would have finished their higher degrees and returned so that no more foreign professors would be necessary. At the end of eight or nine years, there would presumably be twenty-five highly trained Malaysian professors to meet the needs of a growing department at the University of Malaya.

pay the'bills and provide the scholarships for the graduate training required. In this way indigenous universities would be sufficiently strengthened to attract and accommodate local undergraduates, and would be provided with professors and graduate education for their students until they became strong enough to offer excellent graduate programs of their own.

This type of program has decided advantages for the Powers. By providing professors and training future professors for the weaker countries they would be building a large educated public with the similarities of perceptions and value systems so vital for the building of interdependence. In addition the powerful countries would gain large numbers of professors who had lived and taught in the weaker states and in the process acquired greater knowledge and understanding of the cultures and problems of those countries. To some degree, of course, the various student and professional exchange programs currently in existence provide some of what is being recommended here. But those exchange programs are minuscule compared to the need and the opportunity. The suggestion here is for truly massive programs of assistance to help develop the educational facilities of the weaker countries. What the Powers need to recognize is that the foreign policy advantages accruing from large-scale programs would greatly outweigh even very high costs.

The kind of educational program outlined above is precisely what many of the weaker countries feel they need and want. If they are ever going to overcome their educational dependence upon the big Powers they will have to develop their own strong educational institutions. But they cannot do that—at least in the short run—without assistance from the Powers. The one danger they must guard against is overreliance on one major Power. If every department in every school of every university in a weaker country is being developed and taught by the universities of just one Power, the universities in the weak state will become little more than extensions of the Power's university system. Because of language and historical ties this is a very real danger for some countries. The first place to which universities in former French colonies are likely to turn for assistance is France. The first place to which universities in former British colonies are likely to turn for assistance is Britain. Since neither Britain nor France can afford to supply educational assistance on the order of magnitude required, the likelihood is that many of these universities will ultimately turn to the United States, which can afford the kind of assistance envisioned. If America were to comply with all requests (not a very likely prospect) these universities could easily become too dependent upon the U.S. It is not at all likely, however, that the Russians, Germans, and Japanese would sit by and do nothing in this area if the Americans really went at it in a big way, and that is all to the good as far as the weaker countries are concerned. No one state holds a monopoly on wisdom, and the more different approaches the weaker countries can incorporate, the richer and more well-rounded their educational systems will become.

The weak states will also have to be careful to guard against the danger of turning out far more university graduates than their economies can absorb. There is no more destabilizing factor than large numbers of educated unemployed. The weak states will have to build their educational systems to complement the economic growth plans they have for their countries. Most of the countries will need many more engineers, laboratory technicians, nurses, craftsmen, managers, and planners than liberal arts graduates. The trouble is that most students want liberal arts degrees. In order to counter this tendency the weak states will have to offer incentives to get the students to study the subjects needed and disincentives for liberal arts study (for example, they can give scholarships in the fields where there is need, and charge prohibitive tuition for liberal arts degrees). Clearly, the weak states face substantial problems in building their university systems, but in this area, at least, the problems do not seem insurmountable.

Communication Perspectives

As well developed as the Powers' communication channels are, the Powers still do not know as much as they should about the weaker states. If some of the recommendations being offered in this chapter were accepted, much of this need would be met. At the moment, the main defect in the big Power networks seems to be in the quality of their information about developments in the weaker countries. Quality suffers because so very much information is brought in that the system sometimes becomes overloaded and unable to function properly. Which bits of information are to be believed and which discarded? In part this is a technical problem that the big Powers should have no difficulty in solving. In greater part, however, it may be a human problem insofar as the information gatherers in each of the Powers may all (or nearly all) be so biased in their preconceived notions and value systems that they block out information vital to effective decision making and "selectively attend" only to those data that conform to or confirm their preconceived judgments.

One change that seems absolutely crucial, particularly for the

United States (but one suspects also for the Soviet Union) is to separate completely the information-gathering function from decision making and operations. The Central Intelligence Agency (C.I.A.) not only collects information, but processes and acts upon it as well. Given the conservative, nearly paranoid anticommunism of many of the personnel associated with that agency, there is a tendency for its information gatherers to see Communists everywhere, and everyone as at least a potential Communist, and for the agency to act on the basis of those perceptions. If it could be established finally and firmly that the C.I.A. did nothing but gather information, and that all operations were reserved exclusively for the Department of State, there is some chance that the U.S. might engage in fewer wishful-thinking adventures. There is at least some evidence that the Russians may suffer the same problem.

As previously noted, in regard to receiving vital information about the outside world, the weak states have a major problem not easily amenable to solution. None of these states is ever likely to develop an international news agency comparable to those in the powerful countries. None is ever likely to be able to afford the kind of diplomatic representation the Powers have. None is ever likely to develop a far reaching intelligence network. The only possible way for the weak states to alleviate these problems would be to cooperate in some sort of regional (or other) grouping. For example, while none of the states of South Asia or Southeast Asia or sub-Sahara Africa or Latin America could individually afford to establish and operate any but the most limited international news agency, by pooling their resources they might be in a position to establish an effective and meaningful international operation. Certainly they could become the major source of information within their own areas, from which the other international wire services might then buy news. As they grew, and became stronger regionally, each of the regional services could cooperate and/or integrate to provide more extensive coverage.

A start in this direction has already been made in those countries that have established their own national news agencies. Most of these are fairly weak, but they do attempt to cover the local news stories of primary interest to readers, listeners, and (where television exists) viewers in their own countries. Because of the overlapping of salient populations in many neighboring countries, news about events in neighboring countries would be of considerable interest. As the literate population of each of these countries grows, as it is already doing at a fantastic rate, and as these countries become richer and more developed, as some of them are doing, albeit at a slower rate, there will be an expanding market for local news, which these regional news agencies could supply. If effective cooperation on this basis could be established, it would enable the regions to become less dependent on the news agencies of the major Powers and would assist the regional agencies to become interdependent with those more powerful agencies.

Intelligence gathering is a somewhat trickier affair. Since the greatest mistrust often exists among regional neighbors, it is not likely that they could or would establish regional intelligence gathering agencies. Still, to some degree at least, cooperation among national intelligence gathering agencies on matters of common concern already does exist. Perhaps it is not totally unthinkable that in some areas a regional intelligence coordination secretariat could be set up to facilitate exchanges of information, and to expand the realm of what might be considered matters of common concern. It is suspected that concerning cold war matters something of this nature already exists among the Eastern European states (probably with Russian participation), and among SEATO, CENTO, O.A.S., and NATO states (probably with American participation). While regional intelligence coordination would not necessarily be stronger if the Power were kept out, it would certainly be more independent, and might possibly be able to expand the area of common concern beyond the limited cold war context.

As long as the myriad of independent countries continue to retain their individual identities and do not unite into larger, stronger units, there is little chance of their agreeing to have common diplomatic representation abroad. But while each of the weaker countries will certainly continue to have its own diplomatic representatives in the countries it considers important to its national interest, there is no reason why regional representation abroad on matters of common concern to the entire region could not be established. For example, many of the weaker countries find it too expensive to maintain individual tourist bureaus throughout the world. Each wants to encourage tourism in its own state, but knows that the first problem is to get the tourists to come to the region. Accordingly, many regional tourist associations have been established in which all or most of the states in the region cooperate, and to which they each contribute, with representatives in each of the major tourist exporting countries. Some of the countries also maintain' some individual tourist centers, but they join the regional tourist associations in addition to get wider representation. Similarly, there are rubber, tea, oil, cocoa, rice, copper, tin, diamond, and other raw material producer associations to which individual weaker states belong in the hope of ensuring some sort of collective bargaining and to stimulate the promotion

of the particular product. These associations do not replace the
diplomats, but rather supplement their work on a collective basis.
This kind of cooperative representation and communication system
could be expanded into a host of other functional and/or regional
fields to provide the weaker countries collectively with channels
of communication they could not provide individually.

In addition to increasing and improving the sending and receiving of information between weak and powerful states, all of these
cooperative regional communication activities suggested here would
also perform the major function of supplying more interregional
information than is currently available. This would—or should—
help to establish closer communications among the neighbors
themselves, thus increasing the possibility of *their* developing similarities of perception and moving them closer to the day when
some measure of regional integration can become possible.

Economic Perspectives

Implicit in much that has been said in this book is the notion that
economic power is one of the most effective instruments of foreign
policy available to the developed societies. Unfortunately, policy
makers in these countries seem to have failed to grasp the full
significance of this instrument. A genuine mutuality of economic
interest exists between developed and underdeveloped states, which
neither side seems to have exploited to maximum advantage.

Most underdeveloped countries desperately need as much economic assistance as they can get if they are to accelerate their
domestic economic growth. It is imperative that they develop if
overpopulation, mass deprivation, mass discontent, and possibly
mass violence are to be avoided, and the governments of most of
the economically weaker states recognize that imperative. On the
other hand, it is also in the interests of the developed states to give
the underdeveloped countries as much economic assistance as they
can absorb. The United Nations has on several occasions suggested that 1 percent of the Gross Domestic Product of all advanced countries should be devoted to economic development assistance. I would argue that it is in the *political* interests of all
developed countries to offer as much development economic assistance as the poorer countries will take. Further, it is in the
economic interests of the developed countries to provide an amount
equal to as much as 2 to 4 percent of their national income to
speed the economic development of underdeveloped states. Just
as private business in the powerful countries has learned in the
past fifty years that higher wages for the workers mean higher

profits for business generally, so, too, their governments must learn that higher incomes for the populations of underdeveloped countries can mean higher tax revenues for them.

Since the real dollar costs of aid are very low after one discounts the amount that returns to the donor country, economic aid to developing countries could be massive without creating a severe strain on the donor economy. The Marshall Plan to Europe after World War II may have cost the U.S. billions on paper, but in the long run the real cost to the U.S. government may have been nearly nonexistent. Once European recovery was complete and the European countries were again rich enough to buy the products America produced, the U.S. tax on the earnings from the sale of American products in Europe probably came to as much or more than the actual amount of the original aid.[9] (U.S. economic aid to the underdeveloped world has never begun to approach the magnitude of the Marshall Plan. While certain Asian countries, such as South Korea, South Vietnam, and Taiwan, have received inordinate amounts of American aid, most of it has not been for economically productive purposes, but for military equipment, "defense support," or for the kind of outright bribery described by Morgenthau.)

The assistance proposed here is not meant to be aid to specific regimes but rather assistance to countries regardless of regime in power—regardless of whether we agree with the political philosophy of the current government. That is a recommendation very difficult for policy makers in the major Powers to accept. But it is an absolutely essential approach if we are to build an interdependent world. If the policy is to give assistance only to regimes we approve of, or that support us internationally, the judgments will inevitably be made within a cold war context, and every anticommunist dictator will receive help from the U.S. while every anticapitalist dictator will receive help from the U.S.S.R. and/or China. If the arguments presented in Section II of this study mean anything, they mean that the most effective means to transform any society is to assist it to develop in every possible way. The argument that the U.S. or the U.S.S.R. cannot or should not give massive assistance to "hostile" governments simply does not hold up under investigation. Had the U.S. aided the Castro, Nasser, or Kassim regimes in their efforts to develop their countries economically along lines of their own choosing, those countries would

[9] I have seen no concrete figures with which to back up this contention. It is made on the basis of subjective impressions. Hopefully, if they have not already done so, the economists will investigate the relationship between aid and subsequent earnings, and determine exactly how much the U.S. government "lost" or "made" as a result of the Marshall Plan.

be much less anti-American today. Had the U.S. aided Arbenz in Guatemala, Mossadegh in Iran, Goulart in Brazil and others like them who were trying to transform their societies, those countries would be much less likely to be anti-American tomorrow. The same is true whether practiced by the Soviet Union, China, or any other major Power. By refusing to give the kinds of assistance the weaker countries feel they need, the Powers are creating self-fulfilling prophecies: potentially hostile regimes become actively hostile regimes because the Powers did nothing to make them less hostile. If the current elites espouse a philosophy we disapprove of, the way to guarantee that the next generation's elite will espouse one we like better would be to train that elite ourselves, preferably in our own country, so that they can acquire the values, attitudes, and perceptions we prefer.

All of this is not meant to imply that the attractive qualities of economic power are synonymous with "dollar diplomacy." They are not. By definition the Powers have vastly more wealth than the weaker states, and they are going to exercise influence over the weak states no matter what they do or do not do. That being so, my recommendation is that in using their wealth to achieve foreign policy goals, the Powers do so by determining what aspects of that wealth the weaker states need and want to share, and then sharing it with them, rather than by using that wealth to strengthen their own coercive instruments in order to try to force the weaker states to do their bidding. Dollar or ruble diplomacy implies using wealth to maintain the weaker countries in a position of dependence upon the Power. The argument being presented here is that the Powers should use their wealth to help weaker states become interdependent with them. There is a vast difference.

Only one limitation should be placed on the economic assistance a Power offers a weaker state. If the elite in a weaker state is channeling that assistance into its own pocket at the expense of its own population, it would be foolish, and morally and politically wrong, for the Power to continue to support that regime. This is precisely where a multilateral international agency could play a most useful role. Assistance of all sorts will have to flow from the Powers to the weaker states largely on a bilateral basis. But a multilateral agency like the United Nations could advise the weaker country on the type of assistance it should request (including feasibility studies) and it could audit the assistance to see that it was being used for the purposes intended. In that way a presumably impartial multilateral agency would undertake the major functions of assisting the weaker countries to determine the priority of their needs, and then auditing the use of the assistance granted by any of the Powers.

Official governmental aid is not the only, or even the most important economic instrument the powerful countries possess. Governmental economic aid will be needed to build social overhead capital in the weaker countries—the pre- and co-requisites of development like roads, port facilities, dams, schools, and irrigation systems are often simply not profitable enough to attract private capital—but when it comes to building industry, the private sector in the developed countries can probably do it better, at no cost to the governments of either weak or powerful states.

In a modern industrial world becoming increasingly interdependent, overseas markets for certain finished products and overseas producers for certain components are realities of life for businessmen in the growing economies of the developed countries. With full, or nearly full, production in most of these countries, labor has come into relatively short supply and prices have been steadily rising. Many major firms are finding that there are advantages in setting up their factories abroad where they can produce the same products more cheaply. There is no question that private business will continue to seek out and cultivate such mutually beneficial foreign relationships.[10] Businessmen are always searching for lucrative markets for their products, and while they currently find their best markets in their own and other developed economies, as the weaker economies become stronger they will find them commensurately more appealing. It is precisely here that the governments of the Powers can help their own businessmen, the underdeveloped countries, and themselves. By giving tax and various other incentives to businessmen who take the higher risks involved in investing in less developed countries, and by keeping tariffs low on imports from the underdeveloped countries, the governments of the Powers can stimulate their private sectors to take a major role in stimulating economic growth in the weaker countries.

While the largest portion of the capital necessary for the economic development of the underdeveloped countries is going to have to be produced in the weaker countries themselves, few of the weaker countries have, or would want to have, the kind of tight totalitarian control that would be necessary to take vast amounts of capital out of populations having little enough to begin with. It is because of this that foreign capital, both public and private, can perform such a useful function. But this capital is simply not going to come like "manna" from heaven. The weaker countries are going to have to work hard to create the conditions to attract that capital. This may mean, particularly in the short run, increased

---

[10] Provided, of course, that there is no prolonged, major depression, in which case there is likely to be increased pressure for high tariffs to protect home industries.

dependence upon the major Powers, but if the weaker states are really serious about developing their countries rapidly—as they should be—they may have no alternative.

One way to mitigate that dependence is to make a concerted effort to acquire both public and private capital from as many different Powers as possible. Total economic dependence on one Power alone is dangerous for the weaker states. Economic dependence on several Powers is less dangerous. The underdeveloped countries are going to have to convince a number of different Powers that it is in their own best interest to assist the weaker countries to become interdependent with them. They are going to have to make foreign private investment so attractive that the foreign capitalists will not be able to resist the opportunities. Here the governments of the weaker states do have some power—the power of allurement. Unless they use that power constructively and effectively, the private investor will go to other countries that are making investments more attractive.

Of course, there are dangers in dependence on foreign investment. Probably the most effective way to avoid overdependence on foreign investors is not to force them out of the country, as has so often been advocated, but rather to invite more of them in! The more foreign investment in different industries and from different countries an underdeveloped country can attract, the less underdeveloped it will become and the less dependent it will become on one product or one foreign country. What is more, if a favorable climate for foreign investment is created, potential domestic investors may become less skeptical about investing in their own country. Thus massive foreign investment—from many different sources—could produce jobs and create enough domestic markets to generate the necessary economic "steam" to propel the country out of poverty and into economic prosperity.

Marx's warnings, and memories of nineteenth-century imperialist experience, have made the governments of weaker states very suspicious of foreign investments. Certainly, they have cause to be suspicious. But healthy suspicion need not lead to paranoia. While private foreign investment—particularly if it is exclusively in one industry (like oil extraction), or if it is exclusively or predominantly from one country—*could* lead to political domination of a weaker country, there is no reason why it must. The point is that if the leaders of these countries could come to realize that the most effective defense against overdependence on foreign investment is *more* foreign investment—not restrictions—they could effectively emerge from the vicious cycle of general economic dependence in which so many of them are trapped.

This is not meant as a "hosanna" to private capitalism. Rigid adherence to any ideological system is not what matters. What is important for the underdeveloped countries is to attract capital from any source they can. Interestingly enough, many private foreign investors are willing to enter into joint ventures with partly owned government corporations. Private investors are concerned primarily with profits. If a joint venture can ensure those profits the investor will be attracted. In fact, the joint government-private venture is one of the ways in which underdeveloped countries can guarantee the private investor against expropriation. What is more, it is not just private foreign-investors who are interested in overseas investments these days. Socialist countries are often willing and eager to invest in entrepreneurial undertakings in underdeveloped countries in order to gain access to a profitable market.

Nor should foreign investment be totally unrestrained. Unnecessary bureaucratic restrictions on resource allocation and financial and labor management are the bane of the foreign investor, to be sure, and an excess of them can often deter the prospective investor from going beyond preliminary investigations. But government intervention to allow higher profits on industries considered essential, and lower profits on lower priority industries, is a must for balanced growth. Indeed, in many countries incentives to attract foreign investors to particular industries or regions of the country can be and are being built right into development plans for the country.

If the incentives for foreign investors are made attractive enough, the governments of the underdeveloped countries can impose regulations aimed at assisting development without deterring the investors. For example, they can insist that a certain percentage of the raw materials produced in the country be processed there, or that for a given number of years a certain percentage of the profits be reinvested. Particularly in those weaker countries fortunate enough to have much sought after raw materials like oil, copper, and tin, the governments can insist, as a precondition for extraction, that processing plants be built in the country so that primary and secondary processing industries can be generated. They might also find it worthwhile to offer differential "splits" with the extracting companies. For example, on oil shipped abroad for processing, the company might get only 25 percent of earnings, while the government got 75 percent, but on oil processed in the country—thereby helping to develop chemical and plastic industries—the company would get 75 percent and the government 25 percent.

It is true that most foreign investors will tend to gravitate toward the more developed countries where political stability, experienced labor forces, social overhead capital, and profits are more certain. But the underdeveloped countries can, by careful planning and hard work, accelerate their attraction of foreign capital. That there are political as well as economic disadvantages the poorer countries must guard against goes without saying. But overwhelmingly it is in the interests of the governments and the people of the underdeveloped world to attract—and use productively—as much development assistance as they can possibly get, from as many sources as they can.

Military Perspectives

The Powers are going to provide military help to allies they consider important whenever they believe it is in their interest to do so. That is a reality. It is also a reality that they will have large military establishments to protect themselves and their allies from real or imagined enemies. The thrust of the entire argument in this book, however, is that the coercive instrument of power is perhaps the most costly and least effective of all the instruments available to powerful states. In light of the failure of the British and French adventure in Suez, the French failure in Vietnam and Algeria, the U.S. failure in Vietnam, and what may turn out to be the Soviet failure in Czechoslovakia, it does not seem unrealistic to expect that the Powers may soon recognize the greater efficiency of non-coercive instruments of policy, especially in their dealings with the weaker states. As they do, presumably much less attention and money will be devoted to this instrument.

But this is not to say that military power cannot be an effective instrument of foreign policy. Indeed, military power is probably most effective when it is not used in battle. The fact that the U.S. and the U.S.S.R. both have the bomb and could destroy each other probably is a major factor in preventing them from doing so. If it ever came to a test, however, one or both of them would lose, thus proving their military strength less effective in use than as a threat. And as Chapter 7 showed in tracing how military training, like all education, tends to build strong perceptual bonds, the military instrument is even more effective when used for building similarities of perception.

As we have seen, the weaker states believe they need relatively large military forces, and are going to try to build those forces with the assistance of one Power or another. None of the Powers can afford to allow the weaker countries to become totally dependent militarily on what they perceive to be an enemy Power. Thus, as long as there is the cold war or some similar world-wide division, the weaker states can have leverage with a Power by threatening to get their military supplies and training from the competing Power. The Powers can prevent them from applying that leverage by a concerted refusal to supply the weaker states. This has worked in several instances already and it could work in others, but the problem is that it only works in those cases where *all* the major Powers agree to refuse to arm the particular weaker states. Unfortunately, there are not many cases where that is possible, given the current world scene. If and when the major Powers come to recognize the greater efficiency of noncoercive instruments of power and begin to compete and/or cooperate to build greater interdependence, perhaps then they will be able to agree more often to limit the spread of military hardware.

The history books are replete with examples of a weak state's ruler inviting a major Power to intervene militarily in his country to help him defeat challengers to his regime. Almost without exception, once the challenge had been suppressed by the superior coercive strength of the Power, the ruler of the weaker state found that his country and his own authority within the country had become subordinate to the Power he had invited in. There is a lesson here for the weaker countries, and that is for them *never* to invite the military forces of a stronger state into their country. They can more safely ask for assistance in training and equipment, but even then they run an increased risk of a military coup from their own strengthened armed forces. A better strategy for staying in power is for the ruling elite of a weaker country to engage as many different sectors of the society as possible with as many different Powers as possible. It is dangerous to strengthen the military elite of one's country unless all other segments of the society are simultaneously strengthened, thus maintaining the relative balance of competing forces within one's own country.

The weaker countries are tempted to overcome military weakness and dependence by devoting ever-increasing portions of their budgets to military spending, and by buying military hardware and training from as many different Powers as possible. The latter makes sense and is wise policy insofar as the weaker states must buy hardware and training from any source. But there are also dangers inherent in it. Not only does it mean increased expense in order to learn several different technologies, but there is likely to be a temptation to balance one large arms deal by entering into another with a different Power. The desire of the weaker countries to develop the capacity to defend themselves militarily, and to free themselves from overdependence on any one or a combination of major world Powers is certainly understandable. The problem is that the solution they seek—increasing their own military capacity —is based on a fundamental error. The countries most able to defend themselves when faced with an external military threat are not the countries with the most soldiers and military hardware, but those that are economically most developed. Prior to the Six-Day War between Israel and the Arab states in 1967 the latter had considerably more military equipment than the Israelis. The advantage the Israelis had over their opponents, however, was a much higher level of economic development—which implies a level of manpower capable of handling effectively the complex technology of modern military hardware. To be certain, the Israelis may also have had the advantage of surprise in striking first, while Egyptian planes were still on the ground. But Israel was able to strike first—and effectively—because its level of technological development made such a strike possible. The Egyptians had very advanced radar systems (bought from the Soviets) but the indications are that their manpower simply did not have the technological sophistication to use them effectively. That kind of technological development of manpower is only possible in societies that are highly developed economically. Egypt and Jordan would have been better able to protect themselves in the face of an Israeli attack if, instead of having invested millions of dollars on military hardware, they had invested that money in the economic, social, and technlogical development of their countries.

It is not just in the Middle East that these huge sums are being wasted on a narrowly defined military capability. A recent survey conducted by the Stockholm International Peace Research Institute reported that Asian countries, exclusive of China, devoted $6.6 billion to military spending in 1969, while China alone spent $7.8 billion. "In real terms, military spending in Asia, excluding China, increased by 84% in the Sixties—close to double the growth of its national income." [11]

This, then, is the trap into which so many of the weaker countries tend to fall in the name of "defense capacity." Instead of mobilizing every penny for investment in capital-producing industry—thereby increasing the real standard of living of their populations and in the process acquiring a modicum of real ability to defend themselves—almost every one of the newly independent countries is wastefully consuming literally millions of dollars on military hardware. No matter how much these weaker countries spend on armaments, none of them will ever be in a position to stop a military onslaught by one of the major Powers—and they know it. Most of this money is spent on the military not out of fear of the Powers, but out of fear of both neighbors and internal enemies. But if massive investments were made in their own economies,

[11] Cited in *Far Eastern Economic Review,* Vol. LXX, No. 50 (Dec. 12, 1970), p. 3.

producing jobs and the prospect of a decent standard of living, most of the internal enemies would cease to be enemies. Given assurances that these countries intend to live in peace with their neighbors—and there is no better assurance than to maintain only the minimum military establishment necessary for the maintenance of domestic order—the likelihood is that neighboring countries would not feel threatened and hence would feel less need to be threatening themselves. If this sounds incredibly idealistic, observe that Costa Rica has done just this and has less internal or external threat to its security than any other Central American Republic—all the rest of which have large military establishments, and substantial domestic as well as foreign threats to their security. The weaker underdeveloped countries simply cannot afford ever-increasing military expenditures. The sooner they realize this, and the more they divert those expenditures toward rapid industrialization and other economic development, the more security they will gain.

Political Perspectives

The utility to the major Powers of establishing informal political ties with elites and potential elites in the weaker states has already been discussed. Here it remains to examine various ways in which Powers can do so more effectively. Certainly if the recommendations presented thus far in this chapter were to be accepted, the Powers would simultaneously be building informal political ties. The degree of congruence of perceptions, including political perceptions, would increase greatly. Note that the thrust of each recommendation is toward building interdependence, not toward the perpetuation of dependence. Those recommendations, if followed, would go a very long way toward building political interdependence among decision makers in the weak and powerful states.

The trouble is that interdependence of any kind, and particularly political interdependence, is viewed by many policy makers in the powerful countries as something of a bother, as well as not necessarily in the Power's best interest. It implies, after all, that policy makers in the powerful countries must be ready and willing to adjust their own perceptions as much as they expect policy makers in weaker countries to adjust theirs. It implies constant consultation with counterparts in a multitude of weaker states, not only on matters of most concern to the Power, but also on matters of most concern to the weak states. Psychologically, it is much easier for these policy makers to expect the weaker states simply to adjust to them. In fact, however, it may take as much or more effort on the part of the Powers to perpetuate dependence as it would to nurture interdependence. All that interdependence requires is a different approach to the weak states. Once the Power overcame the psychological habit of treating the weaker states as inferiors and started viewing them as equals (or potential equals), there need be no additional work involved at all. It is precisely because policy makers in the powerful countries do view themselves as superior, and as the repositories of political wisdom and savvy, that they must work so hard to persuade decision makers in the weaker states to accept their definitions of political reality. If instead these decision makers could approach their counterparts from the weaker countries in a spirit of openness and willingness to learn, big Power foreign policy could become much more attuned to the needs of the other countries, commonalities of political interest could be widened and much more easily discovered, and concerted policies could be achieved with much less effort.

Interestingly enough, this is not as far fetched and utopian as it might appear. The largest business firms in both Europe and America have for years now spent large sums of money training their top management (including their chief executive officers) in the art of being more open and receptive to ideas, values, attitudes, and feelings of others. This so-called "sensitivity training" utilized by big industrial corporations is aimed precisely at making their executives more sensitive to the needs of others. It has "paid off" for big business to such an extent that sensitivity training in the United States has itself become big business today. Yet the American government generally remains hostile to the entire notion. One American congressman summed up this hostility when he said, in answer to a suggestion that Agency for International Development personnel be selected on the basis of their psychological sensitivity to different ideas and different cultures, "If those people want our help it's up to them to become sensitive to us. We're not going to decide who to send overseas and who not to send, just to suit them." [12] It is precisely this kind of "arrogance of power" that is so terribly self-defeating. Fortunately, it does not extend to every part of the government. One of the reasons the Peace Corps has been as successful as it has, is because the people it sends out are as eager to learn as they are to teach. There are few policy makers—particularly in the more powerful countries— who do not think that they know all there is to know. Changing either the personnel or the attitudes of the personnel in governmental decision-making bodies in the powerful countries so that they are staffed by people more willing to learn about others would

[12] Reported to me in private conversation.

go a long way toward improving political ties between the powerful states and other countries.

But this recommendation for a change in attitude—and all of the other policy recommendations made thus far require that a sweeping *political* decision be made at the very top of the decision-making hierarchy in each of the Powers to change the basic policy toward weaker states. It is the one political decision that will be most difficult to make. Yet unless it is made, it is unlikely in the extreme that any of the policy recommendations proposed here will be implemented. Before any government introduces a major change of policy it has to be convinced that its old policy is not working (or working poorly). Few governments will be willing to admit that the policies they have pursued are not the best possible policies for their countries. It will be especially difficult for a country to accept these policy recommendations if it has been following policies that are the reverse of those suggested here. This is particularly so if the country is currently "at the top of the heap." Decision makers in the United States and the Soviet Union are likely to say, "Look here, in many cases we have followed policies that are absolutely contradictory to those you are suggesting and we are today the two strongest countries in the world. Why should we change course merely because you have a theory that it could be done better?" It has always been exceedingly difficult to convince people who believe themselves successful to do things differently. And it is certainly true that decision makers in the U.S. and U.S.S.R. believe that generally their policies are, and have been, "successful." If they did not believe so, they would already have begun to look for alternatives. Whether it is possible that there will be enough popular discontent with current foreign policy goals and methods in both countries to force the governments to alter their policies remains to be seen.

In countries like Japan, West Germany, and China these policy recommendations stand a much better chance of being adopted. As these countries continue to mobilize their own domestic resources they are increasingly likely to turn their attention outward to questions of their relations with other weaker states. Both Germany and Japan have already experimented with reliance on the coercive instruments of power and have suffered enormously because of it. They—more than any other countries—know that coercion is far less effective than its proponents think. In addition, given their position in world affairs today, it would be difficult for them to attempt again to increase their national power either by making weaker states politically dependent upon them, or through coercive means. Therefore, Germany and Japan—and to a lesser extent China, France, and the United Kingdom (because their resources are not sufficient to give them much choice)—are likely to recognize the advantages of building interdependence with the weaker states, using the attractive instruments of power exclusively. Indeed, there are some indications that they have already begun to do just that. It is almost always the groups or states that are not themselves at the top, but aspire to get there, that are most receptive to innovative techniques to achieve their goals.[13]

One major revision in formal political ties that all Powers could undertake with relative ease would be to adopt the principle of universal diplomatic recognition. By recognizing all governments of the world instead of using diplomatic recognition as a sign of approval of the regime in office, the big Powers could establish formal political ties with a number of governments from which they are currently totally isolated, and this might eventually lead to informal political ties as well. In those cases in which two governments claim to represent all of a particular country, the Powers would do well to recognize and establish formal diplomatic ties with both. Neither side might approve of the Power recognizing its opposition, but if the policy of the Powers were clear and unchanging on this, there would be little that each rival government could do but accept the recognition offered, or run the risk that the opposition would establish more and closer political ties with the Power than it would. Nonrecognition on the part of a Power really gains nothing for the Power, but does limit its potential leverage with that country and inhibit eventual accommodation. Of the major Powers discussed here, only the United Kingdom and France have the policy of more or less universal recognition of states. Japan may ultimately adopt such a policy as it becomes more active politically in world affairs, but it has yet to do so. Both the U.S. and the U.S.S.R. seem to use diplomatic recognition as a weapon in the cold war, without being aware that recognition and a formal diplomatic relationship constitute a more effective weapon than nonrecognition. Each of these Powers refuses to recognize many of the weaker states the other recognizes, having somehow convinced itself that it is punishing the other's associated state by withholding recognition. From all we have seen about how any ties tend to generate other ties, it would appear that withholding this formal political tie hurts the Power far more than it does the government of the weaker state.

On a far more fundamental level, the governments of the Powers need to grant universal recognition to the legitimate human aspirations and concerns motivating all countries. In particular, the United States and the Soviet Union need to recognize that their

[13] For an interesting analogy see E. E. Hagen, *On the Theory of Social Change* (Homewood, Ill.: Dorsey Press, 1962).

major adversaries are not states governed by totally evil ideologies, committed solely to the destruction of the other, but states with interests as complex and humanly valid as their own. In a devastating article entitled "The Hoax That Cost a Trillion Dollars in 25 Years," I. F. Stone said:

> The truth is that we have spent a trillion dollars since World War II on a gigantic hoax. The U.S. emerged from World War II, as from World War I, virtually unscathed, enormously enriched and— with the atom bomb—immeasurably more powerful than any nation on earth has ever been. The notion that it was in danger of attack from a devastated Soviet Union with 25 million war dead, a generation behind it in industrial development, was a wicked fantasy. But this myth has been the mainstay of the military and the war machine.
>
> Until this bogeyman is disposed of, there will always be an ABM. There will always be some new device offered us in panic as necessary to our security. Until the opposition moves from the technical details of weaponry—whether ABM or MIRV—to an attack on this underlying obsession with a Soviet attack, we're never going to bring the arms budget and the arms race under control. At a hearing of his Senate Foreign Relations Committee on MIRV, July 16 [1969], Senator Fulbright put his finger on the essential point when he said the Pentagon experts "seem to assume, I have never been quite clear why, that they [the Russians] have only one object in life and that is to destroy the United States, and everything else is subordinate to that objective. I do not accept that." A psychologist would say that such a view projects on the Rival or Enemy the worst impulses of one's own heart. . . .
>
> All the forces of Light were on our side; all the forces of Darkness, on the other. In a world of demonology, there can be no diplomacy. If both sides are human, equally fallible and fearful, then compromise and accommodation are possible.[14]

Until policy makers in both Super Powers recognize the reality of that argument there can be no hope of moving from the destructive to the creative in international relations. Must the United States suffer the same fate as every other major Power that preceded it, and dissipate its wealth and resources in wars to the point where it becomes at best a second-class Power, or can social science catch up to man's science of destruction and show policy makers how they might build a better world and at the same time a more powerful and secure America? As this is being written the prognosis looks increasingly bleak. Yet there is no reason why America's course could not be changed.

The weaker states, too, are following a course in which rationality does not seem to be a major factor. Regardless of the strides

[14] I. F. Stone, "The Hoax That Cost a Trillion Dollars in 25 Years," *I. F. Stone's Weekly,* Vol. XVII, No. 15 (July 28, 1969), p. 1.

the weaker states make toward rapid economic development, as long as they remain as 120 relatively small political units dealing with two or three or five Super Powers, they will remain comparatively weak. If they could unite into larger units, not only would their chances of achieving economic interdependence with the Powers be enhanced, but they could also begin to aspire to political interdependence. A Europe united into one political unit would be one of the most powerful states in the world, and it would have to be treated as such by every other country. Similarly, a united Latin America, or a united Arab nation, or a united Africa would also mean new power relationships. But as we have already seen, unification does not appear to be even a remote possibility in the foreseeable future.

So many of the individual states seem to be having so difficult a time making themselves into nations that one would presume the job could be made easier—or at least no more difficult—if they involved themselves in larger units. But the weaker states seem to resist this approach. Perhaps it is true, as some scholars have maintained, that these states will have to become nations before they can be concerned about supranationalism. The Arab nation already exists, as do all the elements of a Central American or a Latin American nation. It seems such a pity, in terms of power relationships, to see these nations divided into so many competing states; yet that seems to be a reality that will not easily be overcome.

What is a possibility, however, is a much greater degree of political consultation and accommodation among the weaker states so that they can present more of a united front on issues of common importance to them. In every domestic multiparty political system the smaller parties know that the only chance they have to influence policy is to cooperate (organize) to get a coalition slate elected to office. Similarly, the weaker states must come to realize that the only real chance they have to influence international policy is to cooperate on matters of common concern. On the domestic level the parties in a coalition do not lose their individual identity despite their cooperation with other parties for mutual benefit. Similarly, on the international level there is no reason why the weaker states could not maintain their individual identities while cooperating for mutual political gain. All of the institutional structures for cooperation are there waiting to be used. All the weaker states have to do is use them. The Organization of African States, the Organization of American States, the Association of South East Asian Nations, and the Arab League are just a few of the international structures waiting for effective use by the weaker states. Certainly others could be created if they were needed. But it appears that the weaker states are all so concerned with the priorities of domestic nation building, and so fearful of at least some of their neighbors, that they overlook the opportunities that international cooperation could provide for solving the very problems to which they assign top priority. Certainly nation building would be easier in a state that was developing rapidly. In a rapidly developing state old political and parochial loyalties tend to disintegrate while new national loyalties tend to grow and strengthen. Since it is presumably rational men who influence the destinies of these countries, one would think they would recognize the advantages they could gain by mutual cooperation for rapid development. Any one of the organizations mentioned could be significantly strengthened merely by a conscious decision to do so on the part of the policy makers in each of the member countries. Yet they do not make that decision.

The crucial question seems to be not whether these countries could be developed if their leaders were prepared to make a determined effort, but whether the leaders really do want to see their countries develop rapidly. In many cases, there is considerable evidence that the elites are at best ambivalent. Yes, they would like lower mortality rates, higher employment, higher standards of living, and greater political stability. But many of these political leaders are simply not prepared to make the personal sacrifices that achieving those goals entails. Thus, they will settle for slower rates of growth and continued relative impotence internationally, rather than risk the personal loss—political and/or financial—that accelerating the process of development might bring. Perhaps it is unfair to expect the self-sacrifice, rationality, and foresightedness from leaders of weaker states that are not present among the leaders of the more powerful states.

Until recently, the pressure for change seemed to be greatest in the less developed states. Perhaps now it is as great everywhere. As pressure for change builds up in any country, the leaders are going to have to find ways to channel that pressure into constructive, peaceful, but rapid reform, or face the prospect of destructive, violent change. Frustration is like an infection—it rarely goes away if one simply ignores it. If the current leaders of the weaker states are unwilling or unable to take the kind of political measures that will facilitate change, the odds are overwhelming that they will not be able to remain leaders for long. Everywhere the disadvantaged people are becoming more aware of their condition and they are no longer merely asking for change—they are demanding it. Under the guidance of responsible leaders that demand could be the engine that propels the weaker countries out of a condition of poverty and dependence into one of affluence and interdependence.

Index

of government, 82
instruments of, 5, 60–61, 370–378, 413
international, 39
military, 408
of nongovernment groups, 82
numbers and, 173
of strong states, 367
study of, 3–5
wealth and, 61–69, 73–74
Power and Personality, 53
Powers, colonial, 172–177
major (*see* names of, as United States)
states historically associated with, 56–57, 60; *table,* 94–101
and related states, ties between, 89–177
relative strength of, 82
Super (*see* Super Powers)
weak, 73
and associated states, 168–170, 183, 189
foreign trade of, *tables,* 232–236
(*See also* Weak states)
Western, 206
Predictions, 178
Press Trust of India (PTI), 190
Prestige, 74
United States, 76
Preston, Harley O., quoted, 166
Prime ministers, 201
Production, 59, 64, 210–211
Proletarians, 141
Propaganda, 258
Protective umbrella, 284–285
Protectorates, 36, 93, 104, 277, 338
Protestants, 120–122
Pruitt, Dean G., quoted, 178
Pryor, Frederic, quoted, 346
Psychology, and changing relationships, 45–51
social, 40
Puerto Rico, 106, 170
Punjab, the, 119

Race, 128
attitude toward, 131
definition of, 127
Race perspectives, 389–390
Racial superiority, 130, 133, 174
Racial ties, 127–135
Racism, 131–133
Radio stations, 190

Raw materials, industrial countries and, 209–211
Rebellion, 50
adolescent, 47
Redundancy, 23
Religion, 387
Religious perspectives, 387–388
Religious ties, 108, 119–127, 130
Reuters, 182–183, 190, 205, 207
Rhodesia, 129–130
Riesman, David, 80
Rio Pact, 337, 343
(*See also* Treaty of Rio)
Romania, 85
Roosevelt, Theodore, 344
Rosenstein-Rodan, Paul, 391
Ross, Sanford, quoted, 262
Rostow, W. W., quoted, 263
Rummell, Rudolph, 127–128
Russett, Bruce, 321
quoted, 320
Russia, 143, 146–147, 154, 337, 344
and foreign investment, 262
(*See also* Soviet Union)
Russian Empire, 106, 312, 345, 381
Russian Orthodoxy, 177
Russian revolutions, 62, 394
Rwanda, 238

Satellites, 315, 329
Schecter, Steven, 336
Scholarships, 152, 165
Science, 149–150, 152–153
Scotland, 103–104
Security, collective, 80, 376
military, 251
multilateral "collective," 279–281
Self-defense, 30
Semitic peoples, 129–130
(*See also* Arabs)
Senegal, 103, 383
Sensenig, Barton, 325
Sensitivity training, 412
Servan-Schreiber, J. J., 40
quoted, 262–263
Shannon, Claude, 16
Sierra Leone, 216, 222
Singapore, 284, 296, 321, 396
Singer, Hans, quoted, 368
Singer, J. David, and Melvin Small, 77
quoted, 75
Slavery, 131
Snow, C. P., 149
Social psychology, international relations and, 40